LAW AND SOCIETY IN THE AGE OF THEODERIC THE GREAT

This book explores the evolution of Roman law and society in Italy from 493, with the proclamation of the Ostrogoth Theoderic the Great as King, until about 554, when the eastern Emperor Justinian was able to re-establish imperial authority in the region. Drawing upon evidence from a variety of legal and historical sources, it investigates how Theoderic and his successors attempted to govern the peninsula in the wake of foreign invasions, the collapse of civic administration, the break-up of the Mediterranean economy, and the emergence of new forms of religious and secular authority. It challenges long-held assumptions as to just how peaceful, prosperous, and Roman-like Theoderic's Italy really was. Its primary focus is the *Edictum Theoderici*, a significant but largely overlooked document that offers valuable historical insights into the complex and sometimes contested social, political, and religious changes that marked Italy's passage from Antiquity into the Middle Ages.

SEAN D. W. LAFFERTY is a postdoctoral research fellow at Yale University.

LAW AND SOCIETY IN THE AGE OF THEODERIC THE GREAT

A Study of the Edictum Theoderici

SEAN D. W. LAFFERTY

CAMBRIDGE
UNIVERSITY PRESS

CAMBRIDGE
UNIVERSITY PRESS

University Printing House, Cambridge CB2 8BS, United Kingdom

One Liberty Plaza, 20th Floor, New York, NY 10006, USA

477 Williamstown Road, Port Melbourne, VIC 3207, Australia

4843/24, 2nd Floor, Ansari Road, Daryaganj, Delhi - 110002, India

79 Anson Road, #06-04/06, Singapore 079906

Cambridge University Press is part of the University of Cambridge.

It furthers the University's mission by disseminating knowledge in the pursuit of education, learning and research at the highest international levels of excellence.

www.cambridge.org
Information on this title: www.cambridge.org/9781107028340

First published 2013

A catalogue record for this publication is available from the British Library

Library of Congress Cataloging in Publication data
Lafferty, Sean D. W., 1978–
Law and society in the age of Theoderic the Great : a study of the Edictum Theoderici / Sean D. W. Lafferty.
pages cm
Based on the author's thesis (doctoral – University of Toronto, 2010), under the title: The Edictum Theoderici : a study of a Roman legal document from Ostrogothic Italy.
Includes bibliographical references and index.
ISBN 978-1-107-02834-0
1. Edictum Theoderici Regis. 2. Roman law. 3. Law, Gothic. 4. Theodoric, King of the Ostrogoths, 454–526. 5. Ostrogoths – Legal status, laws, etc. – Italy – History – To 1500. I. Edictum Theoderici Regis. II. Title.
KJA617.L34 2013
340.5′4–dc23
2012043201

ISBN 978-1-107-02834-0 Hardback

Additional resources for this publication at www.cambridge.org/lafferty

Contents

Abbreviations

Amm. Marc.	Ammianus Marcellinus, *Res Gestae*
Anon. Val.	*Anonymi Valesiani pars posterior*
Cass., *Hist.*	Cassiodorus, *Historia ecclesiastica tripartita*
Cass., *Var.*	Cassiodorus, *Variae*
CCSL	*Corpus Christianorum, Series Latina*
CG	*Codex Gregorianus*
CH	*Codex Hermogenianus*
CJ	*Codex Justinianus*
CJC	*Corpus Iuris Civilis*
CLA	*Codices Latini Antiquiores*
Collatio	*Mosaicarum et Romanorum Legum Collatio*
Confess.	Augustine of Hippo, *Confessions*
Cons. Phil.	Boethius, *Consolation of Philosophy*
CSEL	*Corpus Scriptorum Ecclesiasticorum Latinorum*
CTh	*Theodosiani Libri XVI cum Constitutionibus Sirmondianis et Leges Novellae ad Theodosianum Pertinentes*
Dig.	*Digesta*
EMC/CV NS	*Echos du Monde Classique/Classical Views New Series*
ÉFR	*École française de Rome*
EHR	*English Historical Review*
Ep.	*Epistulae*
ET	*Edictum Theoderici*
FIRA	*Fontes Iuris Romani Anteiustiniani*
Fr.	*Fragmenta*
FV	*Fragmenta Vaticana*
Gai., *Inst.*,	Gaius, *Institutiones*
Get.	Jordanes, *Romana et Getica*
Hist. Goth.	Isidore of Seville, *Historia Gothorum Wandalorum Sueborum*

Inst.	*Institutiones*
Itpr.	*Interpretationes*
JECS	*Journal of Early Christian Studies*
JRA	*Journal of Roman Archaeology*
JRS	*Journal of Roman Studies*
LRE	Arnold H. M. Jones, *The Later Roman Empire 284–602: A Social, Economic and Administrative Survey*
LRV	*Lex Romana Visigothorum*
LV	*Leges Visigothorum*
MEFRA	*Mélanges de l'École française de Rome: Antiquité*
MGH	*Monumenta Germaniae Historica*
MGH AA	*MGH Auctores Antiquissimi*
MGH SRM	*MGH Scriptores rerum merovingicarum*
MGH SS	*MGH Scriptores*
Nat. Hist.	Pliny, *Natural History*
Not. Dig.	*Notitia Dignitatum omnium tam civilium quam militarium*
Nov. Anth.	*Novellae Anthemii*
Nov. Maj.	*Novellae Majoriani*
Nov. Val.	*Novellae Valentiniani*
Pan. Th.	Ennodius, *Panegyricus dictus clementissimo regi Theoderico*
PBSR	*Papers of the British School at Rome*
P-Ital	*Die nichtliterarischen Lateinischen Papyri Italiens aus der zeit 445–700*
PL	*Patrologiae Cursus Completus, Series Latina*
PLRE	*The Prosopography of the Later Roman Empire*, vol. 2: AD 395–527
Proc., *BG*	Procopius, *De Bello Gothico*
PS	*Pauli Sententiae*
RE	*Real-Enclopädie der classischen Altertumswissenschaft*
Reg. Ulp.	*Regulae Ulpiani*
RHDFE	*Revue historique de droit français et étranger*
RHS	*Royal Historical Society*
RIDA	*Revue internationale des Droits de l'Antiquité*
SDHI	*Studia et Documenta Historiae et Iuris*
TAPA	*Transactions of the American Philological Association*
V. Epiph.	Ennodius, *Vita Ephiphanii*
ZSS (RA)	*Zeitschrift der Savigny-Stiftung für Rechtsgeschichte (Romanistische Abteilung)*

Acknowledgements

This book would not have been possible without the help and encouragement of many people and institutions. My first debt is to Nicholas Everett, who supervised the thesis that formed the basis of this book, and who has been a source of support and inspiration ever since. For his instruction, kindness, and goodwill, I owe more to him than can be fully expressed here. Earlier drafts were read and commented upon by Giulio Silano, Isabelle Cochelin, Ralph Mathisen, and Andy Orchard, and I have benefited greatly from their advice. To Andy in particular I am profoundly indebted for his unstinting encouragement, mentorship, and friendship.

Thanks also go to the many friends and colleagues who have shared their knowledge and expertise on various aspects of this topic, but I wish to thank especially Tom Noble, Simon Corcoran, Nicholas Terpstra, Jonathan (Scott) Perry, Shane Bjornlie, and Samuel Cohen. Joshua Moukperian, John Duncan, and Emre Gönlügür have encouraged me over the years in more ways than I can recount. For their friendship and camaraderie, I give my warmest thanks.

The Social Sciences and Humanities Research Council of Canada and the University of Toronto generously provided the financial support that assisted me in completing this project. The final stages of writing this book took place while I was a fellow at Trinity College, Toronto, and I should like to express my deep appreciation to the students and staff of this institution who provided me with such a creative and collegial atmosphere to work.

The anonymous referees at Cambridge University Press offered invaluable and detailed feedback for which I am deeply thankful. I am also most grateful to the editorial team at the Press, notably Michael Sharp, Elizabeth Hanlon, and Jodie Hodgson for their professionalism and skill in bringing this book to fruition. All remaining mistakes and infelicities are, of course, my own.

Earlier versions of Chapters 1 and 2 appeared as articles in the *Journal of Late Antiquity* and the *Canadian Journal of History* (both 2010), and I thank the editors for permission to reprint parts of the material here.

To my family – and above all my parents – for their unfailing support and love, I am forever indebted. My final and greatest thanks are to Nathalie, for all she has done and everything else besides. It is to her that I dedicate this book, with all my love.

Introduction

This book explores the evolution of Roman law and society in Italy from 493, with the proclamation of the Ostrogoth Theoderic the Great as King, until about 554, when the eastern Emperor Justinian was able to re-establish imperial authority in the region. Drawing upon evidence from a variety of materials, including extant laws, records of court cases, literary and historical sources, it investigates how Theoderic and his barbarian successors attempted to maintain peace and order in the peninsula in the wake of foreign invasions, the collapse of civic administration, the break-up of the Mediterranean economy, and the emergence of new forms of religious and secular authority. The primary focus is the *Edictum Theoderici*, or *Edict of Theoderic* (hereafter simply *ET*), a largely overlooked law code of unknown date and disputed origin comprising 154 provisions, a prologue, and epilogue. The purpose is to situate this text within its proper historical and legal context, to understand better the processes involved in the creation of new law in the post-Roman world, as well as to appreciate how the law reflected the complex and sometimes contested social, political, and religious changes that marked Italy's passage from Antiquity into the Middle Ages.

A brief history of Italy in Late Antiquity

By the beginning of the sixth century Italy had long been in a period of decline. As early as the third century the peninsula was experiencing significant economic hardship – a situation brought about by the decreasing availability of individuals and resources to work the land, and the tendency of the state to over-tax in a bid to compensate for diminishing revenues. Economic decline was hastened by the barbarian invasions of the late fourth and fifth centuries, which had thoroughly and permanently overturned imperial political control in the other Roman provinces. By 476, the western Roman Empire had become unrecognizable as a political or territorial entity; nearly all of its provinces had been occupied by barbarian forces, and its physical boundaries were reduced to the Italian peninsula. Indeed, this was a Roman Empire in name alone, and so it was fitting that in the same year the last western Emperor, the aptly named Romulus Augustulus ("Little Augustus"), was deposed by Odovacer, a general of Germanic extraction who in turn declared himself King – an event that has traditionally symbolized the end of the Roman Empire in the West. Like Britain, France, Spain, and North Africa before it, Italy had devolved into a barbarian kingdom.

The process by which the provinces of the western Roman Empire came under the control of barbarian warlords and Kings was not one of peaceful transition, but rather one of unprecedented upheaval. Indeed, the period from the battle of Adrianople in 378 to the removal of Romulus Augustulus was one of irrevocable change for the worse for the western Empire.[1] Contemporary and later sources stressed the destructive nature of the barbarian invasions that brought down the imperial administration in the provinces of Britain, Gaul, Africa, and Italy over the course of the fifth century.[2] Italy, in particular, suffered heavily. Between 401 and 412, the peninsula was subjected to sporadic Gothic incursions that left widespread damage. In 410, Rome itself, the true symbol of eternal imperial authority, a city which had not been invaded by a foreign army in roughly eight centuries, was sacked by the Visigothic King Alaric. News of the event reverberated around the Mediterranean world in a violent demonstration of how helpless the western Empire had become in the years following the death of the Emperor Theodosius I in 395. It stunned the imagination of this and later centuries and spurred Augustine, Bishop of Hippo on the coast of North Africa, to compose his apocalyptic *City of God.*

Whatever the psychological effects of the Visigothic looting of Rome, the imperial regime in Italy proved itself remarkably resilient once the threat of a barbarian domination of the peninsula had been removed. Within a year of the sack, the Emperor Honorius dispatched forces to restore imperial

1 For excellent surveys on Rome's dissolution and disintegration in the West, with different emphases on the role played by the barbarian invaders, see Edward A. Thompson, *Romans and Barbarians: The Decline of the Western Roman Empire* (Madison, WI, 1982); Ian Wood, "The Fall of the Western Empire and the End of Roman Britain," *Britannia* 18 (1987), 251–62; Averil Cameron, *The Later Roman Empire,* AD *284–430* (Cambridge, MA, 1993; repr. 2001); Averil Cameron, *The Mediterranean World in Late Antiquity,* AD *395–600* (London, 1993); Michael E. Jones, *The End of Roman Britain* (Ithaca, NY 1996); Walter Pohl (ed.), *Kingdoms of the Empire: the Integration of the Barbarians in Late Antiquity* (New York, 1997); Bryan Ward-Perkins, *The Fall of Rome and the End of Civilization* (Oxford, 2005). For a general summary, see Thomas F.X. Noble (ed.), *From Roman Provinces to Medieval Kingdoms* (London/New York, 2006), 1–27; Clifford Ando, "Decline, Fall, and Transformation," *Journal of Late Antiquity* 1.1 (2008), 31–60.

2 Ward-Perkins, *The Fall of Rome*, chapter 2.

control in at least the southern parts of Gaul; eastern and northern sections remained yet to be resuscitated. Britain, however, had to be left in practice to fend for itself.[3] Nevertheless, the events of 410 were but symptoms of deeper problems within the western half of the Empire, the consequences of which led to a second, much more violent and systematic sack of the Eternal City at the hands of the Vandals in 455, and ultimately the capitulation of the western imperial administration to Odovacer in 476. The main policy of the late Roman government for dealing with barbarian aggression was to grant the offending tribe an area of settlement within imperial territory in return for military service. First made in 382, such grants became a regular occurrence. Their result by the 450s was the emergence of politically autonomous units of Goths, Vandals, and Burgundians within the provinces of the western Empire. Where once there was a *res publica* united under a single authority, there were now competing *regna* ruled by generalissimos and Kings who ultimately retained the upper hand.[4] Of course, barbarian invasions were not the only problem. Throughout the fifth century the western Empire was plagued by bouts of civil war and social unrest. At a time when the Empire required a concerted and united effort against barbarian invaders, what it got instead were usurpations and rebellions, which often were prioritized over foreign threats.

Significantly, the deposition of Romulus Augustulus caused remarkably little stir among contemporary sources. It was, in the words of the Italian historian Arnaldo Momigliano, the "noiseless fall of an Empire."[5] That this event passed almost unnoticed is because the western Empire, and the associations of Roman power that came along with it, had long since disappeared in all but name by the time Odovacer removed the Little Augustus. From 410 onwards, successive Emperors became increasingly incapable of holding on to territory as a consequence of growing military threats and barbarian invasions. In terms of constitutional theory, real authority in all areas relating to the army, military strategy, the making of major political appointments, and civic administration was exercised by imperial appointees in the form of Masters of Soldiers. By the early fifth century, supreme military command was in the hands of barbarian warlords. Odovacer was no different from these generalissimos, save for the fact

[3] Jones, *The End of Roman Britain*; Wood, "The Fall of the Western Empire," 251–62.

[4] On the general subject of barbarian integration into the Roman Empire, see Pohl, *Kingdoms of the Empire*.

[5] Arnaldo Momigliano, "La caduta senza rumore di un impero nel 476 d.C," *Annali della Scuola Normale Superiore di Pisa*, ser. III, vol. III.2 (1973), 397–418 (repr. in his collected essays *Sesto contributo alla storia degli studi classici e del mondo antico*, I (Rome, 1980), 159–79).

that he, like Theoderic afterwards, chose to call himself King rather than Emperor.[6]

Writing to the eastern Emperor Zeno (474–91) shortly after his ousting of the enfeebled Romulus Augustulus, Odovacer proclaimed that Italy no longer required its own Emperor. Instead, he would rule as King and patrician, subordinate to the Emperor's authority. Zeno eventually agreed to this arrangement as he had a number of political and military challenges at home that required his attention. One such problem was how to manage the various warlike bands that had taken up residence in the Balkan provinces of Pannonia, Moesia, and Thrace following the disintegration of Attila's Hunnic Empire in the 450s. Zeno's policy was to play these groups off against each other, using one to fight another. But such diplomatic double-dealing did not alleviate the threat of attack, and Constantinople was frequently besieged by these warbands throughout the 470s and 480s.[7]

One of these warbands was a collection of soldiers and their families based in Pannonia and commonly referred to as the Ostrogoths, or Eastern Goths, as a way of distinguishing them from the Visigoths of Spain and the Gallic kingdom of Toulouse. Their leader was Theoderic, son of Thiudimur, who claimed descent from a royal clan called the Amals. Relying upon the brief *History of the Goths* (or *Getica*) written in Constantinople by Jordanes around 551, many historians have accepted the claim of Theoderic and his family to be of Amal descent. However, it has also been suggested that this was a spurious claim, intended to give *de iure* legitimacy to Theoderic's rule. Nevertheless, in the aftermath of the collapse of the Hun supremacy north of the Danube that resulted from the death of Attila and the defeat of his sons by their subject peoples in the battle of the Nedao River in 454, a number of Germanic groups were admitted into the Empire. Among them were the followers of a certain Valamer, who were settled in Pannonia in the western Balkans by agreement with the Emperor Marcian (450–7). Valamer was killed soon afterwards and his position was taken by his brother Thiudimur, Theoderic's father, thus giving him a claim of legitimacy to rule over the Goths.

Theoderic spent his youth as a hostage at the imperial court at Constantinople from 461 until his return to the Balkans in 471. For the next fourteen years he attempted, through a combination of diplomacy and threat, to secure a permanent homeland for his Gothic followers. In 488,

6 Penny MacGeorge, *Late Roman Warlords* (Oxford, 2002).

7 Patrick Amory, *People and Identity in Ostrogothic Italy, 489–554*, Cambridge Studies in Medieval Life and Thought: Fourth series (Cambridge, 1997), 7.

perhaps as a means of getting rid of him, Zeno petitioned Theoderic to invade Italy as *patricius et magister militum praesentalis* and remove Odovacer. A contemporary historian, the so-called Anonymous Valesianus, reports that pending a successful outcome of his campaign, Theoderic was to rule in Odovacer's place on a strictly interim basis – only until Zeno could return:

> Zeno accordingly rewarded Theoderic for his support, made him a patrician and a Consul, gave him a great sum of money and sent him to Italy. Theoderic came to an agreement with him that if Odovacer should be defeated, in return for his own labors he would rule in Odovacer's place only until the Emperor's arrival.[8]

Officially, Theoderic was to have but limited rights over Roman Bishops and Senators, requiring the consent of the Emperor in most regards. He was unable to appoint offices, and was not authorized to enact laws (*leges*), but only, like a Praetorian Prefect, to issue edicts – legal pronouncements that addressed matters particular to the peninsula and surrounding environs that fell under his jurisdiction.[9] These included Sicily (reconquered by Theoderic in the early 490s), the provinces of Dalmatia and Suavia (504), Provence, the Narbonnaise, and most of Spain, where Theoderic allowed his young Visigothic grandson Amalaric to rule as nominal King, and installed a regent from Italy named Theudis (507).

Presented with the opportunity to rule over a lasting and independent Ostrogothic kingdom in the rich and famous lands of Italy, Theoderic readily agreed to the Emperor's terms. In the following year he led his army – a number comprising some 20,000 troops and sundry hangers-on – across the River Isonzo in Istria and defeated Odovacer at Verona, forcing the latter to retreat to the former imperial capital of Ravenna.[10] For the next four years Italy suffered the ravages of war and famine as Odovacer remained holed up in Ravenna. On 5 March 493, having been unable to breach the dense swamps and heavy fortifications that protected the city,

[8] Anonymous Valesianus 11.49, ed. and trans. John C. Rolfe, *Ammianus Marcellinus*, 3 vols., Loeb Classical Library (Cambridge, MA, 1935–40): "Zeno itaque recompensans beneficiis Thodericum, quem fecit patricium et consulem, donans ei multum et mittens eum ad Italiam. Cui Theodericus pactuatus est, ut, si victus fuisset Odoacar, pro merito laborum suorum loco eius, dum adveniret, tantum praeregnaret."

[9] Arnold H. M. Jones, "The Constitutional Position of Odovacer and Theoderic," *JRS* 52 (1962), 126–30; John Moorhead, "Theoderic, Zeno and Odovacer," *Byzantinische Zeitschrift* 77 (1984), 261–6; John Moorhead., *Theoderic in Italy*, (Oxford, 1992), 39–51.

[10] Thomas S. Burns, "Calculating Ostrogothic Population," *Acta Antiqua Academiae Scientiarum Hungaricae* 26 (1978), 457–64 (estimates 35,000 to 40,000); Herwig Wolfram, *History of the Goths*, trans. Thomas J. Dunlap, 2nd edn. (Berkeley, CA, 1988), 279 (estimates about 100,000); and similarly, Wilhelm Ensslin, *Theoderich der Grosse*, 2nd edn. (Munich, 1959), 62–4.

Theoderic finally capitulated and formalized an agreement with Odovacer by which the two would jointly rule over Italy. Ten days later during a banquet to celebrate the occasion, Theoderic murdered his coregent and assumed supreme control of the peninsula. John of Antioch, writing in the seventh century, provides the most vivid account:

> Theoderic and Odovacer made an agreement with each other to the effect that they both should rule over the Roman Empire and they used to meet each other quite often thereafter. The tenth day had not yet passed when, while Odovacer was visiting Theoderic, two of Theoderic's men approached Odovacer as suppliants and grasped both his hands; at once those who were lying in ambush in the small chambers on either side rushed upon him with drawn swords, but, terrified at the sight, they did not attack him, and so Theoderic leaped forward and struck him on the collar bone with his sword, while Odovacer cried out, "Where is God?" Theoderic replied, "This is what you have done to my people." The blow was mortal for it pierced Odovacer's body through to the lower part of the back, and Theoderic is reported to have said, "This scoundrel does not even have a bone in his body."[11]

The account goes on to say that Theoderic murdered Odovacer's surviving family members and supporters, including his older brother Hunulf, who had sought sanctuary in a church; his wife Sunigilda starved to death while in confinement. One might interpret Theoderic's treacherous act as a sign of primitive barbarism. In fact, Theoderic's actions were decidedly Roman. The fourth-century historian Ammianus Marcellinus, for example, describes no less than five occasions when Roman commanders made dinner invitations an opportunity for dispensing with opponents.[12]

[11] John of Antioch, fragment 214a, ed. and trans. Sergei Mariev, *Ioannis Antiocheni Fragmenta Quae Supersunt Omnia* (Berlin, 2008), 444–5: "῞Οτι Θεοδώριχος καὶ Ὀδόακρος συνθήκας καὶ ξυμβάσεις ἐποιήσαντο πρὸς ἀλλήλους ἄμφω ἡγεῖσθαι τῆς Ῥωμαιων ἀρχῆς, καὶ λοιπὸν ἦσαν αὐτοῖς ἐντεύξεις παρ' ἀλλήλους φοιτῶσι συχναί. Οὔπω δὲ ἠνύετο ἡμέρα δεκάτη, καί, τοῦ Οδοάκρου γενομένου παρὰ τὸν Θεοδώριχον, προσελθόντες τῶν αὐτοῦ ἄνδρες δύω τὰς τοῦ Ὀδοάκρου ἅτείκεται γενόμενοι κατέχουσι χεῖρας, μεθ' ὃ τῶν προλοχισθέντων ἐν τοῖς παρ' ἑκάτερα οἰκίσκοις ἐπελθόντων ἅμα τοῖς ξίφεσιν, ἐκ δὲ τῆς θέας καταπλαγέντων καὶ οὐκ ἐπιτιθεμένων τῷ Ὀδοάκρῳ, Θεοδώριχος προσδραμὼν παίει τῷ ξίφει αὐτὸν κατὰ τὴν κλεῖδα, εἰπόντα δέ· ποῦ ὁ θεός; ἀμείβεται·τοῦτό ἐστιν ὃ καὶ σὺ τοὺς ἐμοὺς ἔδρασας. Τῆς δὲπληγῆς και ρίας καὶ μέχρι τῆς ὀσφύος διελθούσης τὸ Ὀδοάκρου σῶμα, εἰπεῖνφασιν Θεοδώριχονώς· τάχα οὐ δὲ ὀστοῦν ἦν τῷ κακῷ τούτῳ." For Theoderic's victory over Odovacer, see Ennodius, *Pan. Th.*, ed. and trans. Christian Rohr, *Der Theoderich-Panegynicus des Ennodius, MGH* studien und Texte 12 (Hannover, 1995), 14, 25; Ennodius, *Vita Epiphanii*, ed. W. Hartel, *CSEL* 6 (Ennodius, *Opera*) (Vienna, 1882); Jordanes, *Romana et Getica*, 57.289–91, ed. Theodor Mommsen, *MGH AA* 5.1 (Berlin, 1882), 53–138; Proc., *BG* v. i. 9–26, in Procopius, *History of the Wars*, ed. J. Haury and trans. H. B. Dewing, Loeb Classical Library, 5 vols. (Cambridge, MA, 1914–28). See further Wolfram, *History of the Goths*, 278–80; Moorhead, *Theoderic in Italy*, ch. 1; Peter Heather, *The Goths* (Oxford, 1996), 216–20.

[12] *Res Gestae*, 31.5.5–8; 21.4.1–5; 27.10.3; 29.4.2–4; 29.6.5; 30.1.18–21.

In the aftermath of victory, Theoderic emerged the undisputed master of Italy. In response, the Gothic army declared him King, thus signaling the start of a long and successful reign that would last for thirty-three years, until Theoderic's death on 30 August 526. His grand mausoleum, the size and composition of which parallels those of Augustus and Hadrian, stands today outside Ravenna as a testament to a barbarian King who drew inspiration from Rome's glorious past as he attempted to resurrect Italy after more than a century of neglect.[13]

The precise implications of Theoderic's confirmation as King require some consideration. The Anonymous Valesianus describes Theoderic as *rex* only after this event, persistently styling him patrician beforehand, thus implying that it was this election that signified Theoderic's royal status. But there can be no doubt that Theoderic was the "King of the Goths" (*rex Gothorum*) long before he arrived on Italian soil. That he required authorization from Constantinople to continue in that position, any more than did his contemporary counterparts elsewhere in the West, is inconceivable. The kingship in question was presumably over the Romans. Apparently, Theoderic wished to receive the title from the Emperor himself, but unable to secure it on his own terms, allowed the matter to be settled by his Goths. It is clear that by the end of the decade Constantinople had recognized, albeit in ambiguous terms, Theoderic's rule. The Anonymous Valesianus reports (12.67) that in 497 or thereabouts, Theoderic sent an embassy to Constantinople; peace was made concerning Theoderic's assumption of the kingdom, and the Emperor returned to Italy the palace ornaments which had remained in Rome after the attack of the Vandals in 455 and then been transmitted to Constantinople by Odovacer.[14]

If we are to believe his contemporaries, Theoderic's reign was a veritable golden age that contrasted sharply with the dark and distracted period that followed. Over the course of the sixth century, successive generations of Ostrogothic rulers engaged in divisive fratricidal strife, while at the same time the competing kingdoms of the Franks and Vandals began to assert their autonomy and establish dominance in regions once united under Theoderic's rule. Although not as enfeebled as the Merovingian *rois fanéants*, the last of the Ostrogothic Kings were nevertheless unable to maintain the standard of governance and culture which historians associate

[13] Deborah M. Deliyannis, "The Mausoleum of Theoderic and the Seven Wonders of the World," *Journal of Late Antiquity* 3.2 (2010), 365–85.

[14] Jones, "The Constitutional Position of Odovacer and Theoderic," 126–30; Moorhead, "Theoderic, Zeno and Odovacer," 261–6; Moorhead, *Theoderic in Italy*, 39–51; Peter Heather, "Theoderic, King of the Goths," *Early Medieval Europe* 4.2 (1995), 145–73.

with Theoderic's rule. His grandson and successor Athalaric (516–34) was a mere child when he took the throne; effective control rested with his mother Amalasuntha. When the young King died, the throne passed on to Theodahad (534–6), an elderly nephew of Theoderic, who then had Amalasuntha murdered.[15] In the East, the Emperor Justinian (527–65) considered Theodahad a usurper, and using Amalasuntha's death as justification, launched his Gothic War – a massive undertaking that was part of a larger, albeit ultimately futile, endeavor to restore the whole of the Roman Empire.

In 535 an expeditionary force of some 7,500 men, commanded by the general Belisarius, landed on the shores of Sicily. Belisarius quickly took hold of the island, encouraging Justinian to order the invasion of Italy itself. For the next twenty years Gothic and Byzantine forces waged war for control of the peninsula. Belisarius took the early advantage, as he advanced north to Rome without meeting any opposition from the Gothic forces.[16] Incensed by an apparent lack of leadership, high-ranking members of the Gothic army rebelled against Theodahad and elected as King one of their own by the name of Witigis (536–40).[17] On February 21, 537, Witigis and his forces attempted to retake Rome, and for more than a year subjected the city to a brutal siege. Although severely under-manned and beleaguered by hunger and disease, Belisarius was able to hold out and eventually repulse the Gothic army to Ravenna, where he forced Witigis to surrender. But between 542 and 550, the Gothic army, under their newly elected King Totila, reconquered the whole of Italy and Sicily (with the exception of a number of coastal towns including Ravenna) in a series of swift and efficient campaigns. The wars ravaged on until 552, when the Byzantine Eunuch Narses defeated and killed Totila at the battle of Busta Gallorum, as well as the King's successor Teias later in the same year in a final confrontation near Mount Vesuvius. A small contingent of Goths, together with a Franco-Aleman army, continued to fight on until 554, when they agreed to terms that secured them land in return for their allegiance to the Emperor. With their surrender, the Ostrogothic kingdom of Italy officially came to an end.[18]

The Gothic War devastated Italian society and brought about greater ruin to the peninsula than did all of the barbarian invasions of the previous one hundred and fifty years. The sixth-century Byzantine historian Procopius (*c.* 500–65), whose narrative of the conflict fills nearly four volumes of his histories, describes appalling conditions, including widespread famine and

[15] Proc., *BG* v.iv.4–11; Jordanes, *Romana et Getica*, 306. [16] Proc., *BG* v.xiv.1–14.
[17] Proc., *BG* v.xi.1–9. [18] Proc., *BG* VIII. xxix.1–xxxii.36, xxxiii.6–xxxv.29.

disease, as early as 538.[19] Cities and towns were despoiled and populations uprooted. In 550 the city of Rome was entirely depopulated for the first time in its history. Writing in 556, Pope Pelagius I (556–61) described his Italian estates as being desolate.[20] Such was the destruction that after the 550s the Goths disappeared as a nation, leaving no trace of their presence in Italy in the archaeological record.[21] And in 568, when the Lombards invaded and established a kingdom of their own in the north, along with semi-independent duchies based in Spoleto and Benevento in the centre and south, the political unity of Italy as a whole was broken and would not be restored until the nineteenth century.

Given the unprecedented scope of devastation associated with the end of Ostrogothic rule in Italy, it is little wonder that historians, ancient and modern alike, regard Theoderic's reign in such a favorable light. While Belisarius was attacking the Gothic kingdom in 535, Procopius remarked about the dead Theoderic:

> . . . [A]fter gaining the adherence of such of the hostile barbarians as chanced to survive, he [i.e. Theoderic] secured the supremacy over both Goths and Italians. And though he did not claim the right to assume either the garb or the name of Emperor of the Romans, but was called 'rex' to the end of his life (for thus the barbarians are accustomed to call their leaders), still, in governing his own subjects, he invested himself with all the qualities that appropriately belong to one who is by birth an Emperor. For he was exceedingly careful to observe justice, he preserved the laws on a sure basis, he protected the land and kept it safe from the barbarians dwelling round about, and he attained the highest possible degree of wisdom and manliness . . . And although in name Theoderic was a usurper, yet in fact he was truly an Emperor as any who have distinguished themselves in this office from the beginning; and love for him among both Goths and Italians grew to be great, and that, too, contrary to the ordinary habits of men.[22]

[19] Proc., *BG* VI. XX. [20] Pelagius in *MGH Epp.* 3, 72–3.

[21] Chris Wickham, *Early Medieval Italy: Central Power and Local Society 400–1000* (Michigan, 1981), 26.

[22] Proc., *BG* V. i.25–30 (trans. Dewing, 11–13): "ἀπ' αὐτοῦ βαρβάρων τῶν πολεμίων προσποιησάμενος ὅσους περιεῖν ξυνέπεσεν αὐτὸς ἔσχε τὸ Γότθων τε καὶ Ἰταλιωτῶν κράτος. καὶ βασιλέως μὲν τοῦ Ῥωμαίων οὔτε τοῦ σχήματος οὔτε τοῦ ὀνόματος ἐπιβατεῦσαι ἠξίωσεν, ἀλλὰ καὶ ῥὴξ διεβίου καλούμενος (οὕτω γὰρ σφῶν τοὺς ἡγεμόνας καλεῖν οἱ βαρβάροι νενομίκασι), τῶν μέντοι κατηκόων τῶν αὐτοῦ προὔστη ξύμπαντα περιβαλλόμενος ὅσα τῷ φύσει βασιλεῖ ἥρμοσται. δικαιοσύνης τε γὰρ ὑπερφῶς ἐπεμελήσατο καὶ τοὺς νόμους ἐν τῷ βεβαίῳ διεσώσατο, ἔκ τε βαρβάρων τῶν περιοίκων τὴν χώραν ἀσφαλῶς διεφύλαξε, ξυνέσεώς τε καὶ ἀνδρίας ἐς ἄκρον ἐληλύθειώς μάλιστα . . . ἦν τε ὁ Θευδέριχος λόγῳ μὲν τύραννος, ἔργῳ δὲ βασιλεὺς ἀληθὴς τῶν ἐν ταύτῃ τῇ τιμῇ τὸ ἐξ ἀρχῆς ηὐδοκιμηκότων οὐδενὸς ἧσσον, ἔρως τε αὐτοῦ ἔν τε Γοτθοις καὶ Ἰταλιώταις πολὺς ἤκμασε, καὶ ταῦτα ἀπὸ τοῦ ἀνθρωπείου τρόπου."

Perhaps surprisingly, a generally favorable view was also taken by the Anonymous Valesianus:

> For Theoderic did nothing wrong. He so governed two races (Romans and Goths) as one, that although he himself was Arian, he nevertheless attempted nothing against the Catholic religion; he gave games in the circus and amphitheater, so that even the Romans called him "Trajan" or "Valentinian," whose times he took as a model; and because of his *Edict*, by which he established justice, the Goths judged him to be their best King in all respects.[23]

It has generally been assumed that the Goths adhered to a non-Nicene version of Christianity, which maintained that the Divine Son was "like" the Divine Father rather than "of the same essence," as had been asserted by the Council of Nicaea in 325 and later ratified by the Council of Constantinople in 381. Commonly referred to as "Arianism," this is in fact an older version of Christianity that was transmitted, it is believed, to the Goths by the fourth-century missionary Ulfilas, who translated the Bible and various other Christian service books into the Gothic language.[24] Although as Roman in origin as the Nicene Creed, by the sixth century, adherence to "Homoean" (from the Greek word for "like") Christianity, could, and did, serve to undermine relations between Goths and Romans. Despite the fact that Theoderic could show great respect for the Orthodox Church, he actively revived the Homoean Church at the expense of the former, thereby earning the condemnation of many Christian contemporaries.[25] Among these was the Anonymous Valesianus, whose history was intended to show that although he was a great ruler, Theoderic's Arianism ultimately turned him into an enemy of God and brought about his downfall, a turn of events portended by several bizarre and apocryphal events, such as the appearance of devils, a comet, and a woman giving birth to four snakes.[26] Final proof of the Gothic

[23] Anon. Val. 12.60: "Nihil enim perperam gessit. Sic gubernavit duas gentes in uno, Romanorum et Gothorum, dum ipse quidem Arrianae sectae esset, tamen nihil contra religionem catholicam temptans; exhibens ludos circensium et amphitheatrum, ut etiam a Romanis Traianus vel Valentinianus, quorum tempora sectatus est, appellaretur, et a Gothis secundum edictum suum, quo ius constituit, rex fortissimus in omnibus iudicaretur."

[24] On the life of Ulfila and the Gothic Bible (with translations and samples of the text itself), see Peter Heather and John Matthews, *The Goths in the Fourth Century* (Liverpool, 1991), chapters 5–7.

[25] Wolfram, *History of the Goths*, 327–8; Moorhead, *Theoderic in Italy*, 97–100 (concerning Jews); Thomas S. Brown, "Everyday life in Ravenna under Theoderic: an Example of his 'Tolerance' and 'Prosperity'?" in *Teoderico il Grande e i Goti d'Italia: atti del XIII Congresso internazionale di studi sull'Alto Medioevo, Milano 2–6 novembre 1992* (Spoleto, 1993).

[26] Anon. Val. 82–84. See further Sam J. Barnish, "The *Anonymous Valesianus* II as a source for the last years of Theoderic," *Latomus* 42 (1983), 572–96; John Moorhead, "The Last Years of Theoderic," *Historia* 32 (1983), 106–20; Henry Chadwick, *Boethius: The Consolations of Music, Logic, Theory, Philosophy* (Oxford, 1981), 291 n. 67.

King's unsuitability in God's eyes was the fact that he died of dysentery – a fate that befell Arius himself.

Not surprisingly, the impression given by Cassiodorus (*c.* 490–585), Theoderic's minister of propaganda and chief collaborator among the Romans, is a highly laudatory one.[27] According to his *Variae*, a collection in twelve books of 468 letters, proclamations, *formulae* for appointments, and edicts related to the Ostrogothic administration, Theoderic successfully maintained peaceful relations with Constantinople, and achieved harmony between his barbarian followers and the native population by cooperating with Rome's senatorial class and fulfilling Roman expectations of continuity.[28] He maintained the offices of the imperial government, and the care of justice and the revenue was delegated according to the principles, and even the forms, of Roman jurisprudence and organization. He is also said to have revived various ancient and politically significant aspects of the imperial administration, including the free distribution of corn and other foodstuffs to the poor in the city of Rome, and the holding of costly but popular circus games.[29] Perhaps the most extravagant of these were the games held in Rome in 500 to celebrate Theoderic's *decennalia*.[30]

In contrast to the preceding century which witnessed decades of rivalry between ambitious generals, greedy aristocrats, and generally incompetent Emperors that culminated in the deposition of Romulus Augustulus and the seizure of power by Odovacer, Cassiodorus presents Theoderic's reign as an age of peace and prosperity of a kind not experienced since the glory days of the early empire. In large part because of this assessment, modern

27 The standard treatment of Cassiodorus' life and works is that of James J. O'Donnell, *Cassiodorus* (Berkeley, CA, 1979).

28 For the edition of the text: Theodor Mommsen, *MGH AA* 12 (Berlin, 1894), 1–385; trans. (select) by Sam J. Barnish, *The Variae of Cassiodorus Senator*, Translated Texts for Historians, vol. 12 (Liverpool, 1992).

29 Cass., *Var.* 6.18 (concerning Theoderic's arrangement of 12,000 *modii* of grain to be supplied to the people of Rome on an annual basis). On the history of this long-established Roman right, which seems to have gone into abeyance in the fifth century, see Federico Marazzi, "The Last Rome: From the End of the Fifth to the End of the Sixth Century," in Sam J. Barnish and Federico Marazzi (eds.), *The Ostrogoths from the Migration Period to the Sixth Century: An Ethnographic Perspective* (Woodbridge, 2007), 279–302, esp. 295–6. Theoderic also had maintained other free provisions including pork. On this, see Cass., *Var.* 6.18.4; and Sam J. Barnish, "Pigs, Plebeians and *Potentes*: Rome's Economic Hinterland, c. 350–600 AD," *PBSR* 55 (1987), 157–85. Cass., *Var.* 11.34 implies that the supply of pork was provided by Lucania and Bruttium – a situation that seems to have continued from the later Empire. In legislation from the Emperor Valentinian III (*Nov. Val.* 36.1, 4), for example, we learn that the province of Samnium, as well as Lucania and Bruttium, were involved in the meat supply of Rome.

30 *Decennalia* celebrations: Ferrandus Diaconus, *Vita s. Fulgentii*, ed. and trans. G.–G. Lapeyre (Paris, 1929), chapters 9, 55–6. See also Moorhead, *Theoderic in Italy*, 60–3 (who suggests the event marked a military victory).

historians have held a favorable opinion towards the age of Theoderic, treating it as a short interlude of Roman renewal, evoking both nostalgia for a peaceful and prosperous time and regret for the unavoidable fact that it was as fleeting and illusory as an Indian summer.[31]

It is important to remember, however, that inasmuch as it was intended as a semi-official record of the barbarian regime, the *Variae* was a product of political expediency that presents over three decades of Ostrogothic history in a flattering light, in particular the deeds of Theoderic. It was compiled in 537/8 towards the end of Cassiodorus' troubled service as Praetorian Prefect of Italy, while war was raging and the Ostrogothic King Witigis was besieging the Byzantine commander Belisarius in Rome. Its purpose was to instruct members of the Italian civil service through moral and religious exhortation, and to demonstrate their legitimacy and suitability for resuming palatine services following Justinian's reconquest of the peninsula.[32] Throughout, Cassiodorus deliberately glossed over disturbances (such as the downfall and execution of the Senator and philosopher Boethius in 524), and highlighted in deliberate fashion the perception of the order and *civilitas*, that is, the civilized rule of law, associated with Ostrogothic rule.[33] At the same time, he emphasized a connection between the barbarian regime and the late imperial administration both in terms of ideology and organization.

[31] See, e.g., Thomas S. Brown, *Gentlemen and Officers: Imperial Administration and Aristocratic Power in Byzantine Italy,* AD *554–800*, British School at Rome (Rome, 1984), 4; Moorhead, *Theoderic in Italy*, chapter 1.

[32] On the problems surrounding the *Variae* as a propagandistic text, see Shane Bjornlie, "What Have Elephants to Do with Sixth-Century Politics? A Reappraisal of the 'Official' Governmental Dossier of Cassiodorus," *JLA* 2.1 (2009), 143–71; Andrew Gillett, "The Purposes of Cassiodorus' *Variae*," in A. C. Murray (ed.), *After Rome's Fall: Narrators and Sources of Early Medieval History Essays Presented to Walter Goffart* (Toronto, 1998), 37–50. For the religious dimensions of the text see Sam J. Barnish, "Sacred Texts of the Secular: Writing, Hearing, and Reading Cassiodorus' *Variae*," *Studia Patristica* 38 (2001), 363–70. On the authenticity of the *Variae* as part of an actual chancery tradition, see Stefan Krautschick, *Cassiodor und die Politik seiner Zeit.* Habelts Dissertationsdrucke, Reihe Alte Geschichte 17 (Bonn, 1983), 41–5, 118–22; Moorhead, *Theoderic in Italy*, 2–3, 145; O'Donnell, *Cassiodorus*, 59; Gunhild Vidén, *The Roman Chancery Tradition: Studies in the Language of Codex Theodosianus and Cassiodorus' 'Variae'* (Göteborg, 1984), 84, 88, 142.

[33] E.g., Cass., *Var.* 1.1 (a letter in Theoderic's name to the Emperor Anastasius, remarking that the King's rule was in direct imitation of the Emperor's, and noted how his Gothic followers obeyed Roman law); 1.27 (here, the Roman Senate is instructed by Theoderic to uphold the rule of Roman law); 1.44 (a letter to the people of Rome instructing them to obey the authority of the newly-appointed Urban Prefect); 3.17 (a letter in Theoderic's name to the Gothic inhabitants of Gaul, instructing them to obey Roman law); 3.43 (a letter to the same provinces of Gaul, Theoderic reiterates the point that Roman law was to be followed by all provincials). In the preface to the *Variae*, Cassiodorus exclaims how he was frequently encouraged by Theoderic to embrace the laws of the ancient Romans: "hortamini [i.e. Theoderic] me [i.e. Cassiodorus] frequenter, ut diligam senatum, leges principum gratanter amplectar..." For this definition of *civilitas*, see Moorhead, *Theoderic in Italy*, 79; *contra* Amory, *People and Identity*, 43.

From all of this there emerges a highly civilized and Romanized picture of things – a picture that does not necessarily reflect conditions as they actually were, but rather as they were hoped for. A much different and more accurate picture comes to us from the unknown authors of one of the most debated texts of the early medieval era – the *Edictum Theoderici*. This is a significant document that offers valuable historical insights into the formative social, political, and cultural developments taking place on Italian soil during Late Antiquity, as the beliefs, institutions, and customs of the ancient world were slowly transformed or replaced by those of the medieval. It also challenges long-held assumptions as to just how peaceful, prosperous, and Roman-like Theoderic's Italy really was.

Overview

The principal reason for the exclusion of the *ET* as a useful historical source in most modern studies of the period is the fact that historians have been unable to agree upon two important issues surrounding the text – namely, the identity of the individuals responsible for its creation, and when this was carried out. Chapter 1 addresses several questions surrounding the document, including: debates about its authorship and manuscript tradition, the date of its production, the circumstances surrounding its composition, the purposes for which it was created, and the subject matter with which it deals. It is argued that the *ET* was drawn up in accordance with imperial legal tradition by a group of unknown Roman jurists working under the authority of the office of Quaestor, and issued perhaps as early as 500 to coincide with the King's *decennalia* celebrations in Rome. Its purpose was to restore peace and order in the peninsula by reinforcing, clarifying, and, in most cases, updating existing Roman law.

Chapter 2 contextualizes the *ET* in terms of the developments taking place in Roman law and society in Italy from the third to early sixth century, in particular how the text fits within the evolving framework of Roman law in Late Antiquity. Many of the 154 provisions of the *ET* contain words, phrases, and concepts that differ significantly from earlier and contemporary Roman legal texts. Many of these variances reflect the sorts of changes – social, political, economic, and cultural – taking place in Italy as a result of the decline and eventual collapse of Roman rule in the peninsula. Some express an interest in ancient or outmoded customs and practices, and others a concern for present day circumstances. Still others are merely haphazard and of little importance. By way of example the significance of these variations is discussed. The investigation offers a revealing glimpse into the character of Roman law and society in early sixth-century Italy.

Drawing upon evidence from a variety of sources, Chapter 3 provides a detailed account of how a case was initiated, brought to court and heard, and of how judgment was made and executed. It explores how the judicial system in sixth-century Italy was organized, the role of the judge and litigant in legal disputes, and how threats to the public order were dealt with through circumscribed penalties. The focus here is strictly on the court system and the rules of evidence and procedure that appear in the law, not less formal (but by no means less legal) forms of dispute settlement that took place outside of the courtroom. By using late imperial decrees as a model, the investigation demonstrates that while many aspects of the late Roman justice system were selectively appropriated by Theoderic and his successors, many others were re-worked or ignored altogether, thus raising important questions – and doubts – as to just how efficient, organized, and Roman-like the barbarian King's judicial system really was.

The *ET* is a valuable source for the prevailing social and economic conditions of early sixth-century Italy. Provisions pertaining to aspects of private law, including legal status and personality, property (including slaves), contract and sale, ownership and possession, marriage and divorce, succession and inheritance, take up the bulk of the collection. The text also sheds light on such topics as the Ostrogothic monetary system, the commercial activities of merchants and traders, as well as the dangers that threatened the Italian economy, including governmental corruption, counterfeiting, the decline of urban life, and a lack of available men and resources to maintain available income-producing land. Chapters 4 and 5 explore the various and interrelated subjects of Roman private law found in the *ET*. The survey is useful for two reasons. First, it documents extremely well some of the characteristic features of the *ET*: its range, its thoroughness, its reasonableness, its concern with the practical and tangible, its tendency for the particular provision and not the general principle. Second, and more importantly, behind the starkly revealing information yielded by the provisions may be glimpsed, though obscurely, the day-to-day life experienced, or perhaps endured, by the overwhelming majority of inhabitants of Theoderic's Italy – a majority for which there is no other source so informative.

To serve as a reference point and foster further study of the *ET*, a translation of the text is provided in the Appendix. Wherever possible, I have provided notes that contain references to possible sources and analogous texts to individual provisions, brief explanations of technical terms and legal concepts, a discussion of interesting points of the law or debates about its meaning, and specific instances in our sources that involve the operation of the law in question. A brief note concerning the translation: the language and style of the *ET* are essential for understanding its purpose and the audience for which it was aimed. The *ET* was intended to edify not only judges and legal experts, but also the general public at large. To ensure clarity and precision it purposefully lacks the excessively verbose and intricate style of the imperial collections of Theodosius and Justinian, as well as the eloquence on display in the *Variae*. These texts were intended to impress a small, educated elite. To that end, artistic elaboration and grandiloquence was as, if not more, important than the need for the content to be comprehensible for the average person.[34] The translation offered here limits the use of colloquialisms and idioms in an effort to retain, to a worthwhile degree, the original meaning and spirit of the compilers.

Significance

This is first and foremost a study of a Roman legal text from early sixth-century Italy, but the implications extend far beyond the bounds of legal history. For the survival of Roman law is intimately connected with the wider question of the way in which the world of Antiquity came to an end. Traditionally, the removal of Romulus Augustulus in 476 marked the end of imperial rule in the West. But whether this date actually constituted an end of the Roman world is a matter of perspective. Since Edward Gibbon more than 200 years ago wrote his monumental treatise, *Decline and Fall of the Roman Empire*, the degree of disruption or gradual change associated with the end of Antiquity has been debated. Did Rome collapse, or was it merely transformed? Was the Empire destroyed by barbarian invaders, or was its decline a natural and inevitable consequence of immoderate greatness? To be sure, Gibbon concluded that Rome did indeed fall, attributing its fate to a number of contributing internal and external factors, such as the decay of ancient military virtues, the loss of political freedom, the increasing burden of taxation, a weakening moral authority, the development of the Church as the principal object of loyalty for a new governing elite, and of course the barbarians. While he could not provide straightforward answers as to which

[34] Vidén, *The Roman Chancery Tradition*; Nicholas Everett, *Literacy in Lombard Italy, c. 568–774* (Cambridge, 2003), 22, 24; and Barnish, "Sacred Texts of the Secular," 367–8. For the artistic style of Tribonian, the jurist primarily responsible for putting together Justinian's legal corpus, see Tony Honoré, *Tribonian* (London, 1978), 244–5.

of these factors was more important in bringing about Rome's demise, Gibbon nevertheless regarded the period during which Europe was given over to the rule of Goths, Burgundians, Franks, and other barbarians as one of unprecedented destruction and devastation.[35] For Gibbon, influenced as he was by his admiration for all things Roman, the disintegration of the Roman Empire in the West brought about changes which, for the most part, fundamentally changed Europe for the worse; Late Antiquity was a confused and distracted period haunted by the immortal past of a once glorious Rome.

Gibbon's model, which emphasizes the destructive nature of Rome's collapse, has endured for centuries. In the last four decades, however, a number of alternative models have been put forth by scholars attempting to revise the pessimistic view of Gibbon. These scholars prefer to see change and transformation where Gibbon and others only saw destruction. The trailblazer of this revisionist approach is the historian Peter Brown. Beginning with his brief but influential survey *The World of Late Antiquity*, followed soon after by his seminal article "The Rise and Function of the Holy Man in Late Antiquity," Brown changed the way scholars have viewed the end of the Roman world.[36] He articulated a new period, "Late Antiquity," beginning with the accession of the Emperor Diocletian in AD 284 and lasting right up to the eighth century, which was characterized not by the decline and dissolution of the western Roman Empire but by vibrant intellectual, religious, and cultural debate. For Brown, Late Antiquity was a period of transition and transformation in which the fundamental elements of the classical world survived and evolved in different, though no less inferior, forms. Of central importance for this transition were the holy men. Acting as intercessors not only between the increasingly disenfranchised common man and the ruthless, corrupt elite, but also between the earthly and heavenly realms, these "saintly" leaders embraced the spiritual *avant-garde* of the age, and in so doing provided a vital link between the classical and medieval worlds.

[35] Gibbon was not alone in this pessimistic estimation. The French scholar André Piganiol, e.g, declared (*L'Empire chrétien (325–395)*, Histoire Romaine 4 (Paris, 1947), 222) that the Roman Empire did not die a natural death but was assassinated by the Germans. In light of the fact that Piganiol was writing in France so soon after World War II, such sentiment is hardly surprising.

[36] Peter Brown, *The World of Late Antiquity: From Marcus Aurelius to Muhammad* (London, 1971); Peter Brown, "The Rise and Function of the Holy Man in Late Antiquity," *JRS* 61 (1971), 80–101. Other notable works of Brown include *The Making of Late Antiquity* (Cambridge, MA, 1978); *Society and the Holy in Late Antiquity* (Berkeley, CA, 1982); *The World of Late Antiquity: AD 150–750*, rev. edn. (London, 1989); *Power and Persuasion in Late Antiquity: Towards a Christian Empire* (Madison, WI, 1992). On the significance of Peter Brown in the scholarship of Late Antiquity, see James Howard-Johnson and Paul Antony Hayward (eds.), *The Cult of Saints in Late Antiquity and the Middle Ages: Essays on the Contribution of Peter Brown* (Oxford, 1999).

Along a parallel route, some historians have called into question the very notion that the Roman Empire in the West came to an end as a direct result of hostile and violent barbarian invasions. Just as words like "decline" and "crisis" were replaced with "transition" and "transformation" to account for the cultural change in this period, so "accommodation" is now used to explain how barbarians came to live within the Empire and eventually rule it. For these historians, there was no brutal catastrophic onrush of barbarian invaders in the fourth century. Rather, there was a slow evolution during which time the Empire became progressively Germanized while, inversely, the Germans adapted to the mode of existence of the Roman populations. And when, in 476, the western Roman Empire died of exhaustion and not because it was invaded, the new masters in fact understood, or ended by understanding, that they had everything to gain by maintaining rather than upsetting the existing status quo.[37] As Alfons Dopsch put it, "The Germans did not behave as enemies of culture, destroying or abolishing it; on the contrary they preserved and developed it."[38]

Other historians have gone even further than this, notably Walter Goffart, who challenged the very premise of barbarian invasions. Rather than regard the relationship between the Romans and barbarians in terms of conquest and consolidation, Goffart proposed a new paradigm that emphasizes integration and cooperation between the two. The barbarians were incorporated into the fold as protectors of the Roman way of life through an ingenious and effective tax arrangement.[39] In other words, the Romans accommodated the barbarians on essentially Roman terms through existing institutional mechanisms.[40] While allowing for a degree of crisis and disruption, Goffart's model envisions the transition of the Roman world as a relatively peaceful process. The fall of the Roman Empire was, in his words, "an imaginative experiment that got a little out of hand."[41]

37 See, e.g., Brian Croke, "AD 476: The Manufacture of a Turning Point," *Chiron* 13 (1983), 81–119; Raymond Van Dam, *Leadership and Community in Late Antique Gaul* (Berkeley, CA, 1985); Charles E.V. Nixon, "Relations between Visigoths and Romans in Fifth-Century Gaul," in J. Drinkwater and H. Elton (eds.), *Fifth-Century Gaul: A Crisis of Identity?* (Cambridge, 1992), 64–74; Ralph W. Mathisen, *Roman Aristocrats in Barbarian Gaul: Strategies for Survival in the Age of Transition* (Austin, 1993); Pohl, *Kingdoms of the Empire.*

38 Alfons Dopsch, *The Economic and Social Foundations of European Civilization*, trans. M. G. Beard and N. Marshall (London, 1937), 386.

39 Walter Goffart, *Barbarians and Romans: Techniques of Accommodation, AD 418–584* (Princeton, 1980), esp. chapter 3.

40 Goffart reiterates this point in his *Barbarian Tides: The Migration Age and the Later Roman Empire* (Philadelphia, PA, 2006), the title of which reinforces the notion that there was no such thing as a barbarian invasion.

41 Goffart, *Barbarians and Romans*, 35.

In recent years there has been a mini-revival in "disruption" models. The most notable of these is that of Bryan Ward-Perkins.[42] It was the unwelcome arrival of barbarian invaders, Ward-Perkins argues, that brought about a violent and decisive end to the Roman world. In the aftermath of this collapse, civilization sank to a primitive level. For Ward-Perkins, the fall of Rome was a destructive event that marked a decisive break from the classical past and ushered in the Dark Ages. If there was any continuity beyond the fifth century, it failed to live up to the greatness of the preceding era; by whatever standards one might wish to use, life in post-Roman Europe was culturally inferior to, economically retarded by comparison with, and politically backward when measured against the standards of the Graeco-Roman world. While Ward-Perkins' views might be extreme in their elaborations of the social, political, and economic developments associated with Rome's administrative demise, they have reignited the debate among historians wishing to account for Rome's fall or measure its passing.[43]

Scholarship on Ostrogothic Italy has been rooted in these interpretive paradigms. Those interested in the destructive forces of the barbarian invasions have tended to emphasize the "otherness" and "barbarian" qualities of Theoderic and his followers, or point towards "un-Roman" activities within the Ostrogothic regime.[44] Those who support the notion of accommodation have in turn explored a number of angles including the legal mechanisms of the Gothic settlement in Italy; the constitutional position of Theoderic *vis-à-vis* the Roman Empire in the East; and Roman collaborators among the ruling senatorial class who worked together with their barbarian overlords.[45]

This book brings greater clarity to these issues by exploring how Roman law, the institutions of legal administration, and society survived and evolved in Italy long after the official collapse of the western imperial administration, when the maintenance of peace and order was the responsibility of Theoderic and his successors. Despite the fact that scholars have

[42] Ward-Perkins, *The Fall of Rome.*

[43] For a similar view but with less emphasis on the negative impact of the barbarians, see Peter Heather, *The Fall of the Roman Empire: A New History of Rome and the Barbarians* (Oxford, 2006).

[44] E.g., Ward-Perkins, *The Fall of Rome*, 72–3.

[45] E.g., Goffart, *Barbarians and Romans*, chapter 3 (Gothic settlement); Jones, "The Constitutional Position of Odovacer and Theoderic," 126–30; Moorhead, "Theoderic, Zeno and Odovacer," 261–6; Paul S. Barnwell, *Emperors, Prefects and Kings: The Roman West, 395–565* (London, 1992), part 3 (Theoderic's position *viz.* Constantinople); Moorhead, *Theoderic in Italy*; James O'Donnell, "Liberius the Patrician," *Traditio* 37 (1981), 31–72; Sam J. Barnish, "Taxation, Land and Barbarian Settlement in the Western Empire," *PBSR* 54 (1986), 170–95.

focused on the connection that exists in so many respects between the legal conditions prevailing in the successor kingdoms of the Franks, Visigoths, and Burgundians and those of the later Roman Empire, there is as yet no modern legal history of the Ostrogothic kingdom such as that offered here, one that brings together the administrative and judicial features, laws and legal procedures, social and economic conditions of the Italian peninsula, and attempts to put these into a legal-historical perspective.

In this regard the *ET* is an important source that should not be overlooked. On the one hand it fully bears out the longevity of Rome's classical legal heritage. By the early sixth century the imperial administration had largely disappeared, but, however selective and modified, the *ET* was a practical guidebook of Roman law that presupposed a population still concerned with formalities that had their origins in an ancient institution. And with the exception of a few references to barbarians, nothing within the text would suggest that an army of Goths had taken up residence within the Italian peninsula. For many scholars, this sort of continuity is sufficient grounds for concluding that Rome lived on, both as a city and above all as a concept, well after the date that marks its official demise, serving as a model for the relatively primitive Germanic peoples who came to inherit its administration over the course of the fifth and sixth centuries.[46] Proponents for this school of thought have also drawn attention to patterns of land occupation and urban settlements, the social status of nobles and peasants, bonds of kinship, cult practices and religious life, and traditions in education, arguing that in these areas, too, continuity was the rule and not the exception. In so doing they have called into question the notion that the Empire had fallen.[47]

[46] See, e.g., John M. Wallace-Hadrill, *Early Germanic Kingship in England and on the Continent* (Oxford, 1971); John M. Wallace-Hadrill, *The Long-Haired Kings, and Other Studies in Frankish History* (London, 1962), 9; David Ganz, "Bureaucratic Shorthand and Merovingian Learning," in Patrick Wormald with Donald Bullough and Roger Collins (eds.), *Ideal and Reality in Frankish and Anglo-Saxon Society* (Oxford, 1983), 58–75; Ian Wood, "Administration, Law and Culture in Merovingian Gaul," in Rosamond McKitterick (ed.), *The Uses of Literacy in Early Medieval Europe* (Cambridge, 1990), 63–8; Ian Wood, *The Merovingian Kingdoms, 450–751* (London/New York, 1994); Jill Harries and Ian Wood (eds.), *The Theodosian Code. Studies in the Imperial Law of Late Antiquity* (London, 1993); Jill Harries, *Law and Empire in Late Antiquity* (Cambridge, 1999); John F. Matthews, *Laying Down the Law: A Study of the Theodosian Code* (New Haven, CT, 2000); Michael E. Jones, "The Legacy of Roman Law in Post-Roman Britain," in Ralph W. Mathisen (ed.), *Law, Society and Authority in Late Antiquity* (Oxford, 2001), 45–57.

[47] For discussions on the continuity of social order in early medieval Europe, see: Walter Ullman, *The Carolingian Renaissance and the Idea of Kingship* (London, 1969); François L. Ganshof (ed.), *The Carolingians and the Frankish Monarchy*, trans. Janet Sondheimer (Ithaca, NY, 1971); Janet Martindale, "The French Aristocracy in the Early Middle Ages: A Reappraisal," *Past and Present* 75 (1977), 5–45; Edward James, *The Origins of France: From Clovis to the Capetians, 500–1000* (London, 1989), 73–92; Wickham, *Early Medieval Italy*, 80–145. On bonds of kinship,

But to suggest from this sort of continuity alone that Theoderic's Italy constituted a renewed Empire is to overlook far more important questions that the *ET* raises. For instance, how much of the population had access to legal experts and the courts? Were the judges capable of dispensing justice swiftly and equitably? Were they honest and upright? Were the rights of citizens reasonably secure against greedy officials and powerful magnates?[48] To judge from the amount of attention devoted to these kinds of questions in the *ET*, it would seem that the availability of skilled and honest judges who could effectively settle cases at the local level was limited, and this posed a significant challenge for the central administration to maintain peace and order effectively throughout the provinces. The manuscript also casts doubt on the supposed prosperity of Ostrogothic Italy as suggested by some rather ambiguous references in the *Variae*. While the peaceful conditions Cassiodorus attributed to Theoderic's reign certainly allowed for a measure of recovery, such recovery was temporary at best; and it is questionable whether it extended to the entire population. As the *ET* bears witness, Theoderic was unable to remedy certain structural weaknesses that had afflicted the peninsula for more than a century: specifically, the problem of manpower shortage and the insecurity of property in the provinces. Such pressures only served to undermine a superficially stable social fabric that disintegrated completely with the crisis of war that enveloped Italy shortly after Theoderic's death in 526.

Of course, there are problems in using legal materials as an historical source. It is notoriously easy to interpret legal precept as evidence of social practice, and to assume that a measure, by merit of its existence alone, was necessarily enforced. Moreover, it must be appreciated that within these sources it is often the *unusual* that is provided for, especially in those laws that we would classify as criminal. Therefore, our picture may be an exaggerated one or one that never existed, except as an ideal. Despite such

see Joseph H. Lynch, *Godparents and Kingship in Early Medieval Europe* (Princeton, NJ, 1986). For cult practices and religious life, see (in addition to the works of Peter Brown): Raymond Van Dam, *Saints and their Miracles in Late Antique Gaul* (Princeton, 1993); Yitzhak Hen, *Culture and Religion in Merovingian Gaul,* AD *481–751* (Leiden/New York, 1995); Daniel Caner, *Wandering, Begging Monks: Spiritual Authority and the Promotion of Monasticism in Late Antiquity* (Berkeley, CA, 2002). And on continuity in the area of education: Max L. W. Laistner, *Thought and Letters in Western Europe,* AD *500 to 900* (Ithaca, NY, 1966); Rosamond McKitterick, *The Carolingians and the Written Word* (Cambridge, 1989); John Contreni, *Carolingian Learning, Masters and Manuscripts* (Aldershot, 1992); Erich Auerbach, *Literary Language & its Public in Late Antiquity and in the Middle Ages* (Princeton, NJ, 1993); Richard E. Sullivan (ed.), *"The Gentle Voices of Teachers": Aspects of Learning in the Carolingian Age* (Columbus, OH, 1995).

48 Tony Honoré, "Roman Law AD 200–400: From Cosmopolis to Rechtstaat?" in Simon Swain and Mark Edwards (eds.), *Approaching Late Antiquity. The Transformation from Early to Late Empire* (Oxford, 2004), 109–32, at 112.

problems, the rewards in such an approach are entirely justified by the fact that no other source has the evidential value possessed by the law for understanding the objectives and ideals of an ancient society, from the governing elite who created and administered the law to the undifferentiated masses that were subject to its authority. For the law was shaped not by jurists working in isolation, but by wider social and cultural changes. Such social developments in turn affected the form and content of the law through the actions of judges, lawyers, Emperors, Kings, churchmen, and laymen, who were themselves products of their social environment. It is because of this that we can turn to the *ET* for understanding some of the profound social, political, and economic developments associated with Italy's transition from Roman province to barbarian kingdom.

CHAPTER 1

The historical context

Introduction

The *ET* offers us a splendid picture of Italy in the early sixth century. The subject matter is so diverse that virtually no aspect of public and private life is left untouched. The provisions shed light upon the organization and administration of the judiciary, economy, and society; they deal with marriage and guardianship, slavery and manumission, aristocracy and religion; they illustrate the relationship of King and people, of Roman and Goth, of landlord and tenant; they regulate sales and donations, loans and testaments. Topics range from murder to the destruction or theft of property, from necromancy to grave-robbing, from forgery to rape. But continuing disputes over its paternity have limited the potential of this extraordinary document as an historical source. In fact, the list of candidates for authorship is a veritable who's who of the Late Antique world. The most notable include: Eparchius Avitus, western Roman Emperor between 455 and 456; Majorian, who succeeded Avitus and reigned as Emperor between 457 and 461; Theoderic II, who ruled the Visigothic kingdom of Aquitaine in southern Gaul from 453 to 466; Magnus of Narbo, the *Praefectus Praetorio Galliarum* from 458 to 459; Odovacer; and, of course, Theoderic the Ostrogoth.[1] Some scholars have gone so far as to suggest that the *ET* is a forgery, the spurious creation of the sixteenth-century French humanist Pierre Pithou.[2] Any study on the historical significance of the *ET* must therefore begin with the question of authorship.

[1] For a summary of earlier scholarship, see Clausidieter Schott, "Der Stand der Leges-Forschung," *Frühmittelalterliche Studien* 13 (Berlin, 1979), 29–55.

[2] See, e.g., Piero Rasi, "Sulla paternità del c.d. Edictum Theodorici Regis," *Archivio Giuridico* 145 (1953), 105–62; Bruno Paradisi, "Critica e mito dell'editto teodericano," *Bollettino dell'Istituto di diritto romano* 68 (1965), 1–47.

Authorship

The issue of the *ET*'s authorship is a persistent one that stems from problems connected to the uncertainty of the manuscript tradition, the date of composition, and the identity of those who compiled it. In 1579, Pierre Pithou published the first edition of the *ET*. The circumstances of that edition are well known through a letter dated 2 January 1579 and addressed to Eduard Molé, an acquaintance of Pithou.[3] In it, Pithou refers to his recent publication of the *Variae*, and proposes to have published as an accompaniment to that work an edition of the *ET*. According to the letter, Pithou was in possession of a surviving manuscript and obtained a second from Molé: "I wanted the Edict of the wisest prince [i.e. Theoderic] to appear in your name . . . by whose kindness I have obtained another copy."[4] Unfortunately, neither exemplar has survived, leaving Pithou's edition as our only witness to the original text. The relationship between the two manuscripts, and how Pithou drew from them for his own edition, is not known.

Pithou's edition was originally published as part of a larger collection of works, principally those of Cassiodorus. Five subsequent editions of the *ET* were similarly published as part of Cassiodorus' general works: two in Paris in 1588 and 1600 by Marc L'Orry, and three in Geneva in 1609, 1650, and again in 1663. During the eighteenth century the *ET* was republished several times, in each instance as part of a larger collection of various legal sources: Melchior Goldast included a copy in his *Collectio constitutionum imperialium*; Pietro Georgisch in his *Corpus iuris germanici antiqui*; and Paulo Canciani's *Leges antiquae barbarorum* likewise contained the text. In 1816, Gotthard Friedrich Rhon published a new edition of the text complete with commentary. This was soon followed (1824) by a revised edition of Ferdinand Walter in his *Corpus iuris germanici antiqui*, and again by Felix Dahn in 1866, who provided for the first time references to the analogous Roman sources that presumably served as models for individual provisions of the *ET*. Subsequent editions have added to the list of possible analogues, the most comprehensive (and accurate) being that of Friedrich Bluhme, who worked directly from Pithou's original edition. Bluhme's served as the basis for the subsequent editions of Guido Padelletti and Johannes Baviera.

[3] The letter accompanied the 1579 edition (*editio princeps*) as well as subsequent editions of Nivellius (1589), l'Orry (1588, 1600) and Brosse (1600, 1609). See further Giulio Vismara, "Edictum Theoderici," *Ius Romanum Medii Aevi*, part 1, 2 b *aa* α (Milan, 1967), 6–7.

[4] "Edictum vero prudentissimi principis in tuo nomine apparere volui . . . cuius beneficio alterum eius exemplar nactus sum." On the contents of the letter, see Vismara, "Edictum," 6.

The *ET* was last reprinted by Pierre Falaschi in 1966, who also based his edition directly on that of Pithou.[5]

Pithou identified the *ET* as the work of the Ostrogoth Theoderic, referring to his 1579 edition as the *Edictum Theoderici regis Italiae*– a title he apparently derived from the formula that appears at the end of the text: *Explicit Edictum Theoderici Regis.*[6] But the formula does not specify, as Pithou does, that the Theoderic to whom the *Edict* is attributed is King of Italy, only that he is King. In total, there are eight kings known to us from historical sources who ruled under this name. These include two Visigothic kings, Theoderic I (418–51) and Theoderic II (453–66), the Ostrogoths Theoderic Strabo (d. 481) and Theoderic the Great, King of Italy, as well as four Frankish Kings – Theoderic I (511–34), Theoderic II (595–613), Theoderic III, who became King in 679, and Theoderic IV (721–37). Theoderic the Great has always been the main contender for authorship,[7] but a strong case for Theoderic II of the Visigoths has been put forward by Giulio Vismara.

Vismara argues *ex silentio* that although detailed in other respects, sources such as Cassiodorus, Jordanes, Ennodius, and Procopius make no mention of the *ET*, nor do they explicitly cite Theoderic as being responsible for

[5] The most accessible editions are those of Frederich Bluhme (*Edictum Theoderici regis* in *MGH Leges nationum Germanicarum* 5 (Hannover, 1889), 145–79) and J. Baviera (*FIRA*, vol. II, (Florence, 1940); repr. Pier Luigi Falaschi, *Edictum Theoderici regis Italiae* (Milan, 1966), 683–710). For a review of the various editions of the *ET*, see Vismara, "Edictum," 9–11; Baviera, *FIRA*, vol. II, 683.

[6] Pithou again makes this identification in the preface to a selection of his edited works which included the text of the *ET*, a letter of Sidonius Apollinaris, and a panegyric of Ennodius composed in honor of the Ostrogothic King: *Edictum Theoderici regis Italiae – C. Sollii Apollinaris Sidonii Arvenernorum episcopi de Theoderico rege epistola – Ennodii Ticinensis panegyricus Theodericio regi dictus* (c. 356 ed. l'Orry 1588). See Vismara, "Edictum," 7 n. 8.

[7] Supporters of this attribution include most notably: Arnold H. M. Jones, *The Later Roman Empire, 284–602: A Social, Economic and Administrative Survey*, 3 vols. (Oxford, 1964), I, 477; Hermann Nehlsen, "*Edictum Theoderici*," *Zeitschrift der Savigny-Stiftung für Rechtsgeschichte, Germanistische Abteilung* 86 (1969), 246–60; Hermann Nehlsen, *Sklavenrecht zwischen Antike und Mittelalter: germanisches und römisches Recht in den germanischen Rechtsaufzeichnungen I, Ostgoten, Westgoten, Franken, Langobarden*, Göttinger Studien zur Rechtsgeschichte 7 (Göttingen, 1972), 120–3; Herwig Wolfram, *History of the Goths*, trans. Thomas J. Dunlap, 2nd edn. (Berkeley, CA, 1988), 289; Detlef Liebs, *Die Jurisprudenz im spätantiken Italien (260–640 n. Chr.)*, Freiburger Rechtsgeschichtliche Abhandlungen, n.f. 8 (Berlin, 1987), 120–6, and 191–4; Katherine Fischer-Drew, *Law and Society in Early Medieval Europe. Studies in Legal History* (London, 1988), II, 21 (although she contradicts herself at section VII, 2); John Moorhead, *Theoderic in Italy*, 75–6; Renzo Lambertini, *Introduzione allo studio esegetico del diritto romano* (Bologna, 1993), 92; Patrick Amory, *People and Identity in Ostrogothic Italy, 489–554*, Cambridge Studies in Medieval Life and Thought: Fourth series (Cambridge, 1997), 78–82; Patrick Wormald, "The *Leges Barbarorum*: Law and Ethnicity in the Ostrogothic West," in Hans-Werner Goetz, Jörg Jarnut, and Walter Pohl (eds.), *Regna and Gentes: The Relationship between Late Antique and Early Medieval Peoples and Kingdoms in the Transformation of the Roman World* (Leiden/New York, 2003), 21–53.

issuing such a legal pronouncement.[8] Moreover, there are contradictions between the *Variae* and *ET* which Vismara has taken as proof that the *ET* is not of Ostrogothic extraction. For example, we hear from Cassiodorus that Theoderic's nephew Theodahad received a far more lenient punishment for *invasio*, the illegal usurpation of property, than that stipulated in *ET* 10.[9] Such minor points of difference, however, should hardly come as a surprise. In the first place, many of the cases discussed by Cassiodorus represent special intervention on the part of the King, after the regular courts had seen things otherwise. It goes without saying that such cases were by their very nature exceptional, and were not necessarily reflective of the sorts of everyday cases for which the *ET* was intended to apply. Second, it is worthwhile to keep in mind that the *Codex Justinianus*, the single most comprehensive code of law at the time of its promulgation in 533/34, contains countless contradictions of the law, despite Justinian's own claims that his code would eliminate any and all such inconsistencies.[10]

Generally speaking, negative arguments like these are a weak form of proof for this period, especially for a document-type like the *ET* that was not out of the ordinary. But Vismara does not rest his case solely on the absence of evidence. Turning his attention north of the Alps, he argues that the *ET* was the work of the Visigothic King Theoderic II, who quite possibly entrusted the actual writing of the text to the Praetorian Prefect of Gaul, Magnus of Narbo.[11] There are three reasons for this attribution. First, the latest law from which the *ET* borrows is a novel of the Emperor Majorian of 458 (*Nov. Maj.* 7.1). Issued to the Praetorian Prefect Basilius, the novel reaffirms the *temporis praescriptio* for a decurion at thirty years. According to the Roman legal principle of *favor libertatis*, under exceptional circumstances freedom could be attained by an individual who had lived as free for a specified amount of time. Majorian's novel fixed this period

[8] Vismara, "Edictum," 246–8; Felix Dahn also notes the silence of the sources (*Die Könige der Germanen: Das Wesen des ältesten Königsthums der germanischen Stämme und seine Geschichte bis auf die Feudalzeit*, 4 vols. (Leipzig, 1879), 6 n. 1), but does not discount the *ET* as being the work of Theoderic the Great.

[9] Cass., *Var.* 4.39, 5.12. [10] Peter Stein, *Roman Law in European History* (Cambridge, 1999), 32–5.

[11] Vismara, "Edictum," § 28; Giulio Vismara, "Romani e Goti di fronte al diritto nel regno ostrogoto," *Settimanae di studio del Centro Italiano di studi sull'alto medioevo* 3 [= *I Goti in occidente: problemi*] (Spoleto, 1956), 407–63; similarly Hans-Jürgen Becker, "Edictum Theoderici," in *Handwörterbuch zur Deutschen Rechtsgeschichte*, vol. 1 (Berlin, 1971), 802–4; Wolfgang Kunkel, *An Introduction to Roman Legal and Constitutional History*, trans. J.M. Kelly, 2nd edn., based on the sixth German edition of *Römische Rechtsgeschichte* (Oxford, 1973), 160; Hans Schlosser, *Grundzüge der neueren Privatrechtsgeschichte*, 4th edn. (Heidelberg, 1982), 6; Alan Watson, *The Evolution of Western Private Law* (Baltimore, 1985), 77–9.

at thirty years.[12] *ET* 69, based loosely on the novel, recognizes this same thirty-year duration:

ET 69

We order that decurions, guild members, or slaves that clearly have not contributed to their municipality [i.e. through the performance of compulsory public services] are to be retained by property owners who have been in possession of them for a period of thirty years; since We allow the beneficial decree of this thirty-year statute to be disturbed with respect to no one under any pretext, it is fitting that this law [of thirty years] maintain its legal force, in whatever way the laws prescribe, whether in matters involving a private citizen or the fisc. And since We know that such false accusations are frequently stirred up to the ruin of masters when rustics or decurions connive together to say that they have offered a contribution [to their municipality], We grant the following: if it is proven that a contribution was made with the knowledge of the property owner or his procurator or chief tenant if the owner was overseas, this law will remain in full force.[13]

Nov. Maj. 7.1

. . . We sanction that with the exception of those decurions who have assisted their municipalities by some performance of compulsory public services and for that reason are not lost to the municipal senates by any prescription, wherever decurions may be found who have been absent henceforth less than thirty years, the procurators or lessees of the landed estates shall be constrained, the owners of the estates shall be notified, and such decurions, together with their wives, shall be restored to the cities which they had deserted.[14]

[12] The basis for the thirty-year statute of limitations is Valentinian III's voluminous statute (*de triginta annorum praescriptione omnibus causis opponenda*) of 449: *Nov. Val.* 27; esp. §§ 3 and 4.

[13] *ET* 69: "Quisquis curialem, aut collegiatum, aut servum, per triginta annos possederit, qui nullam patriae suae collationem subisse monstratur, eos praediorum dominis iubemus adquiri: quia in nullo tricennalis legis saluberrimum constitutum sub qualibet patimur occasione turbari: quam sive adversus privatum, sive adversus fiscum, suam, quemadmodum leges praecipiunt, obtinere convenit firmitatem. Et quia frequenter scimus tales calumnias in perniciem dominorum, conniventibus rusticis aut curialibus excitari, quo conlationem praestitisse dicantur: hoc eatenus valebit, si sciente possessionis domino, et non reluctante, aut certe procuratore, conductoreque eius, cum dominus in transmarinis fuerit regionibus constitutus, conlationem praestitam, fuerit adprobatum." The *saluber lex* mentioned here seems to be a reference to *Nov. Maj.* 7.1; at the very least it suggests that the compilers had this in mind when they drafted *ET* 69.

[14] *Nov. Maj.* 7.1: ". . . sancimus praeteritae praesumptionis supplicium relaxantes, ut praeter illos, qui patrias suas aliqua munerum collatione iuverunt ac propterea nulla ordinibus praescriptione depereunt, ubicumque intra triginta abhinc retro annos inventi fuerint curiales, constrictis procuratoribus vel conductoribus praediorum dominisque conventis ad urbes, quas deseruerant, cum uxoribus reducantur."

That the *ET* does not borrow from any novel of the Emperor Severus (461–5) provides sufficient justification for Vismara to fix the latest possible *terminus ante quem* for the production date of the *ET* at 461.[15] But given that the perspective in *ET* 69 is quite different from *Nov. Maj.* 7.1, it is unlikely that it came soon after 458. In fact, it is likely that some decades had elapsed between the writing of the two texts. *ET* 69 is focused on landlords. Its purpose was to preserve the thirty-year prescription in favor of those who had acquired decurions, guildsmen, and *servi.* It permits claims *only* if it can be proven that landlords allowed contributions willingly, and not under compulsion, in the thirty-year period; otherwise, the owner would lose possession of the decurion, guildsman, or *servus.* In the novel, however, the emphasis is on the preservation of the rights of the state. Here, the law's purpose is the continued maintenance and protection of civic property and cities against the flight of those who by birth were responsible for their upkeep. The plight of decurions in Late Antiquity is well known, and legal references to attempts by curials to escape their obligations are found as early as the Antonine period.[16] In these, as in Majorian's novel, there is no consideration along the lines of *ET* 69 where the interests of the owner are safeguarded in the event that the decurion or slave should make a false claim (as to his service to the state) in an attempt to escape his servile condition.

Second, there is the testimony of Sidonius Apollinaris (born about 432), who asserts that Seronatus – usually considered to be *vicarius* of Aquitanica Prima around 469 – trampled on the laws of Theodosius and issued the laws of Theoderic: "leges Theodosianas calcans, Theudericanasque proponens."[17] Vismara has taken this to be a reference to the *ET.*[18] But the most that can be taken from this is that Theoderic the Visigoth issued some laws (*leges*), not that he promulgated something along similar lines as the *ET.* That he issued at least individual edicts is attested to in the so-called *Codex Euricianus* – a collection of laws issued by Theoderic's brother and

15 Vismara, "Edictum," 154.

16 E.g., Ulpian: *Dig.* 50.5.1.2; similarly *Dig.* 50.2.1 and *CJ* 10.32.13 for other attempts to escape the decurionate. On the decline of the decurion in general, see: Jones, *LRE*, 2, 737–57 and Arnold H. M. Jones, "The Caste System in the Later Roman Empire," in Peter Brunt (ed.), *The Roman Economy* (Oxford, 1974), 396–418, esp. 397–8 and 413–16; Meyer Reinhold, "Usurpation of Status and Status Symbols in the Roman Empire," *Historia* 20 (1971), 275–302, esp. 299–301; Geza Alfödy, *The Social History of Rome*, trans. David Braund and Frank Pollock (Baltimore, 1988), 201–2; Ramsay MacMullen, *Corruption and the Decline of Rome* (New Haven, CT, 1988), 46–9.

17 Sidonius Apollinaris *Ep.* II 1.3, ed. C. Lütjohanni *MGH Auctor*, vol. VIII (Berlin, 1887), 21–2. On Seronatus: John Martindale, *The Prosopography of the Later Roman Empire*, vol. 2: AD 395–527 (Cambridge, 1980) 995–6. On the dating of the letter, see André Loyen, *Sidoine Apollinaire*, vol. 2 (Paris, 1970), 246 n. 1.

18 Vismara, "Edictum," 180.

successor Euric (466–84). Although Isidore tells us (*Hist. Goth.* 35) that the Goths (i.e. Visigoths) had previously been ruled by customary law alone, this is certainly an exaggeration. An Eurician law expressly refers to a provision of Theoderic I (*CE* 277), and Sidonius' reference to *leges Theodoricanae* is not without justification. But this collection was probably small and composed in the main of measures concerning the division of lands and perhaps some aspects of the internal Gothic regime – nothing as comprehensive as the *ET*.[19] At any rate, the reference here to the *Theodosian Code* is clear, but the second part of the flourish demonstrates Sidonius' penchant for assonance more so than it does the existence of a Visigothic "Code of Theoderic."[20] The whole thing might simply just be an exercise in word play.

Moreover, the *ET* is not a law code consisting of *leges*, but rather a collection of edicts (*edicta*). The issue is one of jurisdiction. By the later Empire, all positive legislation, in the sense of formal law making, was contingent upon imperial authority. Depending on their scope and reach, imperial enactments fell into two types: edicts (or *leges generales*) and rescripts (*leges speciales*). The term *leges generales* (or *edicta imperatorum*) referred to enactments of the Emperor containing legal norms of general application. Imperial edicts were generally binding orders that remained in force for an indefinite period unless they were rescinded by subsequent imperial legislation. An example of this type of enactment is the famous *Edict of Prices* (*edictum de pretiis*) of the Emperor Diocletian of 301. Issued in response to a specific case or request for enlightenment, rescripts were addressed in the Emperor's name to individual officers or private citizens, and were posted up in prominent places wherever the Emperor happened to be at the time. Unlike the edicts of Emperors were those of magistrates, which were limited in time and space according to the jurisdiction of the officer who issued them. It is in this context that the *ET* must be understood. For this was a set of legal rules set forth by someone other than the Emperor. Theoderic, it must be recalled, set out from Thrace as Zeno's official representative, and upon his victory over Odovacer was permitted to issue only edicts. Cassiodorus makes this point clear. Throughout the *Variae* he consistently describes the legal enactments of Theoderic and his successors as edicts or *iura*.[21] One such enactment selected for inclusion in

[19] Paul D. King, *Law and Society in the Visigothic Kingdom* (Cambridge, 1972), 65–70.

[20] This point is noted by Jill Harries, *Sidonius Apollinaris and the Fall of Rome,* AD *407–485* (Oxford, 1994), 126.

[21] Åke Fridh, *Terminologie et formules dans les Variae de Cassiodore* (Stockholm, 1956), 109–10; G. Vidén, *The Roman Chancery Tradition*, 84, 88, 142 with n. 193.

the *Variae* is the *Edict of Athalaric* (*c.* 533–4), which recognizes and upholds the edicts of Theoderic:

> But lest, by addressing a few laws it should be supposed that We do not desire to preserve the rest, We decree that all edicts, both ours and those of our lord grandfather [i.e. Theoderic], which were prepared with venerable deliberation, as well as common public customs, are to be maintained with full force and vigor . . . The ordinary rule of the laws and the integrity of our precepts are to be upheld everywhere.[22]

We do not know if Theoderic the Visigoth was in any *de iure* position to issue an edict in a strictly technical sense. For unlike Theoderic the Ostrogoth, he was a King without any legal or constitutional limitations imposed on him by the East. Despite the fact that he was quickly recognized by his supporters as the King of all Italy, a recognition that was eventually supported by Constantinople, Theoderic the Ostrogoth continued to refer to his laws as edicts – a decision intended to curry favor with both Constantinople and Italy's senatorial aristocracy. Despite the political turmoil of the times, the old noble families of Rome manifested a remarkable capacity for survival. While barbarian army commanders and fainéant Emperors might come and go, through it all the Senators retained their land and power and made themselves indispensable to the administration.[23] Little had changed with the arrival of Theoderic. Wealthy Senators continued to constitute a privileged class, and expected their centuries-old honors and traditions to remain intact. To avoid employing the kind of terminology more readily associated with the legislative activities of an Emperor but rather as a magistrate would certainly go far in appeasing Roman sensibilities.[24]

Third, Vismara's hypothesis that Magnus was the jurist entrusted by Theoderic II to draft the *ET* rests on a text of Sidonius (*Carmina* 5.561–2), the meaning of which is uncertain. Sidonius' poem is a panegyric on Majorian, and in stressing the good qualities of the Emperor's assistants, he says, having just referred to the Prefect Magnus:

[22] Cass., *Var.* 9.18.12: "Sed ne pauca tangentes reliqua credamur noluisse servari, omnia edicta tam nostra quam domni avi nostri, quae sunt venerabili deliberatione formata, et usualia iura publica sub omni censemus districtionis robore custodiri . . . legum usualis regula et praeceptorum nostrorum probitas ubique servetur."

[23] Sam J. Barnish, "Transformation and Survival in the Western Senatorial Aristocracy, *c.* AD 400–700," *PBSR* 56 (1988), 120–55.

[24] On the Roman Senate in Ostrogothic Italy, see Chris Wickham, *Early Medieval Italy: Central Power and Local Society 400–1000* (London, 1981), 15–19. For a more comprehensive study, which includes a prosopographical survey of active senators, see Christoph Schäfer, *Der Weströmische Senat Als Träger Antiker Kontinuät Unter Den Ostgotenkönigen (490–540)* (St. Katharinen, Hamburg, 1991).

> The enemy dressed in skins, who now gives law to the Goths under your judge, admires the hoarse auctioneer.
> (*qui dictat modo iura Getis, sub iudice vestro pellitus ravum praeconem suspicit hostis.*)

Vismara takes the first part (*qui dictat modo iura Getis*) to be a reference to Magnus.[25] But the individual "who now gives laws to the Goths" must grammatically and logically be the same one identified as "the enemy dressed in skins" (*pellitus hostis*), that is, the Visigothic King himself. There is nothing here to suggest that Magnus had anything to do with drafting a law code of the Visigothic King Theoderic.

Vismara's claim that our sources for Theoderic the Ostrogoth are silent on the matter of the *ET* is not entirely accurate. For instance, we are told by the Anonymous Valesianus that Theoderic did in fact issue an edict: "... because of his *Edict,* in which he established justice, he [i.e. Theoderic] was judged by the Goths to be in all respects their best King."[26] Vismara has taken this to mean a code of Gothic law intended for use by Theoderic's Gothic followers only, derived from the so-called *belagines.*[27] Concerning this tradition, Jordanes says that Dicineus, the great and mythical civilizer of the savage Goths, gave them laws by which they learned to live, and which still existed in writing in his day and were referred to as *belagines*: "[Dicineus] gave them laws by which to live naturally; to this day, [the Goths] call these written laws *belagines* ..."[28] That the term only occurs here, in a *quasi*-fictitious context, is hardly proof of a continuing Gothic legal tradition in Italy during Theoderic's time. What the Anonymous Valesianus refers to as an *edictum* that established justice and thus earned the praise of the Goths is less indicative of Theoderic issuing a code of Gothic law than it is a collection of legal pronouncements in keeping with his official position *vis-à-vis* Constantinople.

On the one hand, then, we have the Anonymous Valesianus expressly mentioning an *edictum* of Theoderic, and on the other Cassiodorus, who cites several of the King's individual edicts. Many of these, in fact, correspond with, or seem to make reference to, the *ET*. For instance, in a letter to the distinguished John, Governor of Campania (507–12), Theoderic

25 Vismara, "Edictum," 25–8.

26 Anon. Val. 12.60: "et a Gothis secundum edictum suum, quo ius constituit, rex fortissimus in omnibus iudicaretur." It is perhaps worthwhile to note that both the Anonymous Valesianus and Pithou use the term *Edictum*. Pithou could not possibly have derived the title of his edition from this account, for it was first published in 1636, well after Pithou's 1579 edition.

27 Vismara, "Edictum," 33, 64–75.

28 Jordanes, 11.69: "... naturaliter propriis legibus vivere fecit, quas usque nunc conscriptas belagines nuncupant ..."

addresses the seemingly pervasive problem of *pignoratio* in that region – the practice of seizing someone's property in order to obtain payment of money owed. He instructs John that whereas the seizure of property by a creditor is penalized with forfeiture of his claim, the pledge-holding creditor is permitted to appropriate it:

> Now We have discovered from a complaint of the provincials of Campania and Samnium that some, having neglected the discipline of the times, have given themselves up to the practice of distraint (*pignoratio*). And, as though my edict were forgotten, vices have freely increased among the people... Therefore, in accordance with Our edict (*edictalis programmatis tenore*),[29] We direct the attention of all to the following provision: should anyone violently lay hold of any property to secure an alleged claim, by the authority of the law he shall at once forfeit that claim; nor shall it be permitted for anyone to seize any property (*pignus*) unless it is pledged to him.[30]

The letter seems to be referring to *ET* 123 and 124, which are clearly to be taken together:

> *ET* 123 We deny an individual the permission to seize a pledge on his own unless in a credible case the presiding judge gives him the authority.[31]
>
> *ET* 124 If a creditor forcibly seizes from his debtor property that is not pledged to him, let him restore as penalty fourfold the amount previously taken if he is sued within a year of the offense being committed; but after a year, he will be obligated to pay back the simple sum. Even with respect to produce that has been forcibly removed the rule of law must also be observed.[32]

Like *Var.* 4.10, both *ET* 123 and 124 permit the right to self-help of the *bona fide* creditor when the property concerned was pledged to him; *ET* 124 only prohibits the creditor from seizing property not pledged to him (*sibi*

[29] The term "*edictali programmate*" is also found in Cass., *Var.* 1.31.2; 2.24.5; 2.35.1; 4.10.2; 4.27.5; 5.5.4.

[30] Cass., *Var.* 4.10.1, 3: "Provincialium igitur Campaniae atque Samnii suggestione comperimus nonnullos neglecta temporum disciplina ad pignorandi se studia transtulisse et quasi edicto misso per vulgus licentiam crevisse vitiorum ... Proinde edictalis programmatis tenore comperto spectabilitas vestra in cunctorum faciat notitiam pervenire, ut quisquis quod repetere debuisset pignorandi studio fortassis invaserit, voce iuris amittat nec liceat cuiquam sua sponte nisi obligatum forsitan pignus auferre."

[31] *ET* 123: "Capiendorum pro suo arbitrio pignorum unicuique licentiam denegamus: ita ut, si probabile fuerit, hoc agendi iudicis praestet auctoritas."

[32] *ET* 124: "Creditor si debitori suo res sibi non obligatas violenter rapiat, intra annum criminis admissi conventus, sub poena quadrupli praesumpta restituat: post annum vero in simplum debebit exsolvere. Quod etiam de fructibus violenter ablatis servari debere legum ratio persuadet."

non obligatas). According to *ET* 123, this seizing of pledged goods could be done only with the permission of a judge.

The most telling example of a correspondence between the *ET* and the legislative acts of Theoderic preserved in the *Variae* concerns the treatment of Jews. Cassiodorus documents several instances which together demonstrate that Theoderic's policy towards the Jews was generally positive.[33] In a letter in Theoderic's name to the Jews of Genoa, for example, the King granted them permission to rebuild their synagogue, concluding that the provisions of the old laws concerning them were to continue to apply: "We freely grant your request, that the privileges of the laws which Antiquity has bestowed upon all Jews are to remain intact."[34] In another letter to the populace of Rome in the King's name, Cassiodorus reports that any Romans who took part in the burning of a synagogue at Rome were to be punished, although the cause of their anger towards the Jews was to be investigated; and the synagogue at Milan was to be protected from the attacks of clerics.[35] Around 519 or 520, the people of Ravenna burned down synagogues on two separate occasions. Our source for these events is the Anonymous Valesianus.[36] According to his account, the Jews fled to Verona following the second burning, and made a charge against the Christians before the King. Theoderic conveyed an order by means of Bishop Peter and Eutharic, Consul and heir apparent to the throne until his untimely death in 522, that the entire Roman populace of Ravenna was to pay for the rebuilding of the synagogues. Those who lacked the means to contribute were to be publicly flogged.

[33] On Theoderic's Jewish legislation, see Amnon Linder, *The Jews in the Legal Sources of the Early Middle Ages* (Detroit, 1997), 200–6 (with translation and commentary of Cassiodorus' accounts).

[34] Cass., *Var.* 4.33.2: "deposcitis privilegia vobis debere servari, quae Iudaicis institutis legum provida decrevit antiquitas: quod nos libenter annuimus." The "ancient source" for these laws is most likely *CTh* 2.1.10 (398); and similarly *CTh* 16.8.13 (397).

[35] Rome: Cass., *Var.* 4.43; Milan: Cass., *Var.* 5.37. Cass., *Var.* 4.43 explains that the synagogue was burned down when the Romans learned of an incident of slaves being punished for the death of their masters. Such a reaction can only be understood if we consider that the slaves were themselves Roman, that is, Christian, and the masters Jewish This would indeed be interesting, considering the position of late imperial legislation on the subject, which prohibited Jews from owning Christian slaves (e.g., *CTh* 3.1.5 (384)).

[36] Anon. Val. 14.80–2. See further Moorhead, *Theoderic in Italy*, 98–9; Catherine Morton, "Marius of Avenches, the *Excerpta Valesiana* and the Death of Boethius," *Traditio* 38 (1982), 107–36, esp. 119; Ernest Stein, *Histoire du Bas-Empire, II: De la disparition de l'Empire d'Occident à la mort Justinien (476–565)* (Paris, 1949), 249; Wilhelm Ensslin, *Theoderich der Grosse*, 2nd edn. (Munich, 1959), 302; Henry Chadwick, *Boethius: The Consolations of Music, Logic, Theory, Philosophy* (Oxford, 1981), 58. On the Jewish community at Ravenna see Lellia Ruggini, "Ebrei e Orientali nell'Italia settentrionale fra il IV e il VI secolo d. Cr.," *Studia et documenta historiae et iuris* 25 (1959), 186–308, esp. 228 n. 103.

Likewise, the *ET* accords protection to the Jews by confirming their right – inherited from earlier Roman precedents and reaffirmed in the *Variae* – to live under their own laws:

> The privileges conferred by the laws upon Jews shall be preserved: when disputes arise between those Jews who live in accordance with their own laws, they must have as judges those whom they consider to be teachers of their observance.[37]

We find nothing like this in the legal sources pertaining to other contemporary kingdoms. Visigothic law in particular was decidedly anti-Semitic.[38] In fact, Theoderic's goodwill towards Jews was comparatively unique for this time, and no doubt goes a long way in explaining why the Jews of Naples were among the supporters of the Goths in the city when the forces of Belisarius arrived in 536.

Our sources, then, are hardly silent on the matter of Theoderic issuing a document like the *ET*. There is further evidence from the *ET* itself: three provisions, *ET* 10, 111, and 145, point inescapably to it being a product of Ostrogothic Italy. The first deals with the problem of *invasio*. It requires that judges and their staff, appointed in the provinces or the "Venerable City," who believe themselves incapable of bringing offenders to book, were to notify the *scrinia* so that their decisions could be enforced:

> We command all those judges, appointed in the provinces, or in the Venerable City, and their staffs, to be guardians of this just and lawful decree, in such a manner that if there is any reason they should think themselves incapable of exacting the penalty referred to above, they shall send their report to Our bureaus (*nostra scrinia*) so that, if reason demands it, the penalty may be exacted more strictly by Us.[39]

A rescript of the Emperor Theodosius I of 389 served as the basis for this.[40] But unlike *ET* 10, it contains no reference to Rome. This was clearly an addition on the part of the compilers.

[37] *ET* 143: "Circa Iudaeos privilegia legibus delata serventur: quos inter se iurgantes, et suis viventes legibus, eos iudices habere necesse est, quos habent observantiae praeceptores." Note the parallel between this and Cass., *Var.* 4.33.2: "privilegia legibus delata serventur" = "privilegia . . . debere servari, quae . . . provida decrevit antiquitas."

[38] King, *Law and Society*, 130–44.

[39] *ET* 10: "Cuius decreti iusti atque legitimi omnes per provincias iudices et urbe venerabili constitutos vel eorum officia iubemus esse custodes: ita ut si aliquid extiterit, quo se putent exigendae mulctae superius comprehensae pares esse non posse, relationem ad scrinia nostra transmittant, ut a nobis, si ratio poposcerit, districtius vindicetur."

[40] *CTh* 4.22.3 (addressed to the Count of the Privy Purse Messianus).

A second reference to Rome appears in *ET* 111, which upholds the ancient proscription against the practice of burying corpses within the city's limits:

> Anyone who buries corpses within the city of Rome shall be compelled to allocate a fourth of his patrimony to the fisc; if he is destitute he shall be publicly flogged.[41]

The model for this is *CTh* 9.17.6 (381) of Theodosius I, significant points of which were either altered or ignored completely by the compilers:

> All bodies that are contained in urns or sarcophagi and are kept above the ground shall be carried and placed outside the City, in order that they exhibit an example of humanity and preserve the sanctity of the homes of the residents. But if any person should disregard this regulation or should dare to undertake any such thing after the threat of this precept, let him be fined a third part of his patrimony. Moreover, the office staff which is subject to you will regret to suffer the forfeiture of fifty pounds of gold. That no persons may evade the purpose of this regulation by false and cunning shrewdness and suppose that the resting places of apostles and martyrs are granted for the burial of bodies, let them know and understand that they are excluded from such burial places, just as from the rest of the City.[42]

First, the reference in the original to the existing burial sites of apostles and martyrs was overlooked (a point worthy of note, the Ostrogoths were Arians); and the penalty for contravening the law was decreased from the confiscation of a third of the offender's property to a fourth. Moreover, the compilers made the additional requirement that those unable to pay were to be publicly flogged.

Such a measure as this makes sense only if there was at this time a problem connected with the unlawful burial of corpses within Rome's sacred limits. Since the early fifth century the area around the Colosseum was used as a burial site (an activity no doubt connected with the traumas associated with the Visigothic sack in 410); and, in fact, there is extensive evidence for a renewal of burial activity in that same region in the first half of the sixth century (some tombs feature tiles with stamps bearing the image of

[41] *ET* 111: "Qui intra urbem Romam cadavera sepelierit, quartam partem patrimonii sui fisco sociare cogatur: si nihil habuerit, caesibus fustibus civitate pellatur."

[42] *CTh* 9.17.6: "omnia quae supra terram urnis clausa vel sarcofagis corpora detinentur, extra urbem delata ponantur, ut et humanitatis instar exhibeant et relinquant incolarum domicilio sanctitatem. Quisquis autem huius praecepti neglegens fuerit adque aliquid tale ab huius interminatione praecepti ausus fuerit moliri, tertia in futurum patrimonii parte multetur. Officium quoque, quod tibi paret, quinquaginta librarum auri affectum despoliatione maerebit. ac ne alicuius fallax et arguta sollertia ab huius se praecepti intentione subducat atque apostolorum vel martyrum sedem humandis corporibus aestimet esse concessam, ab his quoque, ita ut a reliquo civitatis, noverint se atque intellegant esse submotos."

Theoderic).[43] In any event, the reference to Rome both here and in *ET* 10 makes it clear that the *ET* was intended to apply to the ancient capital. While Theoderic the Great had authority over matters pertaining to Rome, Theoderic II of the Visigoths did not. That he would issue a code with two provisions dealing specifically with the city is unlikely.

A third indicator of the *ET*'s Italian provenance is *ET* 145, a provision dealing with recalcitrant barbarians. In referring to them it uses the term *capillati*:

> If any barbarian, upon being summoned for a third time by the authority of a judge exercising the appropriate jurisdiction, and duly called upon by judicial directives refuses to come to the judge by whose command he has been summoned, he shall deservedly receive a sentence of contempt after examination of the case; and moreover he shall be judged to have lost the case concerning which he was summoned. There must be these conditions: that either the reliability of the guarantee issued by the defendant shows, or the testimony of freeborn and honorable men confirms, that he who was summoned for the third time was one of the *capillati*; and that it is clearly obvious to those giving testimony that he who lost by judicial decree disdained to give a response and had no wish to come before the court.[44]

The term *capillati*, meaning "long-haired ones," figures prominently in Jordanes' Gothic history.[45] Quoting Dio Chrysostom, Jordanes tells how

[43] See further Neil Christie, *From Constantine to Charlemagne. An Archaeology of Italy* AD *300–800* (Aldershot, 2006), 253; Rossella Rea (ed.), *Rota Colisei: La valle del Colosseo attraverso i secoli*, (Milan, 2002), 85–125; Marios Costambeys, "Burial Topography and the Power of the Church in Fifth- and Sixth-Century Rome," *PBSR* 69 (2001), 169–89, esp. 172–3, 179; John Osborne, "Death and Burial in Sixth-Century Rome," *EMC/CV* 3.2 (1984), 291–9.

[44] *ET* 145: "Si quis barbarorum tertio competentis iudicis auctoritate conventus, et edictis solemniter inclamatus, ad iudicem, cuius praeceptione conventus est, venire neglexerit, merito sub discussione causae sententiam excipiet contumaciae, adeo ut iudicetur de quo conventus est, perdidisse negotium: dummodo tertio quemlibet *capillatorum* fuisse conventum, aut cautionis ab eodem emissae fides ostendat, aut ingenuorum vel honestorum testium dicta confirment, quibus manifeste clareat, auctoritate pulsatum, contempsisse dare responsum nec voluisse ad iudicium convenire."

[45] On the significance of the term see Amory, *People and Identity*, 94, 319, 345–6; Arne Søby Christensen, *Cassiodorus, Jordanes and the History of the Goths: Studies in a Migration Myth* (Copenhagen, 2002), 245–6. As Christensen notes, long hair has been traditionally viewed as a custom of barbarian Kings, who used it as a sign of their sacral right to rule. But it must be noted that long hair was in fact used by Emperors as early as the mid-fifth century, despite classicizing depictions to the contrary. Evidence would seem to suggest that Theoderic himself put little stock in long hair. In the famous Senigallia Medallion, Theoderic only *seems* to be portrayed with long hair. In fact, he has his hair cropped short in the front, with long hair to the back in a style evocative of the modern-day mullet. He is likewise portrayed with short hair in the mosaic in Sant'Apollinare Nuovo – his Arian palace church in Ravenna. For discussion of the mosaic of Sant'Apollinare Nuovo, see Friedrich Von Lorentz, "Theoderich -nicht Iustinian," *Mitteilungen des Deutschen Archäologischen Instituts, Römische Abteilung* 50 (1935), 339–47; Siegfried Fuchs, *Kunst der Ostgotenzeit* (Berlin, 1944), 125–6; Giuseppe Bovini, "Note sul presunto ritratto musivo di Giusttiniano in S. Apollinare Nuovo di

Dicineus instructed the noblest and wisest among the Goths in theology, appointed them priests and called them *Pilleati*. Jordanes believes this name is derived from the manner in which they performed their sacrifices, namely with their heads covered by a headdress called a *pilleus*.[46] Dicineus referred to the remainder of the Goths as *Capillati*, a name, Jordanes says, they still revere and remember in song in the author's day (of course, the Goths of Jordanes' time were those living in Italy).[47] But Jordanes' account was simply an attempt to demonstrate that his Goths possessed a genuine Roman or Italian tradition, since there existed actual living, breathing *Capillati* in Italy as early as the first century. Pliny, for example, used the term to designate a group of people living in the north around the Cottian Alps.[48]

These long-haired people were known in Theoderic's Italy where they are mentioned by Cassiodorus. In a proclamation written in the King's name and addressed to the residents of Siscia and Suavia in the north eastern corner of the peninsula, Cassiodorus includes "long-haired" people among the recipients:

> The King Theoderic sends greetings to all provincials, the *capillati*, the *defensores* and *curials* who reside in the regions of Siscia and Suavia.[49]

In *ET* 145, the term is used to identify those barbarians whose status allowed them to refuse a judicial summons that was otherwise compulsory for all others.[50] According to the provision, the penalties for non-attendance in court would remain in force provided that the reliability of the guarantee issued by the defendant, or the testimony of freeborn and honorable men confirms that the defendant was among those ranks of barbarians designated as *capillati*; and that the defendant's non-attendance was owing to his refusal to appear. The provision leaves room for the interpretation that a

Ravenna," *Annales Universitatis Saraviensis. Philosophie, Lettres* 5 (1956), 50–3; Bryan Ward-Perkins, *From Classical Antiquity to the Middle Ages: Urban Public Building in North and Central Italy, AD 300–850* (Oxford, 1985), 162, 164–5; Mark J. Johnson, "Toward a History of Theoderic's Building Program," *Dumbarton Oaks Papers* 42 (1988), 73–96, esp. 86–7; Maria Andaloro, "Tendenze figurative a Ravenna nell'età di Teodorico," in *Teoderico il Grande e i Goti d'Italia: atti del XIII Congresso internazionale di studi sull'Alto Medioevo, Milano 2–6 novembre 1992* (Spoleto, 1993), 561–2. For parallels of long-haired Roman heads of state in fifth- and early sixth-century statuary, mosaics and diptychs, see Richard Delbrueck, *Die Consulardiptychen und verwandte Denkmäler*, 2 vols. (Berlin, 1929), vol. 2, 42; Amory, *People and Identity*, 344–6.

46 Reports about the Getic-Thracian nobility and their "short hair" date back to the fourth century. See Christensen, *Cassiodorus, Jordanes and the History of the Goths*, 245.

47 Jordanes, *Get.* 40, 71–2.

48 Pliny, *Natural. History*, ed. J. Newsome (Oxford, 1964). 3.5.47. See further Amory, *People and Identity*, 94, 319.

49 Cass., *Var.* 4.49: "universis provincialibus et capillatis, defensoribus et curialibus siscia vel savia consistentibus Theodericus rex."

50 E.g., *ET* 5.

long-haired barbarian could avoid the stipulated penalty for contumacy if his absence was not a willful act of contempt towards the court, but was rather a consequence owing to his status. Presumably, such long-haired Goths were soldiers actively serving in Theoderic's army; long hair, while traditionally viewed as a Germanic custom, had its roots in Roman military custom.[51] That Theoderic's soldiers continued the habit is possible. What is clear is that the term *capillatus* was used exclusively in connection with certain Goths who were living in Theoderic's Italy. There is no evidence for it being used among the Visigoths.

The two references to Rome and this last one to *capillati* at least confirm the Italian provenance of the *ET*.[52] And judging from the disparity between *ET* 69 and *Nov. Maj.* 7.1, it is likely that the *ET* was produced well after 458 (the date of Majorian's novel). This narrows things considerably. When we take into consideration the parallels between it and the *Variae*, and the fact that Cassiodorus confirms that Theoderic issued edicts, it can be reasonably concluded that the *ET* was drafted in Italy sometime during Theoderic's reign. Unfortunately, there is nothing within the text or elsewhere to furnish a reliable *terminus ante quem* by which to secure a more precise publication date other than sometime after 458. Despite this, there have been interesting attempts to do so. For example, the Italian historian Augusto Gaudenzi argued that the silence of Cassiodorus in regards to the *ET* is proof that it was drafted after 511, for it was in that year that Cassiodorus stepped down from his position as *Quaestor sacri palatii* – the imperial office which under Theoderic was responsible for dealing with various legal matters of the *comitatus*.[53] Scholarship on the *Variae* has revealed that this collection of imperial documents was written in three separate phases: 507–11, 523–7, and 535–7. These, we deduce, were the periods during which Cassiodorus himself was at Ravenna holding office, in the first instance as Quaestor, in the second as *Magister officiorum*, and in the third as Praetorian Prefect. The assumption here is that Cassiodorus' activity drafting letters for the King would in each case roughly begin and end with his terms in office, and that he was only involved in the literary activity preserved in the *Variae* during those years when he was appointed to office. Cassiodorus says as much in the preface to

[51] Wolfram, *History of the Goths*, 102–3, 301–2; Herwig Wolfram, "Gotische Studien I/II," *Mitteilungen des Instituts für Österreichische Geschichtsforschung* 83 (1975), 14, 304, 307–8; and also Amory, *People and Identity*, 345–6, who likewise attributes the term to soldiers in Ostrogothic Italy.

[52] Wormald, "The *Leges Barbarorum*," 21–53, esp. 25 n. 10.

[53] Augusto Gaudenzi, *Gli editti di Teodorico e di Atalarico nel Diritto Romano nel Regno degli Ostrogoti* (Bologna, 1884), 29.

his *Variae*, where he notes that he included for publication only that which he wrote while holding the office. Thus, as Gaudenzi argues, it was during Cassiodorus' first such leave of absence, namely between 511 and 523, that the composition of the *ET* took place. To date, however, Gaudenzi's hypothesis has won only a few adherents.[54]

The most promising approach to dating the document concerns *ET* 70, but here, too, we run into difficulty. Derived principally from *CTh* 9.45.5 of the Emperor Theodosius II of 432, the provision addresses the matter of asylum-seeking slaves on the run:

> If a slave of any nation should take refuge in a church, let him be returned immediately upon his owner promising pardon, for We forbid him from staying in that place for more than a single day. If he is unwilling to depart, the archdeacon of that church, or a priest and clerics shall compel him to return to his owner, and deliver him up without delay on the owner pardoning him. But if it happens that the abovementioned religious persons are unwilling to do this, they shall be compelled to give to the owner another slave of equal value; even the slave that remains within the retreats of the church may be claimed by his owner forthwith if he can be captured beyond church limits.[55]

For many historians, the impetus for the inclusion of this provision within the *ET* was the social and political upheaval wrought by the collapse of the Visigothic kingdom of Toulouse in 507.[56] The problem of runaway slaves was a particularly pernicious one in the years immediately following Vouillé. The evidence for this is the occurrence of three successive church councils in Gaul in the first half of the sixth century which convened to address several pertinent topics, including the problem of runaway slaves and in particular those which sought sanctuary. The first of these was the Council of Orléans of 511 which established the following (Canon 3):

54 It was attacked vigorously by Heinrich Brunner, *Deutsche Rechtsgeschichte*, vol. I, 1906, vol. II completed by Claudius Frh. von Schwerin, 2nd edn. (Leipzig, 1906–1928), I, 365; and Richard Schröder, *Lehrbuch der deutschen Rechtsgeschichte* (Leipzig, 1907), 247.

55 *ET* 70: "Si servus cuiuslibet nationis ad quamlibet ecclesiam confugerit, statim domino veniam promittente reddatur: nec enim ultra unum diem ibidem residere praecipimus. Qui si exire noluerit, vir religiosus archidiaconus eiusdem ecclesiae, vel presbyter atque clerici, eundem ad dominum suum exire compellant, et domino indulgentiam praestanti sine dilatione contradant. Quod si hoc suprascriptae religiosae personae facere forte noluerint, aliud mancipium eiusdem meriti domino dari cogantur: ita ut etiam illud mancipium quod in ecclesiae latebris commoratur, si extra ecclesiam potuerit comprehendi, a domino protinus vindicetur."

56 Gaudenzi, *Gli editti di Teodorico*, 29; Brunner, *Deutsche Rechtsgeschichte*, vol. II, I, 365; vol. I, I^2, 527; Schröder, *Lehrbuch der deutschen Rechtsgeschichte*, 247; Dahn, *Die Könige der Germanen*, vol. IV, 11–12; Berhard Kübler, *Geschichte des römischen Rechts* (Leipzig, 1925), 397; Santo Mazzarino, "Si può parlare di rivoluzione sociale alla fine del mondo antico," in *Il passagio dall'antichità al medioevo in Occidente*, Settimane di Studi del Centro Italiano di Studi sull'Alto Medioevo 9 (Spoleto, 1961), 410–25, esp. 421–3; Vismara, "Edictum," 17–18, 100–9.

> A slave who has fled to a church for any fault whatsoever shall be compelled to return immediately to the servitude of his master if he has received pardon from his lord for the admitted fault; however, if after it is documented that the master granted pardon it is proven that he [i.e. the slave] has endured any penalty for those same faults for which he was pardoned, he [i.e. the master] shall be considered a stranger from the communion and community of Catholics on account of his contempt of the church or collusion of the faith, as it has been previously established. If, however, the slave, upon being defended by the church for his own fault, has received pardon from his master for the impunity sought after by the priests, the master shall be permitted to seize that slave who is unwilling to leave.[57]

The conditions outlined here were reiterated by the Council of Epaune (Burgundia) on September 15, 517,[58] and by a second council held in Orléans on October 28, 549.[59] That the issue of asylum-seeking slaves was addressed by three different ecumenical councils within a forty-year period underscores just how serious a problem it was in Gaul at this time.

We hear from Cassiodorus that Theoderic the Great, too, took steps to respond to it. In a letter addressed in the King's name to the sword-bearer (*spatharius*) Unigis, the addressee is charged with a special commission to restore to their owners those slaves who had fled during the Gallic War: "Wherefore, if upon Our army's propitious entry into Gaul, some slaves have abandoned their servitude and taken themselves to new masters, We order that they must assuredly be returned to their former masters[.]"[60] That *ET* 70 was drafted in response to these specific circumstances cannot be ruled out, but neither can it be proved definitively, for the problem of runaway slaves was a persistent one throughout Antiquity. As such, *ET* 70 bears witness to a general phenomenon and not necessarily a specific event.

Despite the lack of any direct evidence for this, it is tempting to place the publication date of the *ET* in the early years of Theoderic's reign, that is,

[57] *Concilia Galliae a. 511-a. 695*, ed. C. DeClercq, *CCSL* 148 (Turnhout, 1963), 5–6: "Servus qui ad ecclesiam pro qualibet culpa confugerit, si a Domino pro admissa culpa sacramenta susceperit, statim ad servitium Domini sui redire cogatur, sed posteaquam datis a Domino sacramentis fuerit consignatus, si aliquid poenae pro eadem culpa, qua excusatur, probatus fuerit pertulisse: pro contemptu ecclesiae vel praevaricatione fidei a communione et convivio catholicorum, sicut superius conpraehensum est, extraneus habeatur. Sin vero servus pro culpa sua ab ecclesia defensatus sacramenta Domini, clericis exigentibus, de impunitate perceperit, exire nolentem a Domino liceat occupari."

[58] *Concilia Galliae a. 511-a. 695*, 34: *Concilium Epaonense* c. 39, ed. C. DeClercq, *CCSL* 148A (Turnhout, 1963).

[59] *Concilia Galliae a. 511-a. 695*, 156 c. 22.

[60] Cass., *Var.* 3.49: "Quapropter cum deo propitio Gallias exercitus noster intravit, si qua mancipia servitium declinantia ad alios se, quam quibus videbantur competere, contulerunt, prioribus dominis iubemus sine aliqua dubietate restitui . . ."

before 512. If we are to take Cassiodorus' mention of "Our edict" (*edictalis programmatis tenore*) in his letter (*Var.* 4.10) to the Governor John as a reference to the *ET*, a fact presupposed by the similarities between the letter and *ET* 123–4 concerning *pignoratio*, then it can be assumed that the promulgation of the *ET* took place sometime before John left office in 512.[61] Taking this one step further, a case could be made for the *ET* being produced as early as 500, for it was in that year when Theoderic celebrated his *decennalia* in Rome.[62] The event was marked by the holding of popular games and festivities. It was also during this visit that Theoderic enjoyed the last western *adventus*, the formal and elaborate imperial ceremony used to signal an Emperor's entrance into a city.[63] A special medal was also issued to commemorate the event. This is the so-called Senigallia Medallion, now in the National Museum at Rome. The obverse bears a portrait of the King making a stylized gesture with his right hand as the pacifier of the world, and carrying in his left a statue of Victory. Inscribed is the legend "REX THEODERICUS PIUS PRINC(EPS) I(NVICTUS) S(EMPER)," ("KING THEODERIC EVER INDOMITABLE PIOUS PRINCE"); and on the reverse "REX THEODERICUS VICTOR GENTIUM," ("KING THEODERIC CHAMPION OF THE GOTHS").[64] Such an occasion as this would have served as an ideal backdrop for Theoderic to issue his *Edict*. Throughout the Empire the promulgation of law by state officials was a very public affair, often celebrated with a great deal of splendor and solemnity. The issuance of the *Theodosian Code* in the West, for instance, took place in the stately home of the Praetorian Prefect of Italy, Anicius Acilius Glabrio Faustus, on Christmas Day 438. According to the edited version of the proceedings, the Senators in attendance received the code with no less than forty-three acclamations, each one of which was repeated eight to twenty-seven times.[65] Given his strong desire

[61] Sam J. Barnish, *The Variae of Cassiodorus Senator*, Translated Texts for Historians (Liverpool University Press, 1992), 76.

[62] Ferrandus Diaconus, *Vita s. Fulgentii*, ed. and trans. G. G. Lapeyre (Paris, 1929), ch. 9, 55–6; Moorhead, *Theoderic in Italy*, 60–3.

[63] For the *adventus* tradition and other victory celebrations in Late Antiquity see Michael McCormick, *Eternal Victory: Triumphal Rulership in Late Antiquity, Byzantium, and the Early Medieval West* (Cambridge, 1986); Mark Humphries, "From Emperor to Pope? Ceremonial, Space, and Authority in Rome from Constantine to Gregory the Great," in K. Cooper and J. Hillner (eds.), *Religion, Dynasty, and Patronage in Early Christian Rome, 300–900* (Cambridge, 2007), 21–58, esp. 30.

[64] Maria R. Alföldi, "Il medaglione d'oro di Teodorico," *Rivista italiana di Numismatica e scienze affini* 80 (1978), 133–41.

[65] See further Matthews, *Laying Down the Law*, ch. 3; Lorena Atzeri, *Gesta senatus Romani de Theodosiano publicando. Il Codice Teodosiano e la sua diffusione ufficiale in Occidente* (Berlin, 2008), who proposes a date

to preserve ancient Roman traditions, Theoderic likely arranged for the promulgation of his *Edict* to be a public spectacle. His visit to Rome would have functioned as the ideal setting for this.

Moreover, it is worth pointing out the fact that the reference of the Anonymous Valesianus to Theoderic issuing an *Edict* appears in the same section (12.60) and immediately after a passage describing how the barbarian King gave games in the circus and amphitheater. This brief note is obviously referring to events taking place in Rome, and could in fact be a specific reference to the *decennalia* celebrations of 500. That the Anonymous Valesianus would mention Theoderic issuing his *Edict* in the same context as this could be taken as proof that the two events were contemporaneous. But again, all of this is simply guesswork. There is nothing in our sources to allow for the secure pinpointing of a precise publication date for the *ET*. Nevertheless, it is a far more likely scenario that this took place sooner rather than later, if for no other reason than the fact that Theoderic would have attempted to consolidate his rule and make a definitive statement as to his authority in the region in the early years of his reign. The issuance of a legal document like the *ET* would have gone far in achieving these ends.

Although the question as to precisely when the *ET* was produced cannot be resolved definitively, it is possible to identify to a certain extent the individuals to whom this task fell. Judging from their intimate knowledge of Roman legal and juristic conventions and concepts, they were experienced Roman jurists. A further indication of this is their use of the term *barbarus* to mean Goth, a term which appears both in the prologue and epilogue, in addition to the following provisions: *ET* 32, 34, 43, 44, 145.[66] In each instance the phrase is a deliberate addition on the part of the compilers.[67] Generally speaking, this was a term used by Romans to describe the Goths, and not by the Goths themselves.[68] Roman sympathizers, too, avoided the term in their description of the Goths. Only on

of May 25 rather than December 25, 438 (based on her emendation of *VIII k. Ian.* to *VIII k. Iun*), which would place the presentation ceremony of the *CTh* in Rome only six months (rather than twelve) after the launch of the code in Constantinople.

66 In both the prologue and epilogue, *barbarus* is juxtaposed with *Romanus* to underscore the fact that both groups were equally required to fulfill the legal obligations imposed upon them by the *ET*: prol. ("barbari romanique"); epil. ("tam barbaris quam romanis . . . barbarorum sive romanorum . . . seu barbari seu romani"). The same juxtaposition is made in the following provisions: *ET* 34 ("nemo aut romanus aut barbarus"); 43 ("nullus ad potentem romanum aut barbarum"); 44 ("nullus se potens romanus aut barbarus").

67 Vismara, "Edictum," 92 n. 312.

68 For the discussion that follows, see Guy Halsall, *Barbarian Migrations and the Roman West, 376–568* (Cambridge, 2007), 332; Amory, *People and Identity*, 59–71; Peter Heather, *Goths and Romans, 332–489* (Oxford, 1991), 52–7.

two occasions does Cassiodorus refer to the Goths as barbarians;[69] elsewhere he makes it clear that they were not.[70] Jordanes, too, implicitly denies that the Goths were barbarians. Yet, for most other Romans of the time, the Goths were barbarians. Pope Gelasius I (d. 496), for instance, viewed the Goths as barbarous; Boethius complains often in his *Consolation* about the avarice of the barbarians; and Procopius certainly regarded them as barbarians.[71]

In the *ET*, *barbarus* is used both in a generic sense as a synonym for Goths, much in the same way as the compilers of the Burgundian *Liber Constitutionum* (517) used the term to designate Burgundians;[72] and in a technical sense to refer specifically to a soldier in Theoderic's army.[73] For example, both *ET* 43 and 44, which clearly are to be taken together, use *barbarus* to refer to a powerful Gothic magnate (*potens barbarus*) who was not necessarily a soldier:

> *ET* 43 No one shall transfer their legal suits under any title to a powerful Roman or barbarian. But if he should do this, let the litigant lose the suit, and he who receives the suit shall be compelled to bear half the value of the matter under dispute as evaluated by the fisc. We stipulate that even those who try to transfer the property in dispute to a person of this sort are to be held by this penalty, since We desire that the litigants contend with the same opportunity when the more powerful person has been removed. But

69 Cass., *Var.* 3.24 (a letter addressed in Theoderic's name to the Romans and barbarians residing in Pannonia); 1.18.2 (a letter of general instruction to the Roman Domitianus and the Gothic Wilia, both recently dispatched to administer justice in their respective jurisdictions, which addresses the problem of *invasio* and refers to any Goth who has committed this crime as a barbarian usurper).

70 Cass., *Var.* 2.5.2 (in this letter concerning soldiers' arrears, Cassiodorus has Theoderic describe other Germanic groups as barbarians); 9.21.4 (in this proclamation of Athalaric, which calls for an increase in the wages of grammarians, Cassiodorus has the King extol the skills of these individuals, and note that while the grammatical art may be lost on other barbarian Kings, it is cherished by legitimate sovereigns, that is members of the Amal royal household).

71 Gelasius, *ep.* 6.1, ed. Andreas Thiel, *Epistulae Romanorum Pontificum genuinae et quae ad eos scriptae sunt a S. Hilaro usque ad Pelagium*, vol. 1 (Brausnberg, 1868; repr. New York, 1974), 325–6. See too *MGH AA* 12.391 *ep.* 8; Boethius, *Cons. Phil.* ed. L. Bieler, *CCSL* 94, 2nd edn. (Turnhout, 1984), 1.4.10; Proc., *BG* v. i. 26, v. ii. 8, 17, 18.

72 *ET* prol., 34, 43, 44, epil. In the Burgundian *Liber Constitutionum*, or *Book of Constitutions* of 517, *barbarus* is frequently used as a synonym for Burgundian: e.g., *Liber Constitutionum* 8,1, ed. L. R. von Salis, *MGH Leges nationum Germanicarum* I (Hannover, 1902), 1–122. See further Ian Wood, "*Gentes*, Kings and Kingdoms – the Emergence of States. The Kingdom of the Gibichungs," in Hans-Werner Goetz, Jörg Jarnut, and Walter Pohl (eds.), *Regna and Gentes*, (Leiden/New York, 2003), 243–69, esp. 260–1; Patrick Amory, "The Meaning and Purpose of Ethnic Terminology in the Burgundian Laws," *Early Medieval Europe* 2 (1993), 1–28; Roger Collins, "Law and Ethnic Identity in the Western Kingdoms in the Fifth and Sixth Centuries," in Alfred P. Smyth (ed.), *Medieval Europeans: Studies in Ethnic Identity and National Perspectives in Medieval Europe* (New York, 1998), 1–28.

73 *ET* 32, and possibly 145.

after the conclusion of the case, We grant to the litigants the power of giving what they won to any person they wish.[74]

ET 44 No powerful Roman or barbarian shall involve himself as a representative (*defensor*) or supporter (*suffragator*) in [another's] trial.[75]

The purpose behind both was to prevent the sorts of abuses that had plagued the provincial courts of the later Empire – namely the exercise of undue influence by magnate patrons.[76] Thus, the *ET* extended the prohibition to include all magnates, whether Gothic or Roman. In *ET* 32, however, the term *barbarus* is used in a qualitative sense to denote a soldier:

> We grant the freedom of making wills to barbarians who are known to have performed military service for the state, in any way they wish and are able, whether they are settled at home or at a military camp.[77]

Here, a barbarian is identified as a soldier in active service of the state; and he is granted the right to draft a will (that is, the soldier's will) wherever he happened to be stationed, just as Roman soldiers were so permitted. The separate soldier's will apparently lived on in Byzantium until the time of Justinian.[78] Like other Romans of their time, the compilers used *barbarus* to refer to Goths. While they were perhaps unaware of some of the ancient negative connotations associated with the word, they clearly did not use it in a pejorative way.[79]

As to the official capacity of these compilers, there is a clue in *ET* 10. According to the provision, judges who were unable to enforce their own judgment were to bring the matter to the attention of *nostra scrinia*, that is, the offices of the palace secretariat, the *Magister officiorum*.[80] In theory,

74 *ET* 43: "Nullus ad potentem Romanum aut Barbarum proprias quolibet titulo transferat actiones. Quod si fecerit, iacturam litis iurgator incurrat, et is qui susceperit, medietatem pretii rei aestimatae fisco cogatur inferre. Qua poena teneri praecipimus etiam eos, qui rem in lite positam in huiusmodi crediderint transferendam esse personam; quoniam volumus, ut remota persona potentioris, aequa iurgantes sorte confligant. Litigantibus vero post caussae terminum, largiendi quod vicerint, cui voluerint personae, concedimus potestatem."

75 *ET* 44: "Nullus se potens Romanus aut Barbarus tanquam defensor aut suffragator negotio misceat."

76 E.g., *CTh* 2.14.1 (400); 1.20.1 (408).

77 *ET* 32: "Barbaris, quos certum est reipublicae militare, quomodo voluerint et potuerint, faciendi damus licentiam testamenti, sive domi sive in castris fuerint constituti."

78 *CTh* 4.4.1, 3 (Constantine ?336). On the soldier's will, see William W. Buckland, *A Manual of Roman Private Law* (Cambridge, 1925), 224; Thomas S. Burns, *A History of the Ostrogoths*, (Bloomington, IN, 1984), 127. On wills in general, see Ulrich Nonn, "Merowingische Testamente: Studien zum Fortleben einer römischen Urkundenform in Frankreich," *Archiv für Diplomatik* 18 (1972), 14–15.

79 As Amory demonstrates (*People and Identity*, 79 with examples), the word was not necessarily a pejorative one in sixth-century Italy.

80 Cassiodorus uses the term *scrinia* in a more generic sense to refer to officers of the imperial administration in general. The following examples are illustrative. In the first three instances, the

the Master of the Offices had the widest range of administrative duties among palatine officials. Cassiodorus, who was himself a holder of the position (523–7), mentions that the officer controlled access to the court, was in charge of the imperial attendants, had authority over provincial Governors, and performed a variety of undisclosed legal functions. But the responsibility for the actual compilation of the *ET* most likely fell to the office of the imperial *Quaestor sacri palatii*. Derived from the distant senatorial *Quaestor candidatus*, who acted as the Emperor's spokesman in the Senate, the imperial Quaestor had become, by the reign of Constantius II (337–61) and Valentinian I (364–75), the Emperor's legal advisor.[81] According to the *Notitia Dignitatum* (*Register of State Dignities*), an official list of all ancient Roman civil and military posts drawn up somewhere between 395 and 427, the Quaestor was responsible for dictating the Emperor's laws (*leges dictandae*), and receiving petitions (*preces*).[82] He had no staff of his own, but rather was expected to rely on the services of the *scrinia*, that is, the notaries and advisors from the three principal secretariats of the *memoria*, *epistulae*, and *libelli*, whose *magistri* were subject not to him but to the *Magister officiorum*.[83] Indicative of the importance of the Quaestor in imperial lawmaking in the later Empire are the *Theodosian Code* and Justinian's *Code, Digest*, and *Institutes*, each the product of imperial Quaestors.[84]

Under Theoderic, the position of the Quaestor remained largely unchanged. In the official scheme of things, this officer was the third-highest-ranking official, immediately behind the Praetorian Prefect of the

reference is to members of the office of the Praetorian Prefect: Cass., *Var.* 11.7 ("universis iudicibus provinciarum senator ppo, 533 ante Sept. I: ad scrinia nostra transmittite"); 12.2 ("universis iudicibus provinciarum senator ppo, 534 ante Sept. I: ad scrinia dirigere"); 12.16 ("canonicaria, 537 ante Sept. I: ad scrinia nostra destinabis"). In the following examples, the reference is to members of the Count of the Sacred Largesse: Cass., *Var.* 7.22 ("formula commonitorii illi et illi scriniariis de binis et ternis"); 9.18 (Edict of Athalaric: "si quis autem de nostris scriniis aliquid crediderit promerendum").

81 Jill Harries and Ian Wood (eds.), *The Theodosian Code. Studies in the Imperial Law of Late Antiquity* (London, 1993), 7.

82 *Not. Dig. Or.* 11.13–16, ed. Otto Seeck (Berlin, 1876; repr. Frankfurt, 1962). On the significance of this document and the problems surrounding it, see Guido Clemente, *La Notitia Dignitatum*, Saggi di storia e letterature 4 (Cagliari, 1968); Michael Kulikowski, "The 'Notitia Dignitatum' as a Historical Source," *Historia* 49.3 (2000), 358–77.

83 *Not. Dig. Or.* 12, *Not. Dig. Occ.* 10.

84 Jill Harries, "The Roman Imperial Quaestor from Constantine to Theodosius II," *JRS* 78 (1988), 148–72; John Matthews, "The Making of the Text," in Jill Harries and Ian Wood (eds.), *The Theodosian Code. Studies in the Imperial Law of Late* Antiquity (London, 1993), 19–44; Tony Honoré, "Some Quaestors of the Reign of Theodosius II," in Jill Harries and Ian Wood (eds.), *The Theodosian Code*, 68–94. The standard work of Tribonian, the Quaestor *par excellence* of the Emperor Justinian, is that of Tony Honoré, *Tribonian* (London, 1978), esp. chapters 1, 2, 5–7.

West and the Prefect of Rome.[85] Cassiodorus' *formula* for appointment, the main points of which are reiterated throughout the *Variae*, describes the Quaestor as being responsible for dealing with appeals and petitions, and the restatement of existing laws in the form of edicts.[86] These were binding rules that reinforced, added to, and in some cases clarified certain points of existing law:

> By necessity this office [i.e. the Quaestor's] is linked intimately to Our [i.e. the King's] thoughts, that it may accurately speak what it knows Us to perceive; it puts aside the judgment of its own will, and so undertakes the will of Our intention that you would think its discourse really derived from Us ... Consider the honor and responsibility you have in equal measure. If We are in doubt as to any matter We ask the Quaestor, who is the treasury of public reputation, a store-room of the laws, ever ready for the unexpected ... Finally, the Quaestor must be such an individual as it befits to bear the image of the prince. For if, as is often the case, We should chance to listen to a suit from documents, how great will the authority of that tongue be which can fulfill Our genius in public? Knowledge of the law and probity of speech must accompany him, so that no one shall criticize what the prince may happen to decide ... For to you, the provinces transmit their petitions; from you, the Senate seeks the aid of the law; from you proven experts seek what they have learned; and you must satisfy all those who may demand legal help from Us.[87]

85 Cass., *Var.* 6 *capitula*, arranged in order of rank. In the index of the *Not. Dig. Or.*, the *magister officiorum* ranks above the Quaestor in importance. In Ostrogothic Italy the evidence would seem to suggest that the order in which individuals could hold these two offices was interchangeable. Cassiodorus, for instance, held the Quaestorship before he was appointed as *magister officiorum.* Eugenes (*PLRE* 2, 414–16) followed a similar career path, but Faustus Niger (*PLRE* 2, 'Faustus 9,' 454–6) was Master of Offices before he was Quaestor. See further Andrew Gillett, "The Purposes of Cassiodorus' *Variae*," in A. C. Murray (ed.), *After Rome's Fall. Narrators and Sources of Early Medieval History. Essays Presented to Walter Gottart* (Toronto, 1998), 41–2.

86 E.g., Cass., *Var.* 5.4 (a letter notifying the Senate of the appointment of Honoratus as Quaestor). See also Cass., *Var.* 8.13 (a letter in Athalaric's name conferring the position of Quaestor on a certain Ambrosius – presumably the same Ambrosius to whom Ennodius addressed his *Paraenesis Didascalica*, containing some important notices of Festus, Symmachus, Boethius, Cethegus, and their contemporaries: see *PLRE* 2, 69); 8.18 (a letter in Athalaric's name appointing Felix to the position of Quaestor); and 10.6 (an appointment letter in Theodahad's name conferring the position of Quaestor on Patricius). Judging by these names, it would seem that the position of the Quaestor was usually reserved for members of the Roman elite.

87 Cass., *Var.* 6.5: "Haec nostris cogitationibus necessario familiariter applicatur, ut proprie dicere possit quod nos sentire cognoscit: arbitrium suae voluntatis deponit et ita mentis nostrae velle suscipit, ut a nobis magis putetur exisse quod loquitur ... Considerate quid ponderis habeatis pariter et decoris. si quid dubitamus, a Quaestore requirimus, qui est thesaurus famae publicae, armarium legum, paratus semper ad subitum ... Talem denique oportet esse Quaestorem, qualem portare principis decet imaginem. nam si nos, ut assolet, causam gestis audire contingat, quae auctoritas erit linguae, quae sub oculis regalem genium possit implere? Adesse debet scientia iuris, cautela sermonis, ut nemo

Aside from the Quaestor himself, however, we know nothing about the individuals who were responsible for the actual composition of the *ET*. Although Cassiodorus included *formulae* for the appointment of notaries in the *Variae*, these documents are rather uninformative, stating only that they were concerned with the writing and recording of royal documents, such as the *ET*.[88]

Purpose and scope

According to its prologue, the *ET* was intended to restore peace to Italy either negatively by what it prohibited, or positively by what it permitted or encouraged. It was, so to speak, the *ius commune* of the provinces – the law common to Goths and Romans residing throughout the peninsula. The prologue states:

> Many complaints have come to Our attention that some people within the provinces are trampling upon the rules of law. Even though the authority of the laws can in no way be used to defend unjust actions, however, We, taking into consideration the [desired] peace of the population, and having before Our eyes the irregularities that can often occur, command that the present edicts be posted for ending matters of this sort, so that both barbarians and Romans, while maintaining the respect due to the public laws and dutifully preserving in their entirety the rights of everyone, may clearly know what they are obligated to follow concerning the items specified in the present edicts.[89]

The King, we are informed, received complaints that laws were not being observed in the provinces. To preserve the desired peace and order, the *ET* was to be posted so that Romans and barbarians would know what was expected of them. To that end, it is likely that copies of the text were distributed in Ravenna and Rome, the larger urban centers such as Milan and Genoa, as well as those places where there was frequent interaction between Goths and Romans. For in much the same way, Athalaric had the Prefect of Rome post his *Edict* in the most conspicuous places for a period of

debeat reprehendere quod principem constiterit censuisse . . . Ad te enim provinciae sua vota transmittunt: a te senatus iuris quaerit auxilium: a te docti probantur expetere quod noverunt, et necesse tibi est omnibus sufficere, quantos a nobis contigerit legum remedia postulare."

88 E.g., Cass., *Var.* 6.16, 17.

89 *ET* prol.: "Querelae ad nos plurimae pervenerunt, intra provincias nonnullos legum praecepta calcare. Et quamvis nullum iniuste factum possit sub legum auctoritate defendere: nos tamen cogitantes generalitatis quietem et ante oculos habentes illa, quae possunt saepe contingere, pro huiusmodi casibus terminandis praesentia iussimus edicta pendere: ut salva iuris publici reverentia et legibus omnibus cunctorum devotione servandis, quae barbari Romanique sequi debeant super expressis articulis, edictis praesentibus evidenter cognoscant."

thirty days: "Let these edicts be read out in the splendor of your assembly, and the Urban Prefect shall have them solemnly published for thirty days in the most frequented places, so that Our good order (*civilitas*) may be recognized, and the hope of truculent men be lost."[90]

To reinforce the solemnity of *ET*, the compilers included an epilogue, declaring rather confidently:

> We have brought together these [edicts], advantageous to all barbarians as well as Romans, as much as Our labors could permit or We could address at this time; all loyal barbarians and Romans must abide by them. Those matters which either the brief scope of the *Edict*, or [Our] attention to [other] public business have prevented Us from including are to be settled as they arise by the usual path of the laws. Let no one with any rank, wealth, power, office or honor presume in any way to oppose these beneficial precepts. We have gathered these laws to some extent from recent law (*lex*) and the sanctity of ancient Roman custom (*ius*). And all judges and those who pronounce the law shall know that if they allow these edicts to be violated in any way, they shall be deservedly struck by the punishment of proscription and exile. But if it happens that a person of considerable influence or his procurator, deputy or even chief tenant, whether barbarian or Roman, does not allow the present edicts (which have been decreed for the good of all) to be heeded in a case of some kind, and the judge involved is unable to withstand or prevent this, let that judge, if he has his own interests at heart, draw up an account of everything, lay aside any appearance of fear, and without delay send a report to Us. Only in this way can he be absolved of blame. For it is the duty of the whole to uphold that which has been provided for the security of all provincials.[91]

[90] Cass., *Var.* 9.19: "Haec in coetus vestri splendore recitentur et per triginta dies praefectus urbis locis celeberrimis faciat sollemni more proponi, ut nostra civilitate recognita spes truculentis moribus auferatur."

[91] *ET* epil.: "Haec quantum occupationes nostrae admittere, vel quae nobis ad praesens occurrere potuerunt, cunctis tam barbaris, quam Romanis, sumus profutura complexi: quae omnium barbarorum, sive Romanorum debet servare devotio. Quae comprehendere nos vel edicti brevitas, vel curae publicae non siverunt, quoties oborta fuerint, custodito legum tramite terminentur. Nec cuiuslibet dignitatis, aut substantiae, aut potentiae, aut cinguli vel honoris persona, contra haec, quae salubriter statuta sunt, quolibet modo credat esse veniendum; quae ex novellis legibus ac veteris iuris sanctimonia pro aliqua parte collegimus: scituris cognitoribus universis ac iura dictantibus, quod si in aliquo haec edicta fuerint violata, se proscriptionis deportationisque poena merito esse feriendos. Quod si forsitan persona potentior, aut eius procurator, vel vice dominus ipsius, aut certe conductor, seu barbari, seu Romani, in aliquo genere causae praesentia non permiserint edicta servari, et iudex, cuius intererit obsistere aut vindicare aut obviare non potuerit, in nostram illico, si sibi consulit, instructa ex omnibus relatione dirigat, deposita totius formidinis suspicione, notitiam. Haec enim sola ratione a culpa esse poterit absolutus. Quia quod pro omnium provincialium securitate provisum est, universitatis debet servare devotio."

Neither ignorance of the law nor the claim that an alleged crime did not figure as the object of a particular ruling constituted a defense, but matters outside the scope of the *Edict* were to be settled as the law required.

The *ET* could be consulted either by judges or litigants themselves in an effort to resolve the sorts of disputes that most often came to the attention of the King. It was to supplement and clarify existing Roman law, which was at this time erratically preserved in sources that were not easily accessible to the general public at large. For instance, the *Theodosian Code*, arguably the most important source for Roman law in the West throughout the early Middle Ages, survives in only ten manuscripts from before the ninth century.[92] This is not a very significant number for such an important legal source, and speaks to the extent to which the preservation and transmission of Roman legal texts as a whole was at this time limited.

For the *ET* to be effective, it had to be feasible, it had to be suited to the time and place of its creation; it had to be clearly expressed, so that there was no danger of ambiguity – especially so, since one of its prime roles was the removal of doubt and uncertainty concerning the law. These were particular attributes of practical and necessary importance, and dictated by the facts of the realities of the early sixth century. In light of this, it is possible to gain valuable insights into the prevailing social conditions surrounding the creation of the *ET* by considering what kinds of topics the compilers selected for inclusion.

The *ET* addresses a wide variety of subjects in a somewhat disjointed and *ad hoc* manner. Unlike the Theodosian model, which groups constitutions chronologically under subject headings, provisions are listed regardless of heading (*titulus*) and with little consideration of subject matter. Topics range from sundry breaches of the criminal law (*crimina*), such as judicial corruption and venality, murder, kidnapping, and tomb violation, to aspects of the private law including contracts, property, marriage, and civil misdemeanors (*delicta*).[93] Table 1 provides a breakdown. Matters of Roman public and criminal law are listed on the left, and issues of private law on the right, with the corresponding provisions of the *ET* noted in parentheses.

[92] In *Codices Latini Antiquiores: A Palaeographical Guide to Latin Manuscripts Prior to the Ninth Century I–XI plus Supplement*, ed. E. A. Lowe (Oxford, 1934–71), Lowe listed nine manuscripts of the *CTh*, or sections of it, one manuscript of a summary of the *CTh*, and one manuscript of the post-Theodosian Novels. Of these, he assigned only one manuscript of the *CTh* to Italy (*CLA* VIII 1212).

[93] For a review of the subject matter, see Ensslin, *Theoderich der Grosse*, 220–36; Becker, "Edictum Theoderic." For an index, see Generoso Melillo, Antonio Palma, and Carmela Pennacchio (eds.), *Lessico dell' «Edictum Theoderici Regis»* (Rome and Naples, 1990).

Table 1

Public law and *Crimina*	Private law and *Delicta*
judicial corruption (1, 2)	unauthorized detention/punishment of a freeman (8, 9)
judicial misconduct (3, 4)	
delivery of a judgment and the conclusion of a legal action (5–7)	temporary seizure of another's property (10)
	right to self defense (15, 16)
rules for laying a criminal accusation (13, 14, 50)	abduction (*raptus*) (17–22)
intestate claims involving the fisc (24, 25, 27)	recovery of lost or stolen property (11, 119, 131, 146, 148)
soldier's will (32)	thirty-year limit by which *de iure* ownership is established (12)
informers in court (*delatores*) (35)	
adultery (38, 39)	intestate claims involving private individuals (23, 26)
perjury (40, 42, 91)	
forgery (30, 41, 90)	robbery and theft (34, 116, 129, 130)
prohibition against the seizure of crown property (47)	wills and inheritance (28, 29, 31, 33)
	illicit marriage (36)
testimony of freedmen, *originarii* and slaves against current and former masters (48, 49)	remarriage of a woman (37)
	prohibition against transferring a legal action to a *potentior* (43)
fiscal liability (51–3, 144)	
rules of appeal (55)	prohibition against the involvement of a *potentior* in another's suit (44)
cattle rustling (56–8)	
removal of public debtors from churches and places of worship (71)	prohibition against the use of titles to indicate ownership (45, 46)
public registration of wills (72)	rules for initiating unilateral divorce (54)
guidelines for the enforcement of judicial decrees (73)	*stuprum* (59–63)
	mixed marriages and slave unions (64–7)
armed brigands (75)	rules of prescription (68, 69)
noxal liability in a criminal context (77, 117, 118, 120)	removal of runaway slaves from churches and places of worship (70)
plagium (78, 81)	liability for bringing forward a frivolous civil action (74)
inciting violence (89)	
arson (97)	restoration of property and temporary possession (76)
homicide (99)	
safeguards for a slave giving testimony in a criminal proceeding (100–2)	enslavement of freemen (79, 82, 83, 96)
	runaway slaves (80, 84, 85, 87)

Table 1 (*cont.*)

Public law and *Crimina*	Private law and *Delicta*
jurisdiction for the prosecution of a crime (103)	immunity from prosecution to the relatives of a rustler, seducer, or thief (88)
rules for the use of oaths in a legal proceeding (106)	misuse/destruction of another's property (86, 150–2)
sedition (107)	betrothal (92, 93)
prohibition against the practice of pagan ceremonies, necromancy, and sorcery (108)	selling/pledging children (94, 95)
	boundary markers (104, 105)
destruction of tombs (110)	improper disposing of a corpse within Rome (111)
theft of public money (115)	
recognition of the privileges of Jews (143)	guidelines for making and recovering loans (121–7, 134, 135)
recalcitrant barbarians (145)	
regulations on the proper use of measures and scales for transaction (149)	noxal liability in a civil context (98, 109, 128)
	rights, property and children of individuals convicted of a criminal act (112–114)
on the proper observance of Sunday and the days of Easter (154)	
	civil actions involving property holders (132)
	financial immunity for women (133, 153)
	ownership involving disputed property (136–8)
	contracts and agreements of sale (139–41, 147)
	right of owners to transfer slaves, *originarii*, and *coloni* (142)

What is immediately clear from all of this is the fact that the *ET* is primarily a handbook of Roman private law, with a total of ninety-four provisions dealing in whole or in part with issues pertaining to the law of persons, property, contract, sale, family, and *delicta* of one sort or another.

One reason for this disparity is the very narrow definition applied by Roman law to what constituted a crime. A crime was a wrongful act that generated a penalty, *poena*, which benefited the community rather than the victim. The penalty itself could vary: it could be flogging, exile, or death, which meant that it affected the status of the wrongdoer exclusively; or it might be sub-capital, which usually involved a fine (*multa*) that was paid not to the victim or his family but to the treasury. Acts which fell under this category included both crimes against the state (for example, treason and sedition) and common law crimes that primarily affected only the injured party, such as murder, forgery, kidnapping, and adultery. This category excludes a number of wrongful acts that we might classify as criminal, such as theft, fraud, injurious behavior, robbery, and some kinds of murder (for example of a slave), as well as actions that we might define as "white-collar crime," such as embezzlement. In these instances, it was the victim alone who benefited from the stipulated remedy. While the state provided the judicial machinery for the settlement of these delicts, it had no vested interest in them.[94]

With such a narrow definition of crime, we emerge with a somewhat restricted and arbitrary list of what constituted a public offense. Even so, the number of provisions in the *ET* that deal in one way or another with criminal matters is significant, and speaks to the document's intended purpose – namely, to bring about peace and order through the suppression of crime. But there can be no doubt that the primary focus of the compilers was on issues such as runaway slaves (*ET* 80, 84, 85, 87), labor shortages, the overworking of slaves or oxen of another (*ET* 150), damaged crops (*ET* 98), shifting boundary markers (*ET* 104, 105), cattle rustlers (*ET* 56–8), and so on – in short, the sorts of perennial problems that plague all agricultural communities. In their selection of topics, they made no reference to the Roman army, its enrollment, means of organization, and provisioning. The whole subject of Roman public works and entertainments was omitted. There is nothing in the *ET* on the repair of aqueducts or roads, public monuments and works of art, theaters, or games. This, despite the fact that according to Cassiodorus, the *cursus publicus* and Flaminian Way were maintained at great expense to the state, aqueducts still flowed, and statues and temples continued to be erected.[95] Of course, walls, roads, and aqueducts continued to be maintained well into the early Middle Ages, at least in the former ancient capital.[96] But this was becoming increasingly a matter of private initiative rather than public policy. In the city of Catana, for example, we are told that the walls and public works (theater and amphitheater) were in such a state of disrepair that the inhabitants petitioned the King, seeking permission to rebuild where possible.[97]

In this process of selection and omission we get a sense as to what kinds of issues mattered in Ostrogothic Italy and how they were to be dealt with. To

94 On this differentiation between crime and delict, see Richard Bauman, *Crime and Punishment in Ancient Rome* (London, 1996); Jill Harries, *Law and Crime in the Roman World* (Cambridge, 2007), 3.

95 Cass., *Var.* 4.47 (*cursus publicus*); 11.12 (Flaminian Way); 3.31 (statues); 5.38, 8.30 (aqueducts).

96 Robert Coates-Stephens, "The Walls and Aqueducts of Rome in the Early Middle Ages, AD 500–1000," *JRS* 88 (1998), 167–78.

97 Cass., *Var.* 3.49.

put it another way, by its silence on certain matters, the *ET* offered a statement of what was no longer important, that is, of the extent to which the institutions that characterized civic life in the later Roman Empire no longer had any practical applications in Theoderic's Italy. As to what kinds of things mattered, the arrival of the Goths on Italian soil created a predictable legacy of boundary disputes that had to be settled within a limited time (*ET* 10). In an effort to control the hostile retinues of powerful warlords, the violent and unlawful seizure of property, the beating of people with clubs or the stoning of them, and the setting of fires were henceforth considered seditious and subject to the harshest penalties (*ET* 47, 75). In addition, this was still a society where members of the upper class could rightly expect, and lawfully demand, preferential treatment in relation to their social inferiors (for example, *ET* 64, 75, 83, 89, 97, 111).

All of these provisions of course had a basis in Roman law. But it does not follow that the compilers, or the judges, lawyers, and practitioners for whom this was a concern necessarily identified some things as Roman and some not, or even understood the complexities of some of the Roman institutions covered in the *ET*. One example of the erosion of understanding of a central Roman institution is what the *ET* made of *patria potestas* (paternal authority). At *ET* 94, children *in potestate* could be sold by their parents:

> Parents who are compelled by necessity to sell their children for the sake of vital necessities shall not prejudice their *ingenuus* status; for the value of a free person is considered inestimable.[98]

What is strange here, and inconsistent with the ancient notion of *patria potestas*, is the use of the term *parens*, which could mean either parent (or any close relation for that matter), and not necessarily *pater*.[99]

[98] *ET* 94: "Parentes qui cogente necessitate filios suos alimentorum gratia vendiderint, ingenuitati eorum non praeiudicant; homo enim liber pretio nullo aestimatur." This is a restatement of a legal opinion of the classical jurist Paul (*PS* 5.1.1), and as such develops Severan juristic arguments from the late third century. See Caroline Humfress, "Poverty and Roman Law," in Margaret Atkins and Robin Osborne (eds.), *Poverty in the Roman World* (Cambridge, 2006), 183–203.

[99] On the decline of *patria potestas* as a viable legal concept in Late Antiquity, see Elisabeth Meyer-Marthaler, *Römisches Recht in Rätien im frühen und hohen Mittelalter* (Zurich, 1968), 131–8; Yan Thomas, "Vitae necisque potestas. Le père, la cité, la mort," in *Du châtiment dans la cité: Supplices corporels et peine de mort dans le monde antique* (Coll. ÉFR 79, 1984), 499–548; William V. Harris, "The Roman Father's Power of Life and Death," in R.S. Bagnall and William V. Harris (eds.), *Studies in Roman Law in Memory of A. A. Schiller* (Leiden, 1986), 81–95. Antti Arjava, "Paternal Power in Late Antiquity," *JRS* 88 (1998), 147–65; Antti Arjava, "The Survival of Roman Family Law After the Barbarian Settlements," in Ralph W. Mathisen (ed.), *Law, Society and Authority* (Oxford, 2003), 33–51.

Conclusions

At some point during Theoderic's reign, and perhaps as early as 500, the office of the imperial Quaestor was instructed by the King to draw up a collection of edicts that spelled out the rules that were to apply to all the inhabitants of Italy. This task ultimately fell to a group of unknown Roman jurists working in one of the offices of the imperial *scrinia*. Drawing upon earlier Roman law, in some instances working directly from a specific text and in others relying on their knowledge of a commonly-held legal or juristic principle, they came up with 154 edicts that together comprised the *ET*. By way of introduction they appended a prologue that explained the purpose behind these legal pronouncements: namely, to restore peace and order to the land. To reinforce the point they included an epilogue with instructions that it was the responsibility of all to uphold the rule of law in equal measure without distinction of ethnicity, condition, age, or sex.

From their selections and omissions we get a sense of what the compilers considered to be most serious and thus requiring immediate remedy. Not surprisingly, the majority of topics concern issues pertaining to life in the countryside. And it was here, in the rural communities that dotted the Italian landscape, where local custom remained strong. The compilers recognized this fact and in many cases adapted existing Roman law according to an evolving provincial setting. In this they were not breaking from imperial tradition. Emperors, Prefects, and jurists had long recognized the benefit of local custom for making the ancient laws of Rome more effective, provided they were compatible with the aims of the Roman government.[100] As we shall see in the pages that follow, the *ET* is both a product of and witness to this legacy.

[100] Paul Barnwell, "Emperors, Jurists and Kings: Law and Custom in the Late Roman and Early Medieval West," *Past and Present* 168 (2000), 6–29.

CHAPTER 2

The legal context

Introduction

The legislation issued by the barbarian Kings who replaced Roman authorities in the former provinces of the defunct western Empire represents their assumption of authority and responsibility for the problems associated with their arrival. Yet, the interplay between Roman and barbarian is a far more complex matter than simple confrontation and eventual replacement of the former by the latter. Barbarian Kings like Theoderic were forced to borrow from and adapt assorted elements of Roman law to establish and maintain sovereignty within their respective kingdoms. Indeed, Roman law was a defining feature within Theoderic's kingdom, just as it was in most other successor states of the post-Roman West. But the legislation issued by Theoderic was not simply a mindless redaction of previous Roman law. It was an amalgamation of different traditions and customs that strove, sometimes together and sometimes apart, towards the simplification and popularization of classical law and jurisprudence.

On the one hand, the *ET* is quite unlike "pure" classical Roman law in terms of its artistic elaboration, rhetorical flourish, and technical precision. While drawing heavily on the Roman civil tradition of three full centuries earlier, the compilers incorporated elements of provincial custom in terms of their emphasis upon reason, flexibility, and judicial discretion, as well as in their desire for specific regulations adapted to the conditions of the time, as opposed to general principles – a characteristic of classical jurisprudence. They also strove for simplicity and clarity of expression, ignoring the standards of artistry and grandiloquence characteristic of the *Theodosian Code* and the crowning achievement of Roman legal science – namely, the *Corpus Iuris Civilis* of the Emperor Justinian.[1] A parallel in the East is the

[1] Ernst Levy, *West Roman Vulgar Law: The Law of Property* (Philadelphia, PA 1952), 7; Fritz Schulz, *History of Roman Legal Science* (Oxford, 1967), 99–261; Wolfgang Kunkel, *An Introduction to Roman*

so-called Farmer's Law, a legal document that was probably drawn up in the late seventh or early eighth century, which incorporated provisions of the early to mid sixth century.[2]

On the other hand, the *ET* did not mark a break from Rome's classical legal heritage. For centuries, Emperors, Prefects, and jurists recognized the need to adapt existing Roman law to better fit current realities. The Emperor Constantine (306–37), for instance, was denounced by his nephew, the apostate Julian (331/32–63), as an "innovator and disturber of the ancient laws and of custom received long ago."[3] Many modern scholars have agreed with Julian's description, viewing Constantine as a radical innovator responsible for the introduction into the Roman legal system of fundamentally non-Roman concepts, derived from Christian and eastern (primarily Greek law) sources.[4] But Constantine was simply acknowledging events that had taken place long before his arrival on the scene: by the beginning of the fourth century, the law which applied in the provinces of the western Empire was an admixture of civil law, local custom, and provincial practice. Differing from region to region and sharing little of the sophistication, complexity, and technical precision of classical jurisprudence, the law that emerged in the post-classical era had a profound influence on the character and style of the earliest law codes of the barbarian successor kingdoms.

Legal and Constitutional History, trans. J.M. Kelly, 2nd edn., based on the sixth German edition of *Römische Rechtsgeschichte* (Oxford, 1973), 135–51; Herbert F. Jolowicz and Barry Nicholas, *A Historical Introduction to the Study of Roman Law*, 3rd edn. (Cambridge, 1972). For the development of Roman law in general, see, e.g., Arnold H. M. Jones, *The Later Roman Empire, 284–602: A Social, Economic and Administrative Survey*, 3 vols. (Oxford, 1964) 1, 470–1, 520–2; Jill Harries, "The Roman Imperial Quaestor from Constantine to Theodosius II," *JRS* 78 (1988), 148–72; Tony Honoré, *Emperors and Lawyers* (London, 1981), *passim*; Simon J. Corcoran, *The Empire of the Tetrarchs: Imperial Pronouncements and Government AD 284–324* (Oxford, 1996); Peter Stein, *Roman Law in European History*, (Cambridge, 1999), 32–6.

[2] Walter Ashburner, "Farmer's Law. I," *JHS* 30 (1910), 68–108; Walter Ashburner, "Farmer's Law. II," *JHS* 32 (1912), 68–95; George Ostrogorsky, "La commune rurale byzantine: Loi agraire – Traité fiscal – Cadastre de Thèbes," *Byzantion* 32 (1962), 140–7; George Ostrogorsky, *History of the Byzantine State*, 2nd edn. (Oxford, 1968), 90–1; John F. Haldon, *Byzantium in the Seventh Century: The Transformation of a Culture* (Cambridge, 1990), 132–5; Mark Whittow, *The Making of Orthodox Byzantium, 600–1025* (Basingstoke, 1996), 115–17.

[3] Amm. Marc., 21.10.8: "novator turbatorque priscarum legum et moris antiquitus recepti."

[4] Most notably Ernst Levy, *Pauli Sententiae: a Palingenesia of the Opening Titles as a Specimen of Research in West Roman Vulgar Law* (Ithaca, NY, 1945); Ernst Levy, "Vulgarization of Roman Law in the Early Middle Ages," *Mediaevalia et Humanistica* 1 (1963), 14–40; Levy, *West Roman Vulgar Law*, esp. 6, 15; cf. many of his papers, gathered together in his *Gesammelte Schriften: Zu seinem achtzigsten Geburstag mit Unterstützung der Akadamien der Wissenschaften zu Göttingen, Heidelberg und München sowie von Basler Freunden ihm dargebracht*, 2 vols. (Cologne, 1963).

Roman law in Late Antiquity

The term "vulgarization" has been key to understanding some of the profound developments taking place in Roman law in the post-classical era. But it is a particularly value-laden concept that traditionally has been used by scholars to draw an artificial dichotomy between the sophisticated classical law of the Roman forum and the primitive custom of the Germanic forests. And it is an especially troublesome term since it is capable of meaning different things. In its most derogatory sense, vulgarization refers to the simplification of Roman law that the barbarian codes like the *ET* can be said to represent. In a more technical sense, vulgarization can be taken to refer to the departure of post-classical law from the classical norms of legal development. The term can also encompass the inevitable divergence between the law practiced in outlying districts of the Empire and that applied in the major civic centers like Rome and Constantinople. And lastly, vulgarization can be understood as the way in which Roman law was practiced over the course of the fourth and fifth centuries in a more crude and unscientific manner than it had been in previous generations.

The expression was first coined by the legal historian Heinrich Brunner in 1880 to designate a body of relatively simple, perhaps customary, law which was not written down, and which governed every day legal business in the western Roman provinces from the fourth to sixth centuries.[5] It was an evolution or, depending upon one's perspective, a degeneration of purely "classical" Roman civil law, that is, the law that originally applied to the city of Rome.[6] But as the application of this law was gradually extended to encompass all Roman citizens living in outlying provinces, it eventually came to take account of, and to be influenced by, custom or provincial practice. Prior to the granting of citizenship to all the

[5] Heinrich Brunner, *Zur Rechtsgeschichte der römischen und germanischen Urkunde I, Das Privaturkunde Italiens; das angelsächischen Landbuch; die fränkische Privaturkunde* (Berlin, 1880), 113, 119; Heinrich Brunner, *Forschungen zur Geschichte des deutschen und französischen Rechtes* (Stuttgart, 1894), 607 n. 1. The fundamental study of the development of Roman law in the East remains that of Ludwig Mitteis, *Reichsrecht und Volksrecht in den östlichen Provinzen des römischen Kaiserreichs: Mit Beiträge zur Kenntniss des griechischen Rechts und der spätrömischen Rechtsentwicklung* (Leipzig, repr. Hildesheim, 1963). Here, the focus is on the influence of peregrine law on classical notions and principles of Roman law. For a review of the scholarship see Detlef Liebs, "Roman Vulgar Law in Late Antiquity," in A. J. B. Sirks (ed.), *Aspects of Law in Late Antiquity* (Oxford: 2008), 35–53.

[6] For this definition and a discussion of *ius civile*, see George Mousourakis, *The Historical and Institutional Context of Roman Law* (Aldershot, 2003), 22–4; Arthur A. Schiller, *Roman Law: Mechanisms of Development* (New York, 1978), 366–8, 525–7; Michael Kaser, *Römische Rechtsgeschichte* (Göttingen, 1976), 130–3.

inhabitants of the Empire, provincial communities were permitted to continue observing their own local systems of law and custom provided they were not incompatible with Roman rule. As citizenship spread to ever increasing numbers of provincials, culminating in 212 with Caracalla's *Constitutio Antoniniana* that granted Roman citizenship to all free inhabitants of the Empire, provincial communities were required to adopt and apply the civil law, the rules and procedures of which were largely unknown to them. Given that the inhabitants of these communities were often reluctant to abandon the norms by which they had been governed in the past, elements of these local systems gradually crept into the civil law. Over time, Rome's law lost its classical "purity" and became "vulgarized."

The most influential voice for defining vulgar law has belonged to Ernst Levy, who drew attention to the vulgarizing tendencies inherent in Roman laws of property that slowly emerged in the West over the course of the third and fourth centuries.[7] Vulgarizing tendencies, Levy exclaims, had existed at all times, but classical jurisprudence kept them in check. Although vulgar law penetrated even the legislation, and was taken over by the elementary books for practitioners and students (for instance the author of the so-called *Pauli Sententiae* (*PS*)), third-century Emperors generally strove against this dissolution of the pure (classical) Roman law. The chief protagonist of this fight was Diocletian (284–305), and with his abdication this imperial policy came to an abrupt end. A corollary to this, Levy asserts, was a decline in legal erudition associated with a drop in the number of skilled legal professionals. The result was the emergence of a new type of law. Adhering neither to traditional niceties nor strict concepts, this law was unable, or simply unwilling to match the standards of the artistic and comprehensive elaboration of logical construction that defined classical jurisprudence.[8]

Roman law, Levy and others maintain, was in the later Empire not just misunderstood or misapplied in places where legal experts were lacking. The official law of the Roman state sank to an almost primitive and unscientific level. For Levy, the law of property in particular suffered a

[7] Levy's theories have found many adherents including, e.g., Katherine Fischer-Drew, "The Germanic Family of the *Leges Burgundionum*," *Mediaevalia et Humanistica* 15 (1963), 5–14; and her "The Barbarian Kings as Lawgivers and Judges," in R. S. Hoyt (ed.), *Life and Thought in Early Middle Ages* (Minneapolis, MN, 1967), 7–29; Tony Honoré, "Ausonius and Vulgar Law," *Iura* 35 (1984), 79–82; Adrian J.B. Sirks, "Shifting Frontiers in the Law: Romans, Provincials and Barbarians," in Ralph W. Mathisen and H. Sivan (eds.), *Shifting Frontiers in Late Antiquity* (Aldershot, 1996), 146–57.

[8] Levy, *West Roman Vulgar Law*, 7.

decline. Fourth- and fifth-century jurists and lawyers could not comprehend even the most basic principles: distinctions between contract and conveyance, ownership and possession, rights *in rem* and *in personam*, and so on. More recent work on late Roman law, however, suggests that it is time to reassess this characterization.[9] To begin, the number of trained lawyers and legal experts all over the later Empire did not decline.[10] Only in the second half of the fifth century did the availability of lawyers, at least in remote areas, become somewhat of a problem.[11] Lawyers and legal experts remained in high demand as assessors in the late imperial *scrinia*; and Cassiodorus, too, attests to the continued importance of skilled lawyers and jurisprudents in the early sixth century.[12] In such a society, bureaucratic and committed to the rule of law, it is hard to imagine that professional standards and legal erudition declined in a dramatic way.

[9] E.g., Franz Wieacker, "Le droit romain de la mort d'Alexandre Sévère á l'avènement de Dioclétien," *RHDFE* 49 (1971), 201–23; Franz Wieacker, "'Vulgarrecht' und 'Vulgarismus'. Alte und Neue Probleme und Diskussionen, lecture in Siena 4th December 1979," in *Studi in onore di Arnaldo Biscardi I* (Milan, 1982), 33–51. Wieacker reiterates his position in his *Römische Rechtsgeschichte*, (Munich, 1988 and 2006), 211–18, noting that the vulgarization of late Roman law was a matter of style rather than an indication of any sort of decline in legal erudition. Moreover, Sarah Vandendriessche in her *Possessio und Dominium im postklassischen römischen Recht. Eine Überprüfung von Levy's Vulgarrechtstheorie anhand der Quellen des Codex Theodosianus und der Posttheodosianischen Novelle* (Hamburg, 2006) demonstrates convincingly that the fundamental classical differentiation between property and simple possession was still well known and respected in post-classical legislation of the fourth and fifth centuries, even if these differences were now versed in non-classical terms. See also Tony Honoré, "Conveyances of Land and Professional Standards in the Later Empire," in Peter Birks (ed.), *New Perspectives in the Roman Law of Property. Essays for Barry Nicholas* (Oxford, 1989), 137–52, who argues against any such notion of vulgarization. Similarly, through a systematic analysis of late imperial juristic literature and the identification of practicing judicial experts between the third and sixth centuries, Detlef Liebs shows that there was no decline in the standard of classical jurisprudence in Late Antiquity. See his *Die Jurisprudenz im spätantiken Italien (260–640 n. chr.)*, Freiburger Rechtsgeschichtliche Abhandlungen n.f. 8 (Berlin, 1987); Detlef Liebs, "Römische Jurisprudenz in Afrika im 4. Jh. n. chr," *ZSS (RA)* 106 (1989), 201–17; Detlef Liebs, (ed.), *Das Gesetz in Spätantike und frühem Mittelalter* (Göttingen, 1992); Detlef Liebs, "Die pseudopaulinischen Sentenzen," *ZSS (RA)* 112 (1995), 151–71; Detlef Liebs, *Römische Jurisprudenz in Gallien (2 bis 8 Jahrhundert)* (Berlin, 2002); and Detlef Liebs, "Roman Vulgar Law in Late Antiquity," 35–53.

[10] Liebs, *Die Jurisprudenz im spätantiken Italien*, 284; Geoffrey Greatrex, "Lawyers and Historians in Late Antiquity," in Ralph W. Mathisen (ed.), *Law, Society and Authority in Late Antiquity* (Oxford, 2001), 148–61.

[11] *Nov. Val.* 32.6 (31 Jan. 451) referring to the lack of lawyers and judges since the time of Alaric's invasion.

[12] E.g., Cass., *Var.* 1.12 (a letter written in the name of Theoderic to the *vir illustris* Eugenius, extolling his skills as an advocate); 4.3 (a letter addressed in Theoderic's name to the *vir illustris* and *comes* Senarius, newly elected to the position of *comes patrimonii*, mentioning his skill as an advocate, and commending his track record as an honest officer to the crown); 5.4 (Honoratus, subject of this letter to the Roman Senate concerning his appointment as Quaestor, is extolled for his service as an advocate in Spoleto, where he had to contend against the corrupt practices of the provincial judges); 5.22 (another letter addressed in the name of Theoderic to the Senate of Rome, concerning the appointment of a certain Capuanus as *rector decurianum*, noting his distinguished service as an advocate before the Senate).

Moreover, evidence from the *ET* argues against any such decline. To take as an example *ET* 147, concerning the conditions that constituted a valid sale:

> A sale agreed upon in good faith and concluded cannot be challenged by the vendor; but he may demand from the buyer any outstanding payment.[13]

If a contract requiring good faith has been made, ownership of the thing has been transferred, and the price paid, the validity of the sale could not later be challenged, for example, on the grounds that the price was too low.[14] There were other factors, however, that might void a sale that was otherwise correctly performed in this aspect. On the one hand, the transaction had to be consensual. A sale performed under duress was *prima facie* void, just as any forced donation was void. To that end, it was illegal for any minor to enter into a contract.[15] On the other, there had to be a specific and authentic title vested in the vendor (or donor). An individual was not permitted to alienate property that was the subject of legal proceedings, which belonged to someone else, or which was physically possessed by another who claimed it as his own.[16] Levy has argued that the transfer of title was the instantaneous consequence of payment, and has taken this provision as proof that the tendency in post-classical times was to conflate two or all of the separate elements that defined sale in the classical period – that is, contract (usually the consensual *emptio–venditio* contract), transfer/conveyance of ownership, and payment of the price.[17] But it is unclear how *ET* 147 runs these incidents of sale together. In the first place, there is the contract requiring good faith (*placita bona fide et definita venditio*). The compilers presuppose the requirement that transfer of the ownership to the buyer is made; but nowhere do they conflate the action with the payment of the price – which is clearly separate, and had no effect on the transfer of ownership.

Similarly, *ET* 141 presupposes all three aspects of the classical sale as being achieved:

> Anyone who sells a slave with a history of escaping to another unaware of this, should the slave then flee the buyer the vendor shall both return the

[13] *ET* 147: "Placita bona fide et definita venditio a venditore rescindi non potest: sed pretium, quod ab emptore debetur, repetendum est."

[14] Ernst Levy, *Weströmisches Vulgarrecht. Das Obligationenrecht*, Forschungen zum römischen Recht (Weimar, 1956), 211.

[15] Cass., *Var.* 4.35. [16] *ET* 10.

[17] Levy, *Law of property*, 156–61 and *Gesammelte Schriften*, 205–6, 213–14.

> payment and compensate [the buyer] for any losses he may have suffered as a result of that [fugitive] slave.[18]

The buyer had the right to recover the price of a slave on the basis that he was a recurrent runaway, along with any expenses he incurred as a result. The crux of the ruling rests on the fact that the contract for the sale of such a runaway slave was *prima facie* void, since it was not made in good faith; and it assumes that the transfer of ownership to the buyer was accomplished (presumably through delivery), and that the payment of the price was given. There is nothing here to suggest that any or all stages of a classical sale were run together.

The *ET* is not a work of vulgar law in the way Levy has characterized it. Nor is it a work of purely classical jurisprudence. While the compilers certainly possessed a rudimentary knowledge of some of the more complex and technical aspects of classical law, it is clear from their selection of topics and the characterization of the provisions which they wrote that such knowledge was no longer necessary, or even practical. They freely adapted the law to better fit the circumstances of their own time. While in many cases this demanded more informality at the expense of technical precision, there is nothing inherently alien or inferior about their work. On the contrary, the *ET* is a work of profound erudition that struck a balance between the strict formalities of classical jurisprudence and the demands of local custom. In this regard, it is a revealing testament to the character and vitality of Roman law in Late Antiquity.

Sources of inspiration and innovation

A study of the *ET* in relation to earlier sources of imperial law and juristic interpretation, as well as the near contemporary legal compilation of the Emperor Justinian (*CJC*), reveals just how much Roman law had evolved in the West since the third century, and the degree to which the law of Theoderic's Italy was unique. As the compilers point out in the epilogue to the text, the authority of the *ET* as a valid source for settling disputes lay in the fact that it was derived from *novellae leges* and *vetus ius*, that is to say, written enactments and ancient custom preserved in imperial codifications and juristic commentaries.[19] In some cases the compilers were working

[18] *ET* 141: "Quicunque fugere solitum vendiderit ignoranti, si emptorem quoque fugerit, et precium venditor reddat et damna sarciat, quae per eundem contigerint fugitivum."

[19] On this distinction between *ius* and *lex*, see Mousourakis, *The Historical and Institutional Context of Roman Law*, 17–18, 357; John F. Matthews, "Interpreting the *interpretationes* of the *Breviarium*," in

directly from a specific text. The basis for identification rests on similarities between the original text and provision in terms of technical subject matter, organization, language, and syntax.[20] Elsewhere, they were simply acknowledging a principle of Roman law or jurisprudence that would have been well understood in the sixth century, and for which no source would have been necessary. In all instances, their perspectives were shaped by the circumstances in which the law was intended to apply. As such, the *ET* is of intrinsic importance for understanding the character of Roman law and society in Theoderic's Italy.

While not specifically cited, the sources for the *ET* include: extracts from the commentaries and legal opinions of the third-century jurists Paul, Ulpian, and Papinian;[21] the late third-century *Gregorian* and *Hermogenian Codes*, sections of which survive in later – oftentimes highly interpolated – versions of the sixth-century *Codex Justinianus* (*CJ*);[22] the fifth-century *Theodosian Code* and some post-Theodosian novels (*novellae constitutiones*) to the exclusion of those of Marcian (450–7), Severus (461–5) and Anthemius (467–72).[23] Of all these, the *Pauli Sententiae*, a post-classical collection of summaries of legal pronouncements and rules attributed to Paul (although not compiled by the jurist himself), and the *CTh* figure most prominently. The former was the source for thirty-five

Ralph W. Mathisen (ed.), *Law, Society and Authority in Late Antiquity* (Oxford, 2001), 11–32 at 16; Stein, *Roman Law in European History*, 4, 28. For similar usages of the terms in later periods, see Rosamond McKitterick, *The Carolingians and the Written Word*, (Cambridge 1989), 38.

20 Bluhme's identifications, which he included in an appendix to his edition (p. 176), have remained standard.

21 On the life and times of these jurists, see Mousourakis, *The Historical and Institutional Context of Roman Law*, 291–305; Stein, *Roman Law in European History*, 20–1; Andrew Borkowski and Paul Du Plessis, *Textbook on Roman Law*, 3rd edn. (Oxford, 2005), 49–50.

22 Under Diocletian, these two collections of imperial legislation, comprising mostly *subscriptiones*, were compiled. The *Codex Gregorianus* covers the period from Hadrian to Diocletian, and the *Codex Hermogenianus* contains legislation from the reign of Diocletian only. These collections provided the model for the *Theodosian Code* and were used by Justinian in his compilation of the *Codex Justinianus*. Although far from certain, it is likely that Diocletian had a hand in the publication of these two collections, which together provided a convenient and accessible reference for local judges and lawyers (as well as other interested parties) to consult as needed. For general discussion on these texts and their survival in Late Antiquity, see Nicole Kreuter, *Römisches Privatrecht im 5. Jh. N. Chr.: Die Interpretatio zum westgotischen Gregorianus und Hermogenianus* (Berlin, 1993); Jean Gaudemet, *La formation du droit séculier et du droit de l'Église aux IVe et Ve siècles*, 2nd edn. (Paris, 1979), 44–8; Corcoran, *The Empire of the Tetrarchs*; Jill Harries, *Law and Empire in Late Antiquity* (Cambridge, 1999), 15.

23 For the edition of the *CTh* see *Theodosiani libri XVI cum constitutionibus Sirmondianis et Leges Novellae ad Theodosianum Pertinentes*, ed. Theodor Mommsen, Paul Meyer, and Paul Krueger, 2 vols. (Berlin, 1905; repr. 1971). For a translation, see Clyde Pharr, *The Theodosian Code and Novels, and Sirmondian Constitutions* (New York, 1952). For the *Novellae*: *Theodosiani Libri XVI*, ed. Mommsen, Meyer and Krueger, vol. 2.

provisions,[24] and the latter supplied the material for a further forty-seven.[25]

For imperial enactments originally collected in the *Gregorian* and *Hermogenian Codes*, as well as the opinions of Papinian and Ulpian, we must rely primarily on later, oftentimes highly interpolated, versions collected in Justinian's *Codex* (*CJ*) and *Digest* (*Dig.*). The former was a collection in twelve books of imperial constitutions intended to update the *Theodosian Code*. The latter was an anthology of extracts from the writings of the great jurists dealing with all subjects of Roman law. It was a work of unprecedented scope, taking three years to complete. In their task the jurists were instructed by Justinian to attribute each fragment to its original source by an appropriate designation. Despite this, however, there is no way of knowing that what they attributed to a particular jurist is what he actually wrote. This is partly because the original discussion had been reduced (oftentimes quite substantially), but also because the compilers were expressly instructed to do away with all contradictions and repetitions. Furthermore, the jurists were permitted to make whatever substantive changes they saw fit to ensure that the final result expressed the law as Justinian desired it – which was a law that both sought to restore the sophistication, precision, and artistry of the Roman law from three centuries before, but also one that could be applied in the Byzantine Empire of his own time. The same rules applied to earlier imperial constitutions collected in the *CJ*.[26]

[24] *ET* 5 (*PS* 5.5a.5–6), 33 (*PS* 5.12.2), 40 (*PS* 1.12.2 (3)), 41 (*PS* 4.7.2), 42 (*PS* 5.15.5; cf. *Dig.* 22.5.16 *Paulus libro 5 sententiarum*), 56 (*PS* 5.18.2; ex *Coll.* 11.2), 57 (*PS* 5.18.1), 58 (*PS* 5.18.4; ex *Coll.* 11.5; cf. *Dig.* 47.14.1, 1), 62 (*PS* 2.26.11), 75 (*PS* 5.26.3), 83 (*PS* 5.30*b*.1), 89 (*PS* 5.25.12), 90 (*PS* 5.25.12, 5, 2), 91 (*PS* 5.25.12), 94 (*PS* 5.1.1), 95 (*PS* 5.1.1), 97 (*PS* 5.20.2; ex *Coll.* 12.2.1), 98 (*PS* 5.20.3–4), 99 (*PS* 5.23.10 (11); cf. *PS* 5.26.1), 100 (*PS* 5.16.3), 101 (*PS* 5.16.7), 102 (*PS* 5.16.9), 104 (*PS* 5.22.2), 107 (*PS* 5.22.1), 115 (*PS* 5.27), 117 (*PS* 2.31.7), 119 (*PS* 2.31.16), 120 (*PS* 2.31.8–10), 123 (*PS* 5.26.4), 124 (*PS* 5.26.4), 130 (*PS* 2.31.25 (24)), 131 (*PS* 5.5a.4), 141 (*PS* 2.17.11), 146 (*PS* 2.31.30; *Dig.* 47.2.83.1), 151 (*PS* 2.31.24 (25)).

[25] *ET* 3 (*CTh* 9.27.3,4 (382)), 10 and 11 (*CTh* 4.22.3 (389)), 12 (*CTh* 4.14.1 (424)), 13 (*CTh* 9.1.11 (368); 9.1.19 (423)), 14 (*CTh* 9.1.15 (385)), 17–19 (*CTh* 9.24.1 pr., 2 and 4 (326)), 20 (*CTh* 9.24.3 (374)), 26 (*CTh* 5.3.1 (434)), 27 (*CTh* 5.2.1 (352)), 28 (*CTh* 4.4.1 (326?)), 35 (*CTh* 10.10.1–3), 37 (*CTh* 3.8.1), 43 (*CTh* 2.13.1 (422)), 44 (*CTh* 2.12.6 (395)), 46 (*CTh* 2.14.1 (400)), 48 and 49 (*CTh* 9.6.3 (397)), 50 (*CTh* 10.10.4 (338)), 51 (*CTh* 8.12.1 (323)), 52 and 53 (*CTh* 8.12.8 (415)), 54 (*CTh* 3.16.1 (331)), 55 (*CTh* 11.30.22 (343); 11.30.42 (384)), 61 (*CTh* 9.25.1 (349)), 65–8 (*CTh* 5.10.1 (419)), 70 (*CTh* 9.45.3 (398); 9.45.5 (432)), 71 (*CTh* 9.45.1 (392); 9.45.3 (398)), 77 (*CTh* 9.10.4 (390)), 84 (*CTh* 5.9.?), 103 (*CTh* 9.1.10 (368)), 108 (*CTh* 16.10.6 (356); 16.10.23 (423)), 111 (*CTh* 9.17.6), 112, (*CTh* 9.42.2 (356)), 113 (*CTh* 9.42.2 (356); similarly, 9.42.24 (426)), 121 (*CTh* 2.30.2 (422); similarly, 2.32.1 (422)), 122 (*CTh* 2.13.1 (422)), 132 (*CTh* 11.39.12 (396)), 134 (*CTh* 2.33.2 (386)), 144 (*CTh* 12.6.18 (396)), 149 (*CTh* 11.8.1 (397); 11.8.3 (409)), 154 (*CTh* 2.8.18; 8.8.3; 11.7.13 (386)).

[26] The instructions given to the sixteen jurists commissioned for the task can be found at *CJ* 1.17.1 (*De auctore*). See also Stein, *Roman Law in European History*, 32–4.

Such interpolations, whether they take away from, add to, or just modify the original text, make the task of identifying the sources of the *ET* a difficult one. Where the compilers of Theoderic were working from a source for which we have only the interpolated version of Justinian's jurists, it is not possible to make a case for positive identification on linguistic or stylistic grounds. That both groups of jurists were working from a common source is entirely possible, but we cannot determine how closely, or if at all, either group was adhering to the original source in question. Nevertheless, we can see in their work how their perspectives differed from each other in terms of what aspects of the same rule or convention they chose to emphasize or ignore (Table 2).

Table 2

Texts from the Pauli *Sententiae* (*PS*)	Provisions of the *ET*
lib. 1 tit. 12 § 3	40
lib. 2 tit. 17 § 11	141
lib. 2 tit. 26 § 11	62
lib. 2 tit. 31 § 7, (8) 10	117, 120
lib. 2 tit. 31 § 16	119
lib. 2 tit. 31 § 24, 25	130, 151
lib. 2 tit. 31 § 30	146
lib. 4 tit. 7 § 2	41
lib. 5 tit. 1 § 1	94, 95
lib. 5 tit. 5*a* § 4	131
lib. 5 tit. 5*a* § 6	5
lib. 5 tit. 12 § 2	33
lib. 5. tit. 5 § 5	42
lib. 5 tit. 16 § 3, 7, 9	100–2
lib. 5 tit. 18 § 2, 1, 4	56–8
lib. 5 tit. 20 § 2–4	97, 98
lib. 5 tit. 22 § 1	107
lib. 5 tit. 22 § 2	104
lib. 5 tit. 23 § 11	99
lib. 5 tit. 25 § 12, 5, 2	89–91
lib. 5 tit. 26 § 1	99
lib. 5 tit. 26 § 3	75
lib. 5 tit. 26 § 4	123, 124
lib. 5 tit.27 § 1	115
lib. 5 tit.30*b* § 1	83
Texts from Book Three of the *Responsa*	**Provisions of the *ET***
fr. 12 *Finium regundor.* (*Dig.* 10.1.12)	105
fr. 49pr. *de iudiciis* (*Dig.* 5.1.49)	139

The works of Paul

Of all the sources of juristic opinion available to them, the compilers turned most often to the works of Paul, most notably his *Sententiae* (*PS*). A further two provisions are analogous to presumably interpolated versions of Justinian's compilers on excerpts taken from Book Three of Paul's *Responsa*, an extensive commentary on the praetorian edict in eighty books which is preserved for us primarily in the *Digest*.[27] The *PS*, a significant work dealing with a broad range of topics relating to both private and criminal law, appears not to have been a genuine work of Paul but rather a summary of his works composed in Africa sometime around 300.[28] It became an extremely popular handbook for students and legal practitioners in the later Empire, and was cited extensively in various other barbarian law codes, including the *Lex Romana Visigothorum*, or Breviary of Alaric II, the Visigothic version of the *Theodosian Code*, produced around the year 506.[29] The original text, however, has not survived. Rather, it has been reconstructed on the basis of extracts included in various post-classical compilations, such as Justinian's *Digest*, the *Lex Romana Visigothorum*, and the *Collatio Legum Mosaicarum et Romanarum* (or *Collatio*) from the early fourth century. But there are enough similarities in terms of language and

[27] *Responsa*: *ET* 105 (*Dig*. 10.1.12), 139 (*Dig*. 5.1.49).

[28] Detlef Liebs convincingly argues that the *Sententiae* originated in Africa sometime around 300; and that the compiler did not draw only on Paul's own works, but also on works by a number of classical jurists as well as the *Codex Gregorianus* and *Codex Hermogenianus*. See his "Römische Jurisprudenz in Afrika, 201–17; Detlef Liebs, "Die pseudopaulinischen Sentenzen," *ZSS (RA)* 112 (1995), 151–71; and most recently his *Römische Jurisprudenz in Africa mit Studien zu den pseudopaulinischen Sentenzen* (Berlin, 2005). Timothy D. Barnes, *Constantine and Eusebius* (Cambridge, MA, 1981), 289 n. 73, notes that the fragment of the full text of the *Sententiae* dates, on paleographical grounds, to around 300, and was most likely written soon after the composition of the original text. For the text, see *FIRA* vol. II, 317–417, 419–432; Maria Bianchi Fossati Vanzetti (ed.), *Pauli Sententiae. Testo e interpretatio* (Padua, 1995). For a useful discussion see Mousourakis, *The Historical and Institutional Context of Roman Law*, 358 (who places it somewhere in the first two decades of the fourth century). For the *Sententiae* as a source of Roman law in the West, see Levy, *Pauli sententiae*; Wieacker, "Le Droit romain de la mort d'Alexandre Sevère à l'avènement de Dioclétien," esp. 218–20; Kunkel, *An Introduction*, 148–50.

[29] The *Lex Romana*, or *Breviary of Alaric*, is a compilation of selections from various Roman sources, including: the *Theodosian Code*, the *Gregorian* and *Hermogenian Codes*, some *Novellae* of Theodosius II and Valentinian III, and some extracts from a *responsum* of Papinian, Paul's *Sententiae* and the complete *Epitome Gai*, the Gallic version of Gaius' *Institutes* (reduced to two books and departing from the original text in many places). Accompanying each part of the collection (with the exception of the *Epitome Gai*) are *interpretationes* – explanatory commentaries that clarify certain points of the original text. For the text see *Lex Romana Visigothorum* (or *Breviarium Alarici*), ed. G. Haenel, *Lex Romana Visigothorum* (Leipzig, 1849; repr. Aalen, 1962), 33–456. On the circumstances surrounding the creation of this text and the identity of those responsible for its compilation, see Matthews, "Interpreting the *interpretationes* of the *Breviarium*," 16–17; John F. Matthews, "Roman Law and Barbarian Identity in the late Roman West," in S. Mitchell and G. Greatrex (eds.), *Ethnicity and Culture in Late Antiquity* (London, 2000), 31–45.

subject matter to suggest that the compilers of the *ET* were working directly from one of the many extant copies of the *Sententiae* that were circulating in the West at this time. In drawing from it the compilers sometimes left the original texts unchanged, or nearly so – presumably because they were already well-suited to the conditions of their time.[30] For example, *ET* 40, a brief provision concerning the matter of testimony, provided immunity to anyone who unknowingly made a false claim in court. Its model is *PS* 1.12.2(3), which is left essentially unchanged:

ET 40	*PS* 1.12.2(3)
Qui falsum nesciens allegavit, ad falsi poenam minime teneatur.	Qui falsum nesciens allegavit, falsi poena non tenetur.

The compilers likewise found no reason to alter *PS* 5.16.9:

ET 102	*PS* 5.16.9
Si servus ad hoc fuerit manumissus ne torqueatur, quaestio de eo nihilominus haberi potest.	Si servus ad hoc fuerit manumissus, ne torqueatur, questio de eo nihilo minus haberi potest.

In the event that a slave was manumitted to prevent him from being tortured under interrogation, the rule here allows for an interrogation concerning him to be held. The basis for this is a non-extant decree of the Emperor Antoninus Pius (138–61), a reference to which is made by the editors of Justinian's *Digest*:

> The deified Pius wrote in a rescript that if a slave is manumitted in order that he not be tortured, then, provided that he is not tortured in a capital case involving his master, he can be tortured.[31]

Here, the freedman was prohibited from being tortured in a capital case involving his master. Neither *ET* 102 nor *PS* 5.16.9 makes any such exception.

Elsewhere, however, there are all sorts of variances and points of difference. To be sure, some of these are haphazard and of no major importance;[32] but others represent significant developments. For example, on the

[30] E.g., *ET* 40, 62, 91, 94, 95, 98, 100, 102, 115, 117, 130, 141.

[31] *Dig.* 48.18.1.13 (Ulpian 8 *de off. Procons.*): "Si servus ad hoc erit manumissus, ne torqueatur, dummodo in caput domini non torqueatur, posse eum torqueri divus pius rescripsit."

[32] E.g., *PS* 5.12.2: aufertur = *ET* 33 auferatur; *PS* 1.12.2 (3): non tenetur = *ET* 40: minime teneatur; *PS* 5.18.4 (ex *Coll.* 11.5): furem magis eum quam abactorem constitui placuit = *ET* 58: furti magis reus

topic of forgery (*falsum*), *ET* 41 closely models *PS* 4.7.2 but departs from it in two important respects:

ET 41	*PS* 4.7.2
Anyone who produces or knowingly uses a forgery, or persuades or compels another to make one, shall suffer a capital penalty.[33]	Not only shall he who tampers with, suppresses, or destroys a testament, but also anyone else who knowingly with *dolus malus* instructs or undertakes this to be done, shall be held liable for the penalty of the Cornelian law [i.e. deportation].[34]

First, unlike the original, which applied exclusively to written forms of testaments, *ET* 41 concerns all manners of forgery. Second, whereas *PS* 4.7.2 treats the offense as capital and punishes the guilty with deportation (presupposed by *PS* 4.7.1), *ET* 41 is purposefully imprecise in fixing a specific punishment, simply stating that the offender would be punished capitally. This could mean any number of things including exile, deportation, and execution (by assorted manner). The basis for all of this is the Cornelian law on forgery (mentioned specifically in *PS* 4.7.2), which was overhauled substantially by Constantine in the fourth century.[35] But Constantine's law applied the maximum penalty (i.e. death) only in the most serious of cases. In most instances the usual punishment was deportation.

As early as the Republic, documentary proofs had acquired administrative significance. In the later Empire, as the administration generally became more dependent on the use of the written word, even greater weight was accorded to the significance of documents as a means of establishing proof. Thus, forgery became a far more serious offense, and was more widely applied to include offenses which under classical law constituted the less serious delictal act of fraud (*dolus*).[36] The corresponding punishment also increased in terms of its severity. The silence in *ET* 41 concerning the penal component would seem to suggest that by the sixth century the

tenendus est; *PS* 5.23.11 (11): ut homicidae puniuntur = *ET* 99: tamquam reus homicidii occidatur; *PS* 5.16.7: poterit interrogari = *ET* 101: debet subiici quaestioni; *PS* 5.5a.4: pignora capi et distrahi possunt = *ET* 131: capi eorum pignora debent et distrahi.

33 *ET* 41: "Qui falsum fecerit, vel sciens falso usus fuerit, aut alterum facere suaserit, aut coegerit, capitali poena feriatur."

34 *PS* 4.7.2: "Non tantum is, qui testamentum subiecit suppressit delevit, poena legis Corneliae coercetur, sed et is qui sciens dolo malo id fieri iussit faciendumve curavit."

35 *CTh* 9.19.2.2 (326).

36 Harries, *Law and Empire*, 108; Borkowski and Du Plessis, *Textbook on Roman Law*, 356–7; Elizabeth A. Meyer, *Legitimacy and Law in the Roman World.* Tabulae *in Roman Belief and Practice* (Cambridge, 2004), 38–43, 209–10, 218–27.

matter had become one of judicial discretion. While the judge could impose a sentence of deportation in accordance with earlier imperial law, he could just as well apply the maximum penalty of death. In other words he was not bound by the fixed limitations of the Cornelian law.

The compilers likewise did away with all outmoded forms of punishment. In *ET* 42, for instance, they omitted the reference in the original (*PS* 5.15.5) to the penal component requiring deportation to an island:

ET 42	*PS* 5.15.5
Those who deliver varying or false testimony or offer such testimony to either party shall be exiled.[37]	Those who deliver testimony falsely or varyingly, or offer [such testimony] to either party shall either be exiled, relegated to an island or removed from the court (local council).[38]

In sixth-century Italy, the punishment of exile did not necessarily entail banishment to an island; although, we hear from Cassiodorus that the curial Jovinus was exiled to the Lipari islands off the coast of Sicily for killing a fellow curial during a heated exchange.[39] Usually, those sentenced to exile were simply banished to another region of the kingdom, and sometimes subjected to a form of imprisonment in a bid to restrict mobility. Illustrative of this is Boethius, who was banished to Calventia (modern Calvenzeno) following his conviction on charges of treason, and there remained under house arrest from 523 until his death in late 525 or early 526.[40] To bring the law up to date, then, the compilers modified each instance where the original source included a penalty that stipulated relegation to an island.[41]

[37] *ET* 42: "Qui varium aut falsum testimonium dixerint, aut utrique parti prodiderint, in exilium dirigantur."

[38] *PS* 5.15.5: "Qui falso vel varie testimonia dixerunt vel utrique parti prodiderunt, aut in exilium aguntur aut in insulam relegantur aut curia submoventur." The editors of the *Digest* reduce this to the following (*Dig.* 22.5.16): "false, inconsistent or double-faced witnesses are appropriately punished by the judge." ("Qui falso vel varie testimonia dixerunt vel utrique parti prodiderunt, a iudicibus competenter puniuntur.")

[39] Cass., *Var.* 3.47. A total of eight provisions of the *ET* include penalties of exile: 18, 42, 75, 83, 89, 95, 97, 108.

[40] Anon. Val. 14.87.

[41] E.g., *PS* 5.23.11 (10): "a judge who accepts a bribe in a capital case shall have his goods confiscated and be deported to an island." ("iudex, qui in caput fortunasque hominis pecuniam acceperit, in insulam bonis ademptis deportatur.") = *ET* 1: "In the first place We have decreed that if a judge accepts money to pass judgment which imperils the life or civil status of an innocent person against the ordinances and provisions of the public law, let him be subjected to a capital penalty." ("Priore itaque loco statuimus, ut si iudex acceperit pecuniam, quatenus adversum caput innocens contra leges et iuris publici cauta iudicaret, capite puniatur."); *PS* 4.7.2: "[a person guilty of forgery] shall be deported to an island." ("...

Other outdated punishments included crucifixion, condemnation to the public mines, and exposure to beasts in the arena. Both execution *ad bestias* and crucifixion are last heard of in legislation of the Emperor Constantine, who condemned to the cross slaves who informed on their masters,[42] and slaves or freedmen convicted of kidnapping were condemned *ad bestias*.[43] Constantine is also credited with formally abolishing crucifixion in favor of hanging.[44] But it would be wrong to think that Christian notions of humanity and compassion diminished the highly public and painful nature of imperial penal policy in any meaningful way. In 323, for instance, Constantine decreed that any soldier who colluded with enemy forces (identified as "barbarians") and caused loss or ruin to another Roman, or otherwise profited from such dealings, was to be burnt alive.[45] Jews and members of other non-Christian sects who punished Christian converts were also put to the flame.[46] And the punishment for homosexuality involving the seduction or rape of a freeborn boy was death by fire.[47]

To account for these developments the compilers made the necessary adjustments. For example, *ET* 104 applied a capital penalty (presumably death) to any slave or tenant farmer (*colonus*) who overturned boundary markers, whether on their own volition or at the request of the master. The compilers glossed over the detail in the original, *PS* 5.22.2, which specified punishment in these instances to be condemnation to the mines:

in insulam deportatur.") = *ET* 41: "[the guilty] shall suffer a capital penalty." ("... capitali poena feriatur."); *PS* 5.20.2: "anyone who sets fire to another's house or villa out of enmity, if they are *humiliores* they shall be condemned to the mines or endure public labor, *honestiores* shall be relegated to an island." ("qui casam aut villam inimicitiarum gratia incenderunt, humiliores in metallum aut in opus publicum damnantur, honestiores in insulam relegantur.") = *ET* 97: "... anyone who sets fire to another's dwelling, house or villa out of enmity, if they are a slave, *colonus*, slave woman or *originarius*, they shall be consumed by fire. If a freeborn should do this, he shall repay any of the costs associated with the fire that he set, and he shall restore the building, and in addition, as a penalty for committing such an act, he shall be compelled to pay the value of the possessions destroyed; but if he is unable to raise this amount on account of his penury, let him be flogged and punished with the banishment of perpetual exile." ("Qui casam, domum, aut villam alienam inimicitiarum causa incenderit si servus, colonus, ancilla, originarius fuerit, incendio concremetur: si ingenuus hoc fecerit, restituat quidquid dispendii acciderit per illud, quod commovit, incendium, aedificiumque renovet, et aestimationem insuper consumptarum rerum pro poena talis facti cogatur exsolvere; aut si hoc sustinere pro tenuitate nequiverit, fustibus caesus perpetui exilii relegatione plectatur.")

42 *CTh* 9.1.5 (314). 43 *CTh* 9.18.1 (315).

44 This is attested by Aurelius Victor, *Liber de Caesaribus* 41.4, ed. Franciscus Pichlmayr (Leipzig, 1911); trans. Harold W. Bird, *Sextus Aurelius Victor: Liber de Caesaribus*, Translated Texts for Historians 17 (Liverpool, 1994). See further Harries, *Law and Empire*, 139.

45 *CTh* 7.1.1. 46 *CTh* 16.8.1 (339). 47 *CTh* 9.7.3 (342), and 6 (390).

ET 104	*PS* 5.22.2
Those who dig up boundaries or plow up property lines, specifically those which designate a perimeter, or destroy trees marking boundaries, if they are slaves or *coloni* and have acted without the consent or authority of their master, they shall be punished capitally. If it is proven that this act was done at the owner's behest, that same owner is to be deprived of a third of his possessions to the benefit of the rights of the fisc; nevertheless, the slave or *colonus* must be punished capitally.[48]	Those who dig or plow up boundaries, or turn over boundary trees, if they are slaves and did so on their own, let them be condemned to the mines; *humiliores* shall be condemned to the public works, and *honestiores*, upon being deprived of a third of their goods, shall be relegated or forced into exile.[49]

Likewise, in *ET* 107 we read that those guilty of sedition (a treasonable offense) were to be burned alive, whereas the original, *PS* 5.22.1, provided varying penalties according to the status of the accused, including crucifixion, exposure to wild beasts, or deportation to an island:

ET 107	*PS* 5.22.1
Anyone who instigates sedition either among the people or in the army is to be burned alive.[50]	Authors of sedition or tumults or disturbers of the populous shall, depending on their status, either be crucified, thrown to wild beasts, or be deported to an island.[51]

Sedition was a treasonable offense, and since acts of treason represented a direct threat against the authority of the Emperor, they were regarded as particularly heinous. The crimes which could constitute a treasonable offense or were regarded as equivalent to treason (specified in the *Lex Iulia*) could vary

48 *ET* 104: "Qui effodiunt terminos, vel exarant limites, finem scilicet designantes, aut arbores terminales evertunt, si servi sunt aut coloni, et sine conscientia vel iussu domini fecerint, [capite] puniantur. Si vero hoc imperante domino factum esse constiterit, idem dominus tertiam partem bonorum suorum perdat, fisci iuribus profuturam: servo ipso aut colono nihilominus capite puniendo."

49 *PS* 5.22.2: "Qui terminos effodiunt vel exarant arboresve terminales evertunt, si quidem id servi sua sponte fecerint, in metallum damnantur: humiliores in opus publicum, honestiores in insulam amissa tertia parte bonorum relegantur aut exulare coguntur." On condemnation to the mines as a capital offense in the Empire, see Fergus Millar, "Condemnation to Hard Labor in the Roman Empire, from the Julio-Claudians to Constantine," *PBSR* 52 (1984), 124–47.

50 *ET* 107: "Qui auctor seditionis vel in populo vel in exercitu fuerit, incendio concremetur."

51 *PS* 5.22.1: "auctores seditionis et tumultus vel concitatores populi pro qualitate dignitatis aut in crucem tolluntur aut bestiis obiciuntur aut in insulam deportantur." Elsewhere (*PS* 5.29) we are informed that whereas the punishment for treason was formerly interdiction from fire and water, "nowadays" (that is, sometime around 300) *humiliores* were condemned to the arena to be devoured by hungry beasts, or burned alive; and *honestiores* were punished capitally.

depending on the discretion of imperial legislators. Hurling insults at an Emperor, for example, might not always be considered treasonable if the abuser was found to be drunk, confused, or simply mad (*CTh* 9.4). While the definition of treason remained (purposefully) ambiguous, and the list of treasonable offenses varied over time, the penalties for the crime were particularly harsh throughout the Empire. As *ET* 107 demonstrates, this remained the case in Theoderic's time.[52]

ET 107 is interesting for another reason. Unlike the original it makes a specific reference to mutineers within the army. And whereas *PS* 5.22.1 required that the guilty be punished according to considerations of status (which could entail deportation), *ET* 107 prescribed death in all such instances. Only in six other places do the compilers specify the manner of execution.[53] Of these, death by fire was the most severe. Treason, as it had been in the Empire, was regarded by Theoderic as an unpardonable offense, particularly in cases involving the military, because of the danger it posed. To not punish the guilty was to condone their behavior, which in turn undermined the stability of the society and the position of the King.

The attention to detail on display in *ET* 107, particularly the specific reference to the army, is a clear indication that the compilers regarded such treasonable acts associated with the military as especially worrisome. This fear is, in fact, echoed by Cassiodorus, who notes several instances where soldiers, improperly or insufficiently supplied, resorted to brigandage in direct defiance of the central authority.[54] Procopius, too, alludes to the challenges Theoderic (and subsequent rulers) faced in securing the loyalty of the army. To ensure allegiance and cohesion among the rank and file of the regular infantry, Theoderic appointed his most trusted followers, an inner élite of several thousand – variously identified by Procopius as "the best" (*aristoi*), "the notable" (*dokimoi*), and "the worthy" (*logimoi*) – to positions of leadership.[55]

This attention to detail is a characteristic trait of the compilers. *ET* 56 concerns cattle rustling – a recurring problem throughout the Empire

[52] On treason in Roman law, see Jill Harries, *Law and Crime in the Roman World* (Cambridge, 2007), 72–85.

[53] There are three instances of punishment by the sword (*ET* 48, 49, 56) and a further three where the offender was to be burned alive (*ET* 35, 61, and 97).

[54] E.g., Cass., *Var.* 3.38, 4.13, 5.13, 12.5.

[55] For specific references to individual *logimoi*, *dokimoi*, and *aristoi*, see respectively: Proc., *BG* v. iv. 13 (*logimoi*); vi. i. 36; vi. xx. 14; vii. xviii. 26; viii. xxvi. 4 (*dokimoi*); vi. viii. 9; vii. i. 46 (*aristoi*). On this policy and some of the challenges encountered by Theoderic in this regard, see the comments of Peter Heather in his "Merely an Ideology? – Gothic Identity in Ostrogothic Italy," in Sam J. Barnish and Federico Marazzi (eds.), *The Ostrogoths from the Migration Period to the Sixth Century: An Ethnographic Perspective* (Woodbridge, 2007), 31–60, esp. 42, 44, 45, 50.

whose pervasiveness rose and fell in response to the prevailing economic conditions of the time. Unlike ordinary theft (*furtum*), it was prosecuted as a public crime whose punishment was generally more severe. The legal force behind this was a decree of the Emperor Hadrian (117–38), the main points of which were reiterated in *PS* 5.18.2. This served loosely as the model for *ET* 56:

ET 56
The rustler of another's animals, flocks and herds, whether he drives them off from stables or pastures, shall be punished by the sword; and the remuneration for the victim's loss, which is to be garnered from the property of the rustler, shall be fourfold. But if the rustler is a slave or *originarius*, his owner, upon being summoned before a judge for these crimes, shall, if he prefer, either compensate [the victim] in accordance with what We have decreed above, or not delay to surrender those accused to a public judge to be punished by death.[56]

PS 5.18.2
Heinous cattle thieves are generally consigned to the sword or the mines, but sometimes to public labor. Heinous [cattle thieves] are those who steal horses and flocks of sheep from a stable or pastures, or if they commit this deed often or with a weapon.[57]

Whereas the punishment in *PS* 5.18.2 varied from the most extreme (i.e. death by the sword or consignment to the mines) to an unspecified form of public labor depending upon the seriousness of the problem in general or the offender specifically, *ET* 56 punished all such thieves with the extreme penalty. Moreover, it went further than the original to require that the victim be compensated in the form of fourfold remuneration, and in accordance with the ancient principle of noxal liability (the responsibility of the *paterfamilias* or owner for delicts committed by his child or slave), that slaves or *originarii* who were condemned for the act

[56] *ET* 56: "Abactor animalium vel gregum atque pecorum alienorum, sive ea de stabulis, sive de pascuis abegerit, gladio puniatur, et in quadruplum amittentis damno de eius substantia consulatur. Quod si servus aut originarius fuerit, dominus pro his conventus legibus, si maluerit, aut, ut supra diximus, satisfaciat, aut impetitos ad poenam mortis iudici publico tradere non moretur."

[57] *PS* 5.18.2: "Atroces pecorum abactores plerumque ad gladium vel in metallum, nonnumquam autem in opus publicum dantur. Atroces autem sunt, qui equos et greges ovium de stabulo vel de pascuis abigunt, vel si id saepius aut ferro conducta mano faciunt."

be surrendered by their owners to be punished capitally. Conversely, the largest fine imposed upon a cattle rustler in the *PS* was threefold the original amount.[58]

Given its severity and attention to detail, *ET* 56 is indicative of the pervasiveness of cattle rustling in sixth-century Italy. As Ulpian noted in his commentary on Hadrian's rescript, the penalty of death applied only in those areas where the crime was most prolific: "Let evil-doers [i.e. cattle rustlers] be punished most severely, but not everywhere and only in those places where the crime is most prolific."[59] *ET* 56 made no such restriction and provided specific remedy for the victims.[60] Cassiodorus, too, confirms that cattle rustling posed a significant problem for Theoderic. In a letter written in the King's name to the provincials, *capillati*, *defensores*, and *curiales* of Suavia concerning the appointment of the Governor Fridibad and the seemingly on-going violence that had been plaguing the land, Cassiodorus has Theoderic proclaim, in rather bold fashion, that the newly-appointed Governor "will punish cattle rustlers with due severity."[61] Here, cattle rustlers were purposefully singled out and threatened with severe sanctions (presumably this meant capitally).

In *ET* 58 the compilers went beyond their source to make explicit the application of the rule of law that was most obviously relevant to conditions in Italy at this time. Based on *PS* 5.18.4, the provision outlines in detail the obligations of an individual who should happen upon another's escaped animal(s):

ET 58	*PS* 5.18.4
Anyone who leads away a cow, horse, or other livestock wandering about must also be held guilty of the crime of theft, and he shall restore fourfold the number of animals or livestock stolen; unless he acknowledges this	Anyone who leads away a wandering cow, horse, or any other kind of livestock, it is pleasing that he be held liable for the actions of a thief rather than those of a rustler.[62]

[58] *PS* 5.18.3.

[59] *Dig.* 47.14.1 pr.:"puniuntur autem durissime non ubique, sed ubi frequentius est id genus maleficii."

[60] Compensation for cattle-rustling is also mentioned at *PS* 5.18.1: whereas *ET* 56 prescribed fourfold remuneration, *PS* 5.18.1 provided twofold or threefold compensation depending on the severity of the crime or the propensity of the offender.

[61] Cass., *Var.* 4.49: "qui [i.e. Fridibad] abactores animalium legitima severitate coerceat . . ."

[62] *ET* 58: "Qui bovem, vel equum errantem, vel aliud pecus abduxerit, furti magis reus tenendus est, et in quadruplum animalia vel pecora sublata restituat: nisi ea ab eo die quo invenerit, septem diebus continuis in publicis celeberrimisque locis, aut ante praetorium iudicis, proposuerit: hoc enim facto nullius poenae damna sustineat."

> fact in public or in well-known places or before the official residence of a judge for seven continuous days since that day he found them; upon completion of this, let him not endure the detriment of any penalty.[63]

The provision obliges anyone who finds strays to make this fact public for a period of seven days, by announcement to the local judge or notification in recognized public places; presumably he was then required to look after them carefully as his own and be compensated for this – but there is no direct evidence for this. Failure to publicize his find rendered him liable to pay the compensation for theft. The basis for this punishment no doubt rested on the grounds that the culpability of the offender yielding to the temptation of a situation which he had not himself brought about should be rated less than that of the man who deliberately chose to assume the charge of strays, but concealed the fact. Presumably after the seven days were up, the animals became the property of the individual who happened upon them, provided he took all necessary precautions. None of this information is found in the original, which simply required that the individual who assumed ownership of another's strays be held liable as a thief rather than a cattle rustler.

Just as the compilers made important additions to reflect specific circumstances, they made equally important omissions. The goal was to render the law more accessible, and therefore more applicable. In most cases the sorts of details that they overlooked were simply extraneous, and made no difference to the effect of the law. For instance, *ET* 83 follows closely *PS* 5.6.14 concerning the unlawful confinement, selling and purchasing of a freeman, but ignores the reference in the original to the source for this – the *Lex Fabia*, a statute of unknown date (presumably the second or first century BC). Similarly in *ET* 123, a brief provision that prohibited creditors from seizing a pledge without the proper authorization of a judge, they ignored the specific reference in the original, *PS* 5.26.4, to the *Lex Iulia de vi privata*. When jurists or legislators mentioned sources like the *Lex Fabia* or *Lex Iulia*, the purpose was to show an accumulation of juristic interpretation of how the principles and expectations of the particular law or statute were intended to apply. This was not simply a matter of mere convention; rather,

[63] *PS* 5.18.4: "Qui bovem vel equum errantem quodve aliud pecus abduxerit, furem magis eius quam abactorem constitui placuit."

it was an affirmation of an ancient legal tradition. If the compilers of the *ET* had wished to continue this tradition, they could have done so by making specific reference to the original sources. But since the compilers were concerned with the application of the law in specific circumstances, they did not need to trifle with details as to ancient precedents, even if these precedents continued to underpin the basic function of the law in the early sixth century.[64]

In *ET* 146 there is a more meaningful omission that reflects significant developments taking place in the area of legal procedure. According to the provision, both the *colonus* and owner – since it was a concern for each – were permitted to bring an action against a person suspected of stealing from the owner's estate. In this, it follows *PS* 2.31.30 (*Dig.* 47.2.83.1) closely:

ET 146	*PS* 2.31.30 (*Dig.* 47.2.83.1)
De frugibus ab aliquo ex fundo cuiuslibet sublatis, tam colonus, quam dominus, quia utriusque interest, agere potest.	Frugibus ex fundo subreptis tam colonus quam dominus furti agere possunt, quia utriusque interest rem persequi.

The basis for this remedy is the classical *actio furti*, concerning which the *PS* makes explicit reference (*furti agere*). In classical terminology *actio* referred to the first stage of a traditional two-stage legal process (the second being *iudicum*), the formulary procedure. Under this system, a plaintiff would bring his complaint to the authorized magistrate who would lay down the rules governing how the case would proceed. The actual judgment was then rendered by a layman, who was guided in all of this by the instructions of the magistrate.[65] During the Principate, and perhaps even earlier, this system was abandoned and replaced by the *cognitio extra ordinem* procedure, in which the judge was a state-appointed professional who heard the whole case. Under the rules of the *cognitio* system, the plaintiff presented his claim to the court in writing. It was then served by a court officer on the defendant, who filed his defense with the court. The parties appeared before

[64] A similar air-brushing out of this Roman legal tradition is found in the *Code of Euric*, and noted by Jill Harries in her "'Not the Theodosian Code': Euric's Law and Late Fifth-Century Gaul," in Jill Harries and Lan Wood (eds.), *The Theodosian Code Studies in the Imperial Law of Late Antiquity* (London, 1993), 39–51 at 47.

[65] On the formulary system in general, see Schiller, *Roman Law: Mechanisms of Development*, 435–7; Jolowicz and Nicholas, *Roman Law*, 199–201; Olivia F. Robinson, *The Sources of Roman Law: Problems and Methods for Ancient Historians* (London, 1997), 84–6; Mousourakis, *The Historical and Institutional Context of Roman Law*, 206–18; Kunkel, *An Introduction*, chapter 6; Barry Nicholas, *An Introduction to Roman Law* (Oxford, 1991), 19–21; David Johnston, *Roman Law in Context*

the judge, who heard arguments on the legal issues, took evidence from witnesses, and then rendered his decision.[66]

The abandonment of the formulary procedure had certain effects on the law – traces of which can be found in *ET* 146 and elsewhere. First, a*ctio* ceased to be conceived in classical terms as a basis of remedy with its own specific set of procedures; no longer did it determine or delimit the demands of the plaintiff or the pleas of the defendant. Second, since it was no longer necessary for a plaintiff to choose a particular formula, it was possible to bring forward an action without identifying precisely what the legal basis of the claim was. Third, now that one judge heard the entire case, the former distinction between the role of the Praetor and *iudex* – a division which was reflected in a division of the law from the facts – became blurred. The legal issues could be brought up gradually as the case proceeded. In the *ET*, the term serves only as a symbol for a substantive legal concept. *Actio* and *agere* are employed chiefly to express the right to sue or as collective expressions for judicially enforceable claims (for example, *ET* 12, 24, 31, 43, 46, 146, 152). Where the compilers name a specific *actio*, for example *actio furti* in *ET* 85, 86, and 120, it is not for the purpose of identifying a particular claim, but rather in a less technical sense to express the object of the action. Whereas in classical law, *actio furti* denoted a penal action through which the plaintiff could claim double or fourfold damages from the defendant, depending on the type of theft that had been committed (i.e., whether it was manifest or not), in the *ET* it refers to the very offense itself.[67] In all instances the compilers either did not specify the nature of the *actio*, as in *ET* 146, or the specific rules associated with a particular claim. Thus, while the language of actions did not die out with the demise of the formulary system, by the early sixth century *actio* had lost its technical meaning, which in turn led to a loss of precision in the law itself.

As the *ET* illustrates, the opinions of Paul remained a popular source of Roman law in Theoderic's Italy just as they had been in the later Roman Empire and other contemporary successor kingdoms. And it is surely significant that given what was available to them, the compilers drew heavily upon this post-classical work, rather than earlier more "classical" juristic writings such as the *Institutes* of Gaius, which was by the middle of the fifth

(Cambridge, 1999), 112–14; Kaser, *Römische Rechtsgeschichte*, 140–2; Michael Kaser, *Das römische Zivilprozesserecht*, 2nd edn. (Munich, 1996), 151–53; Wolfgang Kunkel and Martin Josef Schermaier, *Römische Rechtsgeschichte* (Cologne, 2001), 110–12; Wieacker, *Römische Rechtsgeschichte*, 447–9.

66 On the demise of the *actio* in late Roman law, see Levy, *West Roman Vulgar Law*, 202; Stein, *Roman Law in European History*, 25.

67 Levy, *West Roman Vulgar Law*, 202; Reinhard Zimmerman, *The Law of Obligations: Roman Foundations of the Civilian Tradition* (Oxford, 1996), 200.

century too complicated for lawyers and practitioners and was replaced by an *Epitome Gai* – an abridged version of the *Institutes* that did away with all of Gaius' complex explanations of the law.[68] But even the *PS* required necessary updating.

Digest *and Code of Justinian*

A total of six provisions are analogous to versions in the *Digest* of extracts taken from works of Ulpian and Papinian respectively: five from Ulpian's *de officio proconsulis* (*On the Duties of a Provincial Governor*), and one from a commentary found in Book Two of Papinian's *de adulteriis* (*On Adultery*) (see Table 3).[69]

In each instance the compilers were working directly from the sources themselves; there is sufficient correspondence in terms of technical subject matter between their versions and those preserved in the *Digest* to suggest a common source for both. But since these sources no longer survive in their original form, we cannot determine just how closely this was done.

Not surprisingly, the provisions bear little resemblance to what we find in the *Digest* – the differences between them reflecting the different tasks required of the respective groups of compilers. In consulting the sources, the compilers of the *ET* were guided by considerations for the changed priorities of the time and attempted to render the law in a form that was suitable for conditions particular to sixth-century Italy; whereas Justinian's compilers, guided by the will of the Emperor, consciously looked back to

Table 3

Sources from Ulpian (*de officio proconsulis*)	Provisions of the *ET*
lib. 2 fr. 1 *Quib. ad lib.* (*Dig.* 40.13)	82
lib. 5 fr. 79 pr. *de iudiciis* (*Dig.* 5.1.79 pr.)	74
lib. 7 fr. 7, 4 *de accus.* (*Dig.* 48.2.7.4)	103
lib. 8 fr. 1, 1 *de abigeis* (*Dig.* 47.14.1)	57–8
Sources from Papinian (lib. 2 *de adulteriis*)	**Provisions of the *ET***
fr. 8 *ad legem Iuliam de adulter.* (*Dig.* 48.5.9)	39

[68] Ibid., 27–8.

[69] *De officio proconsulis*: 57 (*Dig.* 47.14.1 pr.), 58 (*Dig.* 47.14.1.1), 74 (*Dig.* 5.1.79 pr.), 82 (*Dig.* 40.13), 103 (*Dig.* 48.2.7.4); *de adulteriis*: 39 (*Dig.* 48.5.9).

the golden age of Roman law and aimed to restore it to the peak it had reached some three centuries earlier, while at the same time ensuring that what was left would be suitable for life in sixth-century Byzantium. These different objectives profoundly influenced how each group approached the same source of law.

To take as an example, *ET* 39 addresses the topic of adultery, specifically targeting individuals who facilitated the crime. For this, the compilers borrowed from Papinian's commentary on Augustus' *Lex Iulia de adulteriis* of 18 BC, an extensive statute which among other things defined cases of adultery as public crimes punishable before a criminal court, the penalties, the forms, and terms of accusation. The text is quite distinct from the version included in the *Digest*:

ET 39	*Dig.* 48.5.9 pr.
Anyone who offers a house or dwelling so that adultery may be committed, or anyone who persuades a wife to consent to adultery, shall be punished capitally.[70]	Anyone who knowingly provides his own house so that an act of *stuprum* or adultery may be committed with another's *mater familias*, or with a male, or makes a profit from the adultery of his own wife, is punished as an adulterer, no matter what his status.[71]

Whereas *ET* 39 focuses exclusively on adultery, the version in the *Digest* includes acts of *stuprum* (illicit sexual behavior) and homosexuality. In the *ET* version, the penal component is extended to include individuals who induced a married woman to commit adultery. Justinian's compilers, on the other hand, address specific instances where the husband pimped his own wife out for profit (*lenocinium*). And while the *ET* specifically notes that this was a capital offense, this fact is only presupposed in the *Digest*.

ET 74 concerns the matter of frivolous lawsuits, and was derived from a fragment of Ulpian's commentary on judges. The provision includes a good deal of information not found in the version of Justinian's compilers (*Dig.* 5.1.79 pr.):

[70] *ET* 39: "Qui ut adulterium fieret, domum vel casam praebuit; quive mulieri, ut adulterio consentiret, suasit, capite puniatur."

[71] *Dig.* 48.5.9 pr.: "Qui domum suam, ut stuprum adulteriumve cum aliena matre familias vel cum masculo fieret, sciens praebuerit vel quaestum ex adulterio uxoris suae fecerit: cuiuscumque sit condicionis, quasi adulter punitur."

ET 74
If a plaintiff launches a wrongful lawsuit over some matter, and is refuted after a just examination, from the day the suit was formally set out the falsely accused shall receive from the plaintiff the costs and expenses of the litigation which he demonstrates he sustained when he was undeservedly sued; this shall be determined by the assessment of a judge or of knowledgeable good men appointed for that purpose. It is right that their sense of justice and deliberations determine what costs and expenses of the suit he who heedlessly led another into a public trial should pay.[72]

Dig. 5.1.79 pr.
He who, it is agreed, has without cause summoned another party to court will be obliged to pay that party's travelling expenses and legal costs.[73]

ET 74 spells out in detail how the victim of a frivolous lawsuit was to recoup his losses. For this, a judge or group of *boni homines* (who were presumably aware of the facts of the case) was to determine what was owed by the plaintiff. Here again, we see the compilers going far beyond Justinian's compilers to include details that were more relevant to the situation in Italy.

Here, the concern for the compilers of the *ET* was to ensure clarity and relevance by including specific details not found in the versions of the *Digest*. Thus, whereas Justinian's compilers might leave the manner of punishment unspecified, or gloss over the details of how a particular rule was to be enforced, Theoderic's took particular notice of these aspects. What they wanted were practical rules that could be easily enforced, without necessarily bothering about their rationale or explaining how they had come to have the form that they did – considerations that loom large in the *Digest*.

[72] *ET* 74: "Si petitor improbe litem cuiuscunque rei alteri forte commoverit, et fuerit sub iusta examinatione convictus, ex die plantati solemniter iurgii, sumptus et litis expensas, quas se pulsatus immerito sustinuisse docuerit, a petitore recipiat, sub aestimatione scilicet iudicis, aut bonorum virorum ex delegatione noscentium: quorum iustitiae et deliberationis erit, quales sumptus litis et expensas eum, qui importune alterum ad publicum deduxerit examen, redhibere conveniat."

[73] *Dig.* 5.1.79 pr.: "eum, quem temere adversarium suum in iudicium vocasse constitit, viatica litisque sumptus adversario suo reddere oportebit."

Gregorian and Hermogenian Codes

The same considerations that are behind the variances between the *ET* and *Digest* explain the sometimes profound differences between the *ET* and *CJ*. In all, there are eight provisions that are analogous to fragmentary and interpolated versions in the *CJ* of imperial decrees originally collected in the late third-century *Gregorian* and *Hermogenian Codes* (*CG* and *CH* respectively) (see Table 4).[74]

Table 4

From the *Gregorian Code*	Provisions of the *ET*
const. Alexandri Severi a. 224 (c. 6 *de furtis*) (*CJ* 6.2.6)	86
const. Gordiani a. 243 (c. 3 *ad legem Cornel. De sicariis*) (*CJ* 9.16.2)	15
const. Diocletiani et Max. a. 287 (*ad legem Fabiam*) (*CJ* 9.20.6)	87
const. Diocletiani et Max. a. 290 (c. 9 *de testamentis*) (*CJ* 6.23.9)	28
From the *Hermogenian Code*	**Provisions of the *ET***
const. Diocletiani et Max. a. 286 (*in fragmentis codicis Greg.* Lib. III tit. 2 c. 4)	138
const. Diocletiani et Max. a. 293 (c. 9 *de noxalib.*) (*CJ* 3.41.4)	109
const. Diocletiani et Max. a. 304 (c. 10 *ad leg. Fabiam*) (*CJ* 9.20.10)	81
const. Diocletiani et Max. a incerti (c. 20 *de locato et conducto*) (*CJ* 4.65.20)	136

[74] *ET* 86 (*CJ* 6.2.6 (224)), 15 (*CJ* 9.16.2 (243)), 138 (*Epitome CG Wisigotica* 3.6(2).4), 87 (*CJ* 9.20.6 (287)), 28 (*CJ* (6.23.9 (290)), 109 (*CJ* 3.41.4 (293)), 81 (*CJ* 9.20.10 (293)), 136 (*CJ* 4.65.20 (?293)). One exception where the original survived in a later version other than the *CJ* is a decree of Diocletian and Maximian from 286 (*in fragmentis codicis Greg.* Lib. III tit. 2 c. 4), which is found in the Visigothic *epitome* of the *CG* (3.6(2).4). The linguistic parallels are noted in italics: "When a sale is made to different people at different times, the one to whom possession was first conveyed is considered the stronger [claimant]." ("*Diversis* temporibus pluribus venum datur, eum *potiorem* esse, *cui* possessio primum *tradita* est.") In *ET* 138 we read: "If the same property is purchased by different people at different times, the one who received it shall have a stronger case and shall more readily acquire ownership." ("Quotiens eadem res a domino *diversis* comparetur, ille *potior* erit et dominium eius magis acquiret, *cui traditam* fuisse claruerit.") In both texts the *dominium* over property claimed by different people was granted to the individual who first acquired possession. Aside from a common adherence to the law, there is insufficient proof in terms of content matter and close verbal affinities to suggest a common source. Both Bluhme and Baviera cite the following as being analogous, but neither suggests that the *CG* or *CH* is the common source. From the *CG*: *ET* 85 (*CJ* 6.2.6 (223)), 96 (*CJ* 7.16.5), 127 (*CJ* 8.41 (42).1 (223)), 82 (*CJ* 7.18.1 (239)), 33 (*CJ* 6.34.2 (285)), 153 (*CJ* 4.12.2 (287)), 5 (*CJ* 7.43.9 (290)), 62 (*CJ* 9.9.22 (290)). From the *CH*: 116 (*CJ* 6.2.14 (293)), 147 (*CJ* 4.44.3 (293)), 148 (*CJ* 8.50 (51),10 (293)), 40 (*CJ* 9.22.20 (294)), 79 (*CJ* 6.16.31 (294)), 127 (*CJ* 8.41 (42).6 (294)), 129 (*CJ* 1.22.2 (294)), 135 (*CJ* 8.13 (14).21 (294)). Vismara, too, is reluctant to identify the *CG* or *CH* as the common source in these instances: "Edictum Theoderici," 135 n. 457.

Some variances were associated with developments taking place in Roman law and administration in the West from the fourth to sixth century. Others were the result of societal changes. While both groups of compilers were concerned with updating, clarifying, and amending previous Roman law, their respective objectives led to significantly different adaptations.

For instance, *ET* 15, a brief provision recognizing the long-held Roman principle of killing in self-defense, bears little resemblance to *CJ* 9.16.2. Both are heavily adapted versions of an imperial decree of the Emperor Gordian of 243:

ET 15	*CJ* 9.16.2
Let the action of one who with a weapon repels an assailant advancing against him not be considered homicide, since someone defending himself is considered in no way to have committed an offense.[75]	He who kills an aggressor or anyone else while in danger of his own life should have no fear of prosecution on account of this action.[76]

Aside from adhering to the same ancient principle of self-defense, the written precedence for which was a Sullan enactment on murderers and poisoners from 81 BC (*lex Cornelia de sicariis et veneficis*), the two texts share little else. First, the language of the *ET* is far less clear; that the person in question actually killed in self-defense is only presupposed by the fact that he is not to be held liable for homicide. Second, the *ET* limits his actions exclusively to the source of the threat, whereas the *CJ* leaves room for the interpretation that a person who was acting in self-defense was not liable for the (presumably unintentional) death of an individual other than the aggressor himself.

Elsewhere, the differences are more substantial. *ET* 87, a brief provision concerning the return of runaway slaves, shares little in common with *CJ* 9.20.6:

ET 87	*CJ* 9.20.6
A slave in flight can neither be sold nor given away.[77]	It is not permitted to sell or give away a slave in flight. Understand that you have

[75] *ET* 15: "Qui percussorem ad se venientem ferro repulerit, non habetur homicida: quia defensor propriae salutis videtur in nullo peccasse."

[76] *CJ* 9.16.2: "Is, qui adgressorem vel quemcunque alium in dubio vitae discrimine constitutus occiderit, nullam ob id factum calumniam metuere debet."

[77] *ET* 87: "In fuga positus servus nec vendi donari potest."

> contravened the law which stipulates that a fixed sum for this sort of delict is to be paid to the fisc; exempt from this are co-heirs and partners to whom it has been permitted to make a bid concerning the fugitive slave in the dividing up of common goods. Thus it is permitted to sell a fugitive slave under this condition; the sale shall be valid whenever the slave, upon his capture, has been demanded by the buyer.[78]

The basis for this legal remedy is the *Lex Fabia* (the chief provisions of which are collected in *Dig.* 48.15.6), which deals with the crime of kidnapping (*plagium*), treating a freeman as a slave, or persuading another's slave to flee. In 287, Diocletian introduced legislation that prescribed the death penalty for *plagium.* It was this rescript that served as the model for both *ET* 87 and *CJ* 9.20.6 – a fact supported by the linguistic echoes between the two texts (marked out here in italics): *ET* 87: *In fuga* positus servus *nec vendi donari* potest = *CJ* 9.20.6: *In fuga* servum constitutum *neque vendere neque donare* licet. For the compilers of the *ET*, this was sufficient. Justinian's compilers, however, elected to reproduce the entire rescript more or less unchanged, including the original requirement, as well as the justification for it, that the (unspecified) fine for contravening this law was to go to the fisc, and that the sale of a fugitive slave could take place under the following conditions: when a co-heir or partner of the owner had a legal claim of ownership to the escaped slave, he could sell him (upon his return) to a willing third party.

To take as another example, *ET* 109 addresses the subject of an owner's liability of a slave for offenses committed by the slave. For this, the compilers drew upon a rescript of the Emperor Diocletian of 293, which survives in *CJ* 3.41.4:

ET 109	*CJ* 3.41.4
If a slave or *colonus* should seize anything violently without the knowledge of his owner, the owner shall be sued fourfold the original	If a slave should violently seize your property without the knowledge of his master, or even if he is aware of it but is unable to prevent it, you can

[78] *CJ* 9.20.6: "In fuga servum constitutum neque vendere neque donare licet. Unde intellegis te in legem incidisse, quae super huiusmodi delictis certam poenam fisco inferendam statuit, exceptis coheredibus et sociis, quibus in divisione communium rerum licitationem de fugitivo servo invicem facere permissum est. Ita vero liceat fugitivum vendere, ut tunc venditio valeat, quando ab emptore requisitus fuerit deprehensus."

amount within a year of the offense, and for the simple sum after a year; or in place of this, should the owner choose the following alternative, let him know that the offending slave or *colonus* is to be delivered up to a judge to be punished: provided that the owner return that which he came into possession of as a result of the violence of the slave. But if the one sued claims that his slave has fled, let it suffice for the claimant to seek legal satisfaction [in accordance with this provision].[79]

bring a suit for fourfold damages against his master before the provincial Governor, if the available year has not yet elapsed; but if this time has passed, you can sue him by means of a simple noxal action. If he prefers to surrender the slave by way of reparation, you will still not be prevented from suing him for the amount which came into his possession from this [robbery]; for if the act was committed with his knowledge and he could have prevented it, he should, by all means, be compelled to pay the amount of the judgment, without taking into consideration the surrender of the slave.[80]

In both, the owner was liable for the theft committed by his slave as well as any damages that may have resulted. Within one year he was required to pay fourfold the value of the damaged property. Afterwards his liability was alternative: either to pay the damages or to surrender the offender to the person injured. Choice here no doubt depended on the value of the slave and the amount of the fine for which the owner was liable to pay. But the owner was still on the hook for the stolen goods. In terms of language and syntax the two texts are nothing alike. There are also significant differences between them in terms of technical precision. Whereas *CJ* 3.41.4 identifies the specific legal action (*noxali iudicio*) for the remedy, *ET* 109 passes over this detail – a further indication of a loosening of legal precision associated with the demise of the formulary procedure. Justinian's compilers also envisaged a situation not covered in the *ET* where the slave has made off

[79] *ET* 109: "Si servus aut colonus domino nesciente violenter aliqua rapiat, dominus eius intra annum in quadruplum, post annum in simplum convenietur: aut pro noxia certe, si hoc magis elegerit, ipsum servum vel colonum noverit ad poenam iudici contradendum: ita ut, quod ad eum ex ipsa servi violentia pervenisse constiterit, reddat. At si conventus eum fugisse dixerit, executionem eius conquerenti dedisse sufficiat."

[80] *CJ* 3.41.4: "Si servus ignorante domino vel sciente et prohibere nequeunte res tuas vi rapuit, dominum eius apud praesidem provinciae, si necdum utilis annus excessit, quadrupli, quod si hoc effluxit tempus, simpli noxali iudicio convenire potes: qui si noxae maluerit servum dedere, nihilo minus cum ipso quantum ad eum pervenit experiri non prohiberis: nam si eo conscio et prohibere valente, detracta noxae deditione conventus ad summam condemnationis solvendam omnimodo compellendus est."

with another's wife and the victim is intending to bring forward a criminal action.

The Roman law of Theoderic's Italy was not the Roman law of Justinian's Byzantium. Although Italy in the sixth century never ceased officially to belong to the Roman Empire, the Ostrogothic King in fact exercised the legislative power independently of the Byzantine Emperor, down to 535 when his rule collapsed under the onslaught of Belisarius' troops. Theoderic's law was unconcerned with the traditional niceties of strict classical jurisprudence, and was governed by social and economic rather than legal considerations; it was a law averse to the standards of classical jurisprudence with respect to artistic elaboration, rhetorical flourish, and technical precision. In contrast to this were the classicizing efforts of Justinian's jurists. These conservative theorists continued to interpret the works of the great classical jurists and the imperial predecessors of Constantine by adhering to outmoded classical standards of precision and artistry in an attempt to resurrect the Roman law from three full centuries earlier. That these jurists may not have known how Roman law was changing in Italy is possible. If they did, they clearly saw no reason why such changes were worthy of their attention.

Theodosian Code

A total of forty-seven provisions, roughly a third of the *ET*, were derived in whole or in part from imperial decrees, postscripts, and rescripts originally collected in the *Theodosian Code* (*CTh*) (see table 5).[81] Begun by the eastern Emperor Theodosius II (408–50) in March 429 and accepted for

[81] Baviera notes similarities between the following: *ET* 3 (*CTh* 9.27.3, 4 (382); not *CTh* 9.27.2 (380) as indicated by Mommsen in his edition of the *CTh*), 10 and 11 (*CTh* 4.22.3 (389)), 12 (*CTh* 4.14.1 (424)), 13 (*CTh* 9.1.11 (368); 9.1.19 (423)), 14 (*CTh* 9.1.15 (385)), 17–19 (*CTh* 9.24.1 pr., 2 and 4 (326)), 20 (*CTh* 9.24.3 (374)), 26 (*CTh* 5.3.1 (434)), 27 (*CTh* 5.2.1 (352)), 28 (*CTh* 4.4.1 (326?)), 35 (*CTh* 10.10.1–3), 37 (*CTh* 3.8.1), 43 (*CTh* 2.13.1 (422)); Alvaro D'Ors, *El Código de Eurico*, (Madrid, 1960) 246 n. 838, cites *CTh* 2.14.1 as a possible source for *ET* 43: the former deals with the transfer of titles and the latter with the transfer of cases, 44 (*CTh* 2.12.6 (395)), 46 (*CTh* 2.14.1 (400)), 48 and 49 (*CTh* 9.6.3 (397)), 50 (*CTh* 10.10.4 (338)), 51 (*CTh* 8.12.1 (323)), 52 and 53 (*CTh* 8.12.8 (415)), 54 (*CTh* 3.16.1 (331)), 55 (*CTh* 11.30.22 (343); 11.30.42 (384)), 61 (*CTh* 9.25.1 (349)), 65–8 (*CTh* 5.10.1 (419)), 70 (*CTh* 9.45.3 (398); 9.45.5 (432)), 71 (*CTh* 9.45.1 (392); 9.45.3 (398)), 77 (*CTh* 9.10.4 (390)), 84 (*CTh* 5.9.?), 103 (*CTh* 9.1.10 (368)), 108 (*CTh* 16.10.6 (356); 16.10.23 (423)), 111 (*CTh* 9.17.6), 112, (*CTh* 9.42.2 (356)), 113 (*CTh* 9.42.2 (356); simil. 9.42.24 (426)), 121 (*CTh* 2.30.2 (422); simil. 2.32.1 (422)), 122 (*CTh* 2.13.1 (422)), 132 (*CTh* 11.39.12 (396)), 134 (*CTh* 2.33.2 (386)), 144 (*CTh* 12.6.18 (396)), 149 (*CTh* 11.8.1 (397); 11.8.3 (409)), 154 (*CTh* 2.8.18; 8.8.3; 11.7.13 (386); 2.8.21 (*CJ* 3.12.7)). The following are cited by both Bluhme and Baviera as possibly sharing a common source: *ET* 4 (*CTh* 9.27.3,4), 6 (*CTh* 4.17.1 (374)), 16 (*CTh* 9.14.2 (391)), 24 (*CTh* 5.1.9), 25 (*CTh* 10.10.27, 30–31), 38 (*CTh* 9.40.1), 45 (*CTh* 2.14.1 (400)), 92 (*CTh* 9.24.1), 94 (*CTh* 5.8.1 (314)), 114 (*CTh* 9.3.5), 143 (*CTh* 16.8.3).

Table 5

From the *Theodosian Code*	Provisions of the *ET*
lib. 2 tit. 8 c. 18	154
lib. 2 tit. 13 c. 1	43, 44, 122
lib. 2 tit. 14 c. 1	46
lib. 2 tit. 30 c. 2	121
lib. 2 tit. 33 c. 2	134
lib. 3 tit. 8 c. incerta a. 380, nunc c. 1 *CJ de secundis nuptiis* (5, 9) et c. 4 ad SC Tertullian (6, 56)	37
lib. 3 tit. 16 c. 1	54
lib. 4 tit. 4 c. 1	28
lib. 4 tit. 14 c. 1	12
lib. 4 tit. 22 c. 3	10, 11
lib. 5 tit. 2 c. 1	27
lib. 5 tit. 3 c. 1	26
lib. 5 tit. 9 c. incerta, nunc c. 4 Iust. *De servis fugitivis* (6, 1)	84
lib. 5 tit. 10 c. 1	65–8
lib. 7 tit. 42 c. 2.	112, 113
lib. 8 tit. 8 c. 3 (sive lib. 2 tit. 8 c. 21)	154
lib. 8 tit. 12 c. 1, 8	51–3
lib. 9 tit. 1 c. 10	103
lib. 9 tit. 1 c. 11, 19	13
lib. 9 tit. 1 c. 15	14
lib. 9 tit. 6 c. 3	48, 49
lib. 9 tit. 10 c. 4	77
lib. 9 tit. 17 c. 6	111
lib. 9 tit. 24 c. 1	17–19
lib. 9 tit. 24 c. 2	61
lib. 9 tit. 24 c. 3	20
lib. 9 tit. 25 c. 1	61
lib. 9 tit. 27 c. 3	3
lib. 9 tit. 45 c. 3. 5	70, 71
lib. 10 tit. 10 c. 2	35
lib. 10 tit. 10 c. 4	50
lib. 11 tit. 8 c. 1. 3	149
lib. 11 tit. 30 c. 42. 22	55
lib. 11 tit. 39 c. 12	132
lib. 12 tit. 6 c. 18	144
lib. 16 tit. 10 c. 6. 23	108

publication in the autumn of 437, the *CTh* comprises sixteen books of imperial edicts and rescripts issued by the Emperors from 313, when Constantine consolidated his power, until 438. Unfortunately we possess only fragments of copies of the complete work, but there is enough to allow for an accurate reconstruction from which we can gauge just how closely the compilers of the *ET* followed it.[82] In fact, nowhere did they leave the original text untouched. In all instances there are superficial differences that reflected the compilers' aim to simplify the law and therefore render it in a more comprehensible and accessible form by doing away with the complex, technical, and rhetorical language of the original texts. In many cases, however, there are substantial differences between the provision and original in terms of what the compilers omitted, added, or altered.[83]

Concerning informers (*delatores*), *ET* 35 was derived from a rescript (*CTh* 10.10.2) of the Emperor Constantine of 312, but differs from it significantly:

ET 35	*CTh* 10.10.2
Anyone who comes forth as an informer to do [what he thinks] necessary as though under the pretext of the public interest, whom nevertheless We affirm We utterly curse, shall be prohibited in accordance with the laws from being heard during a suit, although he may even be reporting factual events; nevertheless, if upon being interrogated during the proceedings he is unable to prove those things which he conveyed to public ears, let him be consumed by flames.[84]	We shall suppress the detestable calamities of informers, the one greatest evil of human life; at the beginning of an attempt he shall be strangled by his very throat, and the tongue of envy shall be cut off from its roots and plucked out, so that judges shall not grant a hearing at all either to such calumny or to the voice of an informer; but if any one should come forth as an informer, he shall be subjected to the capital penalty.[85]

Delatores had long since been held in disrepute by the Emperor and public alike. Concerning the reporting of *caduca* (ownerless land) to the fisc, Paul remarks: "Everyone is completely forbidden to denounce (*deferre*) another and to report a pecuniary matter to the fisc. It does not matter whether

[82] For Books 1–5 of the *Code* the Breviary of Alaric serves as our main source, while there is good support for Books 6–16 from manuscripts 'R' (Paris: Books 6–8) and 'V' (Vatican: Books 9–16). On the manuscript evidence see Matthews, *Laying Down the Law*, passim.

[83] E.g., *ET* 10, 12, 14, 17–19, 28, 35, 43, 44, 46, 48, 50, 51, 52, 54, 61, 68, 70, 71, 103, 108, 111, 134, 144, 149.

[84] *ET* 35: "Is qui quasi sub specie utilitatis publicae, ut sic necessarie faciat, delator existit, quem tamen nos execrari omnino profitemur, quamvis vel vera dicens, legibus prohibeatur audiri: tamen si ea, quae ad aures publicas detulerit, inter acta constitutus non potuerit adprobare, flammis debet absumi."

[85] *CTh* 10.10.2: "comprimatur unum maximum humanae vitae malum, delatorum exsecranda pernicies, et inter primos conatus in ipsis faucibus stranguletur, et amputata radicitus invidiae lingua vellatur, ita ut iudices nec calumniam nec vocem prorsus deferentis admittant; sed si qui delator exstiterit, capitali sententiae subiugetur."

males or females, slaves or free-born or freed people do this, or whether they denounce their own relatives or outside parties; in every case they are punished."[86] Likewise, imperial decrees concerning *delatores* often associate their actions with terms for "calumny" and "betrayal." Only when the information they provided was used against heretics (particularly Manicheans) or other disreputable groups were *delatores* not described in such negative overtones (as in Theodosius I's investigation against the Manicheans launched in 382 (*CTh* 16.5.9)).

While both texts here treat the informer with the utmost contempt, the *ET* does recognize some potential benefit from their services whereas Constantine's legislation did not. To deter them from acting altogether, *CTh* 10.10.2 punished any *delator* who attempted to bring forth an accusation with strangulation and the plucking out of the tongue – particularly grisly and symbolic acts that reflected the disdain which the Emperor had towards this class of people; but *ET* 35 simply barred them from acting in accordance with the laws. The *ET* went much further than Constantine's to allow the informer, presumably in serious cases, to give evidence under interrogation, but always at their extreme peril: an informer who failed to prove his claims was to be burned alive. This is more in keeping with post-Constantinian legislation like that of the Emperors Gratian, Valentinian II, and Theodosius I (*CTh* 10.10.12.2 (380); 28 (418 west)), which limited the number of times an informer could act to a maximum of two. The third time constituted a capital offense.

The compilers also had an eye to matters of credit and debt. As a general rule they favored the interests of the creditor over the debtor. For instance, *ET* 124 granted *bona fide* creditors the right to self-help of pledged properties. This was in sharp contrast to the Roman practice of protecting debtors from overzealous creditors. For instance, a law of Constantine from the early fourth century (315) afforded peasants additional protection that exempted farm implements from any purported pledge.[87] Later in 472, as an attempt to solve the problem of unknown pledges, the Emperor Leo provided a priority for security transactions executed before a public authority.[88] These sorts of protective rules have a long history, appearing in the

[86] *PS* 5.13.1: "Omnes omnino deferre alterum et causam pecuniariam fisco nuntiare prohibentur: nec referrt, mares istud an feminae faciant, servi an ingenui an libertini, an suos an extraneos deferant: omni enim modo puniuntur." On late Roman fiscal *delatores*, see Jones, *LRE*, 1, 486; Harries, *Law and Empire*, 64.

[87] *CJ* 8.16 (17).7. At approximately the same time Constantine expressly provided a preference for a ward's claim against his guardian (*Dig.* 20.4.21 pr.).

[88] *CJ* 8.17 (18).11.

West in the early third century when creditors began to assert maximum discretion to deal with securing pledges – discretionary practices that were abusive compared to the experience of the previous century. And despite the fact that these sorts of measures had a negative effect on the economic growth of the later Empire, they continued to influence imperial policy-making well into the sixth century.[89]

Most illustrative of the compilers' concern for the position of the creditor is *ET* 134. Derived in part from a rescript of the Emperor Valentinian II of 386 (*CTh* 2.33.2), it fixed the maximum rate of interest on money at 1 percent per month:

ET 134	*CTh* 2.33.2
A creditor who presumes to demand from his debtor anything more than the 1 percent [per month] allowed by law shall forfeit his share of the debt.[90]	If any person, taking advantage of a debtor's need, should extort anything beyond the 1 percent [per month] allowed by law, he will immediately, without delay, return what was taken; and he shall be obligated to pay fourfold the original amount.[91]

Valentinian, while recognizing the importance of credit transactions, demonstrates a clear dislike for greedy creditors. But whereas *CTh* 2.33.2 fined creditors fourfold the original sum for extorting *cautiones* at a rate higher than the 1 percent, *ET* 134 punished them with forfeiture of the original debt. Obviously this was a far less punitive measure than the one imposed in the *CTh*; and while direct evidence for this is lacking, we may see in this an attempt on behalf of Theoderic to free up credit and thus encourage commercial activity by making the prospect of lending money more appealing to creditors. This would be in keeping with what we know of the King's efforts to revive the Italian economy through various initiatives designed to encourage private enterprise. Thus, for instance, to foster internal trade he instructed the Praetorian Prefect Abundantius to ensure that the rivers Mincius, Ollius (Oglio), Anser (Serchio), Arno, and Tiber were unobstructed so that "ships can travel through unimpeded."[92] Similar in purpose

[89] Donald E. Phillipson, "Development of the Roman Law of Debt Security," *Stanford Law Review* 20 (1968), 1230–48; Michael Kaser, *Das römische Privatrecht, I: Das altrömische, das vorklassiche und klassiche Recht*, trans. Rolf Dannenbring, *Roman Private Law*, 6th edn. (London, 1968), 130; Fritz Schulz, *Classical Roman Law* (Oxford, 1954), 403–5.

[90] *ET* 134: "Amittat sortem debiti creditor, qui ultra legitimam centesimam crediderit a debitore poscendum."

[91] *CTh* 2.33.2: "quicumque ultra centesimam iure permissam quicquid sub occasione necessitatis eruerit, quadrupli poenae obligatione constrictus, sine cessatione, sine requie protinus ablata redhibebit."

[92] Cass., *Var.* 5.17 (reiterated again in 5.20): "inviolati alvei tractus navium relinquatur excursibus."

was the granting of land to private individuals who undertook to invest in income-producing activities such as the draining of the Pontine marshes and the swamps around Ravenna.[93]

ET 71 departs from the original source in ways that reflect developments in areas involving the Church. Concerning public debtors who sought refuge in a church to avoid payment, the provision requires the relevant Church authority to surrender the debtor immediately; should the debtor refuse and the Church be unable to comply, the archdeacon is here instructed to pay the original debt. The corresponding legislation of Theodosius I (*CTh* 9.45.1 (392)) is much harsher, stipulating that the public debtor is to be forcibly removed from the church whereupon, it is assumed, he was to pay the outstanding debt:

ET 71	*CTh* 9.45.1
If anyone flees to any church whatsoever on account of a public debt, the archdeacon shall compel him to leave in order to render account according to law; but if he is unwilling to do this, he shall deliver forthwith his property which he transferred to the Church. Unless he does this, the archdeacon shall be compelled to pay as much of the debt as involves the public interest.[94]	If public debtors should presume to take refuge in churches, let them be immediately dragged out of their hiding places, or let the payment of their debts be exacted from the Bishops who are proven to have harbored them.[95]

Throughout the later Empire asylum was sought by individuals desperate to escape their financial responsibilities, and criminals hoping to take advantage of laws that considered the sacred boundaries of a church to be immune from secular authority.[96] As a general rule imperial legislators preserved and even reinforced the right of asylum.[97] But in some cases, as with *CTh* 9.45.1, they sought to limit the application of the protection that the Church could afford.

[93] Cass., *Var.* 2.32, 33.

[94] *ET* 71: "Si quis in causa publici debiti ad ecclesiam quamlibet convolaverit, archidiaconus eum compellat egredi, ad edenda legibus ratiocinia sua: aut si hoc facere noluerit, eius substantiam, quam ad ecclesiam detulit, sine mora contradat. Quod nisi fecerit, quanti interest utilitatis publicae, archidiaconus cogatur exsolvere."

[95] *CTh* 9.45.1: "publicos debitores, si confugiendum ad ecclesias crediderint, aut ilico extrahi de latebris oportebit aut pro his ipsos, qui eos occultare probantur, episcopos exigi." Augustine refers to this law in a letter (*ep.* 268) about a certain Fascius who had taken refuge in his church to avoid punishment for an outstanding debt of 17 *solidi*.

[96] Claudia Rapp, *Holy Bishops in Late Antiquity: The Nature of Christian Leadership in an Age of Transition* (Berkeley, CA, 2005), 253–8.

[97] E.g., *CTh* 16.8.19 (409), which treated the violation of asylum as treason.

That *ET* 71 does not go so far as calling for the forcible removal of the debtor from a place of worship reinforces the claims of the Anonymous Valesianus (12.60) that Theoderic was especially respectful of ecclesiastical authority. But such respect was conditional. Criminals, for instance, could not escape the censure of the laws by invoking the solemn rite. The case of Opilio and Gaudentius is illustrative. Both had been arrested for fraud and sentenced to exile by Theoderic, but fled for asylum to a church in Ravenna. Thereupon Theoderic directed that, unless they left by a prescribed date, they should be branded on the forehead and forcibly expelled. It was at this moment that they signed a bill of accusation against Boethius confirming his alleged involvement in the treasonous actions of the Senator Albinus in 524. In return they were granted a reprieve.[98]

ET 77 upholds the basic principle outlined in *CTh* 9.10.4 (390) of the Emperor Valentinian II that an owner was liable should it be discovered that his slave committed violence (*vis*) on his instructions. But it ignores many of the original elements, such as the reference to the testimony of witnesses, the explicit requirement that the offending slave was to be surrendered up, and mention of the *lex Iulia de vi* as the basis for this:

ET 77	*CTh* 9.10.4
If slaves are convicted of inflicting violence, or at the very least they confess to this, and it is proven under a just and diligent inquiry that this was committed through the instruction of the owner, when the owner has been held for the penalty of violence, any stolen incomes shall be returned; slaves, nevertheless, shall be punished by the extreme penalty if it is proven that they committed this violence through their own audacity.[99]	Slaves, who are proven by the testimony of witnesses or by their own confession to have committed violence, if they did so with their master unaware, We decree that they be handed over in order to atone for their transgressions by the supreme penalty. But if they committed the violence either out of fear or the exhortation of the masters, it is clear, according to the *lex Iulia*, that the master shall be pronounced

[98] Hitherto, Albinus had enjoyed a life of vast wealth and a career of distinction: he served as Consul in his youth (493), Praetorian Prefect about 500–3, and then a participant in the negotiations for Church unity at Byzantium under Pope Hormisdas (Hormisdas, *ep.* 104). Albinus denied the charge against him, but Theoderic was inclined to believe it true. At Verona, the King declared the hapless Senator guilty without the legality of a proper trial. For these events see Anon. Val. 14.85; Boethius, *Cons. Phil.* 1.4.14–18.

[99] *ET* 77: "Si servi de irrogata violentia convicti fuerint, aut certe confessi, et hoc domini praecepto factum sub iusta et diligenti cognitione constiterit, domino ad violentiae poenam retento, pervasa reddantur, servis nihilominus extremo supplicio puniendis, si violentiam eos sua temeritate commisisse claruerit."

> infamous and that he cannot use as defense the dignity of his rank or of his birth; but slaves who obeyed the madness of such masters must by this judgment be condemned to the mines.[100]

Interestingly, the compilers do not specify the penalty for slaves that committed the act of *vis* with the knowledge or bidding of the owner. Furthermore, in regards to the complicit owner, they do away with the original penalty of *infamia*, or loss of status, and instead make him liable for criminal violence – a capital offense.[101] *Infamia* deprived the offender of the legal rights of Roman citizenship, which included bequeathing or receiving property in a will, or making a legally binding contract. In the later Empire, it was the standard punishment for such traditional offenses as conniving at the insertion of the name of a powerful person into the titles of a contested property,[102] breaking the conditions of an arbitration agreement by seeking a referral to a judge,[103] or lodging petitions for estates owned by the Emperor.[104] Judges also risked *infamia*, along with a fine of twenty pounds of gold, if they delayed execution of a sentence for a serious crime, or permitted the criminal to be spirited away by clerics.[105] And the religiously incorrect, the Manicheans, Donatists and apostates, were punished with the loss of their testamentary rights.[106] Nowhere in the *ET* is the punishment of *infamia* used, nor does it appear anywhere in the *Variae*. Clearly, as with other outmoded punishments like crucifixion or condemnation to the arena, it was no longer considered a practical deterrent in sixth-century Italy. In a world where one's social standing was not necessarily contingent upon considerations of legal status, this should come as no surprise.

One last example is *ET* 108. Concerning the practice of pagan sacrifices, it borrows elements from two imperial rescripts – *CTh* 16.10.6 (356) of the Emperor Constantius and *CTh* 16.10.23 (423) of the Emperors Honorius and Theodosius II:

[100] *CTh* 9.10.4: "servos, qui fecisse violentiam confessionibus testium aut propriis docebuntur, si id inscio domino commiserint, postremo supplicio deditos luere perpetrata censemus. Quod si illi metu atque exhortatione dominorum violentiam admiserint, palam est, secundum legem iuliam dominum infamem pronuntiandum loci aut originis propriae dignitate non uti, servos vero, quos furoribus talium paruisse constiterit, metallis per sententiam dedi."

[101] *CTh* 9.10.1 (317) of the Emperor Constantine. [102] *CTh* 2.14.1 (400). [103] *CTh* 2.9.3 (395).

[104] *CTh* 5.15.21 (367–70). [105] *CTh* 9.40.15 (392).

[106] *CTh* 16.5.3 (372) and 7 (381) on Manicheans; 16.5.54 (414) and 6.4.3 (405) on Donatists; 16.7.5 (391) on apostates.

ET 108	*CTh* 16.10.6	*CTh* 16.10.23
If anyone is apprehended while sacrificing according to the pagan rite, as well as diviners (*[h]arioli*) and necromancers (*umbrarii*) should they be discovered, upon conviction in a lawful trial they shall be punished capitally; of those individuals who are knowledgeable of the wicked arts, that is sorcerers (*malefici*), *honestiores*, upon being stripped of all their possessions that they might possess, shall be condemned to perpetual exile; and *humiliores* shall be punished capitally.[107]	We command that those who are proven to devote their attention to sacrifices or the worship of images shall be subjected to a capital punishment.[108]	Proscription of their goods and exile shall be the punishment for pagans who survive, if they should at any time be apprehended in the performance of accursed sacrifices to demons, although they ought to be subjected to a capital punishment.[109]

While Theodosius I's famous *cunctos populos* edict of 380 (*CTh* 16.1.2) officially outlawed the ancient religion of Rome, paganism continued to thrive in the more rural districts of the Empire well into the sixth century – a fact owing in part to the conservative attachment of the peasantry for the ancient rites.[110] Following the collapse of the western imperial administration in 476, this task fell to barbarian Kings, who maintained and reissued anti-pagan legislation of the Christian Emperors.[111] The practice of magic

[107] *ET* 108: "Si quis pagano ritu sacrificare fuerit deprehensus, arioli etiam atque umbrarii, si reperti fuerint, sub iusta aestimatione convicti, capite puniantur; malarum artium conscii, id est malefici, nudati rebus omnibus, quas habere possunt, honesti perpetuo damnantur exilio, humiliores capite puniendi sunt."

[108] *CTh* 16.10.6: "poena capitis subiugari praecipimus eos, quos operam sacrificiis dare vel colere simulacra constiterit."

[109] *CTh* 16.10.23: "paganos qui supersunt, si aliquando in execrandis daemonum sacrificiis fuerint comprehensi, quamvis capitali poena subdi debuerint, bonorum proscriptio ac exilium cohercebit."

[110] Peter Brown, *The Rise of Western Christendom. Triumph and Diversity, A.D. 200–1000*, 2nd edn. (Maldon, MA, 2003), 145–54; Patrick Geary, "Peasant Religion in Medieval Europe," *Cahiers d'Extrême Asie* 12 (2001), 185–209.

[111] Jocelyn N. Hillgarth, *Christianity and Paganism. The Conversion of Western Europe, 350–750* (Philadelphia, PA, 1986), 105–10; Brown, *The Rise of Western Christendom*, 149.

was especially opposed by Theoderic and his successors who feared its effect would detract from their own authority. Thus, an edict of Athalaric condemned magicians, describing their activities in treasonous terms and punishing them with death.[112]

Of the two original texts, *ET* 108 follows the language of *CTh* 16.10.23 more closely; but like *CTh* 16.10.6 it applied the maximum penalty to those caught making pagan sacrifices.[113] In connection with this, the compilers made explicit reference to diviners ([*h*]*arioli*), and necromancers (*umbrarii*); and extended the rule to include magicians (*malefici*), which they defined as "those knowledgeable of the wicked arts." The punishment for these varied according to status: *honestiores* were deprived of their possessions and exiled; *humiliores* were punished capitally.[114] None of these categories are mentioned in the original texts. Significantly, the term *umbrarii* appears nowhere in the *Theodosian Code*. An *umbrarius* was a soothsayer, more specifically, one who sought answers from spirits. Augustine refers to it as a sacrilegious mystery – one in which he never took part: "True, the theaters do not now carry me away, nor care I to know the courses of the stars, nor did my soul ever consult answers from a soothsayer; all sacrilegious mysteries I detest."[115] That the compilers use the term and presuppose the fact that it required no explanation or definition is perhaps indicative of a distinctly more doctrinaire understanding of the black arts among rural populations in the West at this time.[116]

As with the other sources of law they consulted, the compilers had no problem modifying the contents of the *CTh* as they saw fit. In all instances where they were working directly from a specific text, they offered a paraphrase, doing away with any unnecessary artistic or rhetorical flourish while upholding the basic meaning of the law. And they frequently made additions and omissions for greater clarity and relevance. The *CTh*, while still an authoritative source of law for Italy in the sixth century, required updating,

112 Cass., *Var.* 9.18.9.

113 The death penalty for pagan sacrifices was reintroduced by the Emperors Theodosius II and Valentinian III in 435 (*CTh* 16.10.25).

114 In the *CTh*, the various terms indicating sorcerers/magicians are used almost synonymously, with little distinction except of degree and intention.

115 Augustine of Hippo, *Confessions* 10.35.56, ed. James J. O'Donnell, 3 vols. (Oxford, 1992): "sane me iam theatra non rapiunt, nec curo nosse transitus siderum, nec anima mea umquam responsa quaesivit umbrarum; omnia sacrilega sacramenta detestor." For a definition: W. H. Maigne d'Arnis and Jacques-Paul Migne, *Lexicon manuale ad scriptores mediae et infimae latinitas* (Paris, 1977), 2240.

116 In noting the variances between *CTh* 9.16.3 and the accompanying *interpretatio*, which includes the specific reference to "invokers of demons," Matthews ("Interpreting the *Interpretationes* of the *Breviarium*," 29) arrives at the same conclusion for early sixth-century Gaul.

at least in those areas where the compilers felt that people required immediate guidance and clarification. When we take into consideration the fact that at the time of its production in 437 (less than a century before the *ET*) the *CTh* represented the most up-to-date body of imperial legislation available at the time, we get a sense as to just how quickly the law was adapting in Italy to keep pace with developments taking place on the ground.

Post-Theodosian novels

Table 6

From the Post-Theodosian Novels	Provisions of the *ET*
novella Theodosii II a. 439 *de paternis bonis*, tit. 14 § 1. 2. 4	54
novella Theodosii II a. 439 *de testamentis*, tit. 16	28, 29
novella Valentiniani III a. 451 *de colonis vagis*, tit. 31 § 1. 2. 5	64, 68
novella Valentiniani III a. 452 *de episcopali iudicio*, tit. 35 § 13	12
novella Maioriani a. 458 *de curialibus*, tit. 7 § 1. 1	69

Seven provisions were derived in whole or in part from imperial constitutions drafted after the publication of the *CTh* in 438 – the so-called post-Theodosian *novellae* (see table 6).[117] The novels themselves never existed in a single standard collection, and it appears that the compilers only had access to texts ranging in date from 439 to 458. Two provisions, *ET* 12 and 68, refer specifically to the novel in question. The first of these is a prohibition against challenges to ownership in the event that the current possessor could demonstrate long and uninterrupted enjoyment of the property for a period of thirty years or more, and grants a five year extension to minors established by "recent law." This is a reference to a novel of the Emperor Valentinian III of 452 (*Nov. Val.* 35.13), which upholds an existing law of Theodosius II (*CTh* 4.14.1 (424)) in regards to the thirty-year rule. In terms of content the two texts are essentially the same:

ET 12	*Nov. Val.* 35.13
Anyone who is proven to be in possession of any property without interruption for thirty years shall be	Just as we have sensibly forbidden that any case whatsoever should be commenced which had not been

[117] *ET* 12 (*Nov. Val.* 35.13 (452)), 28 (*Nov. Th.* 16.2; simil. *Nov. Val.* 21.1.3–4), 29 (*Nov. Th.* 16.3), 54 (*Nov. Th.* 14.1, 2 (439)), 64 (*Nov. Val.* 31.5 (451)), 68 (*Nov. Val.* 31.2), 69 (*Nov. Maj.* 7.1 (458); simil. *Nov. Val.* 27.1). A possible derivation is the epilogue, which follows closely the style and language of *Nov. Val.* 6.2 (443). Both Bluhme and Baviera note the similarity between the following texts (perhaps suggestive of a common source): *ET* 110 (*Nov. Val.* 23.2.3–4 (447)), 142 (*Nov. Val.* 35.18).

> subject to no judicial challenge at all, whether on the part of a private party or the state. Moreover, We decree that the periods [of possession] of a previous holder, or the holder before that, must by law be [calculated] in favor of such a possessor. We add that if a suit has been brought within thirty years, and the end of the thirty years comes about before the suit is concluded, let that end the suit without any further ado; for We believe it is more than sufficient for anyone at all both to institute proceedings properly and bring them to completion within thirty years either through the judgment of a public court or the decision of private arbitration. There is this restriction: the exemptions granted by ancient and recent laws with regard to wards under puberty are to be preserved, and with regard to those persons who begin their cases according to law twenty-five and thirty years after legal action could be taken. In this instance we approve the privilege of a five year extension as added in a recent law.[118]

> initiated within thirty years, so a case which has assumed the beginning of a formal attestation of suit shall be terminated within the aforesaid time, with the exception of the privilege of papillary age, which was granted by a law of Our father, Theodosius, of sainted memory, unless perchance the litigation had been formally attested after the twenty-fifth year from the time when the action began to be available.[119]

Under Theodosius' law on prescription of actions, whoever had possession for a long time without being in some way still subject to legal attack was regarded as the owner. This was upheld by Valentinian's novel, which provided the basis for

[118] *ET* 12: "Qui per triginta annos quamlibet rem iugiter possidere fuerit adprobatus, neque publico neque privato nomine patiatur aliquam penitus quaestionem. Tali autem possessori etiam auctorum proauctorumque suorum tempora secundum legem proficere debere censemus: illud adiicientes ut si intra triginta annos mota lis fuerit, nec finita, superveniens conclusio XXX annorum eandem sine aliqua dubitatione consumat : quia cuivis satis credimus abundeque sufficere, intra XXX annos et actiones suas rite componere et eas publico iudicio vel privata definitione peragere; ita ut circa pupillarem aetatem privilegia antiquis vel novellis legibus concessa serventur, vel circa eos, qui ex quo competere poterant, post vicesimum et quintum annum intra tricesimum suas legibus proposuerint actiones. Cui casui quinquennii beneficium novella lege probamus adiectum."

[119] *Nov. Val.* 35.13: "Sane sicut non coeptam intra tricennium quamlibet causam vetuimus inchoari, ita quae contestatae litis sumpsit exordium, excepto privilegio pupillaris aetatis, quod divae memoriae patris nostri Theodosii lege concessum est, intra eadem tempora terminetur, nisi forte post vicesimum quintum annum, ex quo competere actio coeperat, contestata lis fuerit."

extending the period another five years in cases involving minors. New in the *ET* is the provision that the time of possession could include that of predecessors. Of additional significance is how the compilers defined ownership in terms of lawful *and* physical possession. This same equation between physical occupation and legal ownership appears in *ET* 45 ("possidet iure vel corpore") and 142. This was another consequence associated with the abandonment of the formulary procedure, as the strict hierarchies of rights envisaged by classical Roman property law – rooted as it was in the fundamental distinction between title (*dominium*) and possession – became less clear.[120]

In certain circumstances freedom could be attained by anyone who "for a long period of time, that is, a period of twenty years, had remained in possession of his freedom[.]"[121] By the "*tenore novellae legis,*" *ET* 68 upholds the original twenty-year statute of limitations for reclaiming an *originaria*; and requires that any children born within that period are to remain the property of the former owner. The *novella lex* to which this refers is a novel of the Emperor Valentinian III (*Nov. Val.* 31.2), issued in Rome on 31 January 451 and addressed to the Praetorian Prefect Firminus. The basis for identification rests on similarities between the two texts in terms of subject matter and organization of contents:

ET 68	Nov. Val. 31.2
An *originaria* can be reclaimed by her former owner (*ingenuus*) only within a period of twenty years from the day she departed. But if after a period of twenty years has elapsed, and the *originaria* should be lost to her former owner as a result of this prescription, in keeping with the tenor of the new law any offspring which she gave birth to within this twenty year period must not be lost to her [former] owner.[122]	If a *colona*, who is refused to a petitioner after a period of twenty years, has given birth to any offspring before the designated time limit, such offspring must not be lost to her former master. For it is equitable that the progeny begotten at that time when the woman still belonged to him should return to him, in order that the damage sustained by loss of the mother, which happened because of the passing of years, may be

[120] Stein, *Roman Law in European History*, 25; Levy, *West Roman Vulgar Law*, 28–9, 176–93.

[121] *CTh* 3.8.9: "qui diuturno tempore, hoc est per viginti annorum spatia in libertatis possessione duravit [.]" Justinian upholds earlier legislation of the Emperor Diocletian (*CJ* 7.22.2 (300)) which recognizes this twenty-year period: "those who have lived as *bona fide* free people for an uninterrupted period of twenty years . . . shall become free and Roman citizens." ("qui bona fide in possessione libertatis per viginti annorum spatium sine interpellatione morati essent . . . ut et liberi et cives fiant romani.")

[122] *ET* 68: "Originaria ex quo de ingenuo solo discesserit, intra vicennii spatia repetatur. Quod si originaria, expletis viginti annis, domino sub hac praescriptione perierit, simul eius agnatio, intra viginti annos suscepta a domino mulieris servato novellae legis tenore non pereat."

alleviated at least by the vindication of her offspring.[123]

By the middle of the fourth century, forty years seems to have been the normal period for initiating an action of prescription.[124] Over time this was reduced to thirty years – a period which was granted wider acceptance in the West as the general time requirement for prescription.[125] For instance, Valentinian III issued a voluminous statute that fixed the period at thirty years,[126] thereafter supplementing it with additional provisions that reinforced the thirty-year limit.[127] And as noted already, a rescript of the Emperor Majorian of 458 (*Nov. Maj.* 7.1) used thirty years as the proscribed measure of time. This was upheld in *ET* 69.

Lastly, there is *ET* 64, which concerns the issue of freemen who at one time transferred themselves to the status of *coloni* of estates in order to gain some sort of financial security; and in the process, put the estate in a vulnerable position by forming a relationship with the owner's *originaria* or *colona*. For this, it borrows extensively from section five of Valentinian III's novel of 451:

ET 64	*Nov. Val.* 31.5
Any freeborn man (who is obligated to no municipality in any manner), who defiles another's virgin slave woman or *originaria* of any age, and wishes to be united with her (provided the owner is also willing), he shall acknowledge this in the municipal records and remain under the authority of the woman's owner; [having done this] he shall not abandon the union with the woman he despoiled, nor be able to leave upon her death. If the owner of the slave woman does not consent, or the corruptor is unwilling to acknowledge this [in the municipal records], then he shall either give the	Many times weak and unfortunate immigrants join themselves to the services of certain persons so that, by pretending endurance of labor and services, they may receive food and clothing and thus escape the filth and squalor of poverty. When they have been freed from the confines of their disaster by the humanity and compassion of the individual who receives them, then fully recovered and thinking nothing of misfortune, they choose women who belong to a *paterfamilias* and who are superior in cleverness, beauty, and usefulness. When satiety overtakes them, they leave; they leave with no

[123] *Nov. Val.* 31.2: "colona vero, quae petitori post XX annorum curricula denegatur, si quem partum ante designatum tempus edidit, priori domino eum convenit non perire: aequum est ad eium soboles redeat suscepta tunc temporis, cum adhuc mulier conpetebat, ut damnum amissae matris, quod processu contingit annorum, prolis saltem vindicatio consoletur."

[124] *CTh* 4.11.2 (349). [125] Levy, *West Roman Vulgar Law*, 187.

[126] *Nov. Val.* 27 (449); esp. §§ 3 and 4. [127] *Nov. Val.* 35 (452); esp. §§ 12 and 13, and also § 6.

owner two slaves of equal value should he suffer any financial loss as a result of this; or, if he is unable to fulfill this, upon being flogged most severely with military rods, he shall be judged by a board of magistrates of the nearest city; the judge of that place, mindful of his written statement, will be obligated to ensure that this is carried out.[128]

consideration of their former status, the intimacy of marriage, the sweetness of children, since no law prohibits them. Therefore, if a person who is obligated in no way to a municipality should join himself to the rustic or urban estate of any person and should wish to be united with a woman who is obligated [i.e. as a *colona*], let him declare in the municipal records his intention to reside where he has chosen, so that by the precedence of this bond he may not desert the habitation which he chose nor break up the union with the woman. By this declaration his freeborn status shall remain intact, but he shall not have the right to depart[129]

Part of a larger law that attempted to establish a statute of limitations for the rights of masters of *coloni vagi*, bound tenant farmers who had fled from the estate to which they were bound, section five dealt specifically with freeborn *advenae* (strangers not bound to service) who offered themselves as itinerant laborers, and in so doing formed a relationship with one of the estate's *colonae*. To avoid the sorts of dangers posed by mixing bound and itinerant labor, Valentinian's solution required that the *advena* bind himself to the estate in the event that he took a lover.[130] The compilers followed closely the structure

[128] *ET* 64: "Ancillam alienam virginem vel originariam cuiuslibet aetatis, quisquis ingenuus, nulli tamen quolibet modo obnoxius civitati, corruperit, si dominus voluerit, aut corruptor ipse rogaverit, et apud gesta professus fuerit, mansurus in domini mulieris potestate, eius quam vitiavit contubernium non relinquat, nec, eadem mortua, discedendi habeat facultatem. Quod si dominus ancillae non consenserit, aut ille profiteri noluerit, tunc aut huius meriti duo mancipia domino tradat, eius iuri profutura, si eius substantia patiatur: aut si hoc implere non potuerit, caesus districtissime fustibus vicinae civitatis collegio deputetur: quod iudex eiusdem loci, periculi sui memor, implere et custodire debebit."

[129] *Nov. Val.* 31.5: "Advenae plerumque tenues abiectaeque fortunae quorundam se obsequiis iungunt, ut, simulata laboris et obsequiorum patientia, accepto sumptu ac vestitu inluviem et squalorem egestatis evadant. Ubi de angustiis cladis suae et humanitate et miseratione colligentes fuerint liberati, iam repleti, iam nihil de miseria cogitantes eligunt feminas ad patremfamilias pertinentes, solertia forma utilitate meliores; cum satias ceperit, derelinquunt: non statu priore perpenso, non adsuetudine coniunctionis, non dulcedine filiorum, nulla lege prohibente discedunt. Itaque si nulli quolibet modo obnoxius civitati ad praedium se cuiuscumque rusticum urbanumque collegerit et mulieri obnoxiae sociari voluerit, gestis municipalibus profiteatur habitandi ubi elegerit voluntatem, ut hoc vinculo praecedente nec habitaculum quod placuit deserat nec consortium mulieris abrumpat: qua professione deprompta salva ingenuitate licentiam non habeat recedendi."

[130] Kate Cooper, *The Fall of the Roman Household* (Cambridge, 2007), 130–1.

of the novel while at the same time using much of the original language, suggesting that they were working directly from the text.[131] But there are noticeable differences. For instance, the compilers ignored the preamble in Valentinian's novel concerning the reasons why a freeman would choose to so obligate himself to another in the first place, and focused exclusively on what steps should be taken to safeguard the interests of owners in such instances. And here they offered additional protection to the landowner. We may perhaps see in this a perception that the political and social instability of the time offered increased opportunities for migrant workers to find employment at the expense of others, and for bound tenants to free themselves of their obligations to a landowner.[132]

Another difference here is one of terminology. Whereas the original uses the term *colona*, *ET* 64 uses *originaria*. The same variation appears in *ET* 68. The late Roman term *colonus* could mean either free tenant or owner–cultivator. Since the state taxed them both, and required even independent owners to remain on the land, the law did not always make a distinction between them, and thus it is difficult in many instances to determine whether *colonus* is referring to a free tenant or owner–cultivator. Although the beginnings of the colonate predate Constantine, it was not subject to imperial regulation until his reign. *Coloni* were not to leave their place of birth or to cultivate the land of another; nor was it permitted for *coloni* who belonged to imperial estates to perform additional civic *munera*. However, *coloni* whose masters (*domini*) demanded more of them than had previously been required could approach a *iudex* (the provincial Governor or his subordinate) for help, and if their complaints were proven valid, they were to receive back the excess that was taken from them.[133] For reasons that remain unclear, the compilers of the *ET* elected to replace the term *colona*

[131] Note the following linguistic echoes (marked out in italics): *ET* 64: "*nulli* tamen *quolibet modo obnoxius civitati* . . . et apud *gesta professus fuerit* . . . *non* . . . *discedendi habeat facultatem*" = *Nov. Val.* 31.5: "itaque si *nulli quolibet modo obnoxius civitati* . . . *gestis municipalibus profiteatur* . . . *licentiam non habeat recedendi.*"

[132] Cooper, *The Fall of the Roman Household*, 132.

[133] *CTh* 5.17.1 (332); *CJ* 11.68.2 (no date): *coloni* are not to leave their *origo*; *CJ* 11.68.1 (no date): not to hold *munera*; *CJ* 11.50.1 (no date): *coloni* may seek help for increased demands by *domini*. The laws do not tell us how individuals became *coloni* in the first place, however, and the legal texts are unclear about the status of a *colonus*. Despite the fact that they were required to stay on the land, it is clear that *coloni* did not always do so. There are several instances documented by late Roman legislation of complaints about the flight of *coloni* and the resultant *agri deserti*, ownerless land, which formed a large percentage of the land lost to agriculture at the end of the Empire. See Phillip J. Jones, "L'Italia agraria nell' alto medioevo: problemi di cronologia e di continuità," in *Settimane di studio del Centro italiano di studi sull'alto medioevo, 13* (Spoleto, 1969), 57–92, esp. 67; Campbell Ainsworth Grey, "Revisiting the 'Problem' of *agri deserti* in the Late Roman Empire," *JRA* 20 (2007), 362–76. On the origins of the colonate: Jones, *LRE*, 2, 796–803; Ramsay MacMullen, *Roman Government's Response*

with *originaria*. Used in a generic sense, the term denotes an *origo*, or place of origin. Thus a decurion can be *originalis* (*CTh* 12.1.96). In a technical sense, as in the *ET*, it indicates an attachment to a particular piece of land in much the same way as a *colonus*, and designates that status of ignoble birth.[134]

That copies of post-Theodosian novels were available and being consulted in Italy at this time is confirmed by Cassiodorus. In an edict of Athalaric prohibiting the unlawful seizure of property, Cassiodorus has the King uphold an earlier novel of Valentinian III of 440 (*Nov.* 8.1):

> By the severity of the laws and Our own indignation, We condemn that foremost poison of the human race [i.e. the unlawful seizure of property], under which civil order (*civilitas*) can be neither claimed nor maintained, decreeing that the rule of the divine Valentinian, long seriously neglected, shall rise up against those who despise the order of law, and, in person or by their retinue, dare to expel the owner and violently occupy estates in town or country.[135]

At some point in the nearly one hundred years between the time of its issuance in 440 and the promulgation of Athalaric's edict in 533/4, Valentinian's novel had gone into abeyance. But the Ostrogothic King's legal experts were clearly aware of it and cited it as a relevant source of law, much in the same way the compilers of the *ET* acknowledged the relevance of such post-Theodosian novels, in two instances going so far as to cite the specific text. But again, just as they had with other sources of earlier Roman law, they freely adapted these novels to better suit current realities.

Conclusions

In drawing from earlier sources of Roman law, the compilers expanded upon what they considered important and rejected what they found impractical or unnecessary. Sometimes this meant defining terms that were perhaps no longer familiar, or offering a paraphrase, and occasionally omitting or adding details for clarity and relevance. Some provisions employ

to Crisis AD *235–337* (New Haven, CT, 1976), 175–81; Kyle Harper, *Slavery in the Late Roman World,* AD *275–425* (Cambridge, 2011), 153–5; Campbell Ainsworth Grey, "Contextualizing *Colonatus*: The *Origo* of the Late Roman Empire," *JRS* 97 (2007), 155–75.

134 In a later law of 452 (*Nov. Val.* 35.19) in which Valentinian reaffirms this right of the owner, the term *originaria* is used.

135 Cass., *Var.* 9.18.1: "Primam humano generi noxiam pervasionem, sub qua nec dici potest civilitas nec haberi, severitate legum et nostra indignatione damnamus statuentes, ut sanctio divi Valentiniani adversum eos diu pessime neglecta consurgat, qui praedia urbana vel rustica despecto iuris ordine per se suosque praesumpserint expulso possessore violenter intrare."

different terms or phrases; others are versed in a language and style more succinct and pithy; still others are more elaborate than the original text in question. These variances were fundamentally related to developments that had taken place in the administration of law and justice via the courts from the fourth to sixth centuries. Others, too, were the result of changes in Italian society following the arrival of Theoderic's Goths in the peninsula. To be sure, all of these provisions, whether they clarify, abridge, expand, or merely paraphrase the original text, speak to the purpose for which the *ET* was created, namely, to provide practical solutions for the sorts of everyday problems that arose between Goths and Romans. As such, they offer a revealing glimpse into the prevailing conditions of Italy during a time of profound social, political, and economic change.

CHAPTER 3

Law and order

Introduction

In a highly rhetorical letter to the Roman Senate that was intended to underscore the Solomonesque quality of Theoderic's justice, Cassiodorus has the King proclaim that he was so besieged with petitioners that he was forced to settle cases on horseback:

> It was during Our [i.e. Theoderic's] horse rides that [Cyprian] often obtained from Us that which used to be carried out in the solemn councils (*consistoria*) of long ago. For if at any time it was pleasing to relieve a mind fatigued by the cares of the state, We would turn to horse exercises so that the body's strength and energy might be renewed by the very change of activities. Then, this pleasant reporter would present many cases to Us, and his statement would be esteemed by the judge's wearied mind.[1]

In practice, however, the King rarely tried cases in person, as the nature of his office (like that of the Roman Emperor) did not permit close contact between him and his subjects. Rather, the bulk of cases were handled directly by Theoderic's appointed officials, all of whom were *ideally* versed in the law in some capacity and could thus effectively decide any matter that fell under their jurisdiction. Consisting of members from both the Roman civil service and the Gothic army, this was the judicial bureaucracy that determined the extent to which peace and order would be maintained, and in some cases restored, in the Italian peninsula: for unless reduced to practice, law remained largely symbolic. The questions as to who these individuals were, the mechanisms involved in the administration of their duties, the rules of jurisdiction and procedure that guided them, and the external factors that hindered them, are the focus of attention here.

[1] Cass., *Var.* 5.41: "obtinuit ille saepius in vectationibus nostris, quod in consistoriis agi solebat antiquis. Si quando enim relevare libuit animum rei publicae cura fatigatum, equina exercitia petebamus, ut ipsa varietate rerum soliditas se corporis vigorque recrearet. tunc nobis causas multiplices relator delectabilis ingerebat eratque eius infastidita suggestio sub iudicis animo taedioso."

Judges and courts

Traditionally, scholars have turned to Cassiodorus for the administrative details of Theoderic's government. His *Variae* suggest that the administrative bureaucracy of early sixth-century Italy was a highly differentiated and specialized one comprising civil and military officers with clearly defined and separate functions along similar lines as the late imperial administration. The provincial Governor or his deputy functioned as the judge of first instance in serious cases. His decision could be appealed to the Vicar and in some circumstances, for those with enough time and more importantly money, to the Praetorian Prefect or even the King himself. While the court to which all of these officials were ultimately responsible was that of a King rather than an Emperor, the administrative bureaucracy of Theoderic's government as outlined by Cassiodorus appears to have maintained the essential elements of the late imperial system to a remarkable degree.[2]

The *Variae*, however, was as much a work of political expediency as it was an official record of Ostrogothic rule, and therefore does not necessarily reflect conditions as they actually were, that is, in the aftermath of the collapse of the imperial administration through which the proper and efficient adjudication of disputes could be carried out. The problem for Ostrogothic Italy was that the appointment of provincial Governors was extremely erratic. There are only twelve Governors known for Italy between 476 and 553 – a significant drop from the thirty-three Governors attested for the peninsula in the period 394–476.[3] Even if this scarcity can be partly explained as a problem with the evidence, it is nonetheless clear that Theoderic progressively

[2] On the late imperial court system in Late Antiquity, see Arnold H. M. Jones, *The Lates Roman Empire, 284–602: A Social, Economic and Administrative survey*, 3 vols. (Oxford, 1964), I, 479–493; Jill Harries, *Law and Empire in Late Antiquity* (Cambridge, 1999); Caroline Humfress, *Orthodoxy and the Courts in Late Antiquity* (Oxford, 2007), chapter 2; Herbert F. Jolowicz and Barry Nicholas, *A Historical Introduction to the Study of Roman Law*, 3rd edn. (Cambridge, 1972; repr. 2008), 445–7; Michael Kaser, *Das römische Zivilprozessrecht*, 2nd edn. (Munich, 1996), 517–19; George Mousourakis, *The Historical and Institutional Context of Roman Law*, (Aldershot, 2003), 349–80. On the imperial civil service, see Wolfgang Kunkel, *An Introduction to Roman Legal and Constitutional History*, trans. J. M. Kelly, 2nd edn., based on the sixth German edition of *Römische Rechtsgeschitte* (Oxford, 1973), 141–42; Jolowicz and Nicholas, *Roman Law*, 423–25; Averil Cameron, *The Later Roman Empire,* AD *284–430* (Cambridge, MA, 1993, repr. 2001), 39–41; Kaser, *Römische Rechtsgeschichte*, (Göttingen, 1976), 208–10; Ernst Stein, *Untersuchungen über das Officium der Prätorianerpräfektur seit Diokletian* (Amsterdam, 1962); Andrea Giardina, *Aspetti della burocrazia nel Basso Impero* (Rome, 1977); Roland Delmaire, *Les Institutions du Bas-Èmpire romain, de Constantin à Justinien, I, Les Institutions palatines* (Paris, 1995); Alberto Burdese, *Manuale di diritto pubblico romano* (Turin, 1987, repr. 1994), 222–4; Antonio Guarino, *Storia del diritto romano* (Naples, 1996), 527–9; Mario Talamanca (ed.), *Lineamenti di storia del diritto romano* (Milan, 1989), 564–6.

[3] John Martindale, *The Prosopography of the Later Roman Empire, vol. 2:* AD *395–527* (Cambridge, 1980), 1278–9; Paul S. Barnwell, *Emperors, Prefects and Kings, The Roman West 395–565* (London, 1992), 158.

appropriated the functions of the Roman judges, *iudices*, through such officers as the Gothic *saio* (pl. *saiones*) and *comes* (pl. *comites*).

In the course of the sixth century, military officers like the *comites* and *saiones* began to supersede the traditional civil service (*militia Romana*) in terms of importance in the overall administration. By the close of the century this process was complete: Byzantine Italy was at this time ruled by a military Governor known to us as the Exarch.[4] Cassiodorus, in fact, confirms that the strict division between civilian and military sections of Roman government was already weakening under Theoderic, and officers from both spheres crossed from one branch to another, or operated in both at the same time. For example, to judge by his name the *comes* Colosseus, the Governor of Pannonia Sirmiensis who apparently had troops under his command, was a Roman whose commission encompassed both military and civilian spheres.[5] Similarly, Servatus, Duke of Reate, exercised a jurisdiction that seems to have been both military and civilian in nature.[6] Liberius, the Praetorian Prefect of Gaul, was described by Cassiodorus as a military hero whose imposing appearance was heightened by his visible battle scars;[7] and another Roman, Cyprian, is unambiguously stated to have served Theoderic in both military and civilian capacities.[8] This blurring of boundaries transcended all aspects of life in Theoderic's Italy. The King himself is said to have remarked that "the poor Roman imitates the Goth, the Rich Goth the Roman."[9]

4 Willam Sinnigen, "Administrative Shifts of Competence under Theoderic," *Traditio* 21 (1965), 456–67; Thomas S. Brown, *Gentlemen and Officers: Imperial Administration and Anistocratic Power in Byzantive Italy* AD *554–800* (Rome, 1984), 61–81, 93–101.

5 Cass., *Var.* 3.23.3 (a letter in Theoderic's name confirming Colosseus' appointment as Governor of Pannonia Simiensis).

6 Cass., *Var.* 1.11 (a letter in Theoderic's name to Servatus, concerning on-going violence in the province).

7 Cass., *Var.* 11.1.16. See too Cyprian, Firminus, Viventius, Messianus and Stephen, *Vita Caesarii Arelatensis* (*BHL*, 1508–9), ed. Germain Morin, *S. Caesarii episcopi Arelatensis opera omina*, 2 vols. (Maredesous, Belgium, 1937–42; repr. in *CCSL* 1–3 and 104 (Turnhout, 1953)) 2.10–12, discussed by James O'Donnell, "Liberius the Patrician," *Traditio* 37 (1981), 48–50; and, for his unusual military career under Justinian, see Martindale, *PLRE* 2, 680.

8 Cass., *Var.* 8.21.3; concerning whose life, see Martindale, *PLRE* 2, 332. On the militarization of the Roman bureaucracy, see Brown, *Gentlemen and Officers*, 61–81, 93–101.

9 Anon. Val. 12.61: "Romanus miser imitatur Gothum et utilis Gothus imitatur Romanum." This need not have applied to the aristocracy giving up its military role, or the lower classes filling the ranks of the army, but rather an indication of the convergence of the two cultures, Roman and Gothic, that was taking place in Italy at this time. If the archaeological record is any indication, there is nothing to suggest a distinctly Gothic culture in Italy. On the archaeological invisibility of the Goths in Italy, see Volker Bierbrauer, *Die Ostgotischen Grab- und Schatzfunde in Italien* (Spoleto, 1975); and Gian Pietro Brogiolo, "Dwellings and Settlements in Gothic Italy," in Sam J. Barnish and Federico Marazzi (eds.), *The Ostrogoths from the Migration Period to the Sixth Century: An Ethnographic Perspective* (Woodbridge, 2007), 113–33, esp. 116–17.

An important consequence of this militarization of Italian society was the emergence of the Gothic *saio* as the supreme executive officer of Theoderic's administration, whose authority was second only to that of the King himself. Established perhaps as early as 508 when Theoderic instructed *saio* Nandus to prepare an invasion force for Gaul, the office seems to have emerged in response to the basic need of the King to maintain personal and trusted contacts throughout the peninsula.[10] As a group, *saiones* were remarkably versatile and could be called upon to fulfill any number of functions, including the offering of royal protection (*tuitio*) and the general administration of justice.[11] Our sources contain several examples of their myriad capacities in this sphere. For instance, Theoderic requested the *saio* Fruirarith to judge a case involving a Roman court official.[12] *Saio* Unigilis directed the provisioning for Theoderic's roving court on one of his visits to Liguria.[13] *Saio* Grenoda, along with a special military aide, investigated charges against the ex-Praetorian Prefect Faustus.[14] Duda, a *saio* of exceptional repute, unsuccessfully brought a case against the King's nephew Theodahad, then *dux* in Liguria, and later channeled a troublesome legal case to the proper court.[15] And *saio* Dumerit was sent to Faventia to punish the plunderers of small landholders in the region. It made no difference, according to Cassiodorus, whether the culprits were Goth or Roman.[16]

Like the *saiones*, *comites* played a significant role within Theoderic's administration. Drawn from the rank and file of the Gothic army, *comites* were dispatched throughout the kingdom to maintain peace and order through varying ranks and competences.[17] Some controlled individual cities,[18] some provinces,[19] and others particular groupings of Goths. They

[10] Cass., *Var.* 1.24. See further Ernst Stein, *Histoire du Bas-Empire II; De la disparition de L'Empire d'Occident à la Mort Justinien (476–565)* (Paris, 1949), 122–3; Jones, *LRE*, 1, 255.

[11] Cass., *Var.* 7.39. [12] Cass., *Var.* 2.13. [13] Cass., *Var.* 2.20. [14] Cass., *Var.* 3.20.

[15] Cass., *Var.* 4.32, 34, 39. [16] Cass., *Var.* 9.10.

[17] Kayoko Tabata, "I comites Gothorum e l'amministrazione municipale in epoca Ostrogota", in J.–M. Carrié and R. Lizzi Testa (eds.), *'Humana Sapit'. Études d'Antiquité Tardive Offertes à Lellia Cracco Ruggini* (Bibliothèque de l'Antiquité Tardive, 3) (Turnhout, 2002), 67–78; Herwig Wolfram, *History of the Goths*, trans. Thomas J. Dunlap, 2nd edn. (Berkeley, CA, 1988), 290–2; Herwig Wolfram, *The Roman Empire and its Germanic People*, trans. Thomas Dunlap (Berkeley, CA 1997), 116–17; Dieter Timpe, "Comes," *Reallexikon der germanischen Altertumskunde*, vol. 5 2nd edn. (New York/Berlin, 1982), 63–5; Jones, *LRE*, 1, 366–8; Fischer-Drew, "Law, German: Early Germanic Codes," in J. R. Strayer (ed.), *Dictionary of the Middle Ages*, vol. 7 (New York 1986), 468–75; Ludwig Schmidt, "Die comites Gothorum: ein Kapitel zur ostgotischen Verfassungsgeschichte," *Mitteilungen des Instituts für Österreichische Geschichtsforschung* 40 (1925), 127–33; Otto Seeck, "Comites," *RE* 17 (1900), 622–4.

[18] E.g., Cass., *Var.* 6.22 (*formula* for the *comes* of the city of Syracuse); 6.23 (*formula* for the *comes* of Naples); 7.13 (*formula* for the *comes* of Rome); 7.14 (*formula* for the *comes* of Ravenna).

[19] E.g., Cass., *Var.* 3.23 (a letter to the *comes* Colosseus, Governor of Pannonia Sirmiensis); 7.1 (*formula* for the *comes* of a province).

could be expected to fill posts of specified responsibility at court, sometimes to fulfill regular administrative and judicial functions in the kingdom at large and sometimes to undertake specific tasks as particular problems arose. Cassiodorus records a vast range of activities performed by these special agents. The *comes* Sura was charged with the task of regulating the restoration of public works and monuments of his *civitas*.[20] The *comes* Marabad was entreated by Theoderic to settle a dispute that had been the subject of petition to the King's court.[21] Elsewhere, Theoderic instructed Adila, at once Senator and *comes*, to ensure the protection of the dependents of the Milanese church in Sicily.[22] The *comes* Amabilis was entrusted with the organization of famine relief in Gaul, and the *comes* Simeon undertook the collection of taxes in the province of Dalmatia.[23] And in a rather disturbing case of clerical abuse, Theoderic instructed the *comes* Annas to inquire into allegations of grave-robbing levied against the arch priest Laurentius:

> From the reports of many it has come to Our attention that the arch priest Laurentius dug up the dead in order to search for grave goods among the bodies, and in so doing he, that is the very same individual who ought to preach peace to the living, has disturbed the dead. It is reported that he did not hold back his hands, imbued with the oils of consecration, from such a cruel contagion: carried away by a detestable passion he sought golden riches instead of doing what was right, namely to bestow his own wealth, acquired through honest means, to the needy. Wherefore, We instruct you [i.e. Annas] to inquiry into this matter with diligent consideration so that if you discover these reports to be in accordance with the truth, you shall detain him so that he cannot hide that which he was not permitted to discover. For the honor of the priesthood We leave this wicked deed unpunished, believing that it will be vindicated by a higher power.[24]

In the event that Annas could not complete the task, he could turn to his fellow officers for help. For it was a requirement of all *comites* to assist one another should the need arise.[25]

The *formulae* for the office of the various *comites* preserved in the *Variae* consistently make the point that cases involving just Romans were to be

[20] Cass., *Var.* 2.7. [21] Cass., *Var.* 4.12. [22] Cass., *Var.* 2.29. [23] Cass., *Var.* 4.5; 3.25.

[24] Cass., *Var.* 4.18: "dudum siquidem ad nos multorum suggestione pervenit Laurentium presbyterum effossis cineribus funestas divitias inter hominum cadavera perscrutatum concussionemque mortuis intulisse, quem oportet viventibus quieta praedicare. Non abstinuisse perhibetur tam crudeli contagio piis dicatas consecrationibus manus: aurum exsecrabili quaesisse fertur affectu, quem suam decuisset egentibus dare substantiam vel sub aequitate collectam. Quod te diligenti examinatione praecipimus indagare, ut, si veritati dicta perspexeris convenire, hominis ambitum eo tantum fine concludas, ne possit supprimere quod eum non licuit invenire. Scelus enim, quod nos pro sacerdotali honore relinquimus impunitum, maiore pondere credimus vindicandum."

[25] Cass., *Var.* 3.26.

handled by Roman officials, while the Gothic officers were to handle inter-Gothic disputes. Cases involving both Goths and Romans were to be handled by a pair of judges, the Gothic Count and his Roman counterpart.[26] This jurisdictional division between Roman and Goth followed a functional one between the two groups. As illustrated in the *Variae*, the propaganda of Theoderic's regime consistently presented the incoming Goths as having taken the place of the old Roman army, which was itself becoming increasingly barbarized over the course of the fourth and fifth centuries. There was, in short, a separation of function between Goths and Romans. The Roman role within this system was primarily civilian: paying taxes to support the army. That of the Goths was military: ensuring peace by securing the state against both external and internal threats; in return they received tax and the benefits that Roman society had to offer. On one occasion Cassiodorus observed, "While the army of the Goths makes war, the Romans may live in peace,"[27] and the theme of the Goths fighting while the Romans enjoyed the benefits of peace is one frequently encountered in his *Variae*.[28] In one of his letters (*Var.* 5.29), Cassiodorus refers specifically to a case involving a retired Gothic soldier, Anduit, who complains that his status entitled him to certain rights. In other words, Goths retained their *de iure* status throughout their lives, and not just when they were part of the army.

As in the later Empire, function was an attribute of heredity and caste; functional groups were defined more broadly than just their serving members. Descendants of the clergy, for instance, whether practicing clerics or not, could claim ecclesiastical jurisdiction. The Goths as a whole were supposed to constitute a military caste. And just as Roman soldiers were

[26] E.g., Cass., *Var.* 7.3.

[27] Cass., *Var.* 12.5.4 (an edict of Cassiodorus, drafted during his tenureship of the Praetorian Prefecture, granting various forms of relief to the inhabitants of Lucania and Bruttium).

[28] Historians have long accepted this functional division as broadly true in descriptive terms. For a good modern account see John Moorhead, *Theoderic in Italy* (Oxford, 1992), 71–5, who presupposes that differences between Goths and Romans were inherently obvious, envisaging Theoderic's program as "the imposition of race on a dichotomy which had already existed [viz. soldier-civilian]" (p. 72). See further Theodor Mommsen, *Gesammelte Schriften*, 8 vols. (Berlin, 1904), 6, 436; Stein, *Histoire du Bas-Empire*, 120; James B. Bury, *History of the Later Roman Empire*, 2 vols. (New York, 1958), 1, 455–6; Ludwig Schmidt, "Die comites Gothorum," 127–33 (an attempt to fit the complex administrative framework of Ostrogothic Italy into Theoderic's ethnic ideology). This scholarly consensus has been questioned by Rosario Soraci, *Ricerche sui conubia tra Romani e Germani nei secoli IV-VI* (Catania, 1968; repr. 1974), 85–9; and challenged altogether by Patrick Amory (*People and Identity in Ostrogothic Italy, 489–554*, Cambridge Studies in Medieval Life and Thought: Fourth Series (Cambridge, 1997), esp. ch. 2), who argues that this functional division was in fact an ethnic one, and that barbarian ethnicity was itself an identity that took shape within the context of the break-up of the Empire, one shaped by roles within society (such as churchman, soldier or administrator).

subject to the jurisdiction of their own courts, and in legal terms operated separately from the surrounding civilian population, Goths were to be judged separately by Gothic officials, namely the *saiones* and *comites*.

While *saiones* and *comites* took on a greater role in Theoderic's government, traditional, that is to say imperial, office-holders continued to perform an important, albeit more limited, function in the administration of the law. The highest-ranking of these was the Praetorian Prefect.[29] The *formula* for the position characterizes the officer as a supreme judge with *quasi*-regal status and unappellable jurisdiction over all provinces subject to him:

> For this dignity and Our own [i.e. the King's] there are certain rights shared in common. For it summons men living at a distance to its tribunal without legal limitation; it imposes heavy fines on wrongdoers; it distributes public money at will; by the same authority it grants travel warrants (*evectiones*); it appropriates unclaimed property; it punishes the misdeeds of provincial Governors; it pronounces judgment by word of mouth [whereas all other judges had to read their decisions from their written statement]. What is there which is not entrusted to him whose very speech is a verdict? It is almost as though he can establish laws, since the reverence he garners can settle cases without appeal.[30]

But as Cassiodorus admits in the preface to the letters drafted during his tenure of the Prefecture (535–7), much of the judicial burden of the office was shouldered by his legal expert (*consiliarius*) Felix, and he rarely dealt with legal matters directly.[31] Moreover, parties which considered that they had been wronged by the Prefect's decision could, in fact, appeal. We are told by Cassiodorus of one instance where a Praetorian Prefect was brought before the *saio* Triwila to answer charges of misconduct.[32]

By the beginning of the sixth century the office of the Praetorian Prefect had lost some of its initial prestige. The same is true for the other great prefecture of the western Empire – the Urban Prefect of Rome. For reasons which lay in its past history, Rome was governed on quite different lines

[29] Wolfram, *History of the Goths*, 293.

[30] Cass., *Var.* 6.3: "Quaedam enim huic dignitati et nobiscum iura communia sunt. Exhibet enim sine praescriptione longinquos, magna quantitate multat errantes, fiscum pro sua deliberatione distribuit, evectiones simili potestate largitur, vacantia bona proscribit, delicta provinciarum iudicum punit, verbo sententiam dicit. quid est, quod non habeat commissum, cuius est vel ipse sermo iudicium? Paene est, ut leges possit condere, quando eius reverentia sine appellatione potest negotia terminare." The basis for this is Constantine's *CTh* 11.30.16 of 331.

[31] Cass., *Var.*, *praefatio chartarum praefecturae*, 4, 5; Sam J. Barnish, *The Variae of Cassiodorus Senator*, Translated Texts for Historians (Liverpool, 1992), li.

[32] Cass., *Var.* 3.20.

from other cities of the Italian peninsula. In supreme charge of the city was the *praefectus urbis*. Traditionally, the Urban Prefect functioned as the judge of first instance within the city and for a radius of one hundred miles around it. Within his jurisdiction fell cases involving violations of public order in the city and breaches of building regulations. In this he was assisted by an *officium* consisting of a five-member senatorial subcommittee, the *iudicium quinquevirale*.[33] The office, according to Cassiodorus, was still esteemed highly honorable in the early sixth century, ranking officially below that of Praetorian Prefect, and was normally filled by members of the best families of the senatorial aristocracy.[34]

Judging from a letter drafted in Theoderic's name to the Urban Prefect Argolicus, the officer continued to perform important judicial functions. In the letter we read that Argolicus was instructed by the King to oversee the trial of the two Senators, Basilius (former Consul in 463) and Praetextatus, accused in 510 of practicing the magical arts:

> Thus, by the official report of your greatness, We have discovered that Basilius and Praetextatus, for a long while now polluted by the infection of the sinister art, have been brought before your court because of the charge of certain individuals. Concerning this matter you assert that you look to Our verdict, so that what the authority of Our piety commands may be strengthened. But We, who do not know how to depart from the laws, for whom it is inherent to maintain a moderate justice in all things, decree by this authority that you shall judge this case by legal examination, together with five Senators: namely, the magnificent Patricians Symmachus, Decius, Volusianus, and Caelianus, and the illustrious Maximianus. And in accordance with every legal procedure, if the accusation brought should be proven, let it also be punished by the penalty of the laws themselves, so that hidden and secret culprits, whom uncertain knowledge cannot bring before the laws, may be deterred by this kind of punishment from such sins.[35]

[33] The quinqueviral court was created through legislation of the Emperors Valens, Gratian, and Valentinian of 376 (*CTh* 9.1.3), which was drafted following a notorious hunt for senatorial sorcerers.

[34] See, e.g., Cass., *Var.* 1.42–3 (concerning the elevation of the *vir illustris* and patrician Artemidorus, relative of the Emperor Zeno, to the position of Urban Prefect).

[35] Cass., *Var.* 4.22: "Magnitudinis itaque tuae relatione comperimus Basilium atque Praetextatum, artis sinistrae iam diu contagione pollutos, in accusationem tui examinis personarum intentione deductos. Super qua re nostram te asseris spectare sententiam, ut confidentius fiat quod pietatis nostrae mandat auctoritas. Sed nos, qui nescimus a legibus discrepare, quorum cordi est in omnibus moderatam tenere iustitiam, praesenti auctoritate decernimus, ut quinque senatoribus, id est magnificis et patriciis viris Symmacho Decio Volusiano atque Caeliano nec non illustri viro Maximiano, hanc causam legitima examinatione pensetis. Et per omnia iuris ordine custodito, si crimen quod intenditur fuerit comprobatum, ipsarum quoque legum districtione plectatur, ut rei abditi atque secreti per hoc vindictae genus a culpis talibus arceantur, quos ad leges trahere non potest incerta notitia."

The impression given elsewhere by Cassiodorus, however, is of an officer whose authority was largely ignored. In a letter concerning the ongoing violence that had embroiled Rome as a result of the Laurentian schism (roughly between 502 and 507), Cassiodorus describes how the members of the Senate dismissed the presiding Prefect in the matter. He has the King remind the Senators to forward their complaints to the Urban Prefect Agapitus so that the guilty could be punished in accordance with the laws: "If there is any insult which requires notice, bring it before the Urban Prefect so that any fault can be remedied in accordance with the laws and not through a presumed action that results in injury: for, how does he who strives to take the law into his own hands differ from the one at fault?"[36]

The *praefectus urbis* was further entitled to appoint a deputy who might hear cases in his absence: the *vicarius urbis*. The *formula* for the position describes the *vicarius* as a quasi-military officer who represented the person of the King directly; and the jurisdiction of his office enabled him to hear capital cases, and not just in Rome.[37] Ideally, the Vicar possessed a thorough understanding of the law, but it is clear that this was not always the case. Cassiodorus tells of a certain Joannes, formerly the arch-physician, who was convicted and subsequently pardoned for a crime he did not commit. The basis of his wrongful conviction, Cassiodorus implies, was the inability of the presiding Vicar to detect any wrongdoing on the part of the prosecutor Vivianus:

> You [i.e. Joannes] inform Us that, by the devices of the Spectabilis Vivianus and his superior knowledge of the laws, an unjust judgment was obtained against you, in default, in the Court of the Vicar of the City of Rome: that Vivianus himself, having found God, has now renounced worldly pursuits, and now regrets the charge he brought against you. We therefore (if your statements shall prove to be correct) quash the sentence against you, restore you to your country and your property. . .and that you may be preserved from future molestation, founded on the old sentence against you, We assign you to the guardianship (*tuitio*) of the Patrician Albinus, without prejudice to the laws.[38]

[36] Cass., *Var.* 1.30.4: "Si quod est forte, quod poenam mereatur, admissum, in praefecti urbis notitiam deferatur, ut culpa legibus, non per praesumptam coerceatur iniuriam. quid enim discrepat a peccante, qui se per excessum nititur vindicare?" On the circus factions: Cass., *Var.* 1.27; 1.31–3; 1.44; 3.51.5, 11. On these events in general see Moorhead, *Theoderic in Italy*, 114–39, 239–40.

[37] Cass., *Var.* 6.15.

[38] Cass., *Var.* 4.41: "Data siquidem supplicatione conquereris virum spectabilem Vivianum legum artificio, quo callet, elatum, personam tuam obiectis criminationibus insecutum et eo usque perventum, ut indefensus contra iuris ordinem vicarii urbis Romae sententia damnareris: nunc autem religiosae mentis affectu odia mundana damnasse auctorique suo tuum displicuisse periculum. Et ideo, si nullis impugnationibus enervantur asserta, laesionem non patimur miseris inhaerere, quam

By virtue of his superior knowledge, and by implication the ignorance or inexperience of the Vicar, Vivianus was able to secure a guilty verdict through certain unspecified, but obviously illicit, means. Theoderic here promises the doctor *restitutio in integrum*, and protection from any further molestation under the protection of the patrician Albinus, provided of course that the merits of the doctor's claims are substantiated.

While in the official scheme of things the Praetorian and Urban Prefects were the highest-ranking officers of the Ostrogothic civic administration, it was the provincial Governor who was the linchpin of Theoderic's judicial bureaucracy. Despite the fact that there was a sharp decline in the number of known Governors during this time, Cassiodorus' *formula* for the position underscores the point that the officer was essential for the immediate and effective suppression of crime:

> Antiquity has prudently decreed that judges be sent throughout the provinces, so that the small numbers that come to see us might not increase. For who can endure the audacity of thieves, if they know that the means of establishing order is far away. Violence will everywhere increase unabated, if it is supposed that a litigant's complaint will be dealt with slowly. To repress yet minor quarrels in those regions is far better than defending against hardened crimes [here].[39]

Governors were to be dispatched into the provinces to deal with all matters that would have otherwise found their way to the King's *comitatus*, thereby saving the litigants a long and expensive journey, and effectively extending the King's reach into those areas outside of his immediate control. In a letter to Severinus, Governor of Suavia, Cassiodorus describes how Governors traveled throughout the provinces on yearly circuits: "Judges are to visit each town once in the year, and are not entitled to claim from such towns more than three days' maintenance ... Our ancestors wished that the circuits of the judges should be a benefit, not a burden, to the Provincials."[40] Towards the end of the letter, these circuit judges are

suis constiterit machinatoribus displicere. quapropter in abolitum missa sententia ... patriae te rebusque omnibus nostra reddit auctoritas ... Sed ne cuiusquam forsitan plectenda temeritas in te impetus reparare possit audaciae, patricii Albini salvis legibus tuitio te deputata communiet ..."

[39] Cass., *Var.* 6.21.1: "Omnino provide decrevit antiquitas iudices ad provinciam mitti, ne possit ad nos veniendo mediocritas ingravari. quis enim latronum ferret audaciam, si longe positam cognoscerent disciplinam? Absolute poterat vis permissa grassari, si conquerens tardius crederetur audiri. sed quanto melius in ipsis cunabulis adhuc mollia reprimere quam indurata crimina vindicare."

[40] Cass., *Var.* 5.14.5: "Iudices ... tam de cursu quam de aliis rebus illicita dicuntur possessoribus irrogare dispendia. ...Iudex vero ... propter expensas provincialium, quae gravare pauperes suggeruntur, per annum in unumquodque municipium semel accedat: cui non amplius quam triduanae praebeantur annonae, sicut legum cauta tribuerunt. Maiores enim nostri discursus iudicum non oneri, sed compendio provincialibus esse voluerunt." In a letter (*Var.* 12.15) drafted in his own name as

chastened not to claim from the towns' residents more than that which is lawfully entitled to them – namely, three days' maintenance. To prevent similar such abuses in the future, as well as to protect a judge from possible fraud, all such officers were to enter their proceedings into official registers (*polyptycha*).

As Cassiodorus makes clear, the effectiveness of the system was limited by the inability of the central bureaucracy to interfere systematically in the day-to-day running of local communities. In a letter written in the name of Athalaric, Cassiodorus has the King exhort the provincial Governors to do the job appointed them:

> Although We have, by God's help, appointed you on a yearly basis throughout Our provinces, and throughout all the territories of Italy there is no lack of appointed judges, We learn that an abundance of cases have come [to Us] on account of a lack of justice. Moreover, the blame is clearly a result of your negligence, whenever men are compelled to seek the benefits of the laws from Us.[41]

In two separate letters drafted during his tenureship of the Praetorian Prefecture, Cassiodorus makes similar entreaties.[42] Thus, while the provincial Governor had a clearly defined and significant role within the judicial scheme of things, the impression given by Cassiodorus is of an officer corps that was not always up to the task.

In all instances the Governor possessed executive power throughout his province. While many cases involving small claims could conceivably have reached their courts, such judges were entitled to delegate hearings to deputies, or lesser judges, designated by Cassiodorus (*Var.* 7.26) as *comites secundi ordinis*, Counts of the second order – a clear indication of their subordination to the Counts of the first order, namely the *comites civitatis*.[43] In the later Empire, one of the most important of these lesser judges was the *defensor civitatis*, a municipal official whose function was to

Praetorian Prefect to the right honourable Maximus, *cancellarius* in Lucania and Bruttium, Cassiodorus explains that he is abolishing the travel fees of judges (*pulveratica*) imposed upon the residents of Squillace, the chief city of the region: "Pulveratica quoque iudicis funditus amputantes trium tantum etiam dierum praesulibus annonas praeberi secundum vetera constituta decernimus, suis expensis facta tarditate vecturis."

[41] Cass., *Var.* 9.20: "Cum vos provinciis nostris iuvante deo annua reparatione praestemus nec desint iudicia per universos fines Italiae distributa, intellegimus de inopia iustitiae copiam venire causarum. Culpa siquidem vestrae probatur esse neglegentiae, quotiens a nobis coguntur homines legum beneficia postulare."

[42] Cass., *Var.* 12.2, 6.

[43] Such was the practice throughout the later Empire. See Harries, *Law and Empire*, 54; Jones, *LRE*, I, 50–1.

protect the lower classes against the more powerful, in particular local magnates and governmental officers. He had police, financial, and judicial powers and was an important official of the municipality in the early Empire.[44] In his legislation concerning the creation of the office of *defensor* in Illyricum, the Emperor Valentinian entrusted this officer with the task of protecting the lower classes of the population against the sorts of abuses committed at the hands of great landowners and state officials. To that end, the law specified that *defensores* should be drawn from the ranks of former provincial Governors or other officials from the civil service of sufficient rank. And to ensure the success of the newly-created position, Valentinian stipulated that the final appointment of a candidate for office had to be approved by the Emperor himself.[45] Towards the end of the fourth century, however, the *defensor civitatis* was proving itself to be an increasingly unsuccessful institution, as many of those who held the office often committed abuses themselves or were rendered incapable through bribery or intimidation.

Under Theoderic the office of *defensor* was little more than an additional burden imposed on members of the municipal council. In *ET* 52 and 53, which together concern the matter of tax liability, we learn that the *defensor* was largely responsible for enrolling records in the municipal archives (*gesta municipalia*):

> *ET* 52 But if anyone wishes to willingly make a gift of rural or urban estates, a record of the generosity, confirmed by the signatures of witnesses, shall be registered in the municipal records; provided that three curials or municipal magistrates, and a *defensor civitatis* on behalf of the municipal magistrate together with three decurions or *duumviri*, or *quinquennales* are present as witnesses for the drawing up of the records [of the gift]; but if these are not available, the registering of the transaction shall be fulfilled in another

44 For scholarship on the *defensor civitatis*, see Vincenzo Mannino, *Ricerche sul "Defensor Civitatis"* (Milan, 1984); Jens-Uwe Krause, *Spatäntike Patronatsformen im Westen der römischen Reiches* (Munich, 1987), 289–93; Ramsay MacMullen, *Corruption and the Decline of Rome* (New Haven, CT, 1988), 49; Alexander Demandt, *Die Spätantike Römischen Geschichte von Diocletian bis Justinian 284–565 n. Chr.*, Müller's Handbuch, vol. 3 part 6 (Munich, 1989; repr. 2007), 335, 404; Bärbel Kramer, "Liste der Syndikoi, Ekdikoi und Defensores in den Papyri Ägyptens," *Miscellanea Papyrologica* 19 (Florence, 1990), 305–29; Richard M. Frakes, "Some Hidden *Defensores Civitatum* in the *Res Gestae* of Ammianus Marcellinus," *ZSS (RA)* 109 (1992), 526–32; Richard M. Frakes, "Late Roman Social Justice and the Origins of the *Defensor Civitatis*," *The Classical Journal* 89 (1994), 337–48, where he argues that the office existed as early as 319; Albert Dietl, *Defensor civitatis: der Stadtpatron in romanischen Reliefzyklen Oberitaliens* (Munich, 1998). On the *defensor* in the late Empire, see Richard M. Frakes, *Contra Potentium Iniurias: The Defensor Civitatis and Late Roman Justice* (Munich, 2001).

45 *CTh* 1.29.1 (368). See also *CTh* 1.29.2, 5, 7, 8; 11.8.3 (409).

municipality which has these officials; or let a report of what was given be forwarded to the Governor of that province.[46]

ET 53 Concerning *traditio*, it is necessary for it to be conducted according to the laws in the district: if a municipal magistrate, *defensor*, *duumviri*, and *quinquennales* are not available, three decurions shall be sufficient for executing the records of transfers, provided that the performance of the material conveyance is carried out before knowledgeable men in the neighborhood.[47]

If property changed hands through inheritance, sale, or gift, the new owner was held liable for the tax due the state, although the details for this remain unclear.[48] For the purposes of tax assessment, therefore, all transactions involving movables and immoveables had to be recorded in the *gesta municipalia* before the *defensor* and designated municipal magistrates.[49]

Cassiodorus' *formula* for the appointment of the position also underscores the role of the *defensor civitatis* as being responsible for the equitable collection of all tax revenues.[50] In this capacity, a *defensor* could be expected to fulfill any number of functions. For example, in a letter written in the name of Theoderic to the *possessores*, *defensores* and *curiales* of Aestunae, Cassiodorus has the King instruct the addressees to collect and ship off to Ravenna all unused blocks of marble found within their municipality.[51] Elsewhere, we are told that Theoderic instructed the *defensores* of Pavia to supply the neighbouring Heruli with ships for their voyage to the royal court.[52]

Alongside the *defensor civitatis* there existed certain other municipal magistrates that exercised jurisdiction in minor civil matters within the *civitas*. Both *ET* 52 and 53 mention two such officials – the *duumvir* and

[46] *ET* 52: "Si vero praedium rusticum aut urbanum quisquam libero arbitrio conferre voluerit, scriptura munificentiae etiam testium subscriptionibus roborata gestis municipalibus allegetur; ita ut confectioni gestorum praesentes adhibeantur tres curiales, et magistratus, et pro magistratu defensor civitatis cum tribus curialibus aut duumviri vel quinquennales: qui si defuerint, in alia civitate, quae haec habuerit, allegationis firmitas impleatur, aut apud iudicem eiusdem provinciae, quod donatum fuerit, allegetur."

[47] *ET* 53: "De traditione vero quam semper in locis secundum leges fieri necesse est, si magistratus, defensor, aut duumviri quinquennales forte defuerint, ad conficienda introductionem gesta tres sufficiant curiales: dummodo vicinis scientibus impleatur corporalis introductionis effectus."

[48] The *CTh* contains various regulations on tax records, from how to preserve and record them, to the techniques involved in authenticating them: e.g., *CTh* 5.15.20.1; 8.1.9 (368); 8.2.2 (370); 11.1.3 (366); 11.28.13 (422); 12.1.173 (109); 12.6.20 (386); 13.10.8 (383).

[49] On obligatory transfer of tax liability in the later Empire: *Fragmenta Vaticana* 35 (*c.* 330; *FIRA*, vol. *II*, 469–71); *CTh* 11.3.5 (391); *P-Ital* 10–11 (489). In Ostrogothic Italy: *ET* 144; Ernst Levy, *West Roman Vulgar Law: The Law of Property* (Philadelphia, 1952), 130; see also Walter Goffart, "From Roman Taxation to Mediaeval Seigneurie: Three Notes," *Speculum* 47 (1972), 165–87, esp. 92 n. 68, 170, 203 n. 59, 229 n. 43.

[50] Cass., *Var.* 7.11. [51] Cass., *Var.* 3.9. [52] Cass., *Var.* 4.45.

quinquennalis. The first of these was one of the two heads of the municipal government, which in the later Empire presided over the council, supervised the overall functioning of the municipal administration within individual cities, and provided the city with games and other forms of entertainment. The term *quinquennalis* appears to be a simple abbreviation for the *duumvir quinquennalis*, an official in the municipal administration who was elected every fifth year to perform the local census. As for other members of the municipal government, the *ET* makes no specific distinction, referring to them simply as decurions and curials.[53] Originally, a curial was a member of a municipality whose property and wealth made him eligible to serve as a decurion and as a municipal magistrate. During the Republic and early Empire, municipalities enjoyed a large measure of freedom, as autonomous, self-governing units. But in the later Empire, with the decline of municipalities and their loss of independence, the curial office became primarily a tool of the central government for its administration of the municipalities, for the collection of taxes and the enforcement of various compulsory public services such as the maintenance of the public post by supplying animals and provisions, and other onerous and often ruinous duties that were once the prerogative of the decurion. Such officers sought in every possible way to escape these crushing burdens, but were hunted down, arrested, brought back, and compelled to serve.[54]

As the *ET* confirms and some of the Ravenna papyri attest, city councils continued to function well into the sixth century. In fact, the Ravenna papyri preserve a number of certified copies of proceedings before local *curiae*, including those of Ravenna, Reate, and Syracuse, which range in date from 489 to 625. While documenting some of the minor functions of the *curia*, including the authentication of wills, the registration of conveyances involving real property, the approval of the appointment of guardians, and the performance of similar *quasi*-judicial functions, these records serve

[53] E.g., *ET* 27, 69, 113, 126.

[54] On laws forbidding the flight of curials, and the extreme steps taken by the state to ensure their continued service, see, e.g., *CTh* 12.18.1 (367), 12.1.71 (370), 12.1.76 (=*CJ* 10.32.31 (371)), On the decline of the decurion in general, see: Jones, *LRE*, 2, 737–57 and Arnold H. M Jones, "The Caste System in the Later Roman Empire," in Peter Brunt (ed.), *The Roman Economy* (Oxford, 1974), 396–418, esp. 397–8 and 413–16; Meyer Reinhold, "Usurpation of Status and Status Symbols in the Roman Empire," *Historia* 20 (1971), 275–302, esp. 299–301; Geza Alföldy, *The Social History of Rome*, trans. David Braund and Frank Pollock (Baltimore, MD, 1988) 201–2; MacMullen, *Corruption and the Decline of Rome*, 46–9; John H. W. G. Liebeschuetz, *The Decline and Fall of the Roman City* (Oxford, 2003), 104; Noel E. Lenski, *Failure of Empire: Valens and the Roman State in the Fourth Century* AD. (Berkeley, CA, 2002), 275.

as a striking testimony to the lasting legacy of this quintessentially Roman civic institution in the Italian peninsula.[55]

Ideally, the municipal *curia* were useful for dealing with petty cases, and provided members of the lower classes the means by which to obtain justice cheaply and promptly in their own cities. But this depended on the availability of such magistrates, and there is good reason to suppose that this was not necessarily the case. In *ET* 52 we read that donations involving moveables and immoveables were to be witnessed and a record drawn up in the presence of a specified number of municipal officers. But the provision includes the stipulation that in the absence of these, the witnessing of the transaction was to take place in another municipality where such officers could be found. This was an important departure from earlier Roman law on the subject, which generally required all transactions to be recorded on sight,[56] and speaks to the limited availability of civic magistrates in the rural towns and communities of Italy at this time.

In addition to these regular courts, Cassiodorus lists a large number of special courts that dealt with cases of a particular type or with matters concerning specific categories or ranks of persons. The vast majority of these courts operated under the old Roman principle of *praescriptio fori*, whereby a magistrate had jurisdiction over matters arising out of his departmental duties as well as jurisdiction to deal with his subordinates in matters of discipline.[57] The most important of special administrative courts were those of the imperial treasury. A court of this type was, for example, the court of the *rationalis*, the magistrate who represented the public treasury in a diocese, which tried cases involving disputes relating to taxation and other fiscal issues. A decision of the court of the *rationalis* could be appealed to the *comes sacrarum largitionum*, the minister in charge of state finances.[58] Cases involving disputes over crown property were dealt with by the *comes rei privatae* (or *comes rerum privatarum*), the official entrusted with the administration of the private property of the Emperor and the management of imperial lands.[59]

Apart from these, the other administrative courts were of minor importance. At Rome, the *praefecti annonnae*, for instance, had jurisdiction over

[55] Jan-Olof Tjäder, *Die nichtliterarischen Lateinischen Papyri Italiens aus der Zeit 445–700*, Acta Instituti Romani Regni Sueciae, series in 4° 19, (2 vols.; Uppsala, 1955; repr. Stockholm, 1982). For records of private ownership (no. 2, 178–83); wills (nos. 3, 4, 198–217); gifts (nos. 10–12, 279–99); bills of sale (nos. 29–34, 48–104); manumission (no. 9, 246–9); the appointment of guardians (no. 7, 228–34).

[56] See, e.g., *CTh* 8.12.1 (?323); *CTh* 8.12.8 (415).

[57] Jones, *LRE*, 1, 484–5.

[58] Cass., *Var.* 6.7 (*formula* for the Count of the Sacred Largesses).

[59] Cass., *Var.* 6.8; Wolfram, *History of the Goths*, 293.

matters involving trade and the supply and administration of foodstuffs.[60] The *comes formarum urbis*, Count of the Aqueducts, had judicial authority to settle disputes concerning water rights or the infraction of rules protecting the aqueducts.[61] Both Rome and Ravenna boasted *praefecti vigilum*, night watchmen, whose authority allowed them to deal with minor breaches of the peace. And in both capitals, the Count also possessed certain special jurisdictions: in Rome, the Count could arrest and prosecute anyone found stealing or otherwise defacing public property; the Count of Ravenna had the additional authority to exact a certain amount of forced labor from the owners of merchant vessels.[62]

Alongside these, Cassiodorus mentions several courts that oversaw cases involving individuals of a particular category or rank. In accordance with the rules of *praescriptio fori*, various categories of persons could claim, as defendants in minor cases and exceptionally as plaintiffs in civil proceedings, the jurisdiction of a court other than that of the province of their residence or where the offense was alleged to have taken place. The justification for this was based on the argument that the state was so dependent upon the services of the classes concerned that it could ill afford to have them put aside their duties to attend courts other than those of their chief officer.[63] Senators, for example, could rightly expect and lawfully demand such preferential treatment. Those domiciled within a one hundred mile radius of Rome were entitled to claim trial before the Prefect of the city, whether accused of crimes or sued in civil actions.[64] Doctors, too, received special consideration; disputes involving their number were to be settled by the Count of the Chief Physicians (*comes archiatrorum*).[65]

Members of the cloth were likewise permitted this privilege. In a letter written in Theoderic's name to the Bishop Peter, we are informed that the Bishop's court (*episcopalis audientia*) had jurisdiction over cases involving ecclesiastic officials:

> Therefore, We have come to learn the matter concerning you [i.e. Peter] through the lamentable petition of Germanus, who alleges that you detain from him a part of the property of his father Thomas which legally belongs to him . . . As it is proper that cases which concern you should first be remitted to you (so often employed as judges to settle the disputes of others), we call upon you to inquire into this claim swiftly, and if it be a just one to satisfy

[60] Cass., *Var.* 6.18 (*formula* for the office). [61] Cass., *Var.* 7.6 (*formula* for the office).
[62] Cass., *Var.* 7.7–8 (*formulae* for the Prefect of the Watch for Rome and Ravenna).
[63] Jones, *LRE*, 1, 487. [64] Cass., *Var.* 6.4 (*formula* for the Urban Prefect).
[65] Cass., *Var.* 6.19 (*formula* for the Count of the Chief Physicians).

> it. Know that if you fail to do justice yourself to the petitioner, his cause will be heard by Us.[66]

The Bishop was entitled to claim a portion of the estate in the event that the deceased died intestate.[67] But since no other details are provided, we are left to speculate as to whether or not this was the case

In similar fashion, Athalaric provided that in all civil matters pertaining to the clergy of Rome, the judge of first instance was to be the Pope:

> Therefore, considering both the honor of the Apostolic See and looking after the wish of the petitioners, We by the authority of this letter decree in regular course that if anyone should think that there is probable cause for any priest of the Roman clergy to be prosecuted, let him first present himself for hearing at the court of the most blessed Pope, in order that the latter may either decide between the two in his own holy manner, or may delegate the cause in the hope that it might be settled then.[68]

Anyone found to have circumvented the episcopal court was to be fined ten pounds of gold (to be dispensed to the poor), and any favorable judgment he may have received was to be reversed. Clerics, too, sometimes ignored the jurisdiction of the ecclesiastical court. In a letter to Theoderic's mother Ereliuva, Pope Gelasius complains of two clerics from Nola, Felix and Peter, who in 496 took their case to the King's court, keeping their clerical status

[66] Cass., *Var.* 3.37: "Atque ideo sanctitas vestra a Germano nos aditos flebili allegatione cognoscat, qui se filium legitimum asserit quondam Thomatis, dicens partem facultatis patris sui a vobis detineri sibimet legibus competentem . . . quam monetis, sine observationis longae dispendio debita tribuantur, quoniam causarum vestrarum qualitas vobis debet iudicibus terminari, a quo expectanda est magis quam vobis. imponenda iustitia. Quod si hanc causam sub aequitate vestrum minime definit arbitrium, noveritis supplicis querelam ad nostram audientiam perducendam . . . debita tribuantur, quoniam causarum vestrarum qualitas vobis debet iudicibus terminari." Despite the relative dearth of sources on the functioning of the Bishop's court in Late Antiquity, the subject has received extensive treatment in the secondary scholarship. See generally Claudia Rapp, *Holy Bishops in Late Antiquity: The Nature of Chiotian Leadership in an Age of Transitian* (Berkeley, CA, 2005), 242–52; John C. Lamoreaux, "Episcopal Courts in Late Antiquity," *JECS* 3 (1995), 143–67; Harries, *Law and Empire*, 191–211; Jill Harries, "Resolving Disputes: The Frontiers of Law in Late Antiquity," in R.W. Mathisen (ed.), *Law, Society and Authority in Late Antiquity*, (Oxford, 2007), 68–82; Noel Lenski, "Evidence for the *Audientia episcopalis* in the New Letters of Augustine," in Ralph. W. Mathisen (ed.), *Law, Society, and Authority in Late Antiquity*, (Oxford, 2007), 83–97; Michael Kaser, *Das römische Privatrecht, I: Das altrömische, das vorklassiche und klassiche Recht*, trans. Rolf Dannenbring, *Roman Private Law*, 6th edn. (London, 1968), 526–29. The most extensive work is that of Maria R. Cimma, *L'episcopalis audientia nelle constituzioni imperiali da Costantino à Giustiniano* (Turin, 1989).

[67] *ET* 26.

[68] Cass., *Var.* 8.24: "Atque ideo considerantes et apostolicae sedis honorem et consulentes desiderio supplicantum praesenti auctoritate moderato ordine definimus, ut, si quispiam ad Romanum clerum aliquem pertinentem in qualibet causa probabili crediderit actione pulsandum, ad beatissimi papae iudicium prius conveniat audiendus, ut aut ipse inter utrosque more suae sanctitatis cognoscat aut causam deleget aequitatis studio terminandam."

a secret. Upon discovering their true identities, Theoderic forced the reluctant clerics to follow jurisdictional protocol and be examined by the proper judge, namely Gelasius.[69]

The episcopal court had its drawbacks, the most obvious being the general ignorance of the Bishops in matters of secular law. Thus, as Theoderic makes clear in his letter to the Bishop Peter, a secular claimant who was dissatisfied by the decision of the episcopal court could appeal his case before a secular authority. The purpose of this was to give the Bishop the opportunity of settling the affair himself, and so to prevent the scandal of its appearing in the secular courts, which it assuredly would do if the Bishop were apathetic. Athalaric provided a similar safeguard: "And if, perchance, which it is impious to believe, the reasonable desire of the petitioner shall have been evaded, let him petition before the secular courts when he can prove that his petitions have been spurned by the Bishop of the aforementioned See."[70] But it is clear in this context how easily this would glide into something like immunity from secular tribunals, given that the appellant would have to satisfy the secular judge of a thing which it is almost impiety to believe, namely that the Bishop had spurned his petitions.

Much more important, however, were governmental officials and soldiers (whether they were liable for military service or not).[71] Insofar as officials at Ravenna lived and worked at the court, any jurisdictional privileges that they claimed were unlikely to cause much friction, and did not therefore give rise to legislation. Difficulties arose when they were dispatched into the provinces on official business, and it is in such circumstances that we hear of their privileges. Thus, for example, Theoderic confirmed that officers of the Praetorian Prefect were not subject to the jurisdiction of the provincial Governors: "Among his staff, he [i.e. the Praetorian Prefect] possesses special authority, and is known to command men of such standing that even provincial Governors do not presume to defy them in anything."[72]

As for the military courts, the structure which existed was not so complicated as that of the civil. At the top was the *magister militum*, a position which Theoderic himself took over following the removal of Odovacer from

69 Gelasius: Phillippe Jaffé (ed.), *Regesta Pontificum Romanorum*, 2 vols. (repr. Graz, 1956), 743 = *ep.* "Felix et Petrus," ed. Thiel, *Epistulae Romanorum Pontificum*, *frag.* 13, 490.

70 Cass., *Var.* 8.24.4: "et si forte, quod credi nefas est, competens desiderium fuerit petitoris elusum, tunc ad saecularia fora iurgaturus occurrat, quando suas petitiones probaverit a supradictae sedis praesule fuisse contemptas." Justinian similarly ruled that plaintiffs must first put their claims against the clergy before their Bishop.

71 Cass., *Var.* 5.29.

72 Cass., *Var.* 6.3.5: "in officio suo ius retinet singulare et talibus tantisque noscitur iubere, quos etiam provinciarum iudices non audeant in aliqua parte contemnere."

power.[73] Below this was the duke (*dux*), whose function was primarily one of military leadership, but the preservation of order through the enforcement of law was a concomitant role.[74] Such officers usually heard appeals levied against the decisions of the Gothic Count; and to them the responsibility to take action against the illegal exercise of judicial or executive authority fell. While in theory Theoderic exercised supreme jurisdiction in all matters related to the army, rarely did he do so. In most instances, appeals from the *duces* ran to the head of the civil service, the *magister officiorum*, who was in turn assisted by the Quaestor.

This complex system of special courts and privileged jurisdictions undoubtedly made the plaintiff's task of discovering in what court he should sue his adversary a difficult and daunting one, particularly if the latter belonged – or at least claimed to belong – to one of the various groups protected by the rules of *praescriptio fori*.[75] And judges were often equally confused as to what types of cases they had jurisdiction over. Thus, Athalaric had to remind the *comes* Gildilas of his jurisdictional limitations. In a letter to the Gothic Count the King instructed: "You [i.e. Gildilas] are alleged to have rendered judgment in your own court on matters involving two Romans, even against their will. If you know that these things have been done, do not presume [to do so] anymore, lest while you wish to incompetently seek judgment, you instead seem to be guilty."[76]

Indeed, the system was confusing enough if litigants and governmental officials had kept to the already intricate rules. But confusion no doubt was compounded by the general willingness of certain parties to circumvent the rules. Litigants who were wealthy or influential enough to grease the necessary palms or pull the right strings could secure the legal capacity to summon their adversaries before some court other than the one designated.[77] Ennodius (473/4–521), Bishop of Pavia and an occasional visitor to the court at Ravenna, wrote several letters that document these sorts of practices, and together underscore the importance of patronage in legal affairs.[78] One letter requested

[73] Arnold H. M. Jones, "The Constitutional Position of Odoacer and Theoderic," *JRS* 52 (1962), 128–9; Wolfram, *History of the Goths*, 288; Wilhelm Ensslin, *Theoderich der Grosse*, 2nd edn. (Munich, 1959), 76 and 93–5.

[74] Wolfram, *History of the Goths*, 291–2; Ensslin, *Theoderich*, 192.

[75] Jones, *LRE*, 1, 492.

[76] Cass., *Var.* 9.14.7: "Duorum negotia Romanorum etiam his invitis ad tuum diceris vocare iudicium: quae si cognoscis facta, ulterius non praesumas, ne dum vis iudicium incompetenter quaerere, reatum potius videaris invenire."

[77] Jones, *LRE* 1, 493.

[78] The majority of these letters, composed in Milan, date between 501 and 513. On the career of Ennodius and the dating of this works, see Stefanie A. H. Kennell, *Magnus Felix Ennodius: A Gentleman of the Church* (Ann Arbor, MI, 2000), 6–18; Richard Bartlett, "The Dating of

a Quaestor by the name of Festus to take care of a certain Bassus and assist him to present his petitions to the court.[79] Another asked the same Festus to help Venantius gain justice.[80] This officer's intervention again was sought in a lengthy and intractable lawsuit between a relative of Ennodius by the name of Julian, and one Marcellinus of Milan.[81] Another letter petitioned Festus on behalf of a religious woman;[82] and yet another requested his assistance for a certain Dalmatius who was attempting to establish his rights to a tract of territory in Sicily.[83] And on one occasion Ennodius recommended to his friend Stefanus, an abbot in southern Gaul, to send a representative, supplied with appropriate letters of recommendation, to Faustus at Ravenna in an attempt to forestall an unfavorable judgment, obtainable for a price, being rendered by the Milanese magistrates.[84] As these correspondences attest, friends at court, and more importantly the money to pay them, were crucial elements not only for obtaining a successful outcome, but also for having a case brought forward in the first place.[85]

In the courtroom

Throughout Late Antiquity it was the practice that all hearings, whether civil or criminal, were brought before a judge authorized by the state. In the early Empire this was not normally the case, particularly for criminal hearings where verdicts were delivered by juries. Gradually, however, hearings before a single judge became the standard practice in the provinces for all types of cases.[86] The fact that the same judge was expected to deal with any matter brought before him, criminal or civil provided that it fell within his jurisdiction, led to a merging of the two procedures, although the initial stages of bringing forward the suit retained an important difference: the

Ennodius' Writings," in Edoardo D'Angelo (ed.), *Atti della Seconda Giornata Ennodiana* (Naples, 2003), 53–74; and the introduction in Vogel's *MGH* edition (*AA* 7) (Berlin, 1885). Vogel's numbering system is used, with that of Hartel's supplied in brackets (below).

79 Enn., 25 (= *Ep* 1.20). 80 Enn., 137 (= *Ep*. 4.9). 81 Enn., 90 (= *Ep*. 3.20).

82 Enn., 115 (= *Ep*. 3.33). 83 Enn., 121 (= *Ep*. 4.5). 84 Enn., 150 (= *Ep*. 4.18).

85 All of these letters demonstrate in varying degree the extent to which a patron was expected to act on behalf of his clients – an exercise that entailed writing letters to the Quaestor, and no doubt bribery or other forms of corruption that could lead to the perversion of the course of justice. On the subject of patronage in Ennodius' letters, see Kennell, *Magnus felix Ennodius*, 20, 28, 32, 34, 46–8. On the content of these letters: Moorhead, *Theoderic in Italy*, 156–8; Peter Heather, *The Goths* (Oxford, 1996), 247. For a discussion of patronage and the importance of having court clout (*potentia*) and connections (*gratia*) in Late Antiquity, see Christopher Kelly, *Ruling the Later Roman Empire* (Cambridge, MA, 2004), 129–37. For traditional patronage structures in the Roman world see Andrew Wallace-Hadrill (ed.), *Patronage in Ancient Society* (London, 1989).

86 Harries, *Law and Empire*, 101; Jill Harries, "Violence, Victims, and the Legal Tradition in Late Antiquity," in H. A. Drake. (ed.), *Violence in Late Antiquity: Perceptions and Practices* (Burlington, VT: 2006), 85–102 at 85; Mousourakis, *The Historical and Institutional Context of Roman Law*, 365–78.

accuser in the criminal case had to bind himself by a written undertaking (*inscriptio*) to undergo the same penalty as that which faced the defendant if proved guilty; whereas in civil cases the plaintiff simply had to bear the expenses of the trial if his accusations proved groundless.[87]

From the early fifth century onwards, the preliminary stage in civil proceedings was the summoning of the defendant. When an action was initiated through the making of a formal accusation before a competent judge, it was his duty to summon the defendant and ensure his appearance in court. But there were limitations imposed upon him. For instance, a defendant could not be forcibly dragged to court:

> Let office staffs carry out the directives of any judges, as well as the commands of any office or jurisdiction, provided local custom of the *civitas* is observed; it is enough that the person sued promise to go before the court, and let the *apparitor* dare nothing beyond [extracting this promise – that is, he cannot compel attendance]. And let the *apparitor* of that jurisdiction from which the precepts are issued handle the judgments. But if a *miles* of another jurisdiction should attempt to implement the directive of another, let him be flogged and incur the loss of his position. And the plaintiff shall forthwith lose his case.[88]

Earlier Roman law on the subject included far more restrictions for summoning defendants to court. These included magistrates, priests or other religious officials, judges presiding over a case, litigants involved in another case, lunatics, children, a bride or bridegroom, or the relatives and guests at a funeral.[89] Moreover, a summons could not be issued against the duty to the gods (*pietas*), close relations, and patrons.[90] Defendants could not be forcibly removed from their homes, but could be summoned from the threshold of their houses, baths, or theaters.[91]

Once initiated, cases were to be settled in a timely fashion. Although there is no specific mention in our sources as to a statutory time limit for concluding a case, Cassiodorus has Theoderic remind the *vir spectabilis* Florianus that justice was to be swift: "Lawsuits are not to drag on forever. For how will peace be granted to the litigants, if trials are not settled by

[87] The basis for this is *CTh* 9.10.3 (319).

[88] *ET* 73: "Auctoritates quorumlibet iudicium, vel praecepta cuiuslibet sedis ac potestatis, sola publica servata civitate exequantur officia: et conventum sufficiat promittere, se ad iudicium esse venturum, nihil ultra praesumat apparitor. Et illius sedis apparitor executiones suscipiat, unde praecepta manaverint. Quod si alterius miles, alterius iudicis auctoritatem exsequi forte temptaverit, amissionem cinguli, fustibus caesus, incurrat: litigator autem negotium incunctanter amittat."

[89] *Dig.* 2.4.2–4. [90] *Dig.* 2.4.4–8. [91] *Dig.* 2.4.18.

lawful judgments?"[92] While the aim here was to keep the details of a case fresh in the minds of those involved and thereby ensure a fair conclusion, the course of justice was not always swift. That some delay was the inevitable result of the slowness and uncertainty of communications is clear.[93] Another reason for delay was no doubt the congestion of the courts on all levels – a perennial problem of the late imperial court system. Provincial Governors and lesser magistrates were preoccupied with the administrative duties of their respective offices, from tax collection to the maintenance of public works. That there was some delay in hearing of cases was an inevitable consequence of this.

But for some litigants, to be sure, it was advantageous to have the case drag on, and thus they devoted their efforts and money to ensuring this. This could be done in any number of ways, the easiest of which was simply not appearing to answer a charge in the first place.[94] If the defendant was persistently absent, however, the hearing could take place without him:

> A judgment delivered against parties not present shall be of no consequence, unless it is shown to have been rendered against an individual who, despite being summoned and formally called upon for the third time by judicial directives, has refused to appear [in court].[95]

According to the provision, the accused could not be condemned *in absentia* (but it does not preclude any process from taking place). Second, no one was to be condemned merely on suspicion. Third, where the guilty was deliberately absent, judgment could be rendered against him as it would in a civil case. Under Roman law, penalties that could be imposed on the contumacious absentee could include a fine, loss of status/reputation, and in some cases exile; and for crimes where the punishment was severe, such as condemnation to the mines or death, no reprieve would be given. An exception to this was afforded Goths who could prove their status as soldiers in active military service. At the summons stage they were permitted to provide a written guarantee for appearance. Concerning contumacious barbarians, *ET* 145 makes reference to the reliability of their (presumably

[92] Cass., *Var.* 1.5: "In inmensuns trahi non decet finita litigia. Quae enim dabitur discordantibus pax, si nec legitimis sententiis adquiescant?"

[93] On the challenges of communication in the later Empire and early medieval West, see Kelly, *Ruling the Later Roman Empire*, 115–27; Andrew Gillett, *Envoys and Political Communication in the Late Antique West, 411–533* (Cambridge, 2003).

[94] For this and other kinds of delaying tactics used by litigants in the Empire, see Ernest Metzger, *Litigation in Roman Law* (Oxford, 2005), chapters 5–7.

[95] *ET* 5: "Sententia non praesentibus partibus dicta nullius momenti sit, nisi adversus eum prolata doceatur, qui tertio conventus et edictis sollemniter inclamatus adesse contempserit." Similarly, *ET* 145 (concerning recalcitrant barbarians).

written) guarantee – "*cautionis ab eodem emissae fides.*" Here, a barbarian could avoid the penalties for contumacy provided that the reliability of his guarantee, or the testimony of freeborn and honorable men, confirmed that he was a *capillatus* and that his previous absences were the result of his role as a soldier, and not simply a willful act of contempt towards the court.[96] There is simply no way of telling how prevalent the issue of contumacy was in Late Antiquity. That courts would prefer to levy fines, which could be collected relatively easily from the auctioning off of household goods left behind by the contumacious individual, rather than spend the time and effort in tracking down such individuals is likely.

A further source of delay, according to contemporary opinion, was the ingenuity of the corrupt lawyer. Lawyers, it was believed, fully exploited the ambiguity and uncertainty of the law and the conflicting jurisdictions of the courts to prolong proceedings, whether to increase their own fees or in the interest of clients who had weak cases but deep pockets. For the sorts of time-consuming tactics that could be employed by members of the legal profession, the fourth-century historian Ammianus Marcellinus provides an insightful commentary in his *Res Gestae* (completed at Rome in the 390s):

> A third group [of lawyers] consists of those who, in order to gain eminence in their vexatious profession, sharpen their venal tongues to attack the truth, and with shameless brow and base yelping often gain entrance wherever they wish. When the anxious judges are distracted by many cares, they tie up the business in an inexplicable tangle, and undertake to involve all peace and quiet in lawsuits and purposely by knotty inquisitions they tie up the courts, which, when they operate correctly, are temples of justice, when corrupted, are deceptive and hidden pits: if anyone is ensnared and falls into such pits, he will not escape except after many a term of years, when he has been sucked dry to his very marrow.[97]

An anecdote told of Theoderic, while certainly apocryphal, is revealing of this popular sentiment. A widow of senatorial rank, named Juvenalia, had grown old while awaiting the outcome of a lawsuit against a certain patrician

[96] Wolfram, *History of the Goths*, 102–3, 301–2; Amory, *People and Identity*, 94, 319, 345–6; Arne Søby Christensen, *Cassiodorus, Jordanes and the History of the Goths: Studies in a Migratian Myth* (Copenhapen, 2002), 245–6.

[97] Amm. Mar. 30.4.13: "Tertius eorum est ordo, qui ut in professione turbulenta clarescant, ad expugnandam veritatem ora mercenaria procudentes, per prostitutas frontes vilesque latratus, quo velint, aditus sibi patefaciunt crebros: qui inter sollicitudines iudicum per multa distentas inresolubili nexu vincientes negotia, laborant, ut omnis quies litibus inplicetur, et nodosis quaestionibus de industria iudicia circumscribunt, quae cum recte procedunt, delubra sunt aequitatis: cum depravantur, foveae fallaces et caecae: in quas si captus ceciderit quisquam, non nisi per multa exiliet lustra, ad usque ipsas medullas exsuctus."

named Firmus. Having waited thirty years, she appealed directly to the King to hasten the litigation. Theoderic then issued an ultimatum granting the lawyers only two more days to resolve the dispute. Having been so inspired, they settled the suit forthwith. When Juvenalia came to thank Theoderic shortly thereafter, he promptly summoned the litigators and asked how they could accomplish in two days what was impossible to do in thirty years. Unsatisfied with their response he had them executed.[98]

Before any actual hearing could begin, determination as to the competence of the court and the legal qualifications of the litigants had to be made. With the exception of serious cases and in situations where an individual was permitted special consideration under the privileges of *praescriptio fori*, the general rule was that trials took place in the province or place of residence of the defendant. When the status of the participants was established, the hearing began. As to how the formal arguing of the case proceeded, we are little informed; records of specific cases in the form of charters or *placita* do not survive for early sixth-century Italy. As for the Ravenna papyri, these documents have traditionally received attention more for their form than for their content. Here, the problem lies in distinguishing the form of the recording document from the substance of the recorded dispute. And while they are useful as a record for the continuance of civic involvement in the arbitration of private disputes under the Ostrogothic regime, ultimately they bring us no closer to understanding the actual mechanisms involved. And while law is at best an imprecise guide, both the *ET* and *Variae* provide enough information, in the form of procedural rules and general summaries of cases, to provide a rough outline.

While the burden of proof rested upon the plaintiff,[99] evidence was heard from both sides: "When the claims and proofs of each party have been examined, a judge must render a decision only on that which he perceives to be in accordance with justice and law."[100] Advocates or the litigants themselves put forward the cases, to be sure with the appropriate amount of rhetorical flourish, during which the basic points and arguments were established, followed then by the rebuttal. That advocates played a pivotal

98 On the details of this case, see John Malalas, *Chronographia* 384, ed. Ludwig Dindorf (Bonn, 1831); trans. (with new material and improved apparatus) Elizabeth Jeffreys, Michael Jeffreys, and Roger Scott (eds.), *The Chronicle of John Malalas* (Melbourne, 1986); Jones, *LRE*, 1, 494.

99 Particularly clear from *ET* 13, 74, 96, 100 and 132.

100 *ET* 7: "Iudex discussis utriusque partis suggestionibus atque documentis id solum iudicare debet, quod iuri et legibus viderit convenire."

role in court proceedings is attested to by Cassiodorus, who on several occasions extols their eloquence as a powerful tool for directing the course of affairs.[101] In at least one case the juristic and forensic skills of an ancient day Perry Mason played a determining role in the outcome of the trial. In a letter written in the name of the King to Adeodatus, wrongly convicted for the crime of rape, Cassiodorus attributes the current predicament of the addressee to his being deprived the services of an advocate, and thus rendered defenseless against the rhetorical skills and legal knowledge of his adversaries: "Moreover, [your suit] alleges that justice was unavailable [to you], adding that you were deprived the protection of legal representatives, while your adversaries, flourishing with [legal] skill, were able to entangle you with the laws, despite your innocence."[102]

During the proceedings, various kinds of evidence could be produced to support particular points, accompanied by extensive cross-examination by the *iudex*, who could be aided in this by a team of advisors, or assessors.[103] Witnesses and documents were the prime sources of evidence. Documents had been an essential tool of the Roman government since the Republic.[104] And over the course of the Empire, as the administration became more reliant on the use of documents to manage an increasingly cumbersome bureaucracy, the written word was accorded even greater significance in the courtroom as a means of establishing proof.[105] As some Ravenna papyri illustrate, copies of land records, wills, donations, bills of sale, and any legal decisions indicating rights were regularly filed in the municipal archives both for permanent safekeeping, and in accordance with the rules governing tax liability.[106] But the public records also functioned as archives of legal transactions/agreements of every kind, and could be consulted by any interested party and used in court as a means of verifying claims of ownership or some other legal right/privilege. Together, they demonstrate that documents continued to play an important part in court proceedings in early sixth-century Italy, whether as a

[101] E.g., Cass., *Var.* 1.12; 4.3; 5.4; 5.22.

[102] Cass., *Var.* 3.46: "illud etiam, quod minime iustitia pateretur, adiciens defensorum tibi patrocinia saepius postulanti fuisse subtracta, cum adversarii florentes ingenio etiam innocentem te possent legum laqueis obligare."

[103] Cass., *Var.* 4.12 (on the appointment of assessors). For the use of *assessores* in the imperial judicial system, see the introductory notes of Detlef Liebs in his *Vor den Richtern Roms. Berühmte Prozesse der Antike* (Munich, 2007). On the continuation of this institution in Late Antiquity, see Humfress, *Orthodoxy and the Courts*, chapter 3.

[104] Elizabeth A. Meyer, *Legitimacy and Law in the Roman World.* Tabulae *in Roman Belief and Practice* (Cambridge, 2004), 38–43, 209–10, 218–27.

[105] Meyer, *Legitimacy and Law*, 79–86, 112–20, 227–49; Harries, *Law and Empire*, 99–110.

[106] Tjäder, *P-Ital*: private ownership (no. 2, 178–83); wills (nos. 3, 4, 198–217); gifts (nos. 10–12, 279–99); bills of sale (nos. 29–34, 48–104).

means of establishing proof of ownership or fulfilling some other probative purpose in a trial.[107]

For certain civil matters – including, for example, land claims, testation and inheritance, custody and so on – written documentation was arguably the more common form of evidence for determining points of fact. It is difficult to ascertain the extent of lay education at this time, but the frequency of references in our sources to written documents and records of one sort or another, and to witnesses who signed these in their own hands rather than made their marks (*signum*) upon them, perhaps indicates that elementary instruction in reading and writing was relatively commonplace; or at the very least, that *illiterati* had regular access to one of their number who could meet the basic requirements of the law, which in most cases assumed a rudimentary level of literacy.[108] For example, the suitability of a testator rested in large part on his ability to read and write:

> If a testator is unable to provide his subscription because he is either illiterate or gravely ill, then there shall be summoned on his behalf an eighth witness

[107] The use of municipal records was an extremely formal, albeit elaborate, process that was wholly in keeping with late imperial tradition (e.g., *CTh* 14.15.2; *Nov. Val.* 15.1. and 3). In contrast, the medieval practice was for individuals or institutions to be issued charters by monarchs or other officials of exalted status, such as Bishops. Under these circumstances, archives were largely individualized, if not necessarily private. See further Peter Classen, "Kaiserrescript und Königsurkunde: Diplomatische Studien zum römisch-germanischen Kontinuitätsproblem," vol. 2 *Archiv für Diplomatik* 2 (1956), 1–115; Peter Classen, "Spätrömischen Grundlagen mittelalterlichen Kanzlein," (1974), reprinted in J. Fleckenstein (ed.), *Ausgewählte Aufsätze von Peter Classen*, Vortäge und Forschungen 28 (Sigmaringen, 1983), 67–84; Peter Classen, "Fortleben und Wandel spätrömischen Urkundenwesens im frühen Mittelalter," in Peter Classen (ed.), *Recht und Schrift im Mittelalter*, Vorträge und Forschungen 23 (Sigmaringen, 1977), 13–54; Ernst Posner, *Archives in the Ancient World* (Cambridge, 1972); Harries, *Law and Empire*, 70–1.

[108] A very notable exception appears to have been Theoderic himself. The Anonymous Valesianus alleges (14.79): "Now King Theoderic was illiterate and of such obtuse comprehension that for ten years of his reign he had been completely unable to learn the four letters necessary for endorsing his edicts. Wherefore he commissioned a golden plate with slits to be made, containing the four letters 'legi' ['I have read (it)']; then, if he wished to endorse anything, he placed the plate over the paper and drew his pen through the slits, so that only this subscription of his was seen." ("igitur rex Theodericus illiteratus erat et sic obtuso sensu, ut in decem annos regni sui quattuor litteras subscriptionis edicti sui discere nullatenus potuisset. De qua re laminam auream iussit interrasilem fieri, quattuor litteras 'legi' habentem; unde si subscribere voluisset, posita lamina super chartam, per eam pennam ducebat, ut subscriptio eius tantum videretur.") Procopius relates a similar story of the Emperor Justin. Soon after his accession, the historian claims that the Emperor, because of his illiteracy, had his officials prepare for him a stencil with the Latin word "legi" cut into it. That Theoderic and Justin both used such an implement is unlikely. For discussion see Wilhelm Ensslin, "Rex Theodericus inlitteratus?" *Historisches Jahrbuch* 60 (1940), 391–6; Stein, *Histoire du Bas-empire*, 719–20; Herbert Grundmann, "Litteratus-illiteratus," *Archiv für Kulturgeschichte* 40 (1958), 1–65 at 24–30; Barry Baldwin, "Illiterate Emperors," *Historia* 38 (1989), 124–6. For literacy in the barbarian successor kingdoms, see Peter Heather, "Literacy and Power in the Migration Period," in A. K. Bowman and Greg Woolf (eds.), *Literacy and Power in the Ancient Roman World* (Cambridge, 1994), 177–97.

> whose credibility cannot be challenged in any way. But let witnesses, and particularly the testator himself, know that if, under examination [of the document] anything should be proven false, they shall not be able to avoid the punishment which the authority of the laws concerning forgers stipulates.[109]

In the event that the individual was unable to provide his subscription, an additional witness (of suitable character) was summoned to confirm the validity of the document.

In the later Empire handwriting experts could be used to determine the authenticity of a document.[110] That such forensic skills were available in the sixth century is confirmed by Gregory of Tours. In his account of the trial of Bishop Egidius of Rheims in 590, who was accused of improperly receiving gifts from King Chilperic I (561–84), the historian recounts how the *referendarius* Otto was able to prove on paleographical grounds that the validating signature used to authenticate the Bishop's deed of ownership was a forgery.[111] Egidius was then accused of sending treasonable letters to the same King. This he denied, but an examination of the letters in question proved that they were written by the Bishop.

Despite the importance of the written word, oral testimony remained invaluable. In many instances, to be sure, it was witnesses who provided the bulk of evidence. There is little in our sources concerning witnesses. Obviously, they had to present themselves in person and were questioned by the judge, who then made the decision as to who were the more credible. As to how many witnesses were required to determine a point of fact, there is no mention; but a general rule observed in the later Empire required that more than one witness was necessary for this.[112] Evidently, as was the practice in the later Empire, witnesses in most cases provided sworn depositions of what they knew. In his description of the case of the extravagant widow Aetheria, accused by her former mother-in-law Archotamia of squandering the property of her children, Cassiodorus

109 *ET* 29: "Quod si testator aut literas ignorando aut per necessitatem vicinae mortis propriam subscriptionem non potuerit commodare, tunc octavus testis pro testatore adhibeatur huiusmodi, de cuius fide dubitari omnino non possit: scituris testibus et scriptore praecipue testamenti, quod si quis falsitatis extiterit, sub cognitione decursa se supplicium evadere non posse, quod circa falsarios legum dictat auctoritas."

110 *CTh* 2.27.1; 9.19.2; *CJ* 4.21.20.3.

111 Gregory of Tours, *Decem Libri Historiarum*, 10.19, ed. Bruno Krusch and Wilhelm Levison, *MGH SRM*, 1.1, 2nd edn. (Hanover, 51). For accusations of tampering with wills, see 4.51; 6.46.

112 *Dig.* 22.5.12 (Ulpian), that when the number of witnesses required was not specified, two would suffice.

notes that a copy of the Gospels was to be present in court before the proceedings began – presumably for the swearing in of witnesses:

> Therefore, We, who have been accustomed to turn down the pleas of supplicants (although We neither reject the insinuation of supplicants nor arbitrarily condemn the case of an adversary) have entrusted this case to your judgment to be decided according to the laws; when you have removed all hostility and placed the holy Gospels in the open, with three honorable men knowledgeable in the law and elected by the consent of the parties, fulfill before them that which the precedent of ancient law calls for, while at the same time remaining mindful of the law of Our time, since it does not befit those who deserve to come to Our stewardship to do anything by force.[113]

The two presiding judges, the Goth Marabad, *vir illustris* and *comes*, and the Roman Senator Gemellus, were instructed to restore order to the proceedings (*omni incivilitate summota*) and bring in a copy of the Gospels, in addition to three *assessors* (agreed upon by the litigants) to settle the dispute.

On the use of the Gospels in court proceedings, the Emperor Justinian issued a decree in 530 (*CJ* 3.1.13.4) that required a copy of the text (*scripturae terribiles*) to be present during contumacius proceedings (that is, trials where one of the litigants was absent). The copy was to compensate for the absent litigant. In the same year, he issued a constitution (*CJ* 3.1.14) that required a copy of the *scripturae sacrosanctae* to be placed before the judge where the suit was to be settled according to Roman law; the copy was to remain for the duration of the trial.[114] That the Gospels became the standard text for procedural oath swearing in the sixth century was perhaps due to the fact that they embodied the teachings of Jesus Christ more faithfully than any other text, and in essence became a sort of *Lex Christiana* – a Christian law based on the New Testament – which all faithful and observing Christians

[113] Cass., *Var.* 4.12: "Ideoque nos, qui desideria supplicantum consuevimus remittere ad statuta divalium sanctionum, ut nec insinuationem supplicum renuamus nec adversarii negotium credula facilitate damnemus, sublimitatis vestrae iudicio hanc causam legibus committimus audiendam, ut omni incivilitate summota mediis sacrosanctis evangeliis cum tribus honoratis, quos partium consensus elegerit, qui legum possint habere notitiam, quicquid prisci iuris forma constituit inter eos, considerata disciplina nostri temporis, proferatis, quia non decet per vim eos aliquid agere, qui ad nostra meruerunt regimina pervenire."

[114] Caroline Humfress, "Judging by the Book: Christian Codices and Late Antique Legal Culture," in William E. Klingshirn and Linda Safran (eds.), *The Early Christian Book* (Washington, DC, 2007), 141–58, esp. 148–50. In Lombard law from the middle of the seventh century onwards, greater emphasis was placed on oaths sworn upon a copy of the Gospels, as opposed to the alternative of swearing oaths upon arms. See Nicholas Everett, *Literacy in Lombard Italy (568–774)* (Cambridge, 2003), 171. On the subject of sworn witnesses in Roman law, see Jolowicz and Nicholas, *Roman Law*, 462.

were required to obey, and through which eternal damnation could be secured in the event that they committed perjury.

Attempts were made to ensure fairness by excluding certain categories of witnesses. While the jurists provided an extensive list of excluded categories, including freedmen of the litigants, the under-age, beast-fighters, prostitutes, and advocates involved in the case,[115] the compilers mentioned only slaves, *originarii*, and freedmen, who were prohibited from testifying against their current or former masters and their family:

> We prohibit freedmen, *originarii*, or slaves who inform against their patrons or the children of these patrons from being heard in any matter; for, persons of this sort are incapable of having a legitimate voice in civil or criminal cases involving their patrons, masters, or their children, even if they speak in their defense; those caught in the act must be cut down with swords at the commencement of the suit.[116]

Evidence from slaves occasionally could be admitted in cases involving serious or capital crimes; but, as was the case with earlier imperial legislation, torture was necessary for such testimony to be considered valid.[117] Interestingly, the general prohibition against slaves or freedmen from testifying in matters involving current or former masters seems to have created an unintended consequence whereby individuals sought to achieve some form of immunity through the purchase or sale of a slave for the express purpose of preventing him from testifying. Thus, *ET* 101 voided any such sale, and required the slave to testify under torture against the fraudulent buyer. In the same way, *ET* 102 allowed for a freedman to testify under torture against his manumittor.

Only under exceptional circumstances, when their information was regarded as essential to a case, were informers (*delatores*) permitted to testify, and always at their extreme peril: if an informer was unable to prove the information which he had laid under torture, he was to be burned alive.[118] While these sorts of restrictions were intended to ensure fairness, they are proof of the continuance of one of the long-held peculiarities of the Roman justice system, namely that the credibility of a witness' testimony was based in large part on his or her social status.[119] That this sort of practice could

[115] E.g., *Dig.* 22.5.3.5; 5.9; 5.10; 5.19; 5.25.

[116] *ET* 48: "Libertos originarios, vel servos, dominos aut patronos suos eorumque liberos deferentes, in quolibet negotio prohibemus audiri: quia huiusmodi personae neque in civilibus neque in criminalibus causis contra patronos aut dominos eorumque liberos, etiamsi pro his dicant, vocem possunt habere legitimam; quos in huiusmodi facto deprehensos, in ipso actionis exordio gladiis oportet extingui."

[117] E.g., *ET* 19, 100. [118] *ET* 35. [119] E.g., *CTh* 11.39.3.

easily be abused to the detriment of the poorer and less well-connected litigant goes without saying.

In the event that manifest proof was lacking, the judge could administer an oath. While the details of the process are obscured, *ET* 106 addresses the matter of oath-taking:

> Whenever an oath is used to determine the outcome of some legal matter, whether in accordance with the consent of the litigants or the determination of the judge, the matter cannot be reconsidered; nor is it permitted for anyone to bring an action or start an inquiry concerning the possibility of perjury.[120]

The use of oaths to resolve disputes seems quintessentially barbarian, but it was, in fact, a common procedure in Roman law as well. As Ulpian described the procedure, the defendant was asked by the judge to take the oath. In the event that he refused, he either had to make restitution or to have the judgment go against him. If he agreed, the oath was then offered to the plaintiff, who also had to swear; if he did, he won the case, if not he lost.[121] Here, the purpose of the oath was evidentiary or probative in nature, with its function the basic one of resolving the question as to which party was telling the truth, and therefore deserving of a favorable judgment. Nevertheless, the law recognized that the distant sanction of lost salvation that threatened an oath-taker in the event that he lied, although as effective a deterrent as could be found, was no sure guarantee against perjury. Thus, it was the responsibility of the judge concerned to determine in which cases and by whom an oath should be taken. To maintain the integrity of the institution, a case determined by oath could not be reopened on the grounds that the declarent had committed perjury. There is nothing in our

120 *ET* 106: "Quotiens aliquod negotium consensu litigantium aut sententia iudicis sacramentis fuerit diffinitum, retractari non poterit: nec de periurio agere cuiquam vel movere permittitur quaestionem."

121 *Dig.* 12.2.34 (9). Furthermore, Gaius wrote in his *On the Provincial Edict* (*Dig.* 12.2.1): "Conscientious oath-taking is relied upon as an important means of shortening litigation. Disputes are settled in this way by virtue of agreement between litigants or on the authority of a judge." ("Maximum remedium expediendarum litium in usum venit iurisiurandi religio, qua vel ex pactione ipsorum litigatorum vel ex auctoritate iudicis deciduntur controversiae.") He continues (*Dig.* 12.2.31): "It is a frequent practice of judges in doubtful cases to pronounce, after an oath has been exacted, in favor of the party swearing." ("solent enim saepe iudices in dubiis causis exacto iureiurando secundum eum iudicare qui iuraverit.") The jurist Paul stated that (lib. 18 *ad Edict.* (*Dig.* 12.2.2)): "The taking of an oath is a species of settlement and has greater authority than a judgment." ("Iusiurandum speciem transactionis continet maioremque habet auctoritatem quam res iudicata"); and that (lib. 37 *ad Edict.* (*Dig.* 12.2.38)): "It is an indication of manifest wickedness and an admission to refuse to swear or to counter claim." ("Manifestae turpitudinis et confessionis est nolle nec iurare nec iusiurandum referre.")

sources to suggest that oath-helpers – a necessary component of oath-taking as a legitimate method of proof in most other barbarian law codes – played a role. In Burgundian law, for instance, proof depended entirely on the accused being permitted, prepared, and able to swear with at least twelve other oath-takers (*Liber Constitutionum*, viii.1). This pattern is similar to that in the *Pactus Legis Salicae*, although there are variations in the numbers of oath-takers (*iuratores*) required.[122]

On the basis of evidence, whether in the form of records, testimony of witnesses and exceptionally informers, or the oaths of the participants themselves, the judge then rendered his decision. *ET* 6 required that the verdict be written down, or else it was considered invalid. Concerning this requirement, Cassiodorus remarks in a letter to the tax-collector Joannes: "Rightly did Antiquity ordain that a large store of paper should be laid in by Our bureau (*scrinia*), that litigants might receive the decision of the judge clearly written, without delay, and without avaricious and impudent charges for the paper which bore it."[123] And *ET* 64 instructed the *iudex* to be mindful of his written statement (*periculum*) when carrying out his judgment. An exception to this rule was permitted to the Praetorian Prefect, whose *formula* for appointment (*Var.* 6.3) makes clear that the officer could render his verdict orally (*verbo sententiam dicit*) without the requirement of a written record, since he was considered to be representing the King in person.

There were several reasons for the recording of the verdict. One was to determine that the judge had rendered his decision fairly; if he had failed to do so, he could be held accountable. Second, the transcript would document all the arguments and legal points of the case. Concerned parties undoubtedly kept a record of this in the local archives, to protect themselves in the event of future contestation. The third purpose was to provide a full record for a higher court in the event that the decision was appealed. In theory, all decisions could be appealed before a higher court, but realistically only those with enough time and sufficiently deep pockets could afford the costs that such protracted litigation would entail.

[122] *Pactus Legis Salicae*, ed. K. A. Eckhardt, *MGH Leges nationum Germanicarum* 4.1 (Hannover, 1962), xiv.2, 3; xlii.5; lxxix and cii (*Decretus Childeberti regis*); cxi (*Edictus Chilperici*); ii.5 (*Decretus Childeberti*).

[123] Cass., *Var.* 11.38: "Moderatrix rerum omnium diligenter consideravit antiquitas, ut, quoniam erat plurimis per nostra scrinia consulendum, copia non deesset procurata chartarum, quatinus, cum iudices multis profutura decernerent, odiosas moras dulcia beneficia non haberent." On the use of the written decision in late imperial judicial proceedings, see André Piganiol, *L'Empire chrétien* (Paris, 1947), 378; Classen, "Fortleben und Wandel," 14–15, 51–2; Harries, *Law and Empire*, 110.

Appeal

From Constantine onwards, litigants who were unsatisfied with the decision of the presiding magistrate could appeal their case to the higher courts of the *vicarii* (with authority delegated by the Praetorian Prefects), and above those the courts of the Praetorian and Urban Prefects (all of whom judged in place of the Emperor), and finally the Emperors themselves. To ensure that only those qualified to appeal did so, that procedures were correctly followed, and that delays were minimized, the Emperors issued detailed and complex laws governing the rules of appeal which are preserved in a lengthy section of Book XI of the *Theodosian Code*. Only under exceptional circumstances could a judge refuse to hear an appeal. For instance, an individual convicted on the basis of a confession or manifest proofs could not appeal in a bid to prolong his or her life. To prevent the delay of payment, public debtors were likewise prohibited from appealing. And appeals could only be launched once the whole case had been heard and judgment rendered. Provincial Governors especially were obliged by the law to allow appeals against their judgments, and faced harsh penalties if they threatened defeated parties or ignored their protests.[124]

Such rules demonstrate that the right of appeal was considered by imperial legislators as an essential tool for limiting perceived instances of judicial corruption or misconduct at the local level. In drawing from them, the compilers focused exclusively on the issue of corrupt procrastination or refusal of the provincial Governor to hear an appeal (even superfluous ones):

> Those provincial judges before whom pleas can be petitioned shall hear all appeals; since it befits their unsurpassed knowledge to hear even a superfluous appeal without hesitation, provided that an ordained *cognitor*, upon consideration of the laws, can render a judgment about the merit of an appeal. If a judge should secure his absence so as not to hear appellate petitions, We decree that he who intended to make an appeal must present his petition concerning the absence of the judge, and about his own appeal in well-known places. But let a judge who either refuses to hear an appeal, or at least takes the appellant into custody, or has him flogged or injured by some other grievance, be punished with the loss of ten pounds of gold; this sum We ordain to be amassed by the care of an ordained *cognitor* for the coffers of

[124] E.g., *CTh* 11.30. See also *Dig.* 49.1–13, *CTh* 1.5.1–4, *CJ* 7.62–70, *Nov. Iust.* 23, and *Nov. Iust.* 115.1–2. Federico Pergami, *L'appello nella legislazione del tardo impero, AARC, Materiali per una palingenesi delle costituzioni tardo-imperiali*, serie terza 2 (Milan, 2000); Matthews, *Laying Down the Law*, 201–21; Harries, *Law and Empire*, 111–12; Humfress, *Orthodoxy and the Courts*, 50–1.

> the fisc. Moreover, the office for which this is a concern will be subject to a lawful penalty.[125]

This is in keeping with the emergence in the later Empire of legislation designed to make officials and judges more accountable for their actions – or inactions – as the case may be.

By about the middle of the fourth century, judges and their staff could face fines for delays in forwarding appeals or refusing to hear them altogether. The latter was regarded as a particularly serious offense. In a rescript of 343, Constantius II made the judge answerable to a fine of ten pounds of gold, his staff for fifteen:

> Let all Governors be admonished that if any person should recognize that he has need of an appeal, they must accept the petitions for appeal according to custom and the order of the law, and they must transmit them to those judges who regularly hear appeals. Nor shall they deter appellants by infliction of injuries and deprive them of the assistance of a necessary defense. For We impose the burden of the present fine, namely that the judge who has failed to accept the appeal shall pay ten pounds of gold and his office staff fifteen.[126]

In 385, the Emperors Gratian, Valentinian II, and Theodosius I decreed that if a litigant could prove that his case had been unjustly denied or deferred through a judge's "arrogance" or "favoritism," the judge was fined the value of the sum in dispute (to be paid to the fisc), and the head of his office staff would be deported.[127] Valentinian II followed this up in 392 with a decree that imposed a fine of thirty pounds of gold on the judge, and fifty on his office staff for not properly advising the judge.[128]

ET 55 follows Constantius' imperial rescript of 343 closely. It restricts the liability of the judge to ten pounds and his staff to an unspecified but lawful penalty (presumably the fifteen pounds stipulated in *CTh* 11.30.22).

[125] *ET* 55: "Omnes appellationes suscipiant ii provinciarum iudices, a quibus provocari potest: quando optimae conscientiae conveniat etiam superfluam appellationem sine dubitatione suscipere, dum de appellationis merito sacer possit perpensis legibus cognitor iudicare. Quod si iudex suam absentiam procuravit, ne appellatorios libellos accipiat: in locis celeberrimis, qui appellare voluerit, libellum de absentia iudicis et de sua appellatione exhibere debere censemus. Iudex autem, qui aut suscipere appellationem contempserit, aut certe in custodiam dederit, aut verberaverit, aut aliquo dispendio laeserit appellantem, decem librarum auri amissione feriatur, quas fisci compendiis cura sacri cognitoris praecipimus aggregari; officium quoque, cuius interest, mulctae legitimae subiacebit."

[126] *CTh* 11.30.22: "omnes praesides moneantur, ut, si quis provocatione sibi opus esse cognoscit, iuxta morem ordinemque legum accipiant libellos et ad eos qui consuerunt audire transmittant, nec appellantes iniuriarum adflictatione deterritos a suffragio necessariae defensionis expellant. imponimus enim praesentis multae fascem, ut iudex, qui suscipere neglexerit, auri libras x et officium eius quindecim pendat."

[127] *CTh* 2.1.6. [128] *CTh* 11.30.51.

But there are important points of difference between the two. First, the provision makes a differentiation between judges who simply failed to appear and those who corruptly refused to hear an appellant. In the event of the former scenario, the appellant was required to bring the matter of the no-show judge and the original appeal to the public's attention in well-known places (*in locis celeberrimis*). There is no parallel for this in any of the detailed rules of appeal preserved in the *Theodosian Code*. Second, whereas the rescript of Constantius admonishes judges who deter appellants "by infliction of outrages and deprive them of the aid of necessary defense," *ET* 55 elaborates on this to specify judges who imprison, beat, or otherwise injure the appellant in any way. The provision also goes beyond the rescript by giving a general outline of how the fine was to be exacted. A provincial Governor, *cognitor* (presumably appointed for the task by the office of the Praetorian Prefecture), was to ensure that the fine went to the fisc. The same officer is instructed in the first part of the provision to hold a cognizance trial to determine the merits of the appeal. But we are entitled to ask just how effective such a system was that relied on Governors to watch over and enforce judgment on their own peers.

Crime and punishment

When it came to *crimina*, that is, criminal offenses such as murder, kidnapping, robbery, arson, and so on, the stakes were much higher, both for the accused and accuser. Not only were the prescribed forms of punishment for *crimina* much harsher than those for *delicta*, that is misdemeanors, but judges themselves were permitted much more leeway in determining the facts of a case, including the interrogation of witnesses and suspects, usually under torture (*quaestio*). In addition, the seriousness of the criminal charges suspended privileges otherwise reserved for litigants in civil suits, in particular those concerning *praescriptio fori*, whereby certain classes of individuals were permitted to have their cases tried in a court of their own choosing. Under criminal procedure, the accused, regardless of rank, was to stand trial in the province where the offense was alleged to have taken place.[129] The intention here was to limit any opportunity for the accused to escape custody while being transferred from one province to another.

In the very making of a criminal accusation an individual had to be very sure of his facts. The accuser had to present a subscribed *inscriptio* to the

[129] *ET* 103.

judge promising that in the event of failure he himself would be liable to suffer the fate which would have befallen his opponent, if proved guilty:

> Anyone who considers accusing another with any crime, let him not be heard first, nor let anything concerning the case be judged, unless he undertakes the bond of a preliminary inscription, and guarantees the following before a judge exercising the appropriate jurisdiction: that if he does not prove what he claims, he will suffer a similar penalty which the accused, when convicted according to law, can receive. And let both the accused and accuser be held in similar custody until the outcome of the trial has been reached; unless either the charges are minor, in which cases a guarantor must be produced, or the accused is sufficiently noble or of distinguished enough honor that he ought to be entrusted to his rank.[130]

Unquestionably, not all alleged criminals or accusers were arrested, and certainly not many involved in minor suits. But in many instances, to be sure, the arrest of a defendant, and for that matter the accuser, both before and during a trial must have been necessary in order that the case be heard and judgment executed. It is difficult to believe that a person charged with a serious crime, or the accuser in such a case, was permitted his freedom until the hearings, and thus allowed the opportunity to make good his escape.

Of course, pre-trial custody was no sure guarantee that a trial would ensue. Recounting the case of the Senators Basilius and Praetextatus, we are told by Cassiodorus that before any trial could take place the pair escaped custody: "The Urban Prefect informs Us that Basilius and Praetextatus were alleged by many to be involved in the magical arts; he further reports that they escaped through the stupor (*alienatio*) of the guards."[131] According to a later source, Basilius disguised himself as a monk and fled to Amiternum in Valeria (near L'Aquila), where he was received into a monastery by an unsuspecting abbot by the name of Equitius. Suspicious of his new arrival, Equitius later expelled Basilius believing him to be the devil in disguise. Thereupon he was led back to Rome where he was burned alive by an angry mob.[132]

[130] *ET* 13: "Qui alterum quolibet crimine putaverit accusandum, non prius audiatur nec de exhibitione aliquid iubeatur, nisi se praemissae inscriptionis vinculis obligarit et istud caverit apud competentem iudicem, se eam poenam subiturum, si non probaverit quod intendit, quam possit reus convictus secundum leges excipere : et usque ad eventum iudicii, tam reus quam accusator aequali custodiae sorte teneantur. Nisi forte aut minora sint crimina, in quibus fideiussor praeberi debeat, aut reus adeo nobilis vel splendidi honoris sit, ut suae committi debeat dignitati."

[131] Cass., *Var.* 4.23: "Praefectus igitur urbis sua nobis relatione declaravit Basilium atque Praetextatum magicis artibus involutos impeti accusatione multorum: quos elapsos intimat mentis alienatione custodum..."

[132] Gregory the Great, *Dialogi*, 1.4, ed. U. Moricca (Rome, 1924; repr. Turin, 1960).

Arrest might prove a problem if the accused fled to sanctuary. Asylum might be sought in any church, and was taken advantage of not only by criminals but also by debtors and runaway slaves.[133] As was perhaps an inevitable consequence, the insistence of the Church on its responsibility to protect the weak conflicted with the state's prerogative to protect the public at large. Thus, while Theoderic recognized the principle of ecclesiastical sanctuary established in Roman law (*CTh* 9.45), such recognition was conditional. As the would-be asylum-seekers Opilio and Gaudentius discovered, those accused of particularly heinous crimes or otherwise involved in high-profile cases could not expect to escape the censure of the laws by hiding behind the protection of the Church.[134]

A further problem was that an innocent person could suffer a long term in custody while awaiting the judge's verdict. Boethius, for example, suffered an exceptionally long internment (roughly between 523 and late 525 or early 526) before he was put to death for treason. Doubt concerning his guilt and the need to gain sufficient evidence before execution are possible reasons for such a duration, but it is just as likely that a prolonged, and for that matter public, period of incarceration served a deterrent purpose, particularly in capital cases. Given the severity of the crime with which he was charged, it is unlikely that Boethius was permitted the luxury of house arrest, but it is clear he did not suffer unduly in a dungeon, at least until the very end. For it was during this time that he composed his masterpiece *Consolation of Philosophy*.

Such an individual might not survive at all given what we know about the generally squalid state of prison conditions in the early sixth century. In his *formula* of general amnesty for prisoners (to coincide with Easter), written in his own name as Praetorian Prefect on behalf of the state, Cassiodorus gives a rather stark impression of prisons:

> [T]he prison – that house of Pluto, in which men suffer a living death, from its foul odors, from the sound of groaning which assails their ears, from starvation which destroys their taste, from the heavy weights which weary their hands, from the endless darkness which makes their eyes grow dim – let the prison now be filled with emptiness . . . Never is it so popular as when it is seen to be deserted.[135]

[133] *ET* 70, 71, 126. [134] Anon. Val. 14.85; Boethius, *Cons. Phil.* 1.4.14–18.

[135] Cass., *Var.* 11.40: ". . . cella gemituum, tristitiae domus, apud superos Plutonis hospitium, locus perpetua nocte caecatus, tandem infusione lucis albescat: in quo non unum tormentum sustinet reus, qui antequam incurrat necis exitus, a superis probatur abscisus. Primum pedor ille collega catenarum abominabili maerore discruciat: auditum alieni gemitus et lamenta conturbant: gustum ieiunia longa debilitant: tactum pondera prementia defetigant: lumina diutinis tenebris obtusa torpescunt. Non est

Beyond the rhetoric, it is clear that prisons were not designed with the intention of improving rates of recidivism, but rather to ensure a person's whereabouts through extreme measures.

The intent of the law behind placing the onus on the accuser, requiring him to do all the work himself, and exposing him to a corresponding internment and penalty of the accused if he failed to prove his case, was to limit instances of malicious or false accusation and ensure justice. It goes without saying, of course, that the general requirements concerning the making of a criminal accusation must frequently have deterred private individuals from doing so in all but the most serious of crimes.

In some criminal trials, when the accuser failed to prove his case by direct evidence, the judge had recourse to more coercive tactics to get at the facts; he was entitled to submit slaves, *originarii*, and in some exceptional instances even freemen to torture.[136] In a letter written in Theoderic's name to the Senator Tancila concerning the theft of a brazen statue from the city of Como, Cassiodorus mentions that aside from rewards to witnesses and inducements to accomplices, the King seems to have authorized the use of torture against the workmen of the city, whose experience in working with such things has made them prime suspects. He states: "Inquire from them, under terror, by whose service this [theft] was perpetrated."[137] It is not entirely clear what is meant by the phrase "*sub terrore*." That this could include the use – or at least the threat – of torture is possible, given Theoderic's strong wish, made clear in this and the following letter, to catch the culprits.

The case of Adeodatus is more explicit. Cassiodorus notes that Adeodatus was forced to confess himself guilty of *raptus* despite his being innocent:

> You have alleged that while pressured by the stinging hatred of the *vir spectabilis* Venantius, Governor of Lucania and Bruttium, you were compelled to confess to the abduction of the maiden Valeriana; moreover, that you had preferred rather to die a swift death than to endure anymore the savage tortures [inflicted upon you].[138]

unum clausis exitium: multifaria morte perimitur, qui carceris squalore torquetur . . . atria tua vacuitatibus impleantur. Locus ille perennium lacrimarum quondam tristes incolas perdat. Non sunt inde qui laeti sunt: qui tunc profecto habebit gratiam, si desertus appareat." This concern for prisoners' rights echoes Roman law (e.g., *CTh* 9.3.4 (365); *CTh* 9.2.3 (380); *CTh* 9.3.1 (320); *CTh* 9.3.3 (340); *CTh* 9.2.3 (380); *CTh* 9.2.6 (409); *CTh* 9.3.1 (320); *CTh* 9.3.6 (380); *CTh* 9.3.7 (409) = *CJ* 1.4.9).

136 *ET* 84, 100–2.

137 Cass., *Var.* 2.35: "a quibus sub terrore perquire quo ministro fuerit perpetratum."

138 Cass., *Var.* 3.46: ". . .allegasti viri spectabilis Venantii Lucaniae at Bruttiorum praesulis odiorum te acerbitate compressum, custodiae longo situ laborantem, in confessionem raptus adultae puellae Valerianae fuisse compulsum, ut gratius fuerit spem citae mortis expetere quam tormentorum crudelia sustinere."

According to the petition, no doubt intended to underscore the sorrowful condition of the petitioner, Adeodatus suffered a rather lengthy internment during which he was compelled to wrongly incriminate himself. The method of coercion here was torture, of such an extreme that death was a welcome relief. As the rest of the letter reveals, in the interest of public morality Theoderic did not grant Adeodatus a full pardon but rather reduced his sentence to six months exile, after which he was not to suffer any further recrimination. The original decision of the presiding judge, Venantius, was neither upheld nor reversed.

In some instances, torture could be used to exacerbate the death penalty in particularly heinous crimes, as was the case with Boethius. The Anonymous Valesianus reports that a cord of rope was twisted around his head so tightly that his eyes dislodged from their sockets. A guard then finished him off with a cudgel.[139] Gruesomeness aside, the veracity of these claims seems to be confirmed by an equally terrible account in Procopius' *Secret History* (16.26), where the author says that on Theodora's orders a young man accused of being a homosexual was subjected to torture by leather being bound tightly around his head until his eyeballs had been loosened. For the purposes of interrogation torture was not intended to be gratuitous, but was designed to illicit the truth from those so engaged, in accordance with the long-standing position of Roman jurists that only torture guaranteed truth, even when the testimony was apparently offered voluntarily. But throughout the later Empire, the use of torture was strictly regulated because of its efficacy in extracting confessions of guilt. Its use was further limited, at least in provincial areas, by the lack of skilled operators necessary to both properly carry out the act of torture and then interpret the results.[140]

As for punishment, penalties ranged from the most extreme, that is death (in assorted manner),[141] to exile (which entailed banishment to another region of the kingdom),[142] and flogging, usually carried out in public, and sometimes in lieu of another penalty.[143] Financial penalties varied widely, from confiscations and fines to the benefit of the fisc,[144] to compensation, in money or kind, and established according to a fixed amount (usually

139 Anon. Val. 14.87. See also Henry Chadwick, *Boethius: The Consolations of Music, Logic, Theory, Philosophy* (Oxford, 1981), 55.

140 Edward Peters, *Torture* (Oxford, 1985), 28–30, 33–6. On the use of torture against lower classes of freemen and women in Late Antiquity, see Olivia F. Robinson, *Penal Practice and Penal Policy in Ancient Rome* (London, 2006), chapter 5.

141 *ET* 1, 9, 17, 21, 38–9, 41, 47, 48–9, 50, 56, 63, 78, 91, 97, 104, 107, 108, 110, 120, 125.

142 *ET* 18, 42, 75, 83, 89, 95, 97, 108.

143 *ET* 55, 73, 83, 89, 111.

144 *ET* 3, 10, 22, 24, 55, 73, 83, 84, 104, 111, 112, 115.

fourfold the amount originally and demonstrably taken).[145] Sometimes a particularly gruesome penalty was reserved for an especially heinous crime. For instance, a slave, domestic servant, or freedman who attempted to denounce his master in court was to be "cut down with swords."[146] The instigator of sedition was to be burned alive.[147] The deterrent effect could be further enhanced if the punishment fit the crime. Thus, an arsonist could be "consumed by fire."[148] Such creativity was long a hallmark of Roman penal law. Illustrative of this is a decree of the Emperor Constantine of 326, which aimed at putting a stop to the abduction of minors by targeting complicit nurses with a punishment that was both sadistic and symbolic: "Since the watchfulness of parents is often frustrated by the stories and wicked persuasions of nurses, punishment shall threaten first such nurses whose care is proven to have been hateful and whose talk is proven to have been bought, and the penalty shall be that the opening of their mouth and throat, which elicited destructive encouragements, shall be closed by the swallowing of molten lead."[149]

For lesser offenses and in special circumstances some serious ones, a member of the upper class was afforded preferential treatment in relation to his social inferiors. Thus, for instance, *honestiores* were spared a public flogging where *humiliores* or *viliores* were not.[150] Throughout the Empire, flogging was considered a particularly severe sanction, principally because all forms of corporal punishment were held to be degrading. And Emperors regularly prescribed it upon members of the lower class as an additional penalty in an attempt to further enhance the aspect of physical humiliation.[151] In instances where punishment involved exile, an *honestior* could expect to be banished for up to a period of five years, whereas the *humilior* was exiled for life.[152] For some offenses *honestiores* faced fines or banishment where *humiliores* could be punished capitally. Clearly, this differential treatment was based on the realistic recognition of the enhanced financial status of the individual. Whether or not this differential treatment translated into a preferential one, however, is a matter of perspective. A nobleman, for example, might reasonably conclude that the confiscation of a third of his property was a far greater penalty than the flogging and

145 *ET* 2–4, 10, 11, 64, 70, 71, 80, 84, 97, 109 and 117, 141. 146 *ET* 48, 49. 147 *ET* 107.
148 *ET* 97.
149 *CTh* 9.24.1: "Et quoniam parentum saepe custodiae nutricum fabulis et pravis suasionibus deluduntur, his primum, quarum detestabile ministerium fuisse arguitur redemptique discursus, poena immineat, ut eis meatus oris et faucium, qui nefaria hortamenta protulerit, liquentis plumbi ingestione claudatur."
150 E.g., *ET* 64, 75, 83, 89, 97, 111. 151 Harries, *Law and Empire*, 141. 152 E.g., *ET* 75, 83.

banishment of a mere *humilior*. But there is no doubt that the wealthy and powerful did, in fact, enjoy considerable privileges as a result of their *de iure* status. An assault on a freeborn virgin, for instance, was a capital offense unless the offender was of sufficient means to properly compensate the girl.[153] An *honestior* could similarly avoid being punished capitally if convicted of bribing witnesses or judges, and instead be fined the total sum of his possessions.[154] And whereas all others found to be knowledgeable of the black arts were executed, the *honestior* was instead deprived of his property and exiled.[155] But for a small category of crimes deemed particularly odious or scandalous, a capital penalty was imposed regardless of the wrongdoer's rank. These included actions of violence (*vis*),[156] *raptus*,[157] forgery and counterfeiting,[158] *pervasio*,[159] the destruction of tombs,[160] and assaults on widows.[161]

Just as penalties could vary depending upon one's social status, they could be further complicated by considerations of legal responsibility, which were themselves tied closely to the status of the offender. Slaves, for instance, might act on their own volition or at the behest of their owner, and for some offenses the penalty could vary accordingly. Thus, according to *ET* 77, a slave who committed *vis* on his own account was to be punished capitally; but if in doing so he was following the instruction of his owner, then the owner was held liable, and the implication is that the punishment for the slave, while not explicitly stated, was less severe. An exception to this was *ET* 104, which applied the same penalty (death) to a slave or *colonus* who had destroyed a property marker regardless of whether he acted on his own or at the instruction of his owner. But the likelihood of a slave successfully incriminating his owner if the latter chose to deny prior knowledge under oath would be slim given the prejudice of the law towards the testimony of slaves.

The laws of Theoderic's kingdom enshrined many of the long-standing inequalities of the Roman world, and amply demonstrate that just as in the Empire, inequality or discrimination was an acknowledged feature of Theoderic's legal system. More than simply using his wealth to pay a fine and avoid the otherwise universally stipulated punishment for a given offense, an *honestior* could expect to be spared the more humiliating punishments dealt out to his social inferiors. Generally speaking, his status involved additional legal privileges and responsibilities, and more widely entitled him to protection and favor from the law.

[153] *ET* 59. [154] *ET* 91. [155] *ET* 108. [156] *ET* 9. [157] *ET* 17. [158] *ET* 41. [159] *ET* 47. [160] *ET* 110. [161] *ET* 60.

A contributing factor was the fact that those at the bottom of the social ladder were substantially impeded by their insufficient knowledge of the legal system and lack of resources to initiate proceedings and properly navigate the complicated court system; the unequal distribution of wealth, influence, and legal knowledge prevented them from utilizing the legal system to the same degree as persons of power and rank. And in matters of appeal, such recourse was in practice available only to those litigants who could afford the expense and the inconvenience of a protracted legal process, to those with friends and connections which enabled them to secure an audience before the judge through their (improper) influence with court officials. In law, as in other aspects of life in early medieval Italian society, those most advantageously positioned by virtue of their greater property, power, and status received the foremost privileges and rewards.

This deliberate policy of class inequality, in as much as it could anger those who lacked the means to benefit from it, made very good sense from an administrative standpoint. For the *honestior* was most amply possessed of the means to benefit the state both through his loyal service and as a consequence of his defiance of the law. If, on the one hand, an otherwise law-abiding *honestior* was convicted of an offense, it was in the state's own best interest to secure both short-term and long-term gains through the imposition of penalties that generally targeted the offender's material wealth but not his potential for benefiting the state in the future. On the other, such an individual could not be permitted to defy the law on a continual basis, and in turn undermine the authority of the state. Thus, by targeting possibly substantial portions of his material wealth, the very means of his defiance, the law removed, or at the very least minimized, him as a potential threat.

Judicial enforcement and accountability

It was the responsibility of the judge to ensure the compulsory execution of his judgment through the agency of the *apparitor* or *miles* – a general term that Cassiodorus uses for an officer of the Roman civil service. The *formula* for the position reads as follows:

> Great toils and great perils are the portion of an officer of the courts in giving effect to their sentences. It is easy for the judge to say, "Let so and so be done;" but on the unhappy officer falls all the difficulty and all the odium of doing it. He has to track out offenders and hunt them to their very beds, to compel the contumacious to obey the law, to make the proud learn their

> equality before it. If he lingers over the business assigned to him, the plaintiff complains; if he is energetic, the defendant calls out. The very honesty with which he addresses himself to the work is sure to make him enemies, enemies perhaps among powerful persons, who next year may be his superiors in office, and thus subjects him to all sorts of accusations which he may find it very hard to disprove. In short, if we may say it without offense to the higher dignitaries, it is far easier to discharge without censure the functions of a judge than those of the humble officer (*miles*) who gives effect to his decrees.[162]

Elsewhere, Cassiodorus tells us of an *apparitor* by the name of Ferrocinctus who was instructed by Theoderic to bring the disgraced Praetorian Prefect Faustus to book. He was aided in this task by the *saio* Grimoda.[163] The officer was similarly commanded by Theodahad to assist Gildilas, Count of Syracuse, in enforcing the law in the region: "Wherefore, We command that if Our decrees are being enforced against those defeated in a suit, the enforcer shall receive as much as a reward as Our glorious lord and grandfather [i.e. Theoderic] established that *saiones* ought to accept, in due reference to the ranks of the litigants involved."[164]

In cases where an individual posed a significant flight risk either because of the nature of his crime or the punishment that awaited him, prisons were essential for ensuring that the sentence was carried out. As an addendum to his *formula* for general amnesty for prisoners, Cassiodorus stipulates:

> But let me turn my attention to you, guard. You shall be miserable in the general joy, because you are accustomed to derive your happiness from the misery of many. But as some consolation for your troubles, we remand to

[162] Cass., *Var.* 6.13: "Grandia sunt, quae sustinent excubantes: personas contumaces ad parendum cogunt, latentes in cubilibus suis prudenti sagacitate vestigant, superbis modestiam aequalitatis imponunt: ita quod a iudicibus breviter dicitur, ab ipsis efficacia famulante completur. Notum est quae pericula sustineant, cum ad causas mittuntur alienas. Si segnius agat, petitor queritur: si districte, pulsatus vociferatur. Sic inter utrumque diversum rara laus est invenisse praeconium. Dignitatum pace dicamus, facilius est laudatum iudicem reperire quam militem iniuncta sine offensione complere. Aliud est enim tantum dicere legitima, aliud ad terminum deduxisse iustitiam. Laudabiliter quidem bonum dicitur, sed multo gloriosius statuta complentur. Verba tantum diriguntur a praesulibus, a militibus autem postulator effectus." See also Cass., *Var.* 5.6 (a letter addressed in the name of Theoderic to the court officer Stabularius, instructing the addressee to carry out the decision of the *comitatus* concerning the case of the debtor Thomas, who had hitherto failed to pay back his guarantor, the *vir clarissimus* John). On the office of *apparitor* see further Arnold H. M. Jones, "The Roman Civil Service (Clerical and Sub-Clerical Grades)," *JRS* 39 (1949), 38–55, at 38.

[163] Cass., *Var.* 3.20. Faustus was accused of taking property from the petitioner Castorius.

[164] Cass., *Var.* 9.14: "Unde censemus, ut, si nostra conveniunt decreta pulsatos, tantum commodi percipiat exsecutor, quantum gloriosus domnus avus noster pro honoribus personarum debere saiones accipere expressa quantitate constituit. commodum enim debet esse cum modo."

> your custody those prisoners whom the Law, for very pity's sake, cannot set free – the men found guilty of outrageous crimes, whose liberation would make barbarous deeds frequent. Over these may you continue to exercise your authority.[165]

Even for less serious offenses prisons could be used to help enforce judgment. In a letter addressed in Theoderic's name to the Praetorian Prefect Abundantius, Cassiodorus describes the case of a certain Frontosus, convicted of embezzling public money. While granted what would seem multiple occasions to repay the money, Frontosus failed to satisfy the requirements of the judgment. Such was his intransigence that Theoderic instructed the Prefect to ignore Frontosus' promises and remand him in custody to secure the debt:

> Frontosus ... confessed to having embezzled a large sum of public money, but promised that, if a sufficient interval were allowed him, he would repay it. Countless times has this interval expired and been renewed, and still he does not pay. When he is arrested he trembles with fear, and will promise anything; as soon as he is liberated he seems to forget every promise that he has made ... Since this is his character, when you arrest him, first stop him from making any promises, for his facile nature is ready with all sorts of promises which he has no ability to fulfill. Then, determine what he can actually repay at once, and remand him until he does this.[166]

To limit the possibility of escape, severe penalties awaited anyone who helped in breaking a person out of prison:

> If clerics or any others should forcibly release those who have been adjudged [guilty] and condemned in a criminal proceeding, they themselves shall be penalized or held liable for the fines which the judgment rendered against those convicted had stipulated; and if it is proven that this was perpetrated

165 Cass., *Var.* 11.40.9: "Sed ut tuos quoque gemitus consolemur, illos tibi tantummodo vindica, quos lex pietatis gratia non relaxat, ne, cum truculentis parceret, asperrima facinora levigaret. Solvamur ergo cuncti saecularibus actibus implicati. Patitur omnis homo periculosos nexus, quos festinet evadere. Claustra reos dimittant: nos vincula improbae cogitationis absolvant."

166 Cass., *Var.* 5.34: "Frontosum ... frequenti nobis insinuatione suggestum est pecuniae publicae decoxisse non minimam quantitatem. Quem a diversis iudicibus fecimus iusta examinatione perquiri, ne forsitan, ut assolet, eum non veritas, sed infamaret invidia. Ille omnia confessus reddere se posse constituit. Si ei largae praeberentur indutiae: quibus frequenter emensis immemor prommisionis suae ad constituta semper imparatus occurrit, fugere quidem nescius, sed suae sponsionis ignarus, obliviosus cum relinquitur, trepidus cum tenetur ... Et quia sic notus est, cum facies ad tuum venire iudicium, primum agito, ne promittat, caveto ne constituat, quia levissimi animi mos est polliceri facile quae non disponit implere. Quicquid autem persolvere considerata aequitate potuerit, constrictus sine aliqua dilatione iam reddat, quia post tot falsitates argutiae suae reputare poterit, quod se frequenter illusisse cognoscit."

> through the complicity or collusion of the judge, that same judge shall be compelled to pay five pounds of gold.[167]

It is unclear if the reference here to *clerici* is to priests acting as jailors or to priests breaking people out of prison (*violenter eruerunt*). By the early fifth century the Church had become formally involved in the supervision of prison conditions.[168] In Italy by the sixth century, this could include guard duty. For we hear from the Anonymous Valesianus (14.85) that before their trial, Albinus and Boethius were imprisoned in a baptistery at Verona for an undetermined amount of time. On the other hand, the violence engendered by the Laurentian schism would seem a reasonable context for legislation that targeted jail-breaking priests. But there is no specific mention in our sources of jailbreaks during this affair.

Despite the fact that the central administration accepted some, limited role in the workings of law enforcement through such measures as these, it lacked the ability to maintain a strong presence in the local communities of the provinces where judges operated. In essence, these officers were left on their own to ensure that a criminal was pursued and punished accordingly.[169] In this, their task could be made difficult, if not impossible, by the simple fact that there were those who were prepared to resist and had more effective force at their command than did the judge. Our sources are filled with examples of warlords masquerading as powerful magnates who operated outside the authority of the state with virtual impunity. In his narrative of the Byzantine conquest, for example, Procopius includes several accounts of powerful men who were able to exercise considerable authority in areas that were loosely controlled by the King. One such individual was the nobleman Theudis. After the battle of Vouillé in 507 he was dispatched by Theoderic to command the Gothic army in Spain. Thereupon he raised a private army of about 2,000 soldiers on the estates of a wealthy Hispano-Roman woman whom he married.[170] Even Theoderic's own nephew Theodahad apparently had no aversion to using his men contrary to the

167 *ET* 114: "Si addictos damnatosque iudiciis clerici vel quilibet alii violenter eruerint, ipsi ad poenam, vel ad dispendia teneantur, quae sententia in convictos prolata statuisse monstrabitur: et si conniventia iudicis vel conludio hoc claruerit perpetratum, quinque auri libras idem iudex cogatur exsolvere."

168 E.g., *CTh* 9.3.7 (409).

169 Patrick Wormald, "*Lex Scripta* and *verbum Regis*: Legislation and Germanic Kingship, from Euric to Cnut," in P. H. Sawyer and I. N. Wood (eds.), *Early Medieval Kingship* (Leeds, 1977), 105–38; Hermann Nehlsen, "Aktualität und Effektivität der ältesten germanischen Rechtsaufzeichnungen," in Peter Classen (ed.), *Recht und Schrift im Mittelalter*, Vorträge und Forschungen, xxiii (Sigmaringen, 1977), 449–502.

170 Proc., *BG* V. xii. 50–4.

King's will. Despite being a vast landholder in the Tuscan region, Cassiodorus tells us that the rapacious lord regularly incited his retainers to violently seize what land there remained from his unfortunate neighbors.[171] The *ET*, too, recognized this unfortunate feature of life in early sixth-century Italy. Both *ET* 75 and 89 concern individuals who were capable of raising private armies to enforce their will on the weak and unsuspecting; the epilogue concludes by insisting that where a judge was unable to enforce a decision, he was enjoined to bring the matter to the attention of the *scrinia*.

In many instances, to be sure, the responsibility to ensure that the rule of law was upheld rested with the members of the community at large. To that end, public involvement in court proceedings was essential. Several references in the *ET* make the point that members of the public at large could play a role. Both *ET* 12 and 74 mention public trials specifically; the reference to a *publicum iudicium* in *ET* 12, and similarly to a *publicum examen* in *ET* 74, emphasizes the public aspect of the proceedings, rather than indicating simply the involvement of public authorities. And *ET* 74 makes a further reference to the so-called *boni viri*, who clearly played an important part in the suit. These *boni homines*, who were the large landholders and leaders of the local communities and were presumably knowledgeable in the law, could be assigned as *assessors* by the judge to determine how much was owed a defendant wrongfully brought to trial by a dishonest plaintiff.

Groups of *boni homines* no doubt appeared at nearly every hearing, but we have no records that document their precise activities. While some of the Ravenna papyri list the names of individuals (usually three to four) in attendance who served as witnesses for the signing of documents or transfer of property, such records applied exclusively to relatively minor legal matters that fell under the jurisdiction of the local *curia*.[172] As such, they are of little help for understanding the role played by *boni homines* in more serious civil proceedings, not to mention criminal cases. But the general silence of the sources about their activity should not be taken as a sign of their insignificance. Beyond the fact that they could play an active role, as presupposed here, the very presence of the *boni homines* was an important reflection of participation in the administration of justice by prominent members of communities. This participation offered a guarantee of sorts that court decisions would receive broad support, and the proofs that were

[171] Cass., *Var.* 4.39; 5.12; 10.5. [172] E.g., Tjäder, *P-Ital* no. 7, 228–34.

presented, decisions issued, and oaths taken would be enforced through the collective efforts of the community.[173]

Despite the fact that the justice system was by its very nature an imperfect one, biased in favor of the wealthy, it was nevertheless a legitimate system. Where its integrity came under threat was in areas where the authority of the state was subverted by the exercise of patronage. Those who commended themselves to a patron received from him land on which to live and the means with which to protect it. The patron's participation in this relationship afforded him a means to power, profit, and prestige, that of the client to profit and protection. As the letters of Ennodius make clear, powerful men, following centuries of honorable tradition, continued to use connections at the court to influence, or expedite, the judicial process for the benefit of their clients. The compilers, too, recognized some of the dangers which patronage posed, and attempted to weaken this ancient institution through provisions designed to make it a less attractive venture for patron and client alike. For instance, *ET* 75 and 89 held the leader of an armed group, and here we may presume a patron, personally accountable for crimes committed in his name by members of his retinue. At the same time, the value of a patron to his dependant was diminished by the prohibition in *ET* 43 against a *potentior*, a designation which could certainly apply to patrons, serving as the legal representative of a lesser freeman: a defendant who enlisted the legal services of a patron in order to gain advantage in an impending suit in fact lost his case. Nor was it permitted for a *potentior* to influence the outcome of a trial by making his presence felt in court; or in cases involving land claims, have his name connected with the disputed land in question.[174]

That the law recognized the capabilities of powerful magnates to influence, circumvent, or outright defy the King's justice made it no more effective in preventing them from doing so. For the efficacy of the law lay in the willingness or ability of the judges to properly enforce it, and it was the wealthy and powerful who were most amply possessed of the means to diminish or otherwise impede the capacity of the judge to do his job. Appeals of friendship, patronage, or family, bribes, and even threats were the weapons of choice for the nobleman, and could allow him to unlawfully enjoy privileges at the expense of those who were unable to protect themselves.

173 On *boni homini* in late antique Italy, see generally Philip J. Jones, *The Italian City-State: From Commune to Signoria* (Oxford, 1997), 120–51.

174 *ET* 44, 46.

Judicial incompetence and corruption

It was in the nature of late imperial administration that nearly every officer who held a higher position was at the same time judge over those within his province or sphere of authority. Thus, the military officers (the *duces* and *magistri militum*) sat in judgment over their soldiers, and the heads of regional and local authorities (for example provincial Governor, Praetorian Prefect) presided over Roman provincials. Theoderic maintained this administrative structure: a judge was any officer who held executive authority, such as a Count, Duke, Governor, or Prefect. In other words, there was no branch of government dedicated exclusively to the maintenance of the law.

This lack of a professional judiciary meant that the majority of judges were not selected on the basis of their legal knowledge. That many of them, in fact, knew no law is likely. This was particularly true of the military, financial, and other administrative courts. The *duces* and *magistri militum*, before whom cases involving soldiers had to be heard, even if they were not necessarily illiterate Goths, were normally men who had spent all their lives in the army and were therefore quite unskilled in matters of law. That the situation in the regular courts was undoubtedly better is true enough. As Athalaric proclaimed to his Quaestor Felix: "It is agreeable that the matter of justice be administered by judges experienced in the law, since he who knows fairness nor can easily become soiled by the fault of error can scarcely be able to disregard one who is purged of learning."[175]

But provincial Governors, Urban Prefects, and even Prefects were by no means always learned in the law. Many, if not most, owed their positions to such factors as their wealth and rank, and were generally selected for their noble birth rather than any sort of demonstrable legal knowledge or ability. As Valentinian III remarked in 451 about Italy: "I have learned that both advocates and judges today are rarely if at all knowledgeable of the laws and customs."[176] While the inadequacy of judges was remedied to some extent by the maintenance of the later imperial institution of *assessores*, it would be naïve to think that most judges performed their duties with the benefit of significant legal training or expertise.[177]

[175] Cass., *Var.* 8.18: "Professionem constat esse iustitiae legum peritos iudices ordinare, quia vix potest neglegere qui novit aequitatem nec facile erroris vitio sordescit, quem doctrina purgaverit."

[176] *Nov. Val.* 32.6: "Et causidicos et iudices defuisse hodieque gnaros iuris et legum aut raro aut minime repperiri."

[177] For judicial incompetence in the later Empire, see Jill Harries, *Law and Crime in the Roman World* (Cambridge, 2007), 38–41. For evidence of the problem of judicial incompetence in the successor kingdoms of the Visigoths and Burgundians: *LV* 11.1.21 (Visigothic); *Lex Baiuvariorum*, ed. E. Von Schwind, *MGH Leges* vol. 2 (Hannover, 1926), 11.18 (Burgundian). See further Ramsay MacMullen,

Judicial incompetence undoubtedly played a part in permitting injustice to flourish and the laws to be flouted. But a judge whose perceived impropriety was the result of bribery or favoritism was an altogether different matter. The problem of judicial venality and abuse of power was nothing new. Cicero remarked that there were three types of influence or behavior a judge could exercise on the proceedings that constituted criminal misconduct. These were *gratia*, *potentia*, and *pecunia*.[178] In a judicial context, *gratia* can perhaps be best understood as an improper relationship between the judge and litigant, or the litigant's patron, where the judge renders a verdict out of favor and against the internal content of the law in an attempt to maintain such an alliance.[179] *Potentia* refers not just to power, but to coercion, or oppression. In the context of improper influences in court proceedings, *potentia* could be aimed at the judge, forcing him to render a judgment contrary to justice as a consequence of the fear for doing otherwise; or it may be targeted against a litigant to prevent him from prosecuting his rights to their fullest before a judge. Of all these concepts *pecunia* is the most simple. It refers to outright bribery, to the judge who accepts payment, in money or kind, from a litigant in exchange for rendering a particular judgment or for otherwise affecting the outcome of the trial. This triad of judicial impropriety underpinned all subsequent legislation dealing with judicial corruption, but problems of judicial venality and abuse of power seem to have survived more or less unchecked from Augustus to Charlemagne and after.[180]

The corrupt and venal judge was, in the opinion of contemporaries, an unavoidable feature of the late imperial justice system. Writing in the 380s, an anonymous Christian polemicist complained bitterly about the corruption plaguing Rome, and the greedy judges who flouted the laws with

"Roman Bureaucratese," *Traditio* (1962), 134–6; Wormald, "*Lex Scripta*," 105–38; Pierre Riché, *Education and Culture in the Barbarian West: from the Sixth through the Eighth Century*, trans. from the 3rd French edn. by John Contreni (Columbia, SC, 1962), 229–31.

178 Cicero, *Pro Caecina* ed. and trans. H. Grose Hodge, Loeb Classical Library (Cambridge, MA, 1927), 71 and following. See also John M. Kelly, *Roman Litigation* (Oxford, 1966), 33–4.

179 The concept of *gratia* in Roman political, social and legal thought has been the subject of substantial comment: see Peter Garnsey, *Social Status and Legal Privilege in the Early Empire* (Oxford, 1970); Richard Saller, *Personal Patronage Under the Early Empire* (Cambridge, 1982), esp. 23 and following, where Saller discusses the contractual and reciprocal nature of *gratia* in the Roman social context; Harries, *Law and Empire*, 163–6. It is also important to recognize that in the later Empire, *gratia* came to have significant negative connotations: see John N. L. Myres, "Pelagius and the End of Roman Rule in Britain," *JRS* 50 (1960), 21–36.

180 Michael Hoeflich, "Regulation of Judicial Misconduct from Late Antiquity to the Early Middle Ages," *Law and History Review* 2.1 (1984), 79–104; Harries, *Law and Empire*, chapter 8; Kelly, *Roman Litigation*, 33–4.

impunity. In trying to explain the current state of things, he offered some measure of consolation to his readers:

> So why, here, are sinners kept free from fear by their power, while some make a mockery of the statutes, the poor are oppressed, accusations are framed against the righteous . . . wicked and corrupt men are held in honor, greedy and grasping men grow rich, and the judge is for sale? . . . (in the next world) those who used their power to despise the statutes or made a mockery of the law by sharp practice in their pursuit of wickedness, so puffed up in these ways that they might have appeared to trample on justice itself, they shall be brought low and overthrown and shall be subjected to torments . . .[181]

Similar observations were made by Maximus of Turin (*c.* 400), who noted that "the abuse has grown to such an extent that the laws are sold, statutes corrupted and verdicts habitually venal,"[182] while Zeno of Verona (*c.* 300–71) criticized greedy officials, among them judges, who committed assorted abuses for personal gain.[183]

The problem of corrupt and venal judges was also a concern for Emperors. In 325, following his victory over Licinius at Chrysopolis, Constantine issued a proclamation to the people of Nicomedia encouraging them to forward complaints against provincial Governors or members of the palatine staff directly to him.[184] He followed this up in 331 with a wide-ranging decree in which he threatened to cut off the hands of greedy judges: "The rapacious hands of the functionaries shall immediately cease, they shall cease, I say, for if after due warning they do not cease, they shall be cut off by the sword." The Emperor's frustration continues:

> The chamber curtain of the judge shall not be venal; entrance shall not be purchased, his private chamber shall not be notorious for its bids. The very appearance of the Governor (*iudex*) shall not be at a price; the ears of the judge shall be open equally to the poorest as well as to the rich.[185]

[181] Ambrosiaster, *Quaestiones Veteris et Novi Testamenti* CXXVII 4.2 (ed. A. Souter, *CSEL* 50 (Vienna, 1908); trans. Harries, *Law and Empire*, 153): "ut quid hic peccantes per potentiam secure sunt, alii leges inludunt, pauperes deprimantur, iustis accusatio componitur . . . in iqui et corruptores in honore sunt, avari et raptores locupletantur, iudex venalis est? Illi autem qui per potentiam leges contemperserunt aut tergiversatione inluserunt iniquitatem sectantes, sic gloriosa in his, ut ipsi iustitiae insultare viderentur, ut humiliate et confusi tormentis subiciantur."

[182] Maximus of Turin, *Sermones* 26.103, ed. and trans. Boniface Ramsey, *Ancient Christian Writers* 50 (Mahwah, NJ, 1989).

[183] Zeno of Verona, *Tractatus* ed. B. Loftstedt, *CCSL* 22 (Turnhout, 1971).

[184] *CTh* 9.1.4 (325).

[185] *CTh* 1.16.7 (with 1.16.6; 2.26.3; 3.30.4; 4.5.1; 11.30.16–17; 11.34.1): "Cessent iam nunc rapaces officialium manus, cessent inquam: nam si moniti non cessaverint, gladiis praecidentur. non sit venale iudicis velum, non ingressus redempti, non infame licitationibus secretarium, non visio ipsa praesidis cum pretio: aeque aures iudicantis pauperrimis ac divitibus reserentur."

In 386, three years after the western Emperor Gratian threatened judges who sold verdicts with the penalty for embezzlement (*peculates*),[186] Theodosius I in the East issued an open invitation to all citizens of the Empire to bring forward complaints against judges for extortion, venality, and other acts of injustice.[187] In legislation of the Emperors Arcadius and Honorius, judges who abused their powers were subject to stern moral condemnation as well as a fine of thirty pounds of gold; and those who contrived "venally" to delay the execution of a sentence or abuse the appeals procedure were threatened further.[188]

To compensate for these untrustworthy judges, the state relied more heavily on other organizations. The Church, for instance, became responsible for prison conditions and the return of people enslaved or imprisoned abroad; and Valentinian III recruited decurions in an attempt to enforce the law on tomb violations – a law which was, for the most part, disregarded by the conniving and venal Governors.[189] In addition to these forms of criminal conduct, legislation of the late fourth century was expanded to encompass punishments for judges whose inefficiency or negligence prevented justice from prevailing. Those found to be lazy, negligent or idle were to be punished and replaced if necessary.[190]

It is fashionable nowadays to interpret these kinds of laws not as proof that there was necessarily more corruption in the fourth and fifth centuries than there was in earlier times, but that Emperors were more often prepared to say so in a bid to appear as hardliners against such imperial corruption.[191] But this is an oversimplification of a very complicated issue. Crime and the related matter of judicial corruption was not simply a product of legal rhetoric, but rather a symptom of deep-rooted social and political problems that manifested themselves in different forms in different places, but which all necessitated the development of systematic rules of laws and methods of punishment to reinforce and sometimes create normative forms of behavior. Long before its official demise, the western imperial administration had proven increasingly incapable of maintaining peace and order throughout

186 *CTh* 9.27.5. 187 *CTh* 9.27.6.

188 *CTh* 1.12.8 (400) imposes a fine of thirty pounds of gold for improper delegation; 9.40.15 (connivance with criminals).

189 *Nov. Val.* 23.6 (447). On the role of the Bishop as a provider of political and spiritual leadership in Italy following the collapse of the imperial government, see Rita Lizzi, *Vescovi e strutture ecclesiastiche nella città tardoantica: L'Italia Annonaria nel IV-V secolo d.C.* (Como, 1989); and for the West in general, Rapp, *Holy Bishops in Late Antiquity*, 274–89.

190 *CTh* 1.5.9 (389).

191 E.g., Harries, *Law and Empire*, chapter 8; Walter Pohl, "Perceptions of Barbarian Violence," in H.A. Drake (ed.), *Violence in Late Antiquity. Perceptions and Practices* (Burlington, VT, 2006), 15–26.

the region. And the lawlessness of the times is a frequent complaint of many contemporary authors. Ammianus Marcellinus, Gregory of Tours, and Gildas all speak to an apparent rise in crime in contrast to preceding centuries. Even if one were inclined to dismiss these sorts of complaints as a matter of literary convention, the fact that the subject of judicial corruption receives so much attention in the *ET* – a relatively brief document that is conspicuously devoid of the sort of legal rhetoric found in the *Theodosian Code* or *Variae* – is a strong indicator that it posed a significant problem for Theoderic's administration.

In all, a total of ten provisions of the *ET* deal with related matters of judicial corruption and misconduct. So important was the issue, in fact, that the first seven provisions were dedicated to it.[192] For the compilers, the prime and constant threat was bribery:

> *ET* 1 In the first place We have decreed that if a judge accepts money to pass judgment which imperils the life or civil status of an innocent person against the ordinances and provisions of the public law, let him be subjected to a capital penalty.[193]
>
> *ET* 2 If a judge accepts money in order to render a decision to the detriment of a person's status or property, and is convicted of this crime in a fair hearing, he shall pay fourfold the amount which he previously accepted in his eagerness for corrupt gain; and it will benefit the individual who received an unfair judgment as a result of the bribe.[194]

The compilers made an important distinction between instances of judicial bribery that imperiled another's status or life (*caput*) and those that threatened his property. In the first instance, the judge who took a bribe to secure a conviction faced the death penalty. In the second, he was required to pay fourfold the amount of the bribe to the litigant he attempted to injure. It did not matter if a conviction was secured. Of those who offered the bribe in the first place, offending *humiliores* were punished capitally while *honestiores* suffered the loss of their possessions.[195]

The imposition of the fourfold penalty in *ET* 2 is interesting. In the late fourth century, the fourfold penalty had become standard for *furtum*, both

192 *ET* 1–7, 55, 91, 114.

193 *ET* 1: "Priore itaque loco statuimus, ut si iudex acceperit pecuniam, quatenus adversum caput innocens contra leges et iuris publici cauta iudicaret, capite puniatur."

194 *ET* 2: "Iudex si pecuniam contra statum aut fortunas cuiuslibet ut sententiam proferret, acceperit et ex hac re sub iusta fuerit examinatione convictus, in quadruplum quod venalitatis studio accepit, exsolvat, illi profuturum contra quem redemptus docebitur tulisse sententiam."

195 *ET* 91.

manifestum and *nec manifestum*.[196] Thus, *ET* 2 illustrates not only the persistence in the early sixth century of a notion of civil liability for improper judicial conduct, but it also suggests that conceptually, such misconduct was perceived as tantamount to theft. Therefore, the provision required fourfold restitution of the amount illegally taken. In light of this penalty, it would seem that the judicial liability rule was not primarily compensatory but was rather deterrent in nature. In a compensatory context, one would expect that the penalty paid to the injured party would approximate the amount of his loss. The quadruple penalty, however, would serve primarily to deter a judge from committing the illegal action in the first place.[197]

This is precisely the purpose behind the quadruple penalty imposed on corrupt judges and their staff:

> *ET* 3 A judge that unjustifiably takes anything from provincials shall lose the office which he abused, and shall return at least fourfold the amount to those from whom clearly something was unjustifiably taken; and if the judge has died, let this penalty be sought from his heirs.[198]
>
> *ET* 4 Let the staff of any judge whatsoever that has exacted anything beyond what it has been mandated be compelled, under the penalty of being beaten, to pay fourfold to those from whom property was shown clearly to have been taken.[199]

That the judge's property would serve as bond for his good behavior seems clear; this in itself implies that the *iudex* was a member of the local landowning class. This link between local appointment and property liability can be found in Justinian's *Pragmatic Sanction* of 554, wherein the Emperor provided for the nomination of provincial Governors in Italy from the provinces in which they were to serve. The task of appointing these offices fell on the shoulders of local Bishops and secular magnates, and their property was to guarantee their behavior:

> We order that provincial judges, who are wealthy and capable enough to administer their respective territories, are to be elected by the Bishops and chief men of each of the regions without suffrage from the same provinces

[196] Ernst Levy, *Weströmisches Vulgarrecht. Das Obligationenrecht,* Forschungen zum römischen Recht (Weimar, 1956), 36 and following.

[197] Hoeflich, "Regulation of Judicial Misconduct," 79–104, esp. 97–8.

[198] *ET* 3: "Iudex quod immerito provincialibus rapuerit, amissa dignitate qua male usus est, in quadruplum reddat his duntaxat, quibus immerito constat ablatum: et si defunctus fuerit, ab eius heredibus haec poena poscatur."

[199] *ET* 4: "Officium cuiuslibet iudicii, quod quid ultra quam iussum est exegerit, in quadruplum sub fustuaria poena cogatur exsolvere iis, quibus inclite monstrabuntur ablata."

> they are to administer . . . in such a way that if they are found to have inflicted some injury on the taxpayers, they may make satisfaction from their own property.[200]

ET 3 was undoubtedly in response to the sorts of regional interests reflected by the frequent complaints in the *Variae* to the general maladministration of judges.[201]

The lawless judge, the judge who adjudicated disputes not based upon his legal system's internal content, but rather upon external and therefore unacceptable standards (such as which party provided the largest bribe) posed a major threat to the continued functioning of that system, and was dealt with harshly. To guard against the various dangers posed by the corrupt and negligent judge, Theoderic naturally relied upon those whose loyalty he had no doubt, but this was no guarantee against acts of injustice and lawlessness on their part.[202] That judges sometimes put their own interests before those of justice was an unavoidable consequence of the limitations imposed by Theoderic's bureaucracy, which simply lacked the ability to ensure the integrity of its agents equally throughout the kingdom.

Theoderic was acutely aware of this limitation, but nowhere does he seem to acknowledge the inequity in the fact that his judges were first and foremost servants of the crown. While they were required to render justice impartially and equitably as the law demanded, they were equally, if not more so, obligated to protect the property and privileges of the King. Obviously, these duties were mutually exclusive and this contradiction is made clear on several occasions. The *saio* Duda, for example, was authorized by Theoderic to supervise incidents of grave robbing – a capital offence under *ET* 110 – to ensure that any treasure went to the crown.[203] Elsewhere, we hear that Theoderic's nephew Theodahad, whose wanton acts of violence and plunder had terrorized the landholders of Tuscany, was punished with far less severe sanctions than the laws demanded.[204] But the most

[200] *Novellae*, ed. Rudolf Schoell and Wilhelm Kroll, *Corpus Iuris Civilis*, 3 (Berlin, 1895; repr. 1967), appendix 7, 800–1: "Provinciarum etiam iudices ab episcopis et primatibus uniuscuisque regionis idoneos eligendos et sufficientes ad locorum administrationem ex ipsis videlicet iubemus fieri provinciis quas administraturi sunt sine suffragio . . . ita videlicet ut si aliquam collatoribus laesionem intulisse inveniantur . . . ex suis satisfaciant facultatibus."

[201] E.g., Cass., *Var.* 9.20.

[202] In the early part of his reign, Theoderic, not unlike Odovacer, appointed aristocrats to high office. However, towards the end of the first decade of the sixth century he turned towards *novi homines* (many of whom were Goths) to fill such positions. Not surprisingly, this led to a souring of relations between Theoderic and the traditional lay holders of power in Rome in the second decade of the century. On Theoderic's policies of appointment, see in general Moorhead, *Theoderic in Italy*, 147–58; John Matthews, *Western Aristocracies and Imperial Court,* AD *364–425* (Oxford, 1992), 355, 386–8.

[203] Cass., *Var.* 4.34 (507/11). [204] Cass., *Var.* 4.39, 5.12.

infamous example is the trial of Boethius.[205] In 524 the statesman was charged – in connection with Albinus – with treason for conducting a private correspondence with Constantinople during a time when relations between Theoderic and the eastern court were deteriorating. The matter was forwarded to the *referendarius* Cyprian, whose task was to prepare the case for the King's *Consistorium*, which was the tribunal in charge of hearing cases of treason. Up to this point there is nothing to suggest that there was anything illegal in the procedure. But rather than have the case brought before the Consistory, Boethius and his co-accused were taken to Ticinum (Pavia), south of Milan, where Eusebius, the Prefect of Rome, was summoned by the King to preside over the proceeding. Despite this being a capital case, Boethius was never called to defend himself. In what amounted to little more than a show trial, he was deemed guilty and sentenced to death by a senatorial court sitting in Rome nearly 500 miles away. In 526, after roughly two years of incarceration, he was executed.[206] His fate underscores the fact that the laws could be flouted to protect the interests of the King, and the reality that Theoderic's justice system was inextricably linked to Italy's political landscape, a landscape that towards the end of his reign became increasingly unstable as relations between Ravenna and Constantinople soured.

Conclusions

In Ostrogothic Italy, the rules of law and justice and the courts and officers responsible for maintaining the integrity of the judicial system were essentially the same as those of the later Roman Empire. The provincial courts were administered by the central administration through Roman judges, that is, Governors and their staffs, as well as officers of the local municipalities, including the Roman *defensores*, *duumviri*, *quinquennales*, and the ubiquitous decurions. But it is clear from our sources that this was a much simplified and watered down version wherein the bulk of cases were dealt with by the provincial Governor irrespective of the type of case or considerations of a person's ethnicity. At the same time, the jurisdiction

205 For a full account of these events see Anon. Val. 14.85–7; Boethius, *Cons. Phil.* 1.4.14–18; Proc., *BG* v. i.32–9. There is nothing in our sources to support the claims of Edmund Reiss ("The Fall of Boethius and the Fiction of the *Consolatio Philosophiae*," *The Classical Journal* 77 (1981), 37–47) that these events were fictionalized by Boethius as part of a conversation between himself, the victim, and Philosophy who has come to console him and, indeed, to teach him a proper understanding of happiness. There is enough correspondence between Boethius's own account and those of the Anonymous Valesianus and Procopius to conclude that the account has a basis in historical fact.

206 Anon. Val. 14.87; Chadwick, *Boethius*, 55.

of military officials like the *saio* and *comes* began to supersede that of traditional officeholders, and the authority of lesser officials, like the *defensor*, was significantly curtailed as a result.

Our sources also underscore just how fragile Theoderic's justice system was, and call attention to the dangers that threatened to take it down – dangers that had existed since the early days of the Empire: namely, the exercise of patronage, judicial venality and corruption, and the limitations of government. These problems were not unique to Theoderic's Italy, but rather were endemic throughout the former parts of the western Roman Empire, as different barbarian rulers attempted, with varying degrees of success, to assume the role of supreme lawgiver in the absence of a formal and comprehensive judicial hierarchy.[207] What was different in the case of Theoderic, however, was the King's ability to mask these problems behind a rhetoric of Roman renewal that stressed continuity between his reign and those of other great Emperors like Trajan or Valentinian. But for the ordinary person who had to rely on Theoderic's legal system for some measure of justice, the reality was far less than ideal; for this was a system that was biased in favor of the wealthy and well-connected, and plagued by judges who were either unable or unwilling to enforce the King's laws. Following Theoderic's death the situation only worsened. In a letter of general admonition written on behalf of Athalaric to all the provincial judges, Cassiodorus felt compelled to remind them not to take pleasure in the fact that people were afraid to approach them in the streets.[208]

[207] Wormald, "*Lex Scripta*,"105–38. [208] Cass. *Var.* 9.20; 12.2, 3, 6.

CHAPTER 4

Society and the family

Introduction

One striking but hardly extraordinary feature of early medieval Italian society portrayed in our sources is its class stratification. This should come as no surprise, since the Goths themselves did not practice any principle of democratic egalitarianism prior to their arrival in Italy. At the one extreme they had their equivalent of the Roman *optimates*, at the other their slaves.[1] Procopius in his war narrative, for instance, distinguishes an obviously large class of notables who should also be identified as noblemen.[2] From Cassiodorus we hear of individual Goths insisting that their military service gave them claim to a special freedom and guaranteed their continued independence from any sort of servile condition. Anduit, an elderly veteran of Theoderic's army whose blindness had allowed Gudila and Oppa to reduce him into slavery, successfully claimed that his military service meant that he should continue to enjoy the freedom that his status formerly entailed. Costula and Daila were likewise granted the freedom afforded by their status as Goths, and so were exempt from the servile condition unlawfully imposed upon them by a certain Guduin.[3] The compilers, too, make a distinction between free and unfree, as well as the assorted degrees of freedom: from the greater freemen, identified by the various equivalent terms *potentes/potentiores*, *honestiores*, and *nobiles*; to the lesser freemen, *humiliores*.[4]

Once the Goths had come into regular contact with a class-dominated society like the Romans, in which the social inequalities among freemen

[1] Peter Heather, "*Gens* and *Regnum* Among the Ostrogoths," in Hans-Werner Goetz, Jörg Jarnut, and Walter Pohl (eds.), *Regna and Gentes: the Relationship Between Late Antique and Early Medieval Peoples and Kingdoms in the Transformation of the Roman World* (Leiden/New York, 2003), 88–133, esp. 105.

[2] *Ibid.*, 96–8. [3] Cass., *Var.* 5.29 (Anduit); 5.30 (Costula and Daila).

[4] *Potentes/potentiores*: *ET* 43, 122, epil.; *honestiores*: *ET* 75, 83, 89, 91, 108, 122, 145; *nobiles*: *ET* 13, 59; *humiliores*: *ET* 75, 83, 91, 108; *vilior* is used synonymously with *humilior* in *ET* 89.

were a matter of legal distinction, it is not hard to imagine that their own rudimentary social divisions were both reinforced and refined through laws that benefited those whose status afforded them additional legal privileges at the expense of their social inferiors.[5] This hierarchical ordering, justified as it was by a very real need to manage land as efficiently as possible during a time of chronic labor shortages (itself a product of a series of complex economic patterns that had emerged in the West in the third century), was not a matter of simple social prestige. Rather, the individual's activities and responsibilities were both dictated and circumscribed by personal status that was defined through his or her belonging to a particular class. These distinctions were enshrined in the law's penal regime: while the more important freeman was dealt with one way, the ordinary *ingenuus* suffered differently for the same offense, and the slave differently again. A consequence of a system that allowed the penalty for an offense to be influenced by the social status of the offender was the enforcement of outdated class divisions which in Italy, over the course of the fifth and sixth centuries, became less and less distinguishable in everyday practice.

Legal status and social division

In Roman law, status was determined by three constituent factors – *libertas*, *civitas*, and *familia*, that is, freedom, citizenship, and family.[6] Of these, the most important was freedom, for the loss of liberty entailed the loss of citizenship and family rights as well.[7] Loss of citizenship did not incur loss of freedom, but usually carried with it loss of family. In most instances it occurred as a result of deportation. The loss of family liberties affected status the least. For instance, if a child was emancipated, that is, freed from the legal authority of the *paterfamilias*, the child's legal status transformed

5 Peter Heather, "State, Lordship and Community in the West (c. AD 400–600)," in Averil Cameron, Bryan Ward-Perkins, and Michael Whitby (eds.), *Cambridge Ancient History*, vol. 14, 2nd edn. (Cambridge, 2000), 437–68, esp. 461–3.

6 Andrew Borkowski and Paul Du Plessis, *Textbook on Roman Law*, 3rd edn. (Oxford, 2005), 86.

7 As the jurist Paul remarked (*Dig.* 4.5.11 (lib. 2 *Sab.*)): "There are three kinds of change of civil status: the greatest, the middle, and the least. For there are three things which we have: freedom, citizenship and family. Therefore, when we lose all three . . . the change of civil status is the greatest. But when we lose citizenship and retain freedom, the change of status is the middle. When both freedom and citizenship are retained and only family is changed, it is plain that the change of civil status is the least." ("Capitis deminutionis tria genera sunt, maxima media minima: tria enim sunt quae habemus, libertatem civitatem familiam. igitur cum omnia haec amittimus . . . maximam esse capitis deminutionem: cum vero amittimus civitatem, libertatem retinemus, mediam esse capitis deminutionem: cum et libertas et civitas retinetur, familia tantum mutatur, minimam esse capitis deminutionem constat.")

from one of dependence to one of independence. While the emancipation resulted in the child losing inheritance rights on intestacy, the child also gained legal independence, which could certainly be of advantage in some instances. Together, these three elements of status underpinned all aspects of law and society in the Roman world, and continued to resonate in Theoderic's Italy.

From slavery to freedom

A significant feature of ancient and medieval societies was the widespread existence of individuals who had few or no legal rights of their own. Of these, the lowliest was the slave. Roman law defined a slave as someone who was subject to the ownership (*dominium*) of another against the will of nature.[8] They possessed no rights to speak of, and as such could be acquired, owned, and disposed of at the discretion of their master. They had limited privileges, usually in regards to their *peculium*, that is their *de facto* possession of goods, which they could in some instances use to purchase their freedom; sometimes their families were recognized; sometimes the punishment that their owners could administer to them was restricted by law. But they were defined in law as un-free, in that they had no legal ability to bring forth a complaint to the attention of a judge (with the exception of making a claim that they were illegally enslaved), and possessed no political rights. Simply put, slaves were chattels.[9]

In the later Empire, slaves existed in relatively large numbers, playing a crucial role in agricultural production. At the same time, they had a profound effect on the social relations and cultural values that defined Roman society. Throughout the fourth century, slavery remained a vigorous institution, but as the imperial administration slowly unraveled, slavery became less prominent. But the end of Rome did not witness the end of

[8] *Dig.* 1.5.4–5 (Florentius, lib. 9 *Inst.*).

[9] Chris Wickham, *Framing the Early Middle Ages: Europe and the Mediterranean, 400–800* (Oxford, 2005), 261–65; Chris Wickham, *Land and Power*, (London, 1994), 84–9. For the later Empire see Arnold H. M. Jones, *The Later Roman Empire, 284–602: A Social, Economic and Administrative Survey*, 3 vols. (Oxford, 1964), 2, 793–5; Ramsay MacMullen, "Late Roman Slavery," *Historia* 36 (1987), 359–82; and more recently, Domenico Vera, "Forme e funzioni della rendita fondiaria nella tarda antichità," in A. Giardina (ed.), *Società romana e impero tardoantico*, vol. 3 (Rome and Bari, 1986), 367–447; Domenico Vera, "Schiavitù rurale, colonate e transformazioni agrarie nell'Italia imperial," *Scienze dell'antichità*, VI-VII (1992–3), 291–339; Domenico Vera, "Dalla 'villa perfecta' alla villa di Palladio," *Athenaeum* 83 (1995), 189–211, 331–56; Domenico Vera, "Essere 'schiavi della terra' nell'Italia tardoantica: la razionalitá di una dipendenza," *Studia historica* 25 (2007), 489–505; Andrea Giardina, *L'Italia romana: Storie di un'identità incompiuta* (Rome and Bari, 1997), 223–64; Kyle Harper, *Slavery in the Late Roman World*, (Cambridge, 2011), esp. 60–6.

slavery; there is no shortage of evidence for slaves in the centuries after the fall of Rome.[10] The letters of Gregory the Great, for instance, show him on various occasions attempting to reconcile conflicts between masters and slaves, dealing with episodes of servile violence, handling cases of asylum, and manumitting slaves.[11] And the *ET* provides ample testimony to the continuing importance of slavery in Ostrogothic Italy.

While we are not informed of their exact numbers, the frequency of references in the *ET* and other sources to them – that is *servi*, *familiarii*, *ancillae*, and *mancipia* – confirms that their number was considerable. In all, a total of forty provisions of the *ET* deal with slaves either in whole or in part.[12] The *Variae*, too, document several instances involving slaves, from the theft and return of another's slaves, to the murder of a master at the hands of his household staff, as well as the trading, selling, and purchasing of children and the unfree.[13] Most slaves were certainly such by virtue of their birth. Slavery through birth occurred if the child's mother was a slave when the child was born (the status of the father being irrelevant).[14] But enslavement could also arise from external factors, such as being sold, punished, or captured. Banned since the days of the Republic, the selling of children was revived in the later Empire in limited circumstances, and continued into the early sixth century. According to *ET* 94, newly-born children could be sold into slavery by their parents on the grounds of poverty. But a right of redemption was reserved to the parents should their circumstances improve. When redeemed, the child regained its original (*ingenuus*) status.[15]

10 Heike Grieser, *Sklaverei im spätantiken und frühmittelalterlichen Gallien (5.-7. Jh.): das Zeungis der christlichen Quellen* (Stuttgart, 1997); Pierre Bonnassie, *From Slavery to Feudalism in South-Western Europe*, trans. Jean Birrell (Cambridge, 2009); Hermann Nehlsen, *Sklavenrecht zwischen Antike und Mittelalter: germanisches und römisches Recht in den germanischen Rechtsaufzeichnungen* I, *Ostgoten, Westgoten, Franken, Langobarden*, Göttinger Studien zur Rechtsgeschichte 7 (Göttingen, 1972).

11 For slavery in the letters of Gregory the Great, see Adam Serfass, "Slavery and Pope Gregory the Great," *Journal of Early Christian Studies* 14 (2006), 77–103; Harper, *Slavery in the Late Roman World*, 497–8.

12 *ET* 19, 21, 22, 48, 49, 51, 56, 61, 62, 63, 64, 65, 66, 69, 70, 77, 80, 81, 84, 85, 86, 87, 96, 97, 98, 100, 101, 102, 104, 109, 117, 118, 120, 121, 128, 141, 142, 148, 150, 152.

13 E.g., Cass., *Var.* 1.11 (a complaint concerning a certain Maniarius who alleges that his slaves (*mancipia*) were stolen); 1.30 (concerning slaves accused of murdering their masters); 3.14 (a complaint alleging that the slaves of the venerable Bishop Aurigenes outraged the wife of a certain Julianus and squandered some of his property); 3.18 (a letter of instruction commanding Gemellus, Governor in Gaul, that the property, goods, and slaves are to be restored to a certain *vir spectabilis* Magnus); 3.43 (a letter in Theoderic's name instructing that fugitive slaves are to be restored to their previous owners); 5.1 (here, Cassiodorus has Theoderic extol the Vandal King (Thrasamund) for his gifts of musical instruments and slave boys); 5.15 (on the purchase of slaves for the outfitting of a Gothic navy).

14 *Dig.* 1.5.5.1–2. Similarly *ET* 65.

15 On the selling and pledging of children in Roman law see: *CTh* 5.9.1 and 5.10.1 (Constantine); *Dig.* 20.3.5; 21.2.39.3; *PS* 5.1.1; *CJ* 8.16.1 (197); 7.16.1 (Caracalla); 8.16.6 (293); 2.4.26 (294); 7.16.37 (294).

Concerning the custom, Cassiodorus suggests that it was relatively commonplace, at least in the countryside. In a letter (*c.* 527) addressed in Athalaric's name to the *vir spectabilis* Severus concerning the suppression of violent robberies at Leucothea, a great fair which took place on St. Cyprian's day in the rural suburb of Consilinum, Cassiodorus describes the fair and how freeborn children, boys and girls, were there put up for sale by their parents:

> Though you shall notice the lack of public buildings there, you may yet see the glory of a famous city. Boys and girls are on display, distinguished by their respective sex and age, put up for sale not because of captivity, but freedom: their parents are right to sell them, since they benefit by slavery itself. Indeed, there is no doubt that slaves can be improved by their transference from work in the fields to service in the town.[16]

Despite Cassiodorus' otherwise rosy picture of southern Italy presented in the rest of the letter, it would seem that many were suffering from harsh economic conditions, and thus forced to sell their children – a far better scenario, according to Cassiodorus, than working in the fields as free peasants.

Enslavement could be imposed as a punishment for certain prescribed crimes and actions. Roman law on the subject documents many such instances. In the early Empire, these included crimes where the punishment involved working in the mines or fighting in the arena.[17] Those who evaded paying taxes or fulfilling obligatory military duties could also be enslaved. Similarly, enslavement could result from the failure to pay a debt or stipulated composition. Debt-bondage was not uncommon in some regions of the later Empire, particularly in the East, and it appears to have continued

See also John Boswell, *The Kindness of Strangers: The Abandonment of Children in Western Europe from Late Antiquity to the Renaissance* (New York,1988), 53–137; William W. Buckland, *The Roman Law of Slavery* (Cambridge, 1908), 420–2; Ludwig Mitteis, *Reichsrecht und Volksrecht*, (Leipzig, 1891; repr. Hildesheim, 1963), 358–64; Jaques Ramin and Paul Veyne, "Droit romain et société: Les hommes libres qui passent pour esclaves et l'esclavage volontaire," *Historia* 30 (1981), 472–97.

16 Cass., *Var.* 8.33.4: "Ubi licet non conspicias operam moenium, videas tamen opinatissimae civitatis ornatum. Praesto sunt pueri ac puellae diverso sexu atque aetate conspicui, quos non fecit captivitas esse sub pretio, sed libertas: hos merito parentes vendunt, quoniam de ipsa famulatione proficiunt. Dubium quippe non est servos posse meliorari, qui de labore agrorum ad urbana servitia transferuntur."

17 Such convicts were described as penal slaves (*servi poenae*) and were regarded as the lowest form of slaves. See Joan Burdon, "Slavery as a Punishment in Roman Criminal Law," in Léonie Archer (ed.), *Slavery and Other Forms of Unfree Labor* (London, 1988), 68–83, where the author demonstrates in which cases and to which class of offenders this form of punishment applied; Borkowski, *Textbook on Roman Law*, 89.

in Italy into the sixth century.[18] The *Variae* contain numerous references to the expropriation of properties and subsequent enslavement of the landholders at the hands of wealthy Gothic warlords and powerful Romans; and *ET* 79 gives the impression that a freeman could be held in servitude of another.[19] That these sorts of actions were underpinned by a pre-existing financial arrangement between the two parties, whereby enslavement of the former resulted from his defaulting to the latter, is likely. In any event, Theoderic recognized enslavement as a legitimate penalty, either on its own or in lieu of a stipulated mulct or other punishment, and in exceptional circumstances seems to have permitted private individuals the right to enslave others.[20] Cassiodorus tells us of a certain Crispanus, who killed his wife's lover and was subsequently enslaved by Candax, a relative of the deceased, to work under compulsion (*laborat contra iura publica*) as a means of paying for his deed.[21] Here, the actions of Candax were expressly rejected by the King not because they stood in contrast to any notions of self-help, but because Crispanus was not guilty of committing a crime. Otherwise, Candax would have been well within his rights to enslave Crispanus until the latter could pay off his debt.

Another action that resulted in enslavement was self-sale. Concerning the practice, *ET* 82 reads:

> If a freeborn man is sold, he is not to incur the prejudice of his new status, unless perchance, being of the age of majority, he kept the buyer in the dark by remaining silent about his freeborn status. For he could have brought an action against the seller in defense of himself, or injustices concerning the crime of *plagium*, except that he wanted the money that was given for him to be split between himself and the seller. In that case, he shall incur the prejudice of the condition which he created for himself through deceit and connivance.[22]

18 E.g., at Dura Europos. See further C. Bradford Welles, *The Excavations at Dura-Europos, Final Report* v. *Part* 1*: The Parchments and Papyri* (New Haven, 1959), 12; and generally Geoffrey E. M. De Sainte Croix, *The Class Struggle in the Ancient Greek World* (London, 1981; repr. New York, 1989), 162–9.

19 For examples in the *Variae*: 5.29 (the case of the blind veteran Anduit); 5.30 (addressed in Theoderic's name to the *dux* Guduin, this letter concerns the complaint of two Goths, Costula and Daila, alleging that the addressee has imposed servile tasks (*onera servilia*) on them; 8.28 (a letter in Athalaric's name to Cunigast, *vir illustris*, that concerns the petition of the Romans Constantius and Venerius, which alleges that the Goth Tanca had seized their farm and reduced them to slavery).

20 E.g., *ET* 8, 9. 21 Cass., *Var.* 1.37.

22 *ET* 82: "Si ingenuus distrahatur, nullum praeiudicium sui status incurrit, nisi forte tacendo de ingenuitate sua, emptoris ignorantiam maior aetate circumvenerit. Nam de plagio adversus venditorem pro defensione vel iniuria agere potuit nisi pretium quod pro eo datum fuerit, cum suo voluerit venditore partiri. Tunc enim praeiudicium conditionis incurret, quod sibi ipse dissimulando et consentiendo pepererit."

The context envisaged here is one where the freeman, pretending to be a slave, would arrange for an accomplice to sell him to an unsuspecting customer. After the sale the freeman would establish his freedom (no doubt by means of providing proper documentation) and share the purchase price with the accomplice.[23] But a freeman was prohibited from selling himself into slavery on the grounds that such a sale was *prima facie* invalid since a free person could not in theory be the object of a contract of sale. Paradoxically, attempts to sell oneself in this way were punished with enslavement.[24]

Enslavement was also recognized by Theoderic's successor Athalaric as a useful deterrent. In provision seven of his *Edict* we read that a free woman who offered herself as a concubine to another's husband was to be enslaved to the aggrieved wife:

> But if anyone, having despised married decency in wanton and shameful desire, should prefer to go to the embraces of a concubine, if she is a free woman, she and her children shall, without exception, be made over to the wife under the yoke of slavery. Thus, by an upright judgment she shall experience subjugation to the one above whom she presumed to be placed through her illicit lust.[25]

There is no precedence for this in Roman law, nor is there anything close to it in the *ET*. It appears to have been an innovation of Athalaric's, and it documents just how seriously the King took the matter of adultery.

One final source of slaves was provided through capture, either at the hands of foreign enemies or rapacious lords. Those captured in the course of war became slaves if they were not ransomed.[26] To prevent such a fate from befalling some 6,000 kinsmen who had been captured years earlier by the Burgundian King Gundobad as he campaigned in the northern region of Liguria, we are told that in 496 Theoderic dispatched the Bishops Epiphanius of Pavia and Victor of Turin to secure their release. As the story goes, the Bishops came before the King at Lyons and Epiphanius begged him to have mercy on the prisoners. After consulting with his

[23] While the details for this are lacking, *ET* 96 makes it clear that the burden of proof in such circumstances rested with the claimant.

[24] On this subject in earlier law, see Ramin and Veyne, "Droit Romain et société," 472–97.

[25] Cass., *Var.* 9.18.7: "Si quis autem superflua turpique cupidine coniugali honestate despecta ad concubinae elegerit venire complexus: si ingenua fuerit, iugo servitutis cum filiis suis modis omnibus addicatur uxori, ut illi se per honesta iudicia sentiat subdi, cui per illicitam libidinem credidit posse praeponi."

[26] Roman law on the subject is particularly detailed. See e.g. *Dig.* 28.1.12 (Julian, lib. 42 *Digest*); *Dig.* 49.15.5pr.-1 (Pomp., lib. 37 *Quintus Mucius*); concerning specific cases of Roman citizens being captured and enslaved by barbarians: *CJ* 8.50.1–18; *CJ* 7.14.9.

advisor Laconius, Gundobad ordered the release of many prisoners without payment, while the remainder were to be ransomed.[27] The *ET* contains a provision on the return of captured slaves and *coloni*:

> Slaves or *coloni* that have been captured by enemies and returned shall be restored to their owner: provided that another did not already purchase them when they were sold by enemies in a valid transaction [*commercium*].[28]

The law protected both the interests of the original owner and the rights of the buyer who purchased the captured slave or *colonus* through legal means. In the event that both parties claimed ownership, it is likely that the case was decided in favor of which one could provide the necessary documentation, such as a record of estate holdings or a valid bill of sale, to validate his claims.

Powerful magnates, too, contributed to the number of slaves through the enslavement of freemen. The compilers addressed the issue of unauthorized enslavement directly, targeting those who abducted, sold, or purchased others illegally:

> *ET* 78 Anyone who sells, gives away, or presumes to retain for his own service a freeborn man whom he has taken to another place by means of *plagium*, that is through solicitation, shall be put to death.
>
> *ET* 83 Of those who conceal, sell, or knowingly purchase a freeborn man, *humiliores* shall be flogged and sentenced to perpetual exile; *honestiores* shall be deprived a third of their goods and shall also endure a penalty of exile for a period of five years.[29]

In several instances in the *Variae*, Cassiodorus has the King bemoan the illegal enslavement of freemen. In the matter of Anduit, for example, whose suit alleges that he was dispossessed of his property and reduced to slavery at the hands of two fellow Goths, Gudila and Oppa, Theoderic announced:

> But We, whose special task it is to preserve an impartial justice between equals and unequals, decree by this command that, if he has proved himself free in the court of the aforementioned late Pitzias, you are to banish his

[27] Ennodius, *V. Epiph.* in *Magnis Felicis Ennodii Opera*, ed. Friedrich Vogel, *MGH* AA7 (Berlin, 1885), 136–77. On the dating of this event, see Lellia Ruggini, *Economia e società nell 'Italia annonaria'* (Milan, 1961), 279–80. On Gundobad's campaigning in general, see David Frye, "Gundobad, the *Leges Burgundionum* and the Struggle for Sovereignty in Burgundy," *Classica et Mediaevalia* 41 (1990), 199–212.

[28] *ET* 148: "Servi aut coloni ab hostibus capti et reversi, domino restituantur: si non sunt ante ab altero, vendentibus hostibus, in commercio comparati."

[29] *ET* 78: "Qui ingenuum plagiando, id est sollicitando, in alia loca translatum aut vendiderit, aut donaverit, vel suo certe servitio vindicandum crediderit, occidatur."

ET 83: "Qui ingenuum celaverint, vendiderint, vel scientes comparaverint, humiliores fustibus caesi in perpetuum dirigantur exilium; honestiores confiscata tertia parte bonorum suorum, poenam patiantur nihilominus quinquennalis exilii."

> slanderers immediately. Nor may those, who should have condemned their own intentions when their legal claims were initially quashed, dare to harass him any further with compulsions foreign to his [free] status.[30]

Anduit was fortunate in that his status as a veteran of Theoderic's army merited his case to be heard by the King. To be sure, most were not so fortunate. The various examples cited by Cassiodorus of Romans and Goths alike being forced into servitude by rapacious neighbors speak to the inability of the central authority to deal effectively with the problem, and underscore the point that an individual's freedom largely depended upon his ability to protect himself and his property against the open greed of others.

Concerning its composition, the slave class was by no means homogenous. From the standpoint of economic function, there were two main kinds of slaves: the first was comprised of skilled ones such as the household slave, *familiarius*; and the menial or field type, variously identified by the compilers as *rusticii*, *mancipii*, or the generic *servi* and *ancillae*, constituted the second. As a general rule, household slaves were considerably more valuable than their counterparts in the field, for they could be relied upon to perform a variety of functions that necessitated a degree of expertise beyond the experiences of a menial laborer (thus the insistence of the law that slave-owners be properly compensated according to the value of the lost or damaged slave).[31] While some of the more skilled slaves undoubtedly enjoyed comparatively favorable conditions as a consequence of their position within the master's household, such intimacy also had its drawbacks. For these slaves, often trusted confidents, would have been those who above all suffered on those occasions when the law permitted their torture in cases involving current or former masters.[32]

To be sure, it was the field slaves that constituted the bulk of the slave population. It was certainly these simple farm-laborers, working as they did in more depressed conditions and under less favorable terms, who were more likely to flee. And it was these whom the law took a greater interest in, for their escape posed a far greater economic loss to landholders than the loss of a domestic servant. In all, a total of six provisions of the *ET* deal with

[30] Cass., *Var.* 5.29: "Sed nos, quorum est proprium inter pares se dispares aequabilem iustitiam custodire, praesenti iussione decernimus, ut, si in iudicio supra memorati quondam Pitziae se probavit ingenuum, calumniantes protinus amovete: nec audeant ulterius necessitatibus alienis illudere, quos semel convictos decuerat sua vota damnare." Anduit's was not an isolated incident. See, e.g., Cass., *Var.* 5.30, 8.28. On similar events in Gaul, see Salvian, *De Gubernatione Dei* 5.8, 9, ed. F. Pauly, *CSEL* 8 (Vienna, 1883).

[31] E.g., *ET* 64, 70, 80, 84, 100, 152.

[32] *ET* 100, 101, 102.

runaway slaves.[33] Together, they aimed to put an end to the problem in one of two ways; in the first, by preventing escape through provisions for the punishment of those who incited flight, or knowingly sold or gave away a fugitive slave.[34] *ET* 80, for which there appears to be no precedent in Roman sources, dealt harshly with a person who incited another's slave to flee; those found guilty were required to repay the owner three additional slaves including the absconder together with his *peculium*. In the second, the compilers sought to ensure that a fugitive, deprived of assistance, would be swiftly caught and returned. Here, efforts largely took the form of threats designed to deter anyone from harboring a fugitive slave. *ET* 84 is illustrative of this:

> Anyone who knowingly receives or conceals another's fugitive slave or *colonus* shall render to the owner that fugitive together with his (i.e. the slave's) income and *peculium*, as well as another slave of equal value. But if the one who first received the fugitive allowed him to be received for a second or third time, then that one shall render to the slave's owner three additional slaves in addition to the fugitive along with his income. However, a slave must be tortured in examination lest perchance he has been sent by his owner to the home of the person who received him in order to cleverly and deceitfully profit; so that if through the interrogation of the one testifying it is established that he was fraudulently sent by his owner to another's home, the fisc may at once be compensated.[35]

Anyone who knowingly received another's fugitive slave was to compensate the fugitive's master with another slave of equal value, in addition to the absconding slave where possible, and any property or income amassed by the slave following his escape. Furthermore, in the event that the absconding slave was received for a second or third time by the same individual who provided him employment in the first place, then that person was to pay the fugitive's master three slaves in addition to the absconder, and any income the slave may have accumulated during the intervening period.[36]

To limit the possibility of fraud, the provision required that the slave be tortured as a means to rule out the possibility that his master had, in fact,

[33] *ET* 80, 84–7, 141. [34] *ET* 80, 87, 141.

[35] *ET* 84: "Quisquis servum sive colonum alienum sciens fugitivum susceperit aut occultaverit, ipsum domino cum mercedibus et peculio eius et eiusdem meriti alterum reddat. Quod si secundo aut tertio eundem fugitivum idem apud quem fuerat, suscipiendum esse crediderit, praeter ipsum, cum mercedibus, tres alios domino eius tradat. Mancipium tamen ipsum, ne forte propter capiendum lucrum callide et dolose a domino ad domum eius, qui susceperat, immissum fuerit, oportet in examinatione torqueri: ut si per interrogationem in quaestionem positi constiterit a domino suo ad domum alterius fraudulenter immissum, fisci protinus compendiis adplicetur."

[36] *ET* 85.

contrived his original escape in order to profit. This was a slight variation from *CJ* 6.1.4, the basis for which is a now-lost decree of the Emperor Constantine of 317, which gave the receiver the option of paying the master twenty *solidi* instead of returning the fugitive slave; and provided the receiver the option of compensating the owner two or three slaves in addition to the absconder.

The problem, of course, was how such fugitive slaves could be identified and distinguished not just from other slaves travelling on lawful journeys at the behest of their masters, but also from *originarii*, *coloni*, or even humble freemen who were compelled to travel about in search of employment on the estates of wealthy landholders. Thus, *ET* 80 provided that anyone who took on the services of a stranger was required to direct him to the public records office (*gesta*) where declaration of his (free) status could be made:

> Anyone who induces another's slave to flee shall render to the owner three others of equal value, and the original slave together with his *peculium*. But if anyone is received by another under good faith whereby he claims that he is freeborn, it is necessary for the receiver to take these precautions: namely, to direct the claimant to the records offices where he can declare his freeborn status; upon completion of this, if the claimant is demanded by the owner and proven to be his slave or *originarius*, he shall be returned without any inconvenience to the one who received him [in the first place].[37]

Those who failed to do so, or deliberately concealed the fact that they had received an absconding slave, were criminally liable.[38]

That the compilers devoted such attention to the subject of runaway slaves suggests that it was a serious problem, and forces us to consider why so many slaves fled in the first place. While the *ET* presupposes that they were going to other landlords, the prospects available to such runaways for a better life were few, if any. In economic terms, the most a fugitive could reasonably have expected was a small holding as the tenant of some free landholder. For a slave, of course, the conditions of tenancy might well have been better than those he abandoned, and the stigma associated with servitude, concomitant with its legal disadvantages, would have been lost.[39] But the *ET* makes the point that there was little, if any, difference

[37] *ET* 80: "Qui mancipium alienum sollicitaverit, tres alios eiusdem meriti, et ipsum domino cum peculio suo reddat. Quod si quis a quolibet bona fide suscipitur quo se dicat ingenuum, suscipientis haec debet esse cautela, ut eum ducat ad gesta, et se profiteatur ingenuum: quo facto dum a domino servus aut originarius postulatus fuerit et probatus, solus sine retinentis incommoditate reddatur."

[38] *ET* 85.

[39] See Arnold H. M. Jones, "Slavery in the Ancient World," in Moses I. Finley (ed.), *Slavery in Classical Antiquity*, 1–15, who notes of the later Empire in the West (p. 15): "Where agricultural slavery survived it was a heritage of the past, and the social and economic position of slaves on the land had become

between tenancy and slavery. As a general rule the compilers did not differentiate between slaves, *coloni*, and *originarii*.[40] And in some instances they applied a common penal regime to slaves and lowly tenants – an indication that the frontier between slavery and tenancy was at this time blurred.[41]

In Italy, this blurring of distinction between lower-class freemen and slaves had in fact been going on since the third century.[42] By the sixth century the peninsula had become a region in which rural dependants were mostly unfree. An isolated piece of evidence for Padua in north-eastern Italy, presumably for the church of Ravenna and dating around 560, demonstrates that rent-paying peasants, or tenants (*coloni*), were obligated to perform heavy labor services for their lord one to three days per week (in addition to paying various dues in the form of rent and gifts of lard, honey, eggs and chickens).[43] There is little distinction made here between the position of the *colonus* and that of the slave both in terms of their *de facto* economic autonomy and *de iure* status. It would seem that the situation in the East differed little. For in a piece of legislation from 530, Justinian remarked that he could see no difference between tenant farmers and

indistinguishable from that of free persons. Of course, it mattered enormously to individual tenants whether they were free or not; their capacity to negotiate their rents and to live and work within a wider social context was entirely dependent upon their legal status."

40 The *ET* frequently equates *originarii* with *servi*: 21, 56, 63, 64, 80, 84, 97, 98, 104, 109, 142.

41 E.g. *ET* 21, 48, 56, 63, 64, 65, 66, 67, 68, 80, 97 and 98, 104, 109, 121, 128, 148.

42 M. I. Finley, *Ancient Slavery and Modern Ideology* (Harmondsworth, 1980); Natalie Kampen, *Image and Status: Roman Working Women in Ostia* (Berlin, 1981), 27–32; Beryl Rawson, "*Spurii* and the Roman View of Illegitimacy," *Antichthon* 23 (1989), 10–41. Using Egypt as a case study, Roger Bagnall argues for a similar development in the East. See his *Egypt in Late Antiquity* (Princeton, 1993), 121–7.

43 Tjäder, *Die nichtliterarischen Lateinischen Papyri Italiens aus der Zeit 445–700*, no. 3. The document survives in two columns, the left of which records the dues owed by a set of unidentified tenants; on the right, in a second set, which relates to the territory of Padua, there is listed both the names and dues. The dues are in money, *xenia* (the standard medieval Italian term for symbolic gifts like chickens and eggs, ducks, lard, honey, and milk which are mentioned specifically in the document), and *operae*, that is labor, measured *per ebdomada*, and varying between 0 and 3 days/week. For dating, see the comments of Tjäder, *P-Ital* 185–6. For commentary on the text see John Percival, "P-Ital. 3 and Roman estate management," *Latomus* 102 (1969), 607–15; Vera, "Forme funzioni," 425–30; the former stresses its importance, the latter minimizes it. Other analyses: Philip J. Jones, "L'Italia agraria nell' alto medioevo: problemi di cronologia di continuità," in *Settimane di studio del Centro italiano di studi sull'alto medioevo*, 13 (Spoleto, 1969), 83–4; John Percival, "Seigneurial aspects of late Roman estate management," *EHR* 84 (1969), 449–73, esp. 454–5, 460; Pierre Toubert, *Les structures du Latium médiéval* (Rome, 1973), 466–7; Adriaan Verhulst, "Quelques remarques à propos des corvées de colons à l'époque du Bas-Empire et du Haut Moyen Age," in *Revue de l'Université de Bruxelles* (1977), I, 89–95, esp. 92–3 (now in Adriaan Verhulst, *Rural and Urban Aspects of Early and Medieval Northwest Europe* (Aldershot, 1992), study II); Bruno Andreolli, "La corvée precarolinga," in *Le prestazioni d'opera nelle campagne italiane del Medioevo* (Bologna, 1987), 29–52, esp. 29. See also Jones, *LRE*, 2, 805–6; Wickham, *Framing the Early Middle Ages*, 278–79.

slaves.[44] What remains entirely unclear, however, is whether the tendency of dependent peasants to be unfree was a long-standing feature of late Roman Italy or whether the effects of war, barbarian invasions, or general economic hardship had reduced formerly free *coloni* to serfs.

As property of his master, a slave could not own property. Any acquisition gained lawfully by a slave, from whatever source – earnings, gifts, legacies, even children – was transferred to the ownership of his master.[45] However, masters could grant their slaves a *peculium* – property (whether in the form of moveables or immoveables) that the slave could use and enjoy. The compilers pass over this subject with a few general remarks.[46] In theory, the owner had the right to take possession of the *peculium* at will. This is presupposed by *ET* 84, which instructs the receiver of a fugitive slave to return that slave, along with his *peculium*, to the rightful owner, and *ET* 121, where a creditor who makes a loan to another's slave is to reclaim what he is owed from the slave's *peculium*, and not the owner's property. Moreover, the absence of provisions dealing with offenses committed against the property of slaves suggests that the *peculium* belonged to the slave's owner.[47]

It followed as a consequence of his legal status as property of his owner that any offense committed against a slave was to be dealt with by the owner. Since this was an injury to his property, it was his ultimate right and responsibility to seek redress. The compilers provided several scenarios. For instance, the owner of a murdered slave was given the choice of either prosecuting the offender criminally, or receiving from him two substitute slaves of equal value.[48] The unlawful use of another's slave resulted in a monetary fine.[49] The freeman who defiled another's *ancilla* or *originaria* was required to pay the aggrieved master two slaves of equal value; failure to do so resulted in his being flogged.[50] In all instances, it was the owner who initiated the action.[51]

[44] *CJ* 11.48.21: "What difference can be distinguished between slaves and *adscriptii*?" ("quae etenim differentia inter servos et adscripticios intellegetur. . .?") On the depressed economic and legal status of *adscriptii* in the sixth century, see Wickham, *Framing the Early Middle Ages*, 521. For a general history: Jones, "Slavery in the ancient world," 1–15; Finley, *Ancient Slavery and Modern Ideology*; Kampen, *Image and Status*, 27–32; Rawson, "*Spurii* and the Roman View of Illegitimacy," *Antichthon*, 10–41.

[45] *Dig.* 41.1.10.1 (Gaius, lib. 2 *Inst.*); Ernst Levy, *Weströmisches Vulgarrecht. Das Obligationenrecht*, Forschungen zum römischen Recht (Weimar, 1956), 71–2; Borkowski, *Textbook on Roman Law*, 94.

[46] *ET* 80, 84, 121.

[47] *Dig.* 4.4.3.4; 34.4.31.3; *CJ* 5.18.7 (294); Michael Kaser, *Das römische Privatrecht*, (Göttingen, 1976; repr. 1993), 344.

[48] *ET* 152. [49] *ET* 150. [50] *ET* 64.

[51] There are references only to slave informers and witnesses, not plaintiffs: *ET* 48, 84, 100, 101, 102. A *colonus*, however, was permitted to bring an action against anyone suspected of stealing from his or his master's property (*ET* 146).

Although slaves had no independent legal personality to speak of, the law recognized the independent personality of the slave when he committed a criminal act on his own.[52] The issue of punishment, however, was a difficult one, for it was the master who undoubtedly would have suffered from any compositions or fines imposed upon a criminal slave. Very frequently, therefore, punishment took a corporal or capital form, whereas the same offense committed by a freeman involved his paying in some form or another.[53] But financial penalties for offending slaves did occur, particularly when their actions resulted in the loss or damage to another's property.[54] Under the rules of noxal surrender, an ancient concept dating back to the Republic, the owner had the choice whether to pay for the damage or to surrender the slave to be punished. This rule applied equally to *coloni* and *originarii*.[55] Naturally, the master's decision rested largely on the amount of the sum demanded and the value of the offending slave. We have no direct information on slave-prices in early sixth-century Italy, but an indication is to be found in *Var.* 5.16, where Cassiodorus has Theoderic fix a bounty of two or three *solidi* (depending on their condition) for slaves whose masters commit them to the service of the Ostrogothic navy. But this seems to be an especially low value given that a person who wrongfully employed another's slave was liable to pay one *solidus* for every day he so employed the slave (*ET* 150). In the event that the offending slave was sold or manumitted after the offense, the general rule was that liability followed the wrongdoer, thus making the new owner or the ex-slave liable.[56]

There were also occasions when the participation of slaves was required in legal proceedings. While prohibited from bringing forward a civil or criminal action on his own behalf or that of his owner, a slave could be compelled to act as a witness, under torture, in some civil and criminal proceedings, and in rare instances against his own master. *ET* 19 permits a slave to testify against his owner where a complaint of *raptus* has been concealed. Likewise, a slave could testify to the fact that his owner had connived his escape in order to profit (*ET* 84). Otherwise slaves and freedmen were forbidden, under penalty of death, to give testimony either in defense of or against current and former owners (*ET* 48). Here again, the matter for the compilers was one of practical concern for an owner whose slave was injured or killed as a result of judicial torture. In the event that a

52 *ET* 56, 63, 77, 97, 98, 104, 109, 117. 53 E.g., *ET* 59, 97. 54 E.g., *ET* 98, 117, 118.

55 *ET* 56, 98, 109, 117.

56 *ET* 120. See further Kyle Harper, "Slave Prices in Late Antiquity (and in the Very Long Term)," *Historia* 59 (2010), 206–38.

plaintiff was unable to prove his case through the torture of another's slave, *ET* 100 required him to compensate the owner accordingly:

> Another's slave cannot be tortured [to testify] to the detriment of another, unless the informer or accuser, whose concern it is to prove what he claims, is prepared to stake the amount of the slave's value as determined by his owner.[57]

That a slave was conceived as a possession of his owner was an important consideration for his lowly legal status, but it was not the only one. A related factor was the long-standing prejudice of Roman law that the slave was by his very nature inherently depraved, whereas the freeman was morally superior.[58] This prejudice was enshrined in the *ET*'s restrictions on the admissibility of slave evidence – for the character, position, and economic condition of a witness were all factors that could determine the degree to which he could be trusted, and found palpable expression in the provisions governing sexual relations between free and unfree.[59] The idea of a free-woman willingly cavorting with a slave, whether it was her own or another's, was totally abhorrent, and constituted an act of immorality (*stuprum*). Following *CTh* 9.24.2 of the Emperor Constantius II of 349, the compilers punished the offenders severely, in particular the slave:

> But if any slave commits this crime [*stuprum*], even if he does so with a willing and complicit widow, he shall be burned up by avenging flames; she, too, who was not ashamed to find pleasure with a slave, shall pay the penalty of adultery.[60]

The focus here was on sexual relationships between a free woman and slave, something which Roman society had never favored, partly because children of such unions would be free. A preferred slur of Roman satirists against supposedly respectable women was that they consorted with slaves or low-born males.[61] Under Roman law, sexual relationships between slaves, or

57 *ET* 100: "Servus alienus in alterius caput torqueri non potest: nisi delator, aut accusator, cuius interest probare quod intendit, precium eius, quantum dominus taxaverit, inferre paratus sit."

58 This distinction was a basis of classical law on the subject of slavery, and has been used by some scholars to underscore some of the essential continuities between the classical and medieval worlds. See, e.g, Orlando Patterson, *Slavery and Social Death: A Comparative Study* (Cambridge, MA, 1985); Bonnassié, *From Slavery to Feudalism in South-Western Europe*, 1–59.

59 *ET* 61, 62.

60 *ET* 61: "Si quis vero servus, etiamsi cum volente et adquiescente vidua hoc crimen admiserit, flammis ultricibus exuratur: illa quoque adulterii poena damnanda, quae non erubuit servili subiacere libidini."

61 Amy Richlin, "Approaches to the Sources on Adultery at Rome," in H. Foley (ed.), *Reflections of Women in Antiquity* (New York, 1981), 379–404, esp. 385, 395; Keith R. Bradley, *Slaves and Masters in the Roman Empire: A Study in Social Control* (Oxford, 1987).

those of free people with slaves, had never been recognized as legitimate marriages; and such unions, *contubernia*, lacked all of the legal consequences of marriage, *coniugium*.[62]

Unions involving freemen and slave women, though considered disgraceful to be sure, were not strictly prohibited, in part because children born of such unions would be slaves.[63] For free women, however, the situation was quite the opposite. The general rule from Constantine onwards was that a free woman who cohabitated with another's slave against the will of the master forfeited her free status.[64] As for unions between a free woman and her own slave, the penalty was death for both.[65] Such unions were similarly regarded as heinous throughout most of the barbarian kingdoms. Among the Burgundians, if the woman had not consented, the slave was to be killed; if she did consent, both were to die. For eighth-century Lombard Italy, Rothari stated that intermarriage would result in death for the servile husband and death or slavery for the free wife.[66]

The subject of mixed unions received a good deal of attention by jurists and Emperors alike. The compilers followed in step, applying equally severe measures on the guilty parties. But in light of the fact that such measures were repeated over and over from Constantine to Justinian, it would seem that they met with little success. One reason for the failure, no doubt, rested on the fact that in the provinces, at least, there was a great deal of uncertainty about the legitimacy of mixed unions. Roman law did not necessarily correspond with provincial practice in regards to marriages between free women and slaves, and there is evidence that these sorts of unions did occur in some outlying districts of the Empire well into the fifth century.[67] Further adding to the

62 *PS* 2.19.6; *Reg. Ulp.* 5.5. See also Judith Evans Grubbs, "'Marriage More Shameful than Adultery': Slave-Mistress Relationships, 'Mixed Marriages', and Late Roman Law," *Phoenix* 47 (1993), 125–54; Jane Gardner, *Women in Roman Law and Society* (Bloomington, IN, 1986), 213–18; Beryl Rawson, "Roman Concubinage and Other de facto Marriages," *TAPA* 104 (1974), 279–305; Susan Treggiari, "*Contubernales* in *CIL* 6," *Phoenix* 35 (1981), 42–69. For Roman traditions on marriages between persons of different social status, see generally Paul R. C. Weaver, "The Status of Children in Mixed Marriages," in B. Rawson (ed.), *The Family in Ancient Rome: New Perspectives* (Ithaca, 1986), 145–69.

63 *CJ* 9.9.24 (291). For review and discussion see Treggiari, "*Contubernales*," 53; Weaver, "The Status of Children in Mixed Marriages," 149.

64 *CTh* 4.12.4. Cf. 4.12.1–3 (concerning *contubernium* between free women and imperial slaves).

65 *CTh* 9.9.1 (326). Evans Grubbs, "Marriage More Shameful," 142–7.

66 *Liber Constitutionum*, ed. L. R. von Salis, *MGH Leges nationum Germanicarum* 1 (Hannover, 1902), xxxv, 1–2 (Burgundian); similarly *Pactus Legis Salicae*, ed. K. A. Eckhardt, *MGH Leges nationum Germanicarum* 4.1 (Hannover, 1962), 13, 7–8 (Frankish); Rothari 221, Liutprand 24 (Lombard).

67 See Judith Evans Grubbs, *Law and Family in Late Antiquity* (Oxford, 1995), 269, who cites eastern examples. Wickham cites evidence for this practice continuing in the West well into the ninth century: *Framing the Early Middle Ages*, 405, 560.

problem was the general blurring of social and legal boundaries between free and unfree at this time, and the confusion of status that resulted. For a variety of reasons – legal or otherwise – a freeman one year could find himself a slave in the next, and a resourceful slave could earn his freedom through fortune or reward. This was a general feature of Late Antique society.[68] That people as a result were unsure of their own legal status (or that of other members of their family) or of the validity of their own marriage is clear from the many decrees devoted to questions of status.[69]

It goes without saying that slaves constantly sought to improve their lot in life through the liberation of their bondage and elevation into the ranks of the freed, the *liberti*. Escape was of course a solution, but by no means was it the only one. For freedom could be granted to a slave as a direct consequence of the law in return for services he or she performed for the state, or through the will of the owner in a process of manumission. In Roman law there were three methods of manumission: *vindicta*, *census*, and *testamentum*. *Vindicta*, the oldest of these, required the consent of a magistrate in a formal process involving a ceremonial rod (*Dig.* 40.2.8). In the case of manumission by census, the name of the slave was enrolled in the census with the approval of the master (Gai., *Inst.*, 1.140). And in the most straightforward process, freedom could be granted in the will of the deceased master (*Dig.* 40.4.24).[70]

The compilers passed over the subject of manumission without comment. Instead, they addressed one instance where freedom was rewarded for service:

> If a slave learns that a complaint of abduction (*raptus*) has been concealed by his owners and the crime passed over by connivance, and reports this to the courts, he shall be freed.[71]

We are entitled to ask, however, how such a slave could hope to achieve any success in this action given the position of the law towards informers and

[68] See, e.g., Allen E. Jones, *Social Mobility in Late Antique Gaul: Strategies and Opportunities for the Non-Elite* (Cambridge, 2009), who convincingly demonstrates that Gaul in the fifth and sixth centuries was a flexible society where mobility from one class to another was the rule and not the exception.

[69] E.g., *CJ* 5.18.3 (215); *Dig.* 24.3.22.13 (Ulpian); *PS* 2.21a14. For discussion, see Evans Grubbs, "Marriage More Shameful," 135–6; Evans Grubbs, *Law and Family*, 269–71; Alan Watson, *Roman Slave Law* (Baltimore, 1987), 11.

[70] On the subject of manumission in Roman law, see Jane Gardner and Thomas Wiedemann, *The Roman Household. A Sourcebook* (London, 1991), 145–50, 163–4; Borkowski, *Textbook on Roman Law*, 97–100.

[71] *ET* 19: "Servus vero, si querelam de raptu dissimulari a dominis et pactione crimen senserit definiri atque iudiciis prodiderit, libertate donetur."

slave evidence in general, and the likelihood of the owner simply denying the accusation.

While the *ET* does not expressly address the terms or particular conditions by which manumission could be validly effected, it can be reasonably assumed that one's emancipation was a matter of public record. Included among the Ravenna papyri, for example, is one such declaration of emancipation.[72] Moreover, it was in the freedman's best interest, and that of his heirs, to have his newly-found status formally recognized in some form or another. Of course, a *libertus* was not entirely free, but remained obligated to his manumittor in a number of ways for the balance of his life. Under Roman law his freedom was conditional and always subject to the discretion of his patron or that of the patron's heirs.[73] Unfreedom was thus to be replaced by permanent subjection. And as was the case with many other barbarian law codes, the *ET* underscores the point that the liberty which a slave gained through his manumission was not unconditional.[74] Once freed, the freedman remained bound to his patron and the patronal family under certain defined legal obligations, including the prohibition from testifying against former masters or their heirs.[75]

The evolution of a class of permanently dependent *liberti* was prompted by a variety of reasons. In Visigothic Spain, for example, it has been argued that *liberti* were generated in an attempt to square the demands of Christian ethics with an existing pattern of material, especially landed, wealth. Emerging Christian morality declared the freeing of slaves to be a good thing, particularly for saintly Bishops. This tended to dissipate Church assets, however, since people were as important as land in agricultural production. Permanently dependent *liberti* thus offered Christians – ecclesiastical or lay – the opportunity to make their manumissions while, at the same time, preserving the tied labor force which was central to their wealth.[76]

This is certainly plausible, but there is more to the picture. That *liberti* were connected with the militarization of society in the post-Roman world is likely.[77] According to Visigothic law, it was a requirement that all *liberti*

72 Tjäder, *P-Ital* no. 9, 246–9.

73 See, e.g., *CTh* 4.10.2 of the Emperor Constantine, which prohibited a freedman from showing ingratitude to his former master. Those found guilty were re-enslaved.

74 Visigoths: *LV* v.7.13, 20; Lombards: Rothari 224–6, Aistuulf, 11. See also Wickham, *Framing the Early Middle Ages*, 564–6.

75 *ET* 48.

76 Dietrich Claude, "Freedmen in the Visigothic Kingdom," in E. James (ed.), *Visigothic Spain: New Approaches* (Oxford, 1980), 159–88. For similar arguments in Gaul, see Bonnassie, *From Slavery*, 28.

77 C. Richard Whittaker, "Landlords and Warlords in the Later Roman Empire," in J. Rich and G. Shipley (eds.), *Warfare and Society in the Roman World* (London, 1993), 277–302.

were to fight with their lords during times of war. This prescription applied to only a percentage – 5 percent, raised to 10 percent by King Wamba (672–80) – of full slaves. A similar situation seems to have existed in the Merovingian kingdom, where *liberti* were classified among the arms-bearing groups of society and expected to fight, again under the protection of their lord.[78] And our own sources contain several instances of powerful lords using their dependents in much the same way as a private army.[79] The popularity of freedmen for those able to create them, therefore, may well have been in response to the need to develop a body of armed retainers who possessed the requisite military skill and expertise. As military obligations became more generalized in the course of the fifth and sixth centures, this necessity only grow.[80]

While Roman law made a clear distinction between *liberti* and freemen (*ingenui*) in terms of legal status, this distinction found little expression in the *ET*, at least in terms of punishment: nowhere do the former receive differential treatment.[81] But the *libertus* clearly was not of the same ilk as the slave. Although a freedman did not necessarily lose his inherently depraved nature and gain the rectitude of the freeman immediately upon his liberation, he was not subject to the same impositions or restrictions as was a slave. For instance, there is nothing in the *ET* prohibiting unions between freed and free. Likewise, Constantine's extensive legislation on the subject of mixed unions involving freewomen and slaves did not include a provision on *liberti*. It was not until the Emperor Anthemius 150 years later that such unions were declared illegal, subject to the same harsh penalties as unions between free women and slaves.[82] That the compilers chose to ignore this later development is a good indication that in sixth-century Italy a *libertus*, despite his not being born *ingenuus*, could enjoy many of the privileges that went along with being free. This was not the case for individuals who were subject to the authority of another (*alieni iuris*). Among these included the lowly freeman who was compelled to work as a tenant farmer on another's land, and women and children who lived under the *potestas* of a *paterfamilias*.

The number of provisions that involve one's legal status implies that the preservation of status distinctions in all levels of society continued to be a

78 Visigoths: *LV* 9.2.8–9; Merovingians: *Lex Salica*, ed. K.A. Eckhardt, *MGH Leges nationum Germanicarum* 4.2 (Hannover, 1969), 26.1.
79 E.g., Proc., *BG* V. xii. 50–4; Cass., *Var.* 4.39, 5.12, 10.5; *ET* 75, 89.
80 See further Heather, "State, Lordship and Community in the West," 464–5.
81 Only four provisions mention freedmen specifically: *ET* 19, 30, 48, 103.
82 *CTh* 4.12. *Nov. Anth.* 1 (468).

matter of importance in the early sixth century. A distinct dichotomy between the freeborn, privileged classes, and those of slave or 'base' birth appear in many of the provisions. Of course, the importance of status distinctions in Roman law was hardly a new thing. Considerations of status had always loomed large in Roman society, and legal distinctions between *honestiores* and *humiliores* had a long history behind them. But given the fluidity of late Roman society, wherein it was possible for slaves to become free and *vice versa*, and the fact that among the lower levels of society, and particularly in the provinces, the legal distinction between slave and free was not always acknowledged in everyday practice, one might reasonably expect that concerns of legal distinction would not figure so prominently in the *ET*.[83] That they do speaks to the longevity of such Roman prejudices, which continued to be enshrined in the laws well after they ceased serving any useful purpose. In fact, such artificial legal distinctions between free and unfree remained one of the most conservative elements of early medieval culture, and only after the tenth century did they slowly begin to break down.[84]

Law and the family

The ability to lawfully possess property and meet the fiscal obligations attendant upon it was an important aspect of free status in early sixth-century Italy. But it was not the only one. An important consideration was family, and it is this area of the law in which the compilers took a good deal of interest. In all, a total of twenty-five provisions of the *ET* address specific points of Roman family law, and touch upon virtually every aspect of private and public life: from marriage and divorce, *raptus* and *stuprum*, succession and inheritance, to the rights and responsibilities of parents and guardians, blood relations and in-laws.[85]

The provisions also speak to the importance of the family as a primary social institution of society; and at the same time, underscore the depressed legal status of those individuals who were subject to the *potestas* of the *paterfamilias*, even if such authority of the head of household was by the early sixth century much attenuated. By the fifth century, in fact, *patria potestas* was largely characterized as a restricted and temporary control of the

83 Jones, *Social Mobility in Late Antique Gaul.*

84 Paul Fouracre, "Space, Culture and Kingdoms in Early Medieval Europe," in P. Linehan and J. Nelson (eds.), *The Medieval World* (New York, 2003), 366–80, esp. 370.

85 *ET* 17–20, 23, 24, 36, 37, 38, 39, 54, 59, 60, 61, 62, 63, 64, 65, 66, 67, 92, 93, 94, 95, 153.

marriage property, and the extreme form of a father's authority – namely his right to kill his children (*ius vitae ac necis*), had long been considered obsolete; Christian concepts of humanitarianism left little room for a legal theory where an individual could exercise almost absolute authority over the members of his family, much the same way as a master over his slaves, until his own death. Despite this, it was the *paterfamilias* who benefited the most through his role as husband and father.[86]

Marriage

Marriage serves as a useful starting point for any discussion on the family. To begin, it must be pointed out that what follows is based on the official record of the law, and as such incomplete: for marriage was one area where the law was kept to the periphery. A large obstacle lying in the way of the authorities' efforts in this direction was the persistence of the idea of marriage as consensual, along with a weak formalization of the wedding ceremony itself. The exchange of premarital gifts, the dowry, recording the bride's dowry and property clauses in the event of divorce, the religious ritual, and the family festivities were all moments of social significance and by no means devoid of legal implications. But for many, to be sure, these elements were not essential to the conclusion of a proper marriage. Informal marriages, such as were widely contracted among the poorer classes, were indistinguishable from concubinage, and were not properly addressed by the law. And it was precisely these types of unions which made it difficult to stamp out practices such as bigamy, unjust breaking of the bond, and adultery, and hence to establish the legitimacy of children with any degree of certainty.

In attempting to legislate the marital practices and private behavior of his subjects, Theoderic was simply following long-established imperial tradition. Emperors had attempted to regulate Roman marriage ever since Augustus, whose *Lex Iulia de maritandis ordinibus* and *lex Iulia de adulteriis*

[86] Antti Arjava, "Paternal Power in Late Antiquity," *JRS* 88 (1998), 147–65; Antti Arjava, "The Survival of Roman Family Law After the Barbarian Settlements," in R. W. Mathisen (ed.), *Law, Society and Authority in Late Antiquity* (Oxford, 2001), 33–51; Kate Cooper, *The Fall of the Roman Household* (Cambridge, 2007) 108–11; Yan Thomas, "Vitae necisque potestas. Le pére, la cité, la mort," in *Du châtiment dans la cité: Supplices corporels et peine de mort dans le monde antique*, organisée par L'Ècole française de Rome avec le concours du Centre national de la recherche scientifique (Rome, November 9–11) (Rome, 1984), 499–548; William V. Harris, "The Roman Father's Power of Life and Death," in Roger S. Bagnall and William V. Harris (eds.), *Studies in Roman Law in Memory of A. A. Schiller* (Leiden, 1986), 81–95; Elisabeth Meyer-Marthaler, *Römisches Recht in Rätien im frühen und hohen Mittelalter* (Zurich, 1968), 131–8.

(18 BC) and *Lex Papia-Poppaea* (AD 9) had become the basis for all subsequent marriage legislation over the next five hundred years.[87] The Augustan legislation was originally intended to promote marriage and child-bearing (and to discourage extramarital affairs) among members of the senatorial aristocracy and the wealthier and more socially distinguished classes in general. The main points of the laws were: the treatment of adultery and *stuprum* as public offenses,[88] the regulation of divorce proceedings, the penalization of celibacy and promotion of child-bearing with the rewarding of certain privileges (for example, *ius liberorum*), and the prohibition of certain unions.[89] Augustus' regulations remained more or less unchanged through the third century, with certain revisions and alterations made by various Emperors.[90]

In the fourth century, however, important developments took place. Adultery, for instance, originally entailed a fine and sentence of banishment to an island for those convicted.[91] By Constantine's time, it is generally assumed that convicted adulterers, both male and female, could be

[87] Evans Grubbs, *Law and Family*, 94.

[88] Adultery applied to extramarital sexual relations with or by a married woman; *stuprum* covered illicit sexual relations in general, including adultery and relations with a widow or an unmarried girl or boy of respectable status. For a definition of *adulterium*: *Dig.* 48.5.6.1; 48.5.35.1. Slaves: *Dig.* 48.5.6 pr.; *PS* 2.26.16 (a man who corrupted another's slave could be charged with *iniuria* under the *lex Aquilia*). Prostitutes: *CJ* 9.9.22 (290). On the difference between *adulterium* and *stuprum* in Roman law, see Evans Grubbs, *Law and Family*, 203; Elaine Fantham, "*Stuprum*: Public Attitudes and Penalties for Sexual Offenses in Republican Rome," *EMC/CV NS* 10 (1991), 267–91; David Cohen, "The Augustan Law on Adultery: The Social and Cultural Context," in David Kertzer and R. P. Saller (eds.), *The Family in Italy from Antiquity to the Present* (New Haven, CT, 1991), 109–26; Thomas A. J. McGinn, "Concubinage and the *Lex Julia* on Adultery," *TAPA* 121 (1991), 335–75; Thomas A. J. McGinn, *Prostitution, Sexuality and the Law in Ancient Rome* (Oxford, 1998). For the development of adultery as a public crime, see Joëlle Beaucamp, *Le Statut de la femme à Byzance (4e-7e siècle)*, i. *Le Droit impérial* (Paris, 1990), 139–70; Gillian Clark, *Women in Late Antiquity. Pagan and Christian Lifestyles* (Oxford, 1993), 35–6.

[89] On the Augustan legislation, see Cooper, *The Fall of the Roman Household*, 149; Riccardo Astolfi, *La Lex Iulia et Papia*, 2nd edn. (Padua, 1986); Peter A. Brunt, *Italian Manpower 225* BC–AD *14* (Oxford, 1971), 558–66; Percy E. Corbett, *The Roman Law of Marriage* (Oxford, 1930), 31–9, 119–21, and 133–46; Pal Csillag, *The Augustan Laws of Family Relations* (Budapest, 1976); Richard I. Frank, "Augustus' Legislation on Marriage and Children," *California Studies in Classical Antiquity* 8 (1975), 41–52; Jean Gaudemet, "Le mariage en droit romain: *iustum matrimonium*," in Gaudemet (ed.), *Sociétés et mariage* (Strasbourg, 1980), 46–103; Dieter Nörr, "Planung in der Antike: Über die Ehegesetze des Augustus," in Horst Baier (ed.), *Freiheit und Sachzwang: Beiträge zu Ehren Helmut Schelskys* (Braunschweig, 1977), 309–43; Susan Treggiari, *Roman Marriage: Iusti Coniuges from the Time of Cicero to the Time of Ulpian* (Oxford, 1991), 37–80; and Andrew Wallace-Hadrill, "Family and Inheritance in the Augustan Marriage Laws," *Proceedings of the Cambridge Philological Society* 207 (1981), 58–80.

[90] Evans Grubbs, *Law and Family*, 95–102.

[91] E.g., *PS* 2.26.14 (mentions only the classical penalties of relegation and partial confiscation of property).

punished by death.[92] Over the course of the second and third centuries, restrictions on certain types of marriages were tightened, and the category of prohibited unions was extended.[93] Rules of inheritance were relaxed, and although unpopular, laws penalizing celibacy and promoting child-bearing continued to be enforced. Under Constantine, however, an attempt was made to strengthen, or at least better define rules of inheritance and transactions involving transfer of property within families; and penalties on celibacy as well as rewards for having children, in particular the *ius liberorum*, were abolished.[94]

Cassiodorus' *formula* for the confirmation of marriage characterized *coniugium* as a formal state or union existing as a matter of social fact and created by the will, manifested in the fulfillment of certain prescribed formalities, of particular individuals and the sanction of royal approval:

> With offered prayers you proclaim that the woman whom you have happily chosen [to be your wife] is to be joined to you through Our kindness in honest marriage, so that children borne from her may become legitimate heirs... Wherefore, We ordain that she is to become your legitimate wife; and We desire that children from that marriage, whether they have been conceived or are about to be conceived, shall be lawfully counted as your heirs, so that without any hesitation you may love those whom you know will be your successors. Whereas nature has bestowed upon you children, We have made them most dear possessions through the dispensation of this security.[95]

[92] *CTh* 9.40.1 (314) includes adultery as among the crimes receiving "capitalem ... severamque sententiam." Presumably this meant the death penalty. On the meaning of *capitalis* in this law, see Clémence Dupont, *Le Droit criminel dans les constitutions de Constantin*, ii. *Les Peines* (Lille, 1955), 22–8. On the subject of adultery as a capital offense in Constantine's reign, see generally Theodor Mommsen, *Römisches Stafrecht*, trans. J. Duquesne, *Le Droit pénal romain*, 3 vols. (Paris, 1907), ii, 426; Dupont, *Le Droit criminel dans les constitutions de Constantin*, i. *Les Infractions* (Lille, 1953), 51–2; Richard A. Bauman, "*Leges Iudiciorum Publicorum*," in H. Temporini (ed.), *Aufstieg und Niedergang der römischen Welt* ii., 13 (1980), 103–233, esp. 191 n. 191; Corbett, *The Roman Law of Marriage*, 146; Csillag, *The Augustan Laws*, 196; Treggiari, *Roman Marriage*, 290; Evans Grubbs, *Law and Family*, 95, 216–25.

[93] *Dig.* 47.11.4 (concerning *quasi*-marital relations between a free woman and another's slave); see Gardner, *Women in Roman Law and Society*, 159. Relations between Senators and members of the lower class were prohibited by legislation of the Emperors Aurelius and Commodus: *Dig.* 23.2.16pr. Similarly *Dig.* 23.2.34.3; 23.2.42.1.

[94] Evans Grubbs, *Law and Family*, 103–23.

[95] Cass., *Var.* 7.40: "Oblata itaque supplicatione depromis mulierem quam tibi placitus illigavit amplexus, beneficio nostro iugali honestate debere sociari, ut ex ea liberi nati nomen nanciscantur heredum ... Et ideo illam ... legitimam tibi fieri censemus uxorem et filios ex eadem coniuge, sive qui suscepti sunt sive qui sunt suscipiendi, heredum volumus iura sortiri, ut sub nulla dubietate diligas quos tibi absolute successores futuros esse cognoscas. natura enim tibi praestitit filios, sed nos tali securitate facimus esse carissimos."

Of primary importance was the formality of the dowry. The giving of the *dos* by the man's side was an ancient tradition whose origins lay in the Roman institution of the *donatio nuptialis* (bride-gift).[96] The giving of the *dos* functioned to distinguish the relationship from others of a less binding nature, since the acceptance of the *dos* on the part of the bride's family constituted a formal agreement between the two sides, the betrothal. The compilers recognized the importance of the betrothal, albeit minimally; under *ET* 92, a man convicted of ravishing a girl was granted some leniency if she had been formally betrothed to him.

While the *ET* contains no specific provision on the requirements of a legitimate marriage, it does outline the penalties for contracting an unlawful one:

> If anyone plans to contract an illegitimate marriage, let him not escape the thorough censure of the laws; he shall know that he has neither a just marriage nor legitimate children.[97]

According to this, a prohibited marriage lacked legitimacy, and any children from it were themselves illegitimate, the main consequence of which was that they were barred from making a claim of ownership on their natural father's estate. Examples of prohibited unions include those between free and unfree, and those involving more than two wives were certainly forbidden. Concerning the practice of bigamy, an edict of Athalaric stipulates: "No one shall be married to two wives at one time, for he will know that he is to be punished with the loss of his possessions. For this is either lust, whose enjoyment is not morally allowed; or it is desire, and is legally punished by poverty."[98]

ET 36 is a highly interpolated version of *CTh* 3.12.3, an imperial rescript of the Emperors Arcadius and Honorius of 396. Issued in Constantinople and addressed to the Praetorian Prefect Eutychianus, the rescript concerned one specific type of prohibited marriage, namely those that contravened rules of incest, and outlawed unions between first cousins. Drawing from *CTh* 3.12.3, the compilers took out any reference to incest, a significant

[96] Antti Arjava, *Women and Law in Late Antiquity* (Oxford, 1996), 52–62.; Arjava, "The Survival of Roman Family Law," 40.

[97] *ET* 36: "Si quis ad nuptias non legitimas aspiraverit, legum censuram penitus non evadat; qui nec iustum matrimonium nec filios sciat se habere legitimos."

[98] Cass., *Var.* 9.18.6: "Uno tempore duabus nemo copuletur uxoribus, quia se noverit rerum suarum amissione plectendum. Nam aut libido est, et recte perfrui non sinitur: aut cupiditas, et iure nuditate damnatur."

modification considering the amount of attention the subject received by jurists and imperial legislators. On the subject of incest in general, Ulpian states:

> There is no *conubium* between ascendants and descendants no matter how far removed. Between collateral relatives, at one time marriages could not be contracted up to the fourth degree. But now it is permitted to take a wife also from the third degree – but only a brother's daughter, not a sister's daughter or a paternal or maternal aunt, although they are of the same degree. We cannot take as wife a woman who was our stepmother or stepdaughter or daughter-in-law or mother-in-law. If someone takes a wife who is not permitted, he contracts an incestuous marriage; so the children (of this marriage) are not in his power but are bastards, as if promiscuously conceived.[99]

Under Diocletian, incest seems to have been a capital offense, and by the mid-fourth century, prohibition extended to relations between cousins of the third degree and those between an individual and a relative of his or her previous spouse.[100]

That the compilers did not mention incest specifically in the provision can best be explained by a more relaxed position towards the subject at this time – a position reinforced by Cassiodorus' *formula* for granting legitimacy to unions between first cousins:

> Moved by your request, if you prove that she is joined to you in proximity of blood relations to the extent of first cousin, and no more, We decree that you may be joined in marriage, and order that henceforth you shall not have to undergo any trial . . . By God's favor may you have legitimate heirs from this

[99] *Tituli ex corpore Ulpiani*, ed. and trans. J.T. Abdy and Bryan Walter, *The Commentaries of Gaius and Rules of Ulpian* (Cambridge, 1885), 5.6–7: "Inter parentes et liberos infinite cuiuscumque gradus sint conubium non est. Inter cognates autem ex transverse gradu olim quidem usque ad quartum gradum matrimonia contrahi non poterant: nunc autem etiam ex tertio gradu licet uxorem ducere, sed tantum fratris filiam, non etiam sororis filiam aut amitam vel materteram, quamvis eodem gradu sint. Eam, quae noverca vel privigna vel nurus vel socrus nostra fuit, uxorem ducere non possumus. Si quis eam quam non licte uxorem duxerit, incestum matrimonium conrahit: ideoque liberi in potestate eius non fiunt, sed quasi vulgo concepti spurii sunt."

[100] On legislation see, e.g., *Mosaicarum et Romanorum Legum Collatio* 6.4, ed. J. Baviera, (*FIRA* vol. II, (Florence, 1940), 588–60 (May 1, 295)) of the Emperor Diocletian to the provincials in Damascus), which likened incestuous unions to the mating of cattle or wild beasts (which lacked any respect for modesty), recognized children of such unions as illegitimate, and punished wrongdoers with a penalty of "worthy severity" (presumably death). See also *CTh* 3.12.1–2 (344 and 355) of the Emperor Constantius, issued to the provincials of Phoenicia, which prohibited unions between a man and the former wife of his brother or the sister of his former wife. See further Evans Grubbs, *Law and Family*, 24, 55, 95, 96, 99–101.

> marriage, which, after having been granted our consent, is not culpable but praiseworthy.[101]

Unions that contravened rules of incest clearly continued to be penalized under Theoderic, but the scope of the censure was not nearly as comprehensive as that of earlier Roman legislation. A possible explanation for this more relaxed stance on incest lies in numbers. On the one hand, Italy in the early sixth century simply lacked the sufficient numbers to allow for comprehensive legislation on the subject of incest. That is, the number of eligible candidates for marriage precluded far-reaching legislation on incest of the kind issued in previous centuries. To take as an example, Rome's population by the end of the fifth century was around five hundred thousand – a nearly 50 percent drop from what it had been three centuries before; and it would drop from around half a million to less than forty thousand in fewer than two centuries.[102] At the same time, the central administration lacked sufficient numbers of officers who could effectively regulate such provisions. As the compilers concede the point in *ET* 52 and 53, municipal magistrates were at this time in short supply.

In addition to the subject of prohibited marriages in general, the compilers addressed the particular custom of marriage by abduction (*raptus*).[103] In accordance with established law, in this case a decree of the Emperor Constantine of 326 (*CTh* 9.24.1), abductors of freeborn women or virgins, as well as the complicit victims themselves, were to be executed:

ET 17	*CTh* 9.24.1, 2, 4, 5
We decree, in accordance with established custom, that an abductor of a freeborn woman or virgin, together with his accomplices or assistants, shall be executed once his	If any one who has not previously made a pact with the girl's parents should seize her against her will, or if he should lead her away when she is willing, hoping for protection from

[101] Cass., *Var.* 7.46.2 (*formula qua consobrinae matrimonium legitimum fiat*): "... supplicationum tuarum tenore permoti, si tibi tantum illa consobrini sanguinis vicinitate coniungitur nec alio gradu proximior approbaris, matrimonio tuo decernimus esse sociandam nullamque vobis exinde iubemus fieri quaestionem ... erunt vobis itaque deo favente posteri sollemniter heredes, castum matrimonium, gloriosa permixtio, quoniam quicquid a nobis fieri praecipitur, necesse est ut non culpis, sed laudibus applicetur."

[102] Neil Christie, *From Constantine to Charlemagne: An Archaeology of Italy* AD *300–800* (Aldershot, 2006), 251; Clifford Ando, "Decline, Fall, and Transformation," *Journal of Late Antiquity*, 31–60 at 38; Wickham, *Framing the Early Middle Ages*, 34: "... Rome, which, as a result of the ending of the African taxation [*annona*] which fed the city, experienced its sharpest population fall in precisely this period. Demographic decline in the city of Rome was indeed probably the most important structural change in Italy between 400 and 535."

[103] Roman law did not define rape *per se*, but sexual violence could be prosecuted as *stuprum per vim* (illegal sexual intercourse by force), which was categorized under the *lex Iulia de vi publica*.

crimes have been proven; if the abducted consents to her abductor, she, too, shall be killed.[104]

ET 18

If perhaps the parents or guardian of the abducted (*rapta*) girl neglect to prosecute and take legal measures against the guilty party of such a deed, by making an illicit pact concerning this crime, they shall suffer the penalty of exile.[105]

ET 19

If a slave learns that a complaint of abduction (raptus) has been concealed by his owners and the crime passed over by connivance, and reports this to the courts, he shall be freed.[106]

the response of one whom, on account of the fault of frivolity and the inconstancy of her sex and judgment, our ancestors altogether excluded from making legal complaints and from delivering testimony and from all matters pertaining to courts, the response of the girl shall be of no use to him in accordance with the ancient law, but rather the girl herself shall be held liable as a participant in the crime. (2) And if willing agreement is discovered in the virgin, she shall be punished with the same severity as her abductor . . . (4) But if any slave should report to the public courts that a crime of abduction has been neglected by deception or disregarded be an agreement [between the abductor and the girl's parents], he shall be granted Latinity, or if he is Latin, he shall be made a Roman citizen. If the parents, for whom the punishment of the crime was of particular concern, should show forbearance and suppress their grief, they shall be punished by deportation. (5) We order that partners and accomplices of the abductor also be subjected to the same punishment without regard to sex; and if among these attendants anyone of servile status should be apprehended, we order that person to be burned without consideration of sex.[107]

104 *ET* 17: "Raptorem ingenuae mulieris aut virginis, cum suis complicibus vel ministris, rebus probatis iuxta legem iubemus extingui, et si consenserit rapta raptori, pariter occidatur."

105 *ET* 18: "Si parentes raptae aut curator eius, quae minore aetate rapta est, exsequi et vindicare talis facti culpam forte neglexerit, pactum, quod non licet de hoc crimine faciendo, poenam patiantur exilii."

106 *ET* 19: "Servus vero, si querelam de raptu dissimulari a dominis et pactione crimen senserit definiri atque iudiciis prodiderit, libertate donetur."

107 *CTh* 9.24.1, 2, 4, 5: "Si quis nihil cum parentibus puellae ante depectus invitam eam rapuerit vel volentem abduxerit, patrocinium ex eius responsione sperans quam propter vitium levitatis et sexus

Bride theft involved the capture of an unmarried young woman by a man who was not betrothed to her, with the aim of obtaining her parents' consent to what is essentially a *de facto* marriage. A girl who actively consented was to suffer the same penalty as her abductor. What that penalty actually was is omitted in the text of the *CTh* but not in the *ET*.[108] That this custom was regarded as especially heinous is clear from the provision in both texts that granted freedom to the slave who brings information to the authorities – a significant reward in light of the harsh conditions associated with slavery, and the allowance in both for the use of informers. Given the decidedly dim view Roman law took on the use of informers, and especially slave informers who acted against their masters, these were obviously extreme measures intended to combat what was a particularly abhorrent crime.

A law of the Emperors Valens, Gratian, and Valentinian II of 377 required that any marriage contracted through the crime of abduction was to be prosecuted immediately, either by a relative wishing to avenge the dishonor committed against his family or by a third party inspired by his contempt for the abominable act. However, it also established a five-year statute of limitations on such prosecution. After five years the marriage could not be contested on the grounds that it was illicit, nor could any children borne from it be considered illegitimate.[109] *ET* 20 upholds this five-year statute of limitations, and similarly grants the right of accusation to all:

> Let it be permitted for all to make an accusation of abduction (*raptus*) within a period of five years, but after this period let no one initiate an investigation of this crime, even if it is shown that a legal action could have been brought

mobilitatem atque consilii a postulationibus et testimoniis omnibusque rebus iudiciariis antiqui penitus arcuerunt, nihil ei secundum ius vetus prosit puellae responsio, sed ipsa puella potius societate criminis obligetur. (2) Et si voluntatis assensio detegitur in virgine, eadem, qua raptor, severitate plectatur. . .(4) Si quis vero servus raptus facinus dissimulatione praeteritum aut pactione transmissum detulerit in publicum, latinitate donetur, aut, si latinus sit, civis fiat romanus: parentibus, quorum maxime vindicta intererat, si patientiam praebuerint ac dolorem compresserint, deportatione plectendis. (5) Participes etiam et ministros raptoris citra discretionem sexus eadem poena praecipimus subiugari, et si quis inter haec ministeria servilis condicionis fuerit deprehensus, citra sexus discretionem eum concremari iubemus." See further Judith Evans Grubbs, "Abduction Marriage in Antiquity: A Law of Constantine (*CTh* IX. 24. 1) and its Social Context," *JRS* 79 (1989), 59–83; Denise Grodzynski, "Ravies et coupables: Un essai d'interprétation de la loi 9,24,1 du Code Théodosien," *MEFRA* 96 (1984), 697–726; and Lucetta Desanti, "Costantino, il ratto e il matrimonio riparatore," *SDHI* 52 (1986), 195–217.

108 Evans Grubbs ("Abduction Marriage in Antiquity," 66) speculates that it was *summum supplicium* ("the supreme penalty"), such as condemnation *ad bestias* or burning. See further Beaucamp, *Le Statut de la femme*, 113; Richard Bauman ("*Leges Iudiciorum Publicorum*," 103–233, at 223) suggests the penalty is not specified because it came under the *lex Iulia de vi. Summum supplicium.*

109 *CTh* 9.24.3. Under classical law, *raptus* was dealt with by the *lex Iulia de vi publica*, which did not impose a five-year limit: *Dig.* 48.5.30.9. See further Evans Grubbs, *Law and Family*, 193.

> forward within the period of time prescribed above: particularly since all the children from this marriage [which has been contracted by the crime of abduction] are protected both by the authority and privilege of legitimacy after a period of five years has passed.[110]

The purpose behind the five year limitation was twofold: any marriage that had survived for a period of five years or longer, even one brought about illegally through abduction, essentially constituted a stable union; and should there be any children, their legal status and source of support would at once be put at risk if their parents suddenly faced legal sanction.

The compilers followed Constantine's legislation closely but omitted important sections of it. According to Constantine, because "ancient law" declared that a girl's testimony was invalid in court (on account of the fickleness of her sex), for the same reason, her consent to a marriage with her abductor was also of no legal consequence. The same contempt toward female discretion and disapproval of women's participation in legal affairs are found in several other Constantinian laws,[111] but the *ET* contains no traces of this. While the compilers did not grant more rights to women than did previous Roman legislators, they did so without employing the usual negative rhetoric. *ET* 17 also ignores the penalty (deprivation of the right to inherit from her parents) for girls who did not consent, but did not raise enough clamor to alert their neighbors.[112] Also absent is the provision regarding complicit nurses. In Constantine's legislation, those who convinced the girls under their care to cooperate with their abductors were to be punished by having their mouths and throats (responsible for the 'wicked persuasion') closed shut by the pouring in of molten lead.[113] Of course, such a provision as this would have been a concern only for a small percentage of families that had both the means and opportunity to acquire the services of a nurse. In other words, it was largely meaningless in the context of the *ET*, where the concern of the compilers was with parents who were compelled to sell their children in a bid to escape the crushing burden of poverty (*ET* 94).

Interestingly, in dealing with the subject of marriage by abduction, the compilers ignored a major development in post-Constantinian times of legislation that dealt with the abduction of consecrated Christian virgins or

110 *ET* 20: "Raptum intra quinquennium liceat omnibus accusare, post quinquennium vero nullus de hoc crimine faciat quaestionem, etiam si intra supra scriptum tempus egisse aliquid de legibus doceatur: maxime cum et filii de hoc matrimonio suscepti exacto quinquennio legitimorum et iure et privilegio muniantur."

111 E.g., *CTh* 9.1.3 (322).

112 *CTh* 9.24.1.2. On this penalty, see Paulo Merêa, "Le mariage '*sine consensu parentum*' dans le droit romain vulgaire occidental," *RIDA* 5 (1950), 203–17, esp. 208–10.

113 *CTh* 9.24.1.1.

widows, those who had vowed themselves to a marriage with Christ. In a constitution of 354, for instance, the Emperor Constantius threatened offenders of such divine chastity with "due severity" (presumably death).[114] The culmination of this sort of legislation was a comprehensive law of Justinian of 533, which covered the abduction of all categories of women and paid particular attention to dedicated celibates, virgin and widow alike:

> We decree that the abductors of virgins of honest or ingenuous rank, whether they are married or not, or any widows, and even freedwomen or slaves, have committed the most vile of crimes and shall be punished by the capital penalty: in particular, if they are abductors of virgins or widows dedicated to God (an act which is not only an injury to humankind, but an affront to the omnipotent God, especially when virginity or chastity once corrupted cannot be restored), they shall be deservedly condemned to death, since abductors of this sort shall be held for the crime of homicide.[115]

The silence of the compilers concerning this specific type of *raptus* is suggestive of the fact that sacrosanct virgins or widows were an uncommon feature of rural life in the Italian countryside at this time. Presumably, the hazards of the Italian countryside discouraged individuals from constructing female communities outside the large towns and cities, for all female monasteries were, by the end of the sixth century, located in urban centers of the peninsula. In addition to Rome, Gregory the Great, for example, wrote letters for female monasteries in Naples, Pisa, Lilybitano, Luna, Nola, and the towns of Sicily and Sardinia.[116] The situation was similar in Gaul,

114 E.g., *CTh* 9.25.1 (354). There is no mention in *ET* 17 of the virgin *rapta* being celibate. For widows, the compilers concerned themselves exclusively with acts of *stuprum* (*ET* 60–2): individuals who had sexual relations with a widow (provided she was of respectable status) could be accused of adultery; if the widow was a willing participant, she too was considered guilty. This was standard Roman law.

115 *CJ* 9.13.1: "Raptores virginum honestarum vel ingenuarum, sive iam desponsatae fuerint sive non, vel quarumlibet viduarum feminarum, licet libertinae vel servae alienae sint, pessima criminum peccantes capitis supplicio plectendos decernimus, et maxime si deo fuerint virgines vel viduae dedicatae (quod non solum ad iniuriam hominum, sed ad ipsius omnipotentis dei inreverentiam committitur, maxime cum virginitas vel castitas corrupta restitui non potest): et merito mortis damnantur supplicio, cum nec ab homicidii crimine huiusmodi raptores sint vacui." See further Evans Grubbs, "Abduction Marriage in Antiquity," 77–9; Grodzynski, "Ravies et coupables," 724–6; and Beaucamp, *Le Statut de la femme*, 114–18 for this and later legislation of Justinian.

116 E.g., *ep.* 3.58 in *MGH Epistolae* 1–2, 2 vols. (Berlin, 1887–99), 1, 217–18, and *epp.* 9.54, 11.207 in *MGH Epistolae*, 2, 79, 195–6 (Naples); *ep.* 14.14 in *MGH Epistolae*, 2, 433–4 (Pisa); *ep.* 9.233 in *MGH Epistolae*, 2, 228–29 (Lilybitano); *ep.* 9.114 in *MGH Epistolae*, 2, 119–20 (Luna); *ep.* 1.23 in *MGH Epistolae*, 1, 27 (Sicily); *ep.* 4.101 in *MGH Epistolae*, 1, 243 (Sardinia). The most comprehensive account of monasticism in Italy in this period is to be found in Georg Jenal, *Italia ascetica atque monastica. Das Asketen- und Mönchtum in Italien von den Anfängen bis zur Zeit der Langobarden (c.a. 150/250–604)*, 2 vols. (Stuttgart, 1995), vol. 1, 145–311. See also Georges Duby and Michelle Perrot (eds.), *A History of Women in the West*, vol. II: *Silences of the Middle Ages* (Cambridge, MA, 1992), 188.

where the first significant women's cloisters were situated at Marseilles, Jura, Vienna, Tours, Arles, and Poitiers.[117] In addition to the protection offered by walled towns, urban basilicas, and private households, there was the threat of excommunication. Writing to Bishop Caesarius of Arles in 509, Pope Symmachus (498–514) proclaimed: "We condemn abductors of widows or virgins on account of the inhumanity of such a wicked deed; and are vehement in our pursuit of those who attempt to join themselves in marriage to sacrosanct virgins, whether they be willing or not. Wherefore, because of the barbarity of this most reprehensible crime, We command such perpetrators to be denied communion."[118] At any rate, to judge from the number of provisions in the *ET* dedicated to the subject of *raptus*, it would seem that this practice continued to be regarded as a viable marriage strategy in some parts of Italy throughout Late Antiquity, despite repeated attempts by Emperors and Kings to put a stop to it.

Adultery and divorce

The husband was undoubtedly the dominant partner in the marriage union. Nowhere is the law's discriminatory treatment more evident than in the provisions concerning adultery. Roman law defined adultery as extramarital sexual relations with or by a married woman.[119] The husband could be held liable only in the event that he had sexual relations with a married woman of respectable status; if his lover was an unmarried virgin or widow, and again of respectable status, the crime was classified as *stuprum*. While this was equally reprehensible, it was only because of his lover's status and not because he was married. A man, regardless of if he was married, who had sexual relations with slaves (provided it was not done against the owner's will), prostitutes, or any other woman considered beneath the legal and social definitions of respectability, was acting within the limits of what was deemed acceptable behavior, and was not committing adultery or

[117] Lynda Coon, *Sacred Fictions: Holy Women and Hagiography in Late Antiquity* (Philadelphia, PA, 1997), 121–2.

[118] *Ep.* 5 *ad Caesarium* (*Patrologiae Cursus Completus*, Series Latina, ed. Jacques-Paul Migne (Paris, 1844–91), 62, 53): "Raptores igitur viduarum vel virginum ob immanitatem tanti facinoris detestamur; illos vehementius persequendo qui sacras virgines vel volentes vel invitas matrimonio suo sociare temptaverint. Quos pro tam nefandissimi criminis atrocitate a communione suspendi praecipimus."

[119] Evans Grubbs, *Law and Family*, 203; on the law: *Dig.* 48.2.3, 48.5; *PS* 2.26; *CJ* 9.9. See also Corbett, *The Roman Law of Marriage*, 133–45; Csillag, *The Augustan Laws*, 175–99; Gardner, *Women in Roman Law and Society*, 127–32; McGinn, "Concubinage and the *Lex Julia* on Adultery," 335–75, esp. 340–3; Mommsen, *Römisches Strafrecht*, 414–28; Richlin, "Approaches to the Sources on Adultery at Rome," 379–404; Treggiari, *Roman Marriage*, 277–90; Carlo Venturini, "'*Accusatio Adulterii*' e politica constantiniana (Per un riesame di CTH 9,7,2)," *SDHI* 54 (1988), 66–109.

stuprum. For respectable women, on the other hand, these sorts of relations were strictly prohibited: those who were married were expected to observe strict marital fidelity, and those who were unmarried were to remain celibate.[120] After Constantine, Christian Emperors broadened the definition of adultery to include offenses other than infidelity on the part of the married woman. In 388, for instance, Valentinian II issued a decree that defined marriage between a Christian and a Jew as adultery, and granted the right of accusation to anyone, provided they do so before the appropriate judge.[121] The compilers, however, ignored these sorts of developments and instead continued treating adultery strictly as an act involving an unfaithful wife.

Under the Augustan law, an accusation of adultery could be brought forward by anyone, and the punishment for adulterers was harsh: a woman convicted of adultery was relegated to an island and lost a third of her property and half her dowry, and was prohibited from contracting a valid marriage again; a guilty man was similarly relegated and forfeited half of his property.[122] Constantine, however, restricted the right of accusation to the husband and male relatives exclusively, thus making the preservation of a woman's sexual chastity the responsibility of the male members of the family.[123] Moreover, he seems to have punished convicted adulterers, both male and female, with death.

The compilers further limited the right of accusation to husbands alone (with no mention of male relatives), and treated adultery as a capital offense – a provision that extended to collaborators and anyone complicit in the crime:

> Adulterers and adulteresses, upon being convicted during a trial, shall not escape a violent death; collaborators or those knowledgeable of that crime must be punished in the same way.[124]

In keeping with this, we are informed by Cassiodorus that Theoderic granted the ultimate measure of self-help to Crispanus, who killed his

[120] Despite the fact that this double standard was long criticized by more high-minded pagans and Christians alike, it clearly continued throughout Late Antiquity. See Peter Brown, *The Body and Society: Men, Women and Sexual Renunciation in Early Christianity* (New York, 1988), 23–4. For the objections of pagan philosophers, see, e.g., the first-century Italian *eques* and Stoic philosopher Musonius Rufus (in Cora Lutz, "Musonius Rufus: 'The Roman Socrates'," *Yale Classical Studies* 10 (1947), 3–147, esp. 38–49, 84–101); Evans Grubbs, *Law and Family*, 62.

[121] *CJ* 1.9.6. On the subject of Jewish–Christian marriages in Late Antiquity, see Hagith S. Sivan, "Why Not Marry a Jew? Jewish–Christian Marital Frontiers in Late Antiquity," in Ralph W. Mathisen (ed.), *Law, Society, and Authority in Late Antiquity*, (Oxford, 2001), 208–19.

[122] *PS* 2.26.14. [123] *CTh* 9.7.2.

[124] *ET* 38: "Adulteri et adulterae, intra iudicia convicti, interitum non evadant; ministris eiusdem criminis aut consciis pariter puniendis." See also *ET* 39 (on facilitating adultery).

wife's lover when he caught the pair *in flagranti delicto*. In explaining his decision to grant the cuckolded husband immunity for his action, the King remarked: "While the crime of murder is abominable . . . it is necessary to consider the circumstances in which the act was perpetrated. For, what man would punish another according to the laws if he had attempted to violate the sanctity of his marriage?"[125] And in a rather imaginative move ostensibly intended to curb such wanton acts, Athalaric proclaimed:

> If a man, by punishable seduction, strives to break up another's marriage, his own union shall be considered unlawful, so that he may instead experience for himself that which he malignly attempted to inflict on another. But should he be without the love of a wife, We deny him the right of a future marriage, since he who dared to carry on in dividing the marriage bed does not deserve to obtain the rewards of conjugal reverence.[126]

The subject of adultery ties in closely with the provisions of the law concerning the dissolution of the marriage bond. Unions ended for a variety of reasons, death of course being one of them. Both a widower and widow were permitted the right to remarry, with the exception of the requirement that the latter wait for a period of one year, the *tempus luendi*, after her husband's death before contracting a new union. Concerning the woman's right to remarry, *ET* 37 upholds the fixed time of mourning after which a widow could lawfully remarry, as outlined by a decree of the Emperor Theodosius I of 381 (*CTh* 3.8.1):

> No woman shall marry for a second time within a year of her husband's death; and she shall not associate herself secretly with the man to whom she shall be married after a year's time; for, in so doing she seems to have been willing to circumvent the laws. For this reason, We stipulate that each one of them is guilty of *stuprum*. We grant this complaint to children and near relatives alone so that they may carry out what is lawfully admissible in such matters.[127]

[125] Cass., *Var.* 1.37: "Quamvis homicidii facinus primus detestetur auditus . . . tamen iustitiae consideratione librandum est, qua cuique fiat iniuria necessarium scelus: qui nova infelicitate fortunae tunc erit detestatio cunctorum, si se servet innoxium. quis enim ferat hominem ad leges trahere, qui matrimonii nisus est iura violare?"

[126] Cass., *Var.* 9.18.4: "Qui suasione plectenda matrimonia dividere nititur aliena, ipsius coniugium habeatur illicitum: ut magis contigisse sentiat sibi, quod in altero malignus exercere temptavit. Sive pro coniunctionibus caritate privatur, futurum illi matrimonium iure denegamus, quia non meretur iugalis reverentiae praemia consequi, qui in genialis tori ausus est divisione grassari."

[127] *ET* 37: "Intra annum mortis mariti nulla ad secundas nuptias migret: sed nec furtim se misceat illi, cuius post annum erit uxor futura, quia leges videtur circumscribere voluisse. Idcirco utramque personam stupri ream esse praecipimus. Quam querelam damus tantum filiis et propinquis, ut quod in talibus causis legibus competit, exsequantur."

While an ancient concept going back to early Roman mores and law, the requirement that a widow observe a proper mourning period (*tempus luendi*) went into abeyance by the late Republic, but reappears in several later laws of Theodosius I. Its purpose was to avoid confusion over the paternity of any child the woman might have afterwards.[128]

Divorce, however, was an altogether different matter. Under classical law, either spouse could initiate a unilateral divorce provided they notify their partner by means of a written repudiation (*repudium*). While such an action required no justification or formal legal undertaking, the declaration of divorce had to be made publicly in the presence of seven witnesses for it to be considered fully valid.[129] If the divorce was the fault of the wife (or that of her *paterfamilias*), the husband was entitled to retain the dowry. If, on the other hand, the divorce was due to the husband's actions, he was obligated to repay the dowry in full.[130] These rights, however, were subject to certain conditions: family property, that is property associated exclusively with the marriage, and conjugal gifts could not be disposed of freely by either man or woman if there existed children between them. For the law guaranteed children succession rights to parental property through inheritance or conjugal gift.

Apart from these requirements, and the punishments for which an adulterous wife was liable, divorce entailed no legal sanctions until Constantine, who in 331 issued a new divorce law that was to be universally upheld.[131] Addressed to the Praetorian Prefect Ablabius, *CTh* 3.16.1 represents a complete overhaul of the procedures for unilateral divorce in effect since the time of Augustus. This served as the model for *ET* 54:

ET 54	*CTh* 3.16.1
We do not permit marriages to be dissolved indiscriminately. Wherefore, upon the issuance of a divorce notice, neither a wife nor husband shall withdraw from the marriage bond except on proven grounds which the laws recognize. Divorce is permitted only on the following grounds: if a wife proves in trial	It is pleasing that a woman not be permitted to send a notice of divorce (*repudium*) to her husband because of her own depraved desires for some carefully contrived cause, such as the fact that he is a drunkard or gambler or a philanderer, but neither should husbands be permitted to divorce their own wives for

128 Legislation: *CJ* 5.9.1, together with *CJ* 6.56.1 (Theodosius, 380); and 3.81. See further Michel Humbert, *Le Remariage à Rome: Étude d'histoire juridique et sociale* (Milan, 1970), 113–31, 378–87; Treggiari, *Roman Marriage*, 493–5; Evans Grubbs, *Law and Family*, 94.

129 Evans Grubbs, *Law and Family*, 226–7.

130 *Ibid.*; Treggiari, *Roman Marriage*, 352, 463–4.

131 On the subject of divorce in Roman law after Constantine, see Cooper, *The Fall of the Roman Household*, 158–60; Evans Grubbs, *Women and the Law in the Roman Empire* (London, 2002), 184, 202–10; Evans Grubbs, *Law and Family*, 253–60.

that her husband is a murderer, sorcerer, or a destroyer of tombs. A husband, too, may rightfully divorce his wife who is convicted of these crimes: that is, if he is able to prove in a trial that she is an adulteress (*adultera*), or sorceress (*malefica*), or what is commonly referred to as a procuress (*aggagula*). When these facts have been disclosed clearly, a husband shall both gain back the dower and receive or retain the dowry; and in accordance with the laws, We order him to preserve intact property of both himself and his former wife for the children of that marriage. And in like manner, if a wife proves that her husband has been involved in the aforementioned crimes, she shall receive both the dowry and dower as profit. But she is required to retain only the dower for the children of that marriage; and in accordance with ancient customs, she shall obtain the freedom to marry again or not.[132]

just any reason whatsoever. But in the sending of a *repudium* by a woman the following crimes alone shall be investigated: if she has proven that her husband is a murderer or a preparer of poisons (*medicamentarius*) or a disturber of tombs, so that not until then shall she earn commendation and receive back her entire dowry. But if she has sent a *repudium* to her husband on grounds other than these three crimes, she must leave everything, even to her last hairpin (*acucula capitis*) in her husband's home and be deported to an island in return for her supreme self-confidence. Also in the case of men, if they should send a *repudium*, inquiry shall be made as to the following three crimes: if they wanted to repudiate an adulteress (*moecha*) or a preparer of poisons or a go-between (*conciliatrix*). For if he has ejected a woman who is innocent of these crimes, he must restore her entire dowry and not marry another woman. But if he should do this [i.e. marry another woman], the power shall be given to the first wife to enter his house and transfer the entire dowry of the second wife to her own possession in return for the injury inflicted upon her.[133]

132 *ET* 54: "Passim matrimonia dissipari non patimur. Ideo uxor a marito, aut maritus ab uxore, nisi probatis causis, quas leges comprehendunt, omisso repudio, a iugali vinculo non recedant. Causae autem debent esse divortii: si maritus aut homicida, aut maleficus, aut sepulchrorum violator ab uxore in examine fuerit adprobatus. Maritus quoque his criminibus convictam merito dimittat uxorem, si adulteram, vel maleficam, vel etiam quam vulgus adpellat aggagulam, in iudicio potuerit adprobare. Quibus edoctis, maritus, et dotem lucretur, et sponsalitiam recipiat vel sibi habeat largitatem, et tituli utriusque proprietatem secundum leges filiis eum iubemus servare communibus. Pari etiam modo, si mulier maritum superioribus criminibus involutum a iudicatione convicerit, et dotem recipiat, et sponsalitiam lucro habeat largitatem. Cuius tamen sponsalitiae tantum donationis proprietatem liberis communibus etiam ipsa conservet: et nubendi vel non nubendi licentiam pro constitutis veteribus sortiatur."

133 *CTh* 3.16.1: "Placet, mulieri non licere propter suas pravas cupiditates marito repudium mittere exquisita causa, velut ebrioso aut aleatori aut mulierculario, nec vero maritis per quascumque occasiones uxores suas dimittere, sed in repudio mittendo a femina haec sola crimina inquiri, si homicidam vel medicamentarium vel sepulcrorum dissolutorem maritum suum esse probaverit, ut ita demum laudata omnem suam dotem recipiat. nam si praeter haec tria crimina repudium marito miserit, oportet eam usque ad acuculam capitis in domo mariti deponere, et pro tam magna sui confidentia in insulam deportari. In masculis etiam, si repudium mittant, haec tria crimina inquiri conveniet, si moecham vel medicamentariam vel conciliatricem repudiare voluerit. Nam si ab his

In terms of subject matter and organization of content, the two texts are similar, but there are important differences between them. According to both, a spouse could initiate a unilateral divorce with impunity only if the other partner was guilty of a particularly heinous crime. In the case of the wife, she had to prove that her husband was one of three things: a murderer, sorcerer, or disturber of tombs. For the husband, it was necessary to prove that his spouse was an adulteress, sorceress, or procuress. That one party or both were otherwise willing to agree to the dissolution of the union was seemingly immaterial. Divorce by mutual consent was not subject to legislation until 542, when it was prohibited by a law of the Emperor Justinian (*Nov.* 117.10), and subsequently annulled by his successor Justin (*Nov.* 140).

There are significant variations in terminology between the two texts. In Constantine's law, the word for an adulteress is *moecha*; a preparer of poisons/dealer in magic is a *medicamentaria/us*; and a procuress or go-between is a *conciliatrix*. In the *ET*, the corresponding terms are *adultera*, *malefica/us*, and *aggagula*, which for clarity the compilers note is a colloquial expression (*quam vulgus adpellat aggagulam*). Given the similarity between them, it would be tempting to see *aggagula* in *ET* 54 as a misreading of *acucula* in *CTh* 3.16.1, meaning "hairpin." In replacing these terms the compilers clearly regarded them as obscure. For the vocabulary of Constantine's law is very unusual and is unlike that found in other contemporary legal works as well later imperial constitutions. In particular, eight words in Constantine's law appear nowhere else, including *medicamentarius/a*, *acucula*, and *moechus/a*.[134] Thus, the compilers took it upon themselves to update the original language in an effort to make the law more understandable for a larger audience that was presumably not familiar with the sort of terminology found in this particular law of Constantine.

There are other important differences between the two texts. Whereas *ET* 54 treats the husband and wife on more or less equal terms, Constantine's legislation is clearly much harder on the wife who attempted an illegal divorce than on the husband. A woman who repudiated her husband for any reason other than those explicitly permitted was to be

criminibus liberam eiecerit, omnem dotem restituere debet et aliam non ducere. quod si fecerit, priori coniugi facultas dabitur, domum eius invadere et omnem dotem posterioris uxoris ad semet ipsam transferre pro iniuria sibi illata."

134 On the unique vocabulary of this law, see Evans Grubbs, *Law and Family*, 258; Edoardo Volterra, "Intorno ad alcune costituzioni di Costantino," *Rendiconti dell'Accademia Nazionale dei Lincei. Classe di Scienze morali, storiche e filologiche*, series 8, vol. 13 (1958), 61–89; Edoardo Volterra, "Quelques remarques sur le style des constitutions de Constantin," *Mélanges Levy-Bruhl* (Paris, 1959), 325–34.

deprived of her dowry (including her last hairpin!) and be banished to an island. The husband, however, was simply required to give back the dowry (just as he had been under classical law) if there were no children between them and he was unable to prove that his wife was guilty of being an adulteress, sorceress, or procuress. The only new stipulation introduced by Constantine's legislation, which the compilers chose to ignore, was that the husband was not supposed to remarry. While, in fact, there was nothing expressly prohibiting him from doing so, if he did he risked having his former wife enter his new home and confiscate the dowry of his second wife. Exactly how this was to be done is unclear, and the fact that the compilers ignored it altogether is a good indication of its impracticality.

Children

Within the family household a child remained subject to the disciplinary authority of its parents. Short of death, the law did not impose any restrictions on parents in this regard. It was their responsibility to ensure filial obedience through the imposition of certain summary forms of punishment. Earlier imperial legislation on the subject provided that a father could support children *in potestate* by more or less regular allowances. Alternatively, he could set aside for them a *peculium*, a sum of money or other property which they could control independently.[135] That the threat of taking away such a child's *peculium*, should he have any, or disinheriting him altogether, served as a useful deterrent in some cases is possible, given the child's dependent status and the fact that he could lose his inheritance rights on certain statutory grounds.

Justinian provided a list of offenses that justified disinheritance.[136] For example, a child who renounced the Catholic faith or practiced a shameful profession gave just cause for disinheritance. These examples demonstrate that *patria potestas* alone did not suffice for the father to have his way. Although punitive disinheritance is sometimes mentioned by late antique writers, it appears to have been after all a rare and dramatic occurrence. Sidonius Apollinaris, for example, grouped it together with crucifixion and

[135] E.g., *Dig.* 2.13.28.2; 34.4.31.3; 41.2.14.pr; 42.8.12; 46.2.34.pr. More generally on the *peculium* and property relations between fathers and sons, see Yan Thomas, "Droit domestique et droit politique à Rome: Remarques sur le pécule et les honores des fils de famille," *MEFRA* 94 (1982), 527–80; Aaron Kirschenbaum, *Sons, Slaves and Freedmen in Roman Commerce* (Washington, DC, 1987). For Late Antiquity, see Arjava, "The Survival of Roman Family Law", 33–51.

[136] *Nov.* 115.3. Similarly, in Visigothic Spain a child could be disinherited if he or she had been convicted of physical assault upon, or had lodged a (presumably false) accusation against, the parent: *LV* 4.5.1.

drowning, traditional punishments for parricide.[137] And Libanius laments that fathers, who were otherwise powerless against the unruly behavior of their sons, did not even threaten to use it.[138]

A father's authority also included the right of arranging his child's marriage, the *potestas de coniunctione*.[139] Theoderic himself exercised this privilege, marrying two of his daughters to the Kings of the Visigoths and Burgundians respectively. In 493 he gave Thiudigotho in marriage to the Visigothic King Alaric II, and in 493 or thereabouts, he betrothed his second daughter Ostrogotho to Sigismund, future King of the Burgundians.[140] Upon the father's death this authority presumably passed to his widow, and when she died or remarried, to the child's brothers or, if they were of insufficient age or otherwise incapable, to the paternal uncle.[141] How far those in possession of the *potestas de coniunctione* were inclined to impose their authority upon an unwilling child depended on certain factors. In most cases, to be sure, the child was sufficiently young enough to accept the decision of a parent or relative in the matter of an arranged marriage. And it is unlikely that parents routinely ignored the wishes of their child and arranged a match that the latter opposed. Nevertheless, instances must have arisen where the wishes of the parents or relatives were at variance with those of a child. When it came to a young woman, *ET* 93 is clear: the possessor of the *potestas de coniunctione* did not require her consent. As for male children the law is silent, but there is no reason to suppose that they were in any position to decide the matter of their betrothal without the approval of those who retained betrothal rights over them. Only when children reached the age of majority could they legally marry whomever they wished. Legal ability was of little importance, however, if a person lacked the means to present a sufficiently suitable dowry to their intended; and such means undoubtedly depended upon the willingness of their family to consent to the union.[142]

137 *Ep.* 4.23.

138 Libanius, *Orations* 62.24–5, ed. R. Foerster, *Libanii opera*, 4 vols. (Leipzig, 1903–8); ed. and trans. A. F. Norman, *Selected Works* II (Cambridge, MA, 1977). Similarly, Theodoret of Cyrrhus, *Historia Ecclesiastica*, ed. L. Parmentier, *GCS* 44, 2nd edn. (Berlin; 1954), 3.17; and Cass., *Hist.* 6.44. See further Arjava, "The Survival of Roman Family Law, 43–5; Arjava, "Paternal Power in Late Antiquity," 154.

139 *ET* 93.

140 Herwig Wolfram, *History of the Goths*, trans. Thomas J. Dunlap, 2nd edn. (Berkeley, CA, 1988), 309–13; Cass., *Var.* 5.43 (for the account of Ostrogotho).

141 Cass., *Var.* 1.38 (the case of a certain Senator by the name of Baion, who was the erstwhile legal guardian of his nephew).

142 For the early Empire, see Richard P. Saller, *Patriarchy, Property and Death in the Roman Family* (Cambridge, 1994), 71–153.

Only through marriage or upon its reaching the age of majority did a child escape from this parental control. Legal age for males in Roman law was twenty-five, although children could be released from *potestas*, through a procedure called *emancipatio*, which severed most legal ties with paternal relatives. For males, this could be granted at the age of twenty-one; for females at nineteen.[143] Theoderic offered a similar grant. According to Cassiodorus' *formula* for adulthood (*formula aetatis veniae*), a minor could petition to be recognized as a legal adult and be granted full authority to decide over all matters pertaining to his property:

> Wherefore, if it is evident that you have reached that age at which you can lawfully petition for *venia aetatis*, in solemn accordance with ancient custom concerning these matters, We shall not deny your request, and further provide that you shall have authority over the alienation of your property, whether it be in the country or city.[144]

The *formula* provided the legal means for children *in potestate* who were looking to get out from under the thumb of a *paterfamilias*, but it did not provide the necessary practical means. If we take into account the nature of property holding of the later Empire, the majority of the upper and middle classes depended, directly or indirectly, on income from inherited property. A young adult male, even if recognized legally as an adult, could not readily acquire the necessary wealth to support himself, let alone a family, if he had not inherited his parents' estate. Like it or not, he would have been totally dependent on his father, whether *in potestate* or not.[145]

While the authority of parents was considerable, it was also limited by rules and safeguards that sought to protect children against possible abuses. Infanticide, and the particularly gruesome practice of exposure – in Gibbon's words "the prevailing and stubborn vice of antiquity"[146] – was nowhere accorded any legal justification. As a preferable alternative, the law conditionally permitted parents to sell their children; but such children

143 *CTh* 2.16.2 (319); *CTh* 2.17.1, 2 (321; 324). See also Cooper, *The Fall of the Roman Household*, 111; Hugh Lindsay, *Adoption in the Roman World* (Cambridge, 2009), 98–9; Arjava, *Women and Law*, 117; Arjava, "Paternal Power," 161–3, on *emancipatio*.

144 Cass., *Var.* 7.40: "Atque ideo, si id tempus constat elapsum, quo ad hanc veniam accedi iura voluerunt, nos quoque probabilibus desideriis licentiam non negamus, ut in competenti foro ea quae in his causis reverenda legum dictat antiquitas, sollemniter actitentur, ita ut alienandis rusticis vel urbanis praediis constitutionum servetur auctoritas."

145 Alan Watson, *Society and Legal Change* (Edinburgh, 1977), 27–8; Peter Garnsey and Richard P. Saller, *The Roman Empire: Economy, Society and Culture* (Berkeley, CA, 1987), 47–8.

146 Edward Gibbon, *The History of the Decline and Fall of the Roman Empire*, 6 vols., ed. and abbr. Hans-Friedrich Mueller, Modern Library (Toronto and New York, 2003), 4, 779.

were not to suffer the loss of their *ingenuus* rank.[147] The pledging of children was altogether prohibited.[148] Creditors who knowingly received children as surety for the parents' debt were to be exiled; remarkably, no penalty is prescribed for the offending parents. In similar legislation passed by the Emperor Justinian in 529, all exposed children were guaranteed the condition of freedom and those who received them were denied the power to enslave them or reduce them to any other form of dependence, or even to place them in a relationship of patronage. At the same time, those abandoning a child were to be denied the right to recover him with the object of enslaving him.[149]

That Theoderic was concerned for the overall welfare of children is undeniable. For the law put in place various safeguards designed to protect the vulnerability of their position against possible abuses. Perhaps nowhere is the practical form of this concern more apparent than in the statutory rights afforded minors when they were orphaned or otherwise refused the legal support of parents. A child bereft of both parents, for instance, was appointed a legal guardian whose responsibilities and liabilities were presumably the same as the deceased parents. In most cases, we may assume, relatives undertook the role of guardian, and selection thereof was ultimately a family decision. On at least one occasion, however, the appointment of a guardian became the matter of royal prerogative. Upon the death of a certain Benedictus, Cassiodorus reports that Theoderic appointed Theriolus as legal guardian of the orphaned children.[150] Elsewhere, we are told that the King placed under his special protection (*tuitio regii nominis*) two orphaned minors, Maurentius and Paula respectively, who had been (falsely) charged with a variety of offenses.[151]

Further protection was afforded children in matters of inheritance. Under Roman law children were guaranteed a statutory right of inheritance to the property of the mother, the *bona materna*. In 315, Constantine ruled that the widowed father was forbidden from alienating anything from the

[147] *ET* 94. [148] *ET* 95.

[149] *CJ* 8.51.3 (similarly *Nov.* 153 at n. 34). The wide range of laws dealing with infant exposure attests to how pervasive the phenomenon was, for it continued well into the Middle Ages, even surviving in early modern history with the development of industrial urbanism. On the practice of exposure in the Roman world and beyond, see Judith Evans Grubbs, "Hidden in Plain Sight: *Expositi* in the Community," delivered at the Vth Roman Family Conference: *Secrets de familles, familles secretes: mémoire et identité familiales* (Université de Fribourg, 15 June 2007), SSRN, 1–17; Andrea Giardina, "The Family in the Late Roman World," in Averil Cameron, Bryan Ward-Perkins and Michael Whitby (eds.), *The Cambridge Ancient History*, vol. 14: *Late Antiquity: Empire and Successors*, AD *425–600* (Cambridge, 2000), 392–415, esp. 408; Boswell, *The Kindness of Strangers*.

[150] Cass., *Var.* 1.36. [151] Cass., *Var.* 4.9.

bona materna, but had to preserve the whole of it for the children; although he retained both control, *dominium*, and what was called *potestas utendi fruendique*, or essentially a lifelong usufruct of the estate.[152] A divorced mother, too, was required by a law of Theodosius I (*CTh* 3.8.2 (382)) to make provisions for her children in her will. A law of Theodosius II of 439 reiterated this point, but also made the same requirement of husbands.[153] Similarly, in *ET* 54 the husband who retained his wife's dowry after divorce was required to pass it on to any children they had together, and the wife was likewise obligated to retain the dower for any children. In the event that a widow disregarded the rules of the *tempus luendi*, she forfeited all conjugal proceeds to her husband's relatives or heirs (*ET* 37). The stipulation that husbands were legally obligated to provide for the financial well-being of their children is in contrast to earlier legislation on the subject, illustrated by a rescript of Theodosius I of 382 (*CTh* 3.8.2.3) which simply admonished husbands to do so by appealing to their sense of morality. That such moral appeals were eventually replaced with binding legal sanctions is strong proof that they largely fell on deaf ears.

Indicative of the law's concern for children's rights in matters of inheritance is the case of Aetheria, the details of which are recorded by Cassiodorus: "The illustrious Lady Archotamia, saddened over the loss of her grandson, alleges that her (grand)daughter-in-law Aetheria, having put aside the love of her [former] husband and subsequently marrying a certain Liberius, and eager to appear more embellished in her new marriage, has enriched herself from the inheritance of her children, for whom this property was suitably intended."[154] The case presupposes that the children had a right to the *bona materna*; should the presiding judges, the Goth Marabad and the Roman Gemellus, have found Aetheria guilty of squandering the property in question, she would have been obligated to compensate her children accordingly.

[152] *CTh* 8.18 pr. See further Arjava, *Women and Law*, 100–5. On the problems of the legal terminology (including the act of *cretio*, through which the child and the father together demanded the inheritance), see, e.g., Pasquale Voci, "Il diritto ereditario Romano nell'età di tardo impero: il IV secolo (prima parte)," *Iura* 29 (1978), 17–113, esp. 56–79; and Pablo Fuenteseca, "Maternum patrimonium (Revisión de CTh. 8,18,1 y 8,18,2)," *Atti dell'Accademia Romanistica Costantiniana: IX Convegno internazionale* (Naples 1993), 331–47.

[153] *Nov. Th.* 14.1, 2.

[154] Cass., *Var.* 4.12: "Arcotamia itaque illustris femina flebiliter ingemiscens nepotis sui calamitatem tali conquestione deploravit . . . asserens Aetheriam nurum suam, mariti postposita dilectione, cuidam se Liberio iugali foedere sociasse et cum ornatior cupit novis thalamis apparere, studuerit prioris viri facultates evertere, allegans ditatam filiorum spoliis, quibus magis decuit congregari." The case is mentioned again in Cass., *Var.* 4.46.

The *ET* provides no details as to how property was to be transferred from parents to children or other direct descendants, or how it was to be divided between children. If the Visigothic evidence is any indication of the state of Roman inheritance law in Italy at the beginning of the sixth century, the benefits afforded children of the marriage were quite generous. According to Visigothic law, a husband was obligated to preserve for his children two-thirds of their maternal estate when they married, or one half when they reached the age of twenty; the remainder he kept for himself in usufruct.[155] As for the widowed mother, she was required to yield power and control over her share of the paternal estates upon her remarriage; and although nowhere expressly stated, the remaining shares were likely transferred to the children under the same terms as was the maternal property.[156] Visigothic inheritance provisions went so far as to guarantee children four-fifths of all conjugal gifts, excepting the dowry, and four-fifths of the family inheritance held by, or due to, each parent: of the dowry, two-thirds had to be reserved.[157]

Family property

The issue of inheritance brings us to the related matter of family property in general. Roman law governing the transfer of property within families, particularly between parents and children, comprises a considerably complex and detailed set of rules and regulations, which for the most part are preserved in Book IV of the *Theodosian Code*.[158] These were passed over by the compilers except for a few very general clauses on inheritance and donation.[159] Property was normally inherited either under a will or as the result of an intestacy. The law of intestacy applied when there was no operative will, which occurred if a person failed to make a will or made one that lacked legal effect (for example, for want of proper form or heirs).[160] *ET* 28 deals with the issue of legitimacy, and concedes testamentary rights to all those whom the laws recognize as being legally able to draft

155 *LV* 4.2.13 (= *CE* 321).

156 Fischer-Drew, "The Family in Visigothic Law," in her *Law and Society in Early Medieval Europe. Studies in Legal History* (London, 1988), VII, 10–12.

157 *LV* 5.2.4; 5.1; 4.5.2: Fischer-Drew, "The Family in Visigothic Law," VII, 10–12.

158 For a useful review see Evans Grubbs, *Law and Family*, 112–18; Joshua C. Tate, "Inheritance Rights of Nonmarital Children in Late Roman Law," *Roman Legal Tradition* 4 (2008), 1–36; Lindsay, *Adoption*, chapter 7; Andrew M. Riggsby, *Roman Law and the Legal World of the Romans* (Cambridge, 2010), chapter 15.

159 *ET* 23–4, 28–33, 51–2, 72. *ET* 26 and 27 deal with intestate clerics and decurions respectively.

160 Lindsay, *Adoption*, 100–1.

a will. *ET* 29 specifies what steps are to be taken should the testator be illiterate or otherwise unable to sign the document, and warns against forgers; and *ET* 30 qualifies the issue of forgery even further. Together, these three provisions functioned together as a general edict on testacy:

> *ET* 28 We grant the universal right to make a will to all whom the laws permit to do so: provided that seven or five witnesses who are freeborn and of adult age shall at his request and at the same time sign the document in the presence of the testator.[161]
>
> *ET* 29 If a testator is unable to provide his signature because he is either illiterate or gravely ill, then there shall be summoned on his behalf an eighth witness whose credibility cannot be challenged in any way. But let witnesses, and particularly the testator himself, know that if, under examination [of the document] anything should be proven false, they shall not be able to avoid the punishment which the authority of the laws concerning forgers stipulates.[162]
>
> *ET* 30 Moreover, let an appointed heir, legatee, or freedman know that if anything of this sort is attempted through their complicity or knowledge, not only will they be deprived of the very profit and income of that testamentary provision, but also, they will not be able to avoid the penalty of forgery. Anyone who makes an effort or applies himself to drafting such testaments will be guilty of this offense, since We wish that the desire of the dead to remain unimpeded, and nothing should be appropriated for another's benefit because of a difference of opinion [concerning the validity of the document].[163]

ET 28 fails to specify the particular grounds for establishing the capacity of a testator, referring only to the *leges* that have already done so. For the most part these are outlined in the juristic works of Labeo, Gaius, and Ulpian. According to Labeo: "in the case of someone who is making his will, at the time when he makes the will, soundness of mind is required, not health of

[161] *ET* 28: "Faciendorum testamentorum omnibus quos testari leges permittunt, damus late licentiam: ita ut septem aut quinque testes ingenui ac puberes in conspectu testatoris, uno tempore, eodem rogante subscribant."

[162] *ET* 29: "Quod si testator aut literas ignorando aut per necessitatem vicinae mortis propriam subscriptionem non potuerit commodare, tunc octavus testis pro testatore adhibeatur huiusmodi, de cuius fide dubitari omnino non possit: scituris testibus et scriptore praecipue testamenti, quod si quis falsitatis extiterit, sub cognitione decursa se supplicium evadere non posse, quod circa falsarios legum dictat auctoritas."

[163] *ET* 30: "Sciat autem scriptus heres vel legatarius aut libertus, quod si eis conniventibus aut scientibus, tale aliquid temptatum fuerit, se non solum emolumento ipso vel fructu eius scripturae esse privandos, verum etiam falsi poenam declinare non posse. In hoc reatu erit quisquis operam aut studium faciendis adhibuerit talius testamentis: cum voluntates velimus esse liberas mortuorum et nihil ibi sibi aliena debeat persuasio vindicare."

body."[164] As Labeo makes clear, the testator was required to have mental capacity (but not physical) at the time he made the will. The basic requirements for capacity to make a will were that the testator should be a citizen of full age, i.e., over the age of puberty, and *sui iuris*. Gaius adds: "a person in parental power has not the right to make a will, and this is so much the case that even if his father gives him permission, he still cannot thereby lawfully make the will."[165] Persons judged to be *intestabiles* also lacked capacity to make a will (*Dig.* 28.1.26), but any will made before the interdict was considered valid (*Dig.* 28.1.18 pr.).[166]

Under Constantine, for a will to be legally recognized as valid, it had to be signed before five, and sometimes seven witnesses.[167] *ET* 28 allowed for the document to be signed before seven or five witnesses in the same way Constantine's law had – five according to the older civil law, seven according to the modifications introduced by the Praetor and known as the praetorian law, or the honorary law.[168] *ET* 29 ignores this differentiation completely, requiring seven witnesses and an eighth in the event that the testator was not up to the task. It also expands upon this to include the application of the penalty for forgery, which was most obviously a pressing issue for the compilers. Both this and the following provision warn the forger and the witnesses who knowingly signed a forged deed that they would not escape the thorough censure of the laws concerning forgery. According to *ET* 41, this was a capital offense. To guard against these sorts of actions, and at the same time to establish tax liability, wills were to be registered in municipal archives (*gesta municipalia*) as the laws required.[169] As for the soldier's will mentioned in *ET* 32, it is likely that a good deal of liberty was afforded those granted this option: for many such documents were necessarily written and subscribed by soldiers who were stationed on the front lines in the absence of sufficient or suitable witnesses. Presumably,

164 *Dig.* 28.1.2: "In eo qui testatur eius temporis, quo testamentum facit, integritas mentis, non corporis sanitas exigenda est."

165 *Dig.* 28.1.6 pr.: "Qui in potestate parentis est, testamenti faciendi ius non habet, adeo ut, quamvis pater ei permittat, nihilo magis tamen iure testari possit."

166 On the issue of capacity see John A. Crook, *Law and Life of Rome* (London, 1967), 120–1.

167 *CTh* 4.4.1 (?326).

168 Ian Wood ("Disputes in late fifth- and early sixth-century Gaul: Some Problems," in Wendy Davies and Paul Fouracre (eds.), *The Settlement of Disputes in Early Medieval Europe* (Cambridge, 1986), 7–22, esp. 19) has argued that this admixture of procedures reflected a general misunderstanding of earlier classical forms, and that such incoherency is the hallmark of vulgar law. But there is no reason to interpret this admixture of procedures as a decline in legal standards in Late Antiquity. In fact, it could be taken as an inventive solution to the fact that in many areas of the Empire the availability of suitable witnesses was limited.

169 *ET* 72. See also *ET* 52.

as was the case in the Empire, probate here depended upon the satisfactory comparison of the handwriting of the document with that of surviving examples of the alleged testator's script.[170] And although there is no indication that testaments were subject to a statute of limitations, it is unlikely that a potential beneficiary or successor could profit should a significant amount of time elapse between the reception and presentation of the deceased's will.

There is nothing in the *ET* as to the internal form which the will was to take – details that were of paramount importance for establishing the authenticity of the document as a genuine expression of the deceased's final wishes. This, combined with the interest of the compilers on the subject of intestacy and intestate succession, is indicative of the fact that in Italy in the early sixth century the act of making a will was not a particularly common one.[171] Despite the variety of reasons for testation, it cannot be maintained that will-making was the norm in the late Roman world as well. It is true that juristic discussion in the *Digest* of problems arising from wills overwhelmingly exceeds that devoted to intestacy, but this is hardly conclusive; the law relating to wills was more extensive and complex than the laws of intestacy.[172]

In classical law, the order of succession to the estates of an intestate person was children, heirs-at-law other than children (such as agnates), cognates, and if there were not claimants with the previous classes, the surviving spouse was entitled to *bonorum possessio* (possession of property) of the whole or part of the estate.[173] Under *ET* 23, the order of succession was children (including grandchildren), then followed by agnates and cognates. That surviving spouses could inherit if there was no successful claimant among these is presupposed by *ET* 24, which concerns the rights of the fisc over caducous land. Citing the precepts of ancient laws and desiring this prerogative to be universal in accordance with the will of the Emperors, the

[170] *CTh* 2.27.1; 9.19.2; *CJ* 4.21.20.3. This type of testament – that is the holograph testament – presented judges in the Empire with the greatest problems for determining authenticity. See further Elizabeth A. Meyer, *Legitimacy and Law in the Roman World.* Tabulae *in Roman Belief and Practice* (Cambridge, 2004), 274–5.

[171] In all, a total of five provisions deal with the topic of intestacy and intestate succession: *ET* 23 and 24, 26, 27, 33.

[172] David Daube, "The Preponderance of Intestacy in Rome," *Tulane Law Review* 35 (1964–65), 253–62; David Cherry, "Intestacy and the Roman Poor," *Traditio* 64 (1996), 155–72.

[173] John A. Crook, "Women in Roman Succession," in B. Rawson (ed.), *The Family in Ancient Rome: New Perspectives* (Ithaca, NY, 1986), 58–82, esp. 60; Christopher J. Smith, *The Roman Clan: the Gens from Ancient Ideology to Modern Anthropology* (Cambridge, 2006), 29; Lindsay, *Adoption*, 100.

provision permitted the fisc to assume ownership of property in the absence of a suitable heir, such as a surviving spouse:

> In accordance with the precepts of the ancient laws, the fisc shall act at that time when neither a parent, child, grandchild, relative, kin, wife, or husband can be found to succeed: provided that whenever the fisc discovers an instance that it has a right to succession, or seeks something which it has a legal right of ownership to, it shall put forth an action [to claim it] without the formality of titles or benefice; for the fisc can deservedly, and without causing injury through the oppression of another, demand for itself any property whatsoever, provided that during a proper hearing a judgment was rendered in its favor. And We desire, just as the Emperors willed also, that this [property] law be universal.[174]

Along these lines Theoderic instructed the Senator Epiphanius to reclaim for the fisc property hitherto belonging to a certain Joanna who was intestate upon her death, "since the laws have established as a precaution that caducous property is to be claimed by Our fisc."[175] But the King insisted that Epiphanius hold an inquiry into the matter. If it was determined that those who had appropriated the land had a legal basis for doing so, then their claims would be upheld: "Inquire into these allegations as it does not befit Our eminence to be defrauded, for it is a weakness borne out of negligence to forfeit that which the laws require [Us] to take away. But if you find the facts different to these, by all means leave the present owners in quiet possession, since Our patrimony consists of those lands which are lawfully reclaimed from Our subjects."[176]

[174] *ET* 24: "Fiscus tunc agat, quando nec parentum nec filiorum nec nepotum nec agnatorum nec cognatorum nec uxoris et mariti, quae succedat, extare comperitur persona, secundum legum veterum constituta: ita ut fiscus quotiens locum successionis invenerit vel aliqua sibi competentia repetit, actionem, remota titulorum vel officii praesumptione proponat, quia tunc fiscus unamquamque rem merito potest et sine oppressionis alienae iniuria vindicare, dum intercedente sententia pro ipso fuerit iudicatum. Nobis enim, sicut et principes voluerunt, ius cum privatis volumus esse commune." The final clause of this provision is similarly expressed in *CJ* 6.22.7 of the Emperors Valentinian, Valens, and Gratian (371): "cum heredes instiluuntur imperator seu Augusta, ius commune cum ceteris habeant: quod et in codicillis vel fideicommissariis epistulis iure scriptis observandum erit. Et sicuti prisci legibus cautum est, imperatori quoque vel Augustae testamentum facere liceat et mutare." Likewise, *CTh* 11.30.68 of Theodosius II and Valentinian III (429): "ius nobis cum privatis non dedignamur esse commune."

[175] Cass., *Var.* 5.24: "quia caduca bona fisco nostro competere legum cauta decreverunt . . . substantia a diversis nullo legitimo iure suffultis usurpatione voluntaria suggeritur possideri."

[176] Cass., *Var.* 5.24.2: "Rogari enim in talibus causis, non fraudari principem decet, quia neglegentiae vitium est praesumptiones relinquere, quas iura praecipiunt amputare. Si quid autem contra reppereris, quietos dominos habere patieris, quia magis illa nostra sunt patrimonia, quae a subiectis legitime possidentur." For the practice of the imperial fisc in regards to seizing caducous property, the relevant legislation is *CJ* 6.51, a constitution drafted by the Quaestor Tribonian in 534, and

Family property could also be transferred between parents and children in the form of a gift. In the matter of gifts, late classical law had grown fairly complicated. To perform a *donatio perfecta* effectively, various and complex rules had to be followed. To simplify the process, Constantine introduced legislation in 323 which constituted a complete reworking of the ancient Roman law of donations.[177] According to Constantine's law, the Emperor had learned that gifts were not being made according to the correct legal procedure, and as a result, many lawsuits had arisen in part due to the inconsistency of previous imperial legislation on the matter. Henceforth, gifts had to be publicly recorded, with the name of the donor, the property being given, and the donor's right to that property put down in writing. Strictly speaking, the matter became one of public law. The physical transfer and acceptance of the object or property donated had to be carried out before neighbors and other witnesses; and to eliminate instances of fraud, a record of the transaction had to be registered in the public *acta* in the presence of the provincial Governor or, in his absence, of local magistrates. In making donation a matter of public record, Constantine was adhering to long-held practice.[178] Since the third century the imperial chancellery and the leading jurists recognized that the public registration of a donation, or simply the documentation of it, or the support of it through the delivery of documents had become a basic feature of the process of donation.

A possibly unintentional but impractical consequence of Constantine's law was that every gift, including occasional and petty ones, was to be registered in the public archives. The compilers, however, saw nothing impractical about Constantine's law. But they did make certain allowances that differed slightly from both Constantine's and subsequent legislation. Both Constantine and later adaptations of the law required that the record of the transaction be registered before the provincial Governor or, in his absence, local magistrates. A later law of the Emperor Honorius allowed the registration to take place in the presence of the defender of the people from

entitled *de caducis tollendis* ("Concerning the abolition of the forfeitures of successions to the State"), which summarizes all imperial legislation on the matter since the *lex Papia Poppaea* of Augustus. On this constitution see further Michel Kaplan, *Les propriétés de la couronne et de l'église dans l'empire byzantin (Ve-Vie siècles)* (Paris, 1976), 76; Tony Honoré, *Tribonian* (London, 1978), 110 (who notes forty-six characteristic traits of Tribonian within this constitution).

177 This is preserved in part at *CTh* 8.12.1, where it is addressed to the Urban Prefect Valerius Maximus. Since he was *praefectus urbi* from 319 to 323, the law is dated to probably 323. See Otto Seeck, *Regesten der Kaiser und Päpste für di Jähre 311 bis 476 n. Chr* (Stuttgart, 1919; repr. 1964), 88; Evans Grubbs, *Law and Family*, 118 n. 64. On the content of the law, see Clémence Dupont, "Les Donations dans les constitutions de Constantin," *RIDA* 9 (1962), 291–324, esp. 292–4, 298–304; Ernst Levy, *West Roman Vulgar Law: The Law of Property* (Philadelphia, PA, 1952), 137–46.

178 E.g. *Dig.* 41.2.48 (Papinian); *Dig.* 6.1.77 (Ulpian); *FV* 263, 265, 268, 281, 288, 297, 314; *CJ* 4.19.18; also *CJ* 4.21.12.

any municipality in the event that local magistrates could not be found.[179] The compilers, on the other hand, required the registration to be performed before witnesses (identified in *ET* 52 as "knowledgeable men from the neighborhood") and at least three municipal magistrates. In the absence of these, the record of transaction could be registered before a *defensor civitatis* together with three decurions, *duumviri*, or *quinquennales*. And should these officers be lacking, the compilers allowed for the witnessing to take place in another municipality that had such officers, but added that a report of the events must also be forwarded to the Governor of that province.[180]

Conclusions

Topics of Roman private law, a detailed and complex subject that had the potential to impact nearly every aspect of an individual's life, comprise the bulk of the content of the *ET*. Throughout, the compilers display a keen interest in, an ability to understand, and a desire to preserve many of the ancient concepts that defined Roman society. The legal conditions and consequences of freedom and unfreedom, aspects of private land ownership, the general system of succession and inheritance, rules over marriage and divorce, and many other features of Roman private law were transmitted, perhaps somewhat simplified, but still in easily recognizably Roman form. At the same time, they felt it prudent to observe local custom in their efforts to update the law. Strict prohibitions against incest, which figured prominently in imperial legislation of the late fourth and fifth centuries, were purposely overlooked, and we are told by Cassiodorus that close-kin marriages of first cousins were permitted. This is hardly evidence of a breakdown in ancient social structures or the development of a new concept of the family, but simply a testament to the persistence of certain provincial marriage practices that had long been considered abhorrent to Roman morals and legal standards.[181]

The compilers also ignored the derogatory tone against women that is such a defining feature of Roman family law. They also emphasized the importance of a woman's chastity (provided she was above a certain legal and social standing),[182] just as Roman law had, but ignored the significance

[179] *CTh* 8.12.8 (415). [180] *ET* 53.

[181] An argument made by Evelyne Patlagean in regards to the eastern provinces of the late Empire. See her *Pauvreté économique et pauvreté sociale à Byzance 4e–7e siecles* (Paris, 1977), 113–28.

[182] E.g., *ET* 62.

placed on divine chastity by later imperial legislation. That these sorts of omissions are indicative of a general change in social attitudes and mores toward the position of women in public and private life is certainly possible. But more than likely they are simply reflective of the realities of rural life of the smaller towns and countryside for which the *ET* was drafted, just as earlier Roman laws on the subject reflected a more sophisticated urban culture of the large cities of the Empire.[183] This is reinforced by the amount of detail the compilers devoted to such issues as abduction, marriage, or the selling of children, issues that were more relevant to the rural lower classes than matters of testation and inheritance, subjects which were passed over with a few very general remarks since they concerned primarily the urban, wealthier, more sophisticated classes, that is, those who had enough wealth or property that the details of the law were important to know.

Just as the *ET* bears witness to the evolution of Roman private law in Late Antiquity, it also, and more importantly, speaks directly to the kinds of issues that mattered most to the average person in Theoderic's Italy, preoccupied as they were with such issues as incidents of land tenureship and ownership, rights over, and obligations to, slaves and farmhands; and matters closer to home, like a wife's infidelity, the rights of a spouse in matters of marriage and divorce, some of the responsibilities and obligations of parents to their children, the conveyance of property through succession and inheritance, and so on. It was provisions such as these with which ordinary persons most often had to deal while going about their daily lives, even if at times they testify to the exception more so than they do the rule.

[183] On the sorts of differences reflected in Roman law between urban culture and country living regarding issues of women, see Evans Grubbs, *Law and Family*, 333–6.

CHAPTER 5

The economy

Introduction

The economic conditions of Ostrogothic Italy are difficult to assess with any certainty. In general terms, however, it is clear that for some centuries the peninsula had been in decline, with respect to both the role it played in long-distance trade and its internal situation, and this for reasons not directly connected with the political turmoil of the times.[1] We should be right to think in terms of a considerable ruralization of life and economy, a state of affairs reflected in large measure in the *ET*, where preoccupation with the resolution of agricultural problems is a predominant feature. It would be wrong, however, to conceive of the economy as based so completely upon the land that external trade had virtually dried up and the

[1] On the economic decline of Italy from the fourth to sixth centuries, see Chris Wickham, *Land and Power: Studies in Italian and European Social History, 400–1200* (London, 1994), 101; Chris Wickham, *Framing the Early Middle Ages*, (Oxford, 2005) 34, 203–5 (with a focus on the decline of the senatorial elite – a good indicator of overall economic decline according to the author); Bryan Ward-Perkins, "Land, Labor and Settlement," in Averil Cameron, Bryan Ward-Perkins, and Michael Whitby (eds.), *The Cambridge Ancient History*, vol. 14: *Late Antiquity: Empire and Successors, AD 425–600* (Cambridge, 2000), 315–46; Bryan Ward-Perkins, "Specialized Production and Exchange," in Averil Cameron *et al.* (eds.), *The Cambridge Ancient History*, 346–91, esp. 354–5; Federico Marazzi, "The Destinies of the Late Antique Italies," in Richard Hodges and William Bowden (eds.), *The Sixth Century. Production, Distribution and Demand* (Leiden/New York, 1998), 119–59. On the archaeological evidence of economic decline in Italy, see Gian-Pietro Brogiolo, "Dwellings and Settlements in Gothic Italy," in Sam J. Barnish and Federico Marazzi (eds.), *The Ostrogoths from the Migration Period to the Sixth Century: An Ethnographic Perspective* (Woodbridge, 2007), 128–30; Alastair M. Small and R. J. Buck, *The Excavations of S. Giovanni di Ruoti*, I (Toronto, 1994), 121; Timothy W. Potter and Andrew C. King, *Excavations at the Mola di Monte Gelato* (London, 1997), 76–7, 121. For evidence of decline both in terms of the distribution and sophistication of fine pottery during this period, see Paul Arthur and H. Patterson, "Local Pottery in Southern Puglia in the Sixth and Seventh Centuries," in L. Saguì (ed.), *Ceramica in Italia: VI–VII secolo. Atti del convegno in onore di J. W. Hayes*, May 11–13, 1995. Arch. Medievale 14 (Florence, 1998), 511–30, esp. 507; Helga Di Giuseppe, "La Fornace di Calle di Tricarico," in Saguì (ed.), *Ceramica in Italia*, 735–52. For discussion on the general decline of western Europe from the fourth century to the eighth, see Paul Fouracre, "Space, Culture and Kingdoms in Early Medieval Europe," in Peter Linehan and Janet Nelson (eds.), *The Medieval World* (New York, 2003), 366–80, esp. 367.

towns taken on the character of mere markets for the interchange of bartered goods. Not only direct evidence bearing on urban and commercial life, but also the constant role that money compositions and transactions play in the *ET* argues conclusively against any such view.

That there was at least some modest revival in production, trade, and civic life during this time is clear.[2] We are, in fact, told, though perhaps with some exaggeration, that on one occasion Theoderic ordered the construction of a thousand ships, and that he arranged for the exportation of grain (at great expense to the state) from the ports of Campania and the upper Adriatic to relieve a severe food shortage in Liguria and Provence.[3] We also learn from the annals of the first Gothic War that Naples was an active center of trade and the residence of many merchants from the East, especially Jews, who urged the population to resistance during Belisarius' siege in 536 with assurances that they could keep the town adequately supplied.[4] Some account must also be taken of Theoderic's reform of the coinage and fixing of corn prices,[5] or the many building programs which he undertook.[6] The degree to which these and other economic policies instituted by Theoderic were successful can be gleaned from a careful reading of the *ET*, which in its selection of topics suggests that no amount of government involvement could completely rid Italy of the problems that had been plaguing it for more than a century: specifically, the manpower shortage on the land, the insecurity of property, and the violent overbearing of the small proprietors and laborers by the great magnates. All of this was compounded by the occurrence of periodic but devastating droughts and famines, and the greed and corruption of government officials who readily took advantage of a weak central administration.[7]

[2] Marazzi, "The Destinies of the Late Antique Italies," 132–4.

[3] Cass., *Var.* 5.16, 17 (construction of fleet); *Var.* 1.34; 2.26; 4.5, 7; 5.35 (ended in failure); 9.3.4, 5; 10.27 (grain transportation and distribution). On the movement of grain, on trade in general, and on the type of ships used, see the excellent discussion of Dietrich Claude, *Der Handel im westlichen Mittelmeer während des Frühmittelalters*. Abhandlungen der Akademie der Wissenschaften in Göttingen, Phil.-hist. Kl. III 144 (Göttingen, 1985), esp. 71–3. See also Lellia Ruggini, *Economia e società nell' "Italia annonaria"* (Milan, 1961), 292–4.

[4] Proc., *BG* V. viii. 41, v. x. 24–6.

[5] Cass., *Var.* 10.27; 2.26 and 12.27 (emergency measures to combat rising prices). See Ludo Moritz Hartmann, *Geschichte Italiens im Mittelalter*, 2 vols. (Leipzig, 1897; repr. 1923), I, 128, n. 20; Wolfgang Hahn, *Moneta Imperii Byzantini*, 3 vols. (Vienna, 1973), I, 77–91; II, 25–32, which contains an excellent discussion of the Ostrogothic monetary system.

[6] Anon. Val. 12.71. On Theoderic's building program in general, see Mark J. Johnson, "Toward a History of Theoderic's Building Program," *Dumbarton Oaks Papers* 42 (1988), 73–96.

[7] For the negative effects of droughts and famines in the peninsula: Cass., *Var.* 4.5 (a letter addressed in Theoderic's name to the *comes* Amabilis, concerning the supply of provisions to the famine-stricken province of Gaul); 4.7 (apparently, some of the supply ships sent to Gaul to relieve the famine sank. Here, Theoderic instructs the *comes privatarum* not to penalize any merchants whose loss was no fault of their own); 10.27 (written in Theodahad's name, this letter

Currency and counterfeiting

The regular imposition of monetary fines as a legitimate penalty for certain prescribed crimes presupposes the use of currency in Ostrogothic Italy.[8] The largest single imposed fine which appears in the *ET* is truly staggering: ten pounds of gold, or approximately 665 *solidi*, for any judge who refused to hear a case or otherwise abused an appellant in any way.[9] Significant financial penalties are also attested to by Cassiodorus. Nowhere in the *Variae* is provision made for payment less than a *solidus*, and in some instances, the total composition could often amount to several hundred *solidi*. For example, an individual who unlawfully used a horse of the public post could be fined as much as 100 *solidi* for each offense.[10]

Certainly, it is not to be supposed that the ordinary freeman would easily, if at all, have been able to find the sums required in composition for more serious offenses, even assuming financial assistance from his near kinsfolk. But it would be to attribute to Theoderic and his advisors either a grotesque lack of realism, or the deliberate aim of bringing about the mass enslavement of the free population to suppose that the mulcts imposed for lesser offenses could not normally have been met. Thus, we come across provisions that take into account the inability of a freeman to pay a composition, and in turn impose a sentence of flogging or banishment rather than enslavement in place of the fine.[11] Of course, the fact that a composition was expressed in monetary terms does not mean that it was necessarily paid in coin. The *ET* contains numerous provisions that allow for payment to be made in kind by the delivery of land, animals, or slaves for a given offense.[12] But even if this was the case, the commodity concerned could fulfill its role as a substitute for cash only if it had a monetary value put upon it as a result of the willingness of someone, somewhere, eventually to exchange coin for it.

It is clear, moreover, that the apparatus for a developed economic and commercial life based upon money transactions existed and needed regulation. Edicts governing sales are witnessed, and loans at interest were

concerns the supply of corn to the depleted regions of Liguria and Venetia); 12.25 (a letter in Cassiodorus' own name concerning the famine that struck Italy in 538). The famine is mentioned again in 12.28. Corrupt government officials: Cass., *Var.* 9.12, 9.14.

8 *ET* 2, 4, 10, 55, 71, 97, 98, 109, 115, 124, 126, 149, 150; Cass., *Var.* 1.32; 2.26; 3.46; 4.47; 5.5; 6.3, 13; 7.42; 9.2, 18.1; 10.28; 11.11–12.

9 *ET* 55. 10 Cass., *Var.* 4.47 11 E.g., *ET* 64; similarly Cass., *Var.* 4.10.

12 E.g., *ET* 56, 57, 58, 64, 70, 80, 84, 117, 119, 141, 151, 152.

strictly regulated.[13] According to Cassiodorus, it would seem that no interest was paid on money lost by no fault of the borrower, although the capital had, of course, to be repaid. In a letter addressed in the name of Theoderic to the Praetorian Prefect Faustus, Cassiodorus instructs the addressee that the merchants of the city of Sipontum (in Apulia) are to be granted a two-year amnesty from paying taxes – in consideration of the destruction caused by hostile incursions (presumably a reference to the Byzantine fleet in 508). Creditors are similarly instructed to provide the same indulgence:

> We have no pleasure in gains which are acquired by the misery of our subjects. We are informed that the merchants of the city of Sipontum have been grievously despoiled by hostile incursions. Let your Magnificence therefore see to it that they are for two years not vexed by any claims for purveyance (*coemptio*) on the part of our Treasury. But their other creditors must give them the same indulgence, in so far as they may reclaim the debt after the two years, but not to the detriment of the debtors.[14]

After the designated two-year period, creditors could take action against defaulting borrowers, including, presumably, the imposition of the stipulated interest.

Our sources point inescapably to the conclusion that not only was currency used, but in fact, that it was used extensively. Indicative of this is Theoderic's concern to ensure the purity of the coinage. Adulteration, clipping, and counterfeiting of coins were all capital offenses:

> Those who erase, change, add to or take away, burn or expunge another's testament, codicil, records, accounts, transcripts of registered instruments, documents, bonds, or letters in any place for the purposes of fraud, or give, sell, or substitute gilded bronze, silver or iron for gold, and those who substitute tin for silver, or cut around the outer circle of a *solidus*, or those who prescribe or take pains that this may be done, shall endure the stipulated penalty for the crime of forgery [i.e. death].[15]

[13] *ET* 134, 139, 140 and 147.

[14] Cass., *Var.* 2.38: "Urbis itaque Sipontinae negotiatores hostium se asserunt depopulatione vastatos: et quia egentium levamina nostras potius divitias aestimamus, illustris magnificentia vestra per hoc iuge biennium nuncupatos nulla faciat coemptione vexari . . . ne in hoc biennii spatio quicquam de credita summa existiment postulandum, quatenus sub induciis supradictis et datam possint reparare pecuniam et aliquatenus debitorum valeat respirare substantia."

[15] *ET* 90: "Qui testamentum, codicillum, tabulas, rationes, gesta, libellos, cautiones, epistolas in fraudem alterius, quocumque loco deleverint, mutaverint, subiecerint, subrepserint, incenderint, raserint, aut aes, argentum, vel ferrum inauratum scientes pro auro dederint, vel vendiderint, vel subposuerint, quique pro argento stamnum subiecerint, vel exteriorem circulum solidi praeciderint, quive, ut id fieret, iusserint operamve dederint, poenam sustineant falsi crimini constitutam."

To facilitate the prosecution of suspected counterfeiters, the *ET* permitted the use of torture of slaves to substantiate the validity of an accusation *pro falsa moneta* levied against a freeman.[16]

The perceived severity of the penalty reflects the seriousness of the crime. Counterfeiting posed a direct threat to the economic stability of the kingdom, and thus had to be dealt with harshly. To that end, the *formula* for the Master of the Mint warns the officer in highly rhetorical fashion against tampering with the coinage in any way:

> You must preserve in whole the purity of the money, upon which Our image is impressed and where public advantage is found. For, what will be left unharmed, if Our likeness is blemished and that which the public ought to venerate wholeheartedly, is violated by a sacrilegious hand? Add to the fact that public sale and trade would be destroyed if the currency is corrupted.[17]

Despite such measures as these, however, it would seem that counterfeiting remained a serious problem. In a letter written in the name of Theoderic to the patrician and *vir illustris* Boethius, Cassiodorus refers to a complaint made to the King by the horse and foot guards (*domestici patres equitum et peditum*) of their being paid by improperly weighted *solidi*:

> The horse and foot guards, who are seen to keep constant watch over Our court, have made this complaint to Us in a joint petition, which is the usual result of serious grievances: they do not receive *solidi* of full weight as their customary wages from the Prefect's treasurer, and they suffer heavy losses in the number of coins. Therefore, let your wisdom, trained by learned texts, expel this wicked fraud from the company of truth, so that no one shall be tempted to diminish that purity.[18]

Trade and commerce

Currency brings us to the related matter of trade and industry. Despite the considerable evidence for trading relations between Italy and other regions – or, at least, of maritime links which argue for the strong

16 *ET* 100.

17 Cass., *Var.* 7.32: "Tamen omnino monetae debet integritas quaeri, ubi et vultus noster imprimitur et generalis utilitas invenitur. nam quid erit tutum, si in nostra peccetur effigie, et quam subiectus corde venerari debet, manus sacrilega violare festinet? additur quod venalitas cuncta dissolvitur, si victualia metalla vitiantur[.]"

18 Cass., *Var.* 1.10.2: "Domestici partis equitum et peditum, qui nostrae aulae videntur iugiter excubare, quod ex magnis fieri doloribus solet, adunata nobis supplicatione conquesti sunt ab illo arcario praefectorum pro emolumentis sollemnibus nec integri ponderis solidos percipere et in numero gravia se dispendia sustinere. Quapropter prudentia vestra lectionibus erudita dogmaticis scelestam falsitatem a consortio veritatis eiciat, ne cui sit appetibile aliquid de illa integritate subducere."

probability of trade – the *ET* reveals next to nothing concerning this industry.[19] Nevertheless, what little information there exists is revealing in its own right. The implications of the territorial nature of Roman law in Ostrogothic Italy (as stated at the outset of the *ET* and further reinforced by the epilogue) were such that overseas merchants doing business in Italy were necessarily subject to its provisions. To that end, the law protected the interests of a buyer if the validity of a sale was later challenged in court.[20]

Of internal trade we know very little from the *ET* itself. Travel by river, in those places where the geography permitted, was facilitated by Theoderic who insisted upon the free navigation of the larger rivers used by fishing boats and trading vessels.[21] For those travelling by road, some protection was afforded against brigands. In a letter written in the name of Athalaric to the *vir spectabilis* Severus, presumably the Governor of Lucania and Bruttium, Cassiodorus tells the story of a certain *vir sublimis* Nimfadius who, while traveling through the region on his way to the royal court, had his animals stolen by the local inhabitants there:

> While the *vir sublimis* Nimfadius was making his way to the most sacred *comitatus* to plead a case of his, he grew wearied by the long journey, and attempting to rest his tired animals, chose to make a stopover at the fountain of Arethusa, located in the region of Squillace (Scillacium) . . .while resting here, Nimfadius asserts that his packhorses were taken by the local inhabitants. . .We decree that you diligently inquire into the matter, whose authority derives both from Our palace and the laws. . .lest such a miracle [the fountain of Arethusa] is spoiled by the excesses of thieves.[22]

Severus was instructed to find the culprits and bring them to justice. While the rights of Nimfadius were no doubt a concern for Athalaric, the

[19] Cass., *Var.* 4.19 (tax immunity on traders of corn, wine and oil); 7.9 (*formula* for the Count of the Port of Rome, with reference to trade to and from the city); Anon. Val. 12.71–3 (on the economic policies of Theoderic in general, including his efforts to increase commercial ties with neighboring nations). On trade in general see Claude, *Der Handel*, 71–3; Knud Hannestad, *L'évolution des ressources agricoles de l'Italie du quatrième au sixième siècle de notre ère*. Historisk-filosofiske Meddelelser af det Koneglige Danske Videnskabernes Selskab 40/41 (Copenhagen, 1962), 28–41.

[20] *ET* 139.

[21] Cass., *Var.* 5.17 (addressed to the Praetorian Prefect Abundantius; reiterated again in 5.20).

[22] Cass., *Var.* 8.32: "Cum Nymphadius v. s. pro causis suis ad comitatum sacratissimum festinaret, itineris longinquitate confectus, animalia fessa reparare contendens, ad fontem Arethusae in Scyllacino territorio constitutae elegit ponere mansionem . . . hic cum mansionem supradictus Nymphadius habuisset, insidiis rusticorum abactos sibi asserit caballos . . . quod vivacitatem tuam diligenti censemus examinatione discutere . . . quae et de palatio nostro auctoritatem et de legibus visa est iustitiam collegisse . . . ne latronum excessibus vitetur tale miraculum[.]"

real issue at hand was the potential for economic loss to the region – a tourist draw noted for its famous spring which *prisca superstitio* had formerly named after the goddess Leucothea – if such acts of highway robbery went unpunished.

The story of Nimfadius presupposes that there existed certain legal obligations and responsibilities of local municipalities and private landholders towards the erstwhile traveler. This was certainly the case in most other successor kingdoms.[23] Among the Visigoths, for instance, a traveler might pull down a fence or wall which he found obstructing a highway or vicinal road,[24] and was entitled to use unenclosed land, and even uncultivated land marked off as private by ditches, for pasturing his animals: permission from the owner was required only when he stayed for more than two days. Small trees might be felled for fodder, and the branches of others lopped, and the owner of the land was penalized if he impounded or drove out the animals.[25] If cultivated land near a river-crossing was not enclosed, the traveler was not responsible for damage which he or his animals might cause,[26] and the same probably applied when the land was near a highway.[27] In any case, the traveler was not liable for damage caused by his entry on to cultivated land when passage was otherwise impossible.[28] He might light a fire with wood from the place where he rested, although he had to be careful to prevent it from spreading and causing injury or damage, for which he was, of course, accountable.[29] He received some compensation for injuries inflicted by snares or pits, and was extended protection against unlawful detention, manhandling, theft, or robbery.[30] In Burgundy, travelers might claim the protection of a roof, and a Burgundian refusing the shelter or referring him to a Roman was subject to a fine.[31]

While these examples are indicative of a considerable volume of internal trade and travel within these regions, what evidence we have for Ostrogothic Italy suggests that Theoderic was chiefly concerned with the interests of crop-raisers over travelers. Repeated royal grants in the *Variae* which awarded farmers for losses suffered as a consequence of the Gothic army travelling through their lands underscore this concern. On

[23] Felix Dahn, *Die Könige der Germanen: Das Wesen des ältesten Königsthums der germanischen Stämme und seine Geschichte bis auf die Feudalzeit*, 4 vols. (Leipzig,, 1879), VI, 286–7; Teophil Melicher, *Der Kampf zwischen Gesetzes- und Gewohnheitsrecht im Westgotenreich* (Weimer, 1930), 183–4; Ernst Levy, *West Roman Vulgar Law: The Law of Property* (Philadelphia, PA, 1912), 125–6.

[24] *LV* 8.4.24. [25] *LV* 8.3.9; 4.26, 27. [26] *LV* 8.4.28.

[27] Cf. *LV* 8.4.25 (requiring the fencing or ditching of land adjoining the clear stretches on both sides of the roads. But the immediate aim was probably to prevent the encroachment of cropland).

[28] *LV* 8.3.9. [29] *LV* 8.2.3. [30] *LV* 8.4.22, 23. [31] *LB* 38.7.

one occasion the extraordinarily large sum of 1,500 *solidi* was awarded as compensation. In a letter to the Bishop Severus concerning damage done to the Alpine region by his army (presumably traveling en route to Gaul), Theoderic proclaimed:

> Therefore, considering the action suitable to your merits, We inform you that We have sent your holiness, through Montanarius, 1,500 *solidi*. In so far as you know any of the provincials to have suffered loss from the passage of Our army in this year, you are to distribute the money to them, having already made an estimate of the damage, so that no one who has suffered by his losses will be a stranger to Our generosity.[32]

Town and country

That there was an overall decline in civic life in post-Roman Italy can hardly be doubted. Many towns had been in a period of decline long before Odovacer removed the enfeebled Romulus Augustulus in 476, and although his tenureship was brief (476–89), it only added to the misery. Even if we are to believe that Odovacer and his followers were not invaders who seized land but rather were accommodated as guests through some sort of allocation of tax revenue, the results could hardly have been pleasant for the native inhabitants. Ennodius is particularly critical, noting on several occasions that Odovacer's officials caused a great deal of misery on local communities through their ineptitude and corruption.[33] The situation was made worse in 489 when Theoderic was dispatched by Zeno to remove the barbarian upstart. Several towns throughout the peninsula were devastated as a result of the four-year-long contest for power between Theoderic and

[32] Cass., *Var.* 2.8: "Proinde aptam considerantes vestris meritis actionem significamus nos per Montanarium sanctitati vestrae mille quingentos solidos destinasse, quos provincialibus, prout quemque praesenti anno exercitu nostro transeunte dispendium pertulisse cognoveris, habita laesionis aestimatione distribuas, ut nullus a nostra munificentia reddatur alienus, quem sua damna gravaverunt." See also Cass., *Var.* 4.36 (a letter in Theoderic's name to the Praetorian Prefect Faustus, concerning the remission of taxes to the provincials of the Cottian Alps as a consequence of the damage caused by the army of Ibbas passing through the region in 508 to fight Clovis).

[33] On the negative impact of Odovacer's tenureship in Italy, see Ennodius' treatment in his *Vita Epiphanii*, 107 (concerning the suffering of the landowners of Liguria at the hands of the corrupt Praetorian Prefect Pelagius); *Pan Th.*, which not surprisingly stresses the corruption and ineptitude of Odovacer's officials and soldiers (e.g. *Pan. Th.* 23–4, 25, and 37). For a more sympathetic treatment of Odovacer's reign, see John Moorhead, *Theoderic in Italy* (Oxford, 1992), 8–9, 29–31; and Maria Cesa, "Odoacre nelle fonti letterarie dei secoli V e VI," in Paolo Delogu (ed.), *Le invasioni barbariche nel meridione dell'impero: Visigoti, Vandali, Ostrogoti: atti del convegno svoltosi alla Casa delle culture di Consenza dal 24 al 26 luglio 1998* (Soveria Mannelli, 2001). On the edition of the *Panegyric*, see *Panegyricus dictus clementissimo regi Theoderico*, ed. and trans. Christian Rohr, *Der Theoderich-Panegyricus des Ennodius. MGH* Studien und Texte 12 (Hannover, 1995).

Odovacer, and others were despoiled or abandoned altogether during the sixth century.[34] But all was not bad. Ravenna arose in new splendor, and according to one sixth-century *vita*, Rome continued to inspire awe in many who visited the *caput mundi* during Theoderic's *decennalia* celebration in 500.[35] And we know of a few cities actually being founded by Theoderic, and not in every case for a military purpose. One of these was a town in Reate bearing the King's name – the mysterious (insofar as its precise location remains unknown) Theodericopolis.[36]

We are ill-informed as to the quality of life in the towns. Judging from what little evidence we have, public spectacles and theaters remained popular, and patrons continued to flock to the local baths, but not to the scale of the later Empire.[37] Cassiodorus' description of the amphitheater and baths of Rome implies that they were far too large for contemporary needs:

> It is evident how great the population of the city of Rome had been . . . for the vast extent of the walls bears witness to the crowds of citizens, as do the swollen capacity of the buildings of entertainment, the wondrous size of the baths, and that great number of water-mills which was clearly provided especially for the food supply.[38]

The decline of town life is further underscored by Theoderic's repeated calls to put a stop to the theft of public statues and other bronze and marble

[34] E.g., Cass., *Var.* 3.49 (on the deteriorating state of the city of Catana). *Contra* Thomas S. Brown, *Gentlemen and Officers: Imperial Administration and Aristocratic Power in Byzantine Italy, AD. 554–800* (Rome, 1984), 1–2.

[35] Ravenna: Cass., *Var.* 1.6. See also the monumental work of Friedrich Wilhelm Deichmann, *Ravenna: Hauptstadt des spätantiken Abendlandes*, vol. 1 (Wiesbaden, 1969). Rome: Cass., *Var.* 2.7; 3.29–31; 7.15. Ferrandus Diaconus, *Vita s. Fulgentii*, ch. 9, 55–6; Moorhead, *Theoderic in Italy*, 60–3.

[36] Wilhelm Ensslin, *Theoderich der Grosse*, 2nd edn. (Munich, 1959), 244–62. The foundation of a city near Trent is decreed in Cass., *Var.* 5.9. On the building activity see Anon. Val. 12.71. The city of Chur has long been identified as the Theodericopolis of the Anonymous Geographer of Ravenna, but the evidence for this is far from conclusive. On Theodericopolis, see Ravennas Anonymus, *Cosmographia* IV 26.45, ed. Joseph Schnetz in *Itineraria Romana*, vol. 2: *Ravennatis Anonymi Cosmographia* (Leipzig, 1929–40; repr. 1990); Ensslin, *Theoderich*, 142 n. 1; Herwig Wolfram, "Gotisches Studien I/II," *Mitteilungen des Instituts für Österreichische Geschichtsforschung* 83 (1975), 1–28, esp. 16 n. 97; Otto P. Clavadetscher, "Churrätien im Übergang von der Spätantike zum Mittelalter nach den Schriftquellen," *Vortäge und Forschungen* 25 (Sigmanngen, 1979), 164. On the interest in geography under Theoderic, see Franz Staab, "Ostrogothic Geographers at the Court of Theoderic the Great: A Study of Some Sources of the Anonymous Cosmographer of Ravenna," *Viator* 7 (1976), 27–64.

[37] Games: Cass., *Var.* 1.20, 1.27, 1.30, 3.51, 5.42, 6.4, Anon. Val. 12.60, 67; theater: *Var.* 7.10; pantomimes: 1.31 and 32; actors: 7.10 and 9.21; baths: 2.37, 5.38, 6.4, 7.6, 8.31, 9.6, 10.29.

[38] Cass., *Var.* 11.39.2: "Apparet, quantus in Romana civitate fuerit populus . . . Testantur enim turbas [Romanorum] civium amplissima spatia murorum, spectaculorum distensus amplexus, mirabilis magnitudo thermarum et illa numerositas molarum, quam specialiter contributam constat ad victum."

works from civic buildings and monuments, as well as his insistence that temples and public places be restored to their former glory. In a letter penned by Cassiodorus, the King bemoaned the ruinous state of Rome and his inability to put a stop to the continued destruction of the ancient capital:

> We strive to restore all things to their original condition, the improvement of the city of Rome still binds Us to a special concern; there whatever is spent on adornment is furnished for the joy of all . . . Bronze moreover – no small weight of it – and soft lead, which is very vulnerable to theft, are reported to have been removed from the adornments of the public buildings, although their inventors dedicated them to the service of the ages. . .Furthermore, temples and public places which, at the request of many, We assigned for repair, have instead been given over to demolition.[39]

The *formulae* for the Prefect of the Watch of Rome (*Var.* 7.7) and Ravenna (*Var.* 7.8), as well as that of the Count of Rome (*Var.* 7.13) mention these sorts of problems specifically.[40] Of course, such abuses were nothing new. The Emperor Majorian's fourth novel, an imperial ordinance on public buildings addressed in 458 to the Roman Senate, responded at length to the deteriorating state of the city, including the purposeful destruction of buildings to give materials for the repair of others: "While stones are supposed to be necessary for public works, the beautiful arrangement of ancient buildings [in particular pagan temples and shrines] is being scattered, and in order that something small may be repaired, great things are being demolished."[41] Although by the beginning of the sixth century Rome had long since become a political and economic backwater, it remained a potent symbol of the vitality of Empire, the significance of which was not lost on Theoderic. Despite this, the barbarian King, like

[39] Cass., *Var.* 3.31: "Tamen Romanae civitatis sollicitiora nos augmenta constringunt, ubi quicquid decoris impenditur, generalibus gaudiis exhibetur . . . aes praeterea, non minimum pondus, et quod est facillimum direptioni, mollissimum plumbum, de ornatu moenium referuntur esse sublata, quae auctores suos saeculis consecrarunt . . . templa etiam et loca publica, quae petentibus multis ad reparationem contulimus, subversioni fuisse potius mancipata."

[40] Similarly Cass., *Var.* 2.35 (concerning the theft of a brazen statue from the city of Como).

[41] *Nov. Maj.* 4: "Dum necessaria public opera saxa finguntur, antiquarum aedium dissipater speciosa constructio et ut parvum aliquid reparetur, magna diruuntur." On the re-use of public materials, see in general Bryan Ward-Perkins, *From Classical Antiquity to the Middle Ages: Urban Public Building in North and Central Italy, AD 300–850* (Oxford, 1985), chapter 3; Joseph Alchermes, "Spolia in Roman Cities of the Late Empire: Legislative Rationales and Architectural Reuse," *Dumbarton Oaks Papers* 48 (1994), 167–78. On the deterioration of the monumental center of Rome, see Federico Marazzi, "The Last Rome: From the End of the Fifth to the End of the Sixth Century," in Sam J. Barnish and Federico Marazzi (eds.), *The Ostrogoths from the Migration Period to the Sixth Century* (Woodbridge, 2007), 279–301; Brogiolo, "Dwellings and Settlements in Gothic Italy," 127.

Majorian and other Emperors before him, was unable to prevent further destruction to the city's once glorious temples and monuments.

Just as civic buildings and monuments were plundered for valuable adornments, so, too, were tombs. Under *ET* 110, which preserves the most severe Roman tradition dealing with the protection of burial places and the dead, the destruction of a tomb qualified as a capital offense and was punishable by death. It made no difference if the offense involved the theft of grave goods or was simply the result of damage associated with the appropriation of funerary stones or ornaments for reuse elsewhere. To be sure, early medieval sepulchers proved tempting targets to thieves precisely because of the costly grave goods and decorative ornaments associated with them; and the lucrative nature of grave robbery helps explain the popularity of the practice despite the risks and penalties it involved.[42] Theoderic, too, recognized the potential of graves for increasing revenue. In a letter of instruction to the *saio* Duda, the King proclaimed:

> It is the custom of prudence to reclaim treasures hidden in the earth for humane purposes, and to designate it for the business of the living and not the dead, since these buried items are of no use to Us and are of no advantage to the dead when left behind. The circulation of precious metals is certainly a comfort for men . . . Wherefore, by this just command We decree that you [i.e. Duda] proceed in public view to any place where valuable materials are said to be buried. And if any gold or silver should happen to be found through your investigation, you will faithfully vindicate it for the public treasury, but only under this condition: namely, that you abstain from laying your hands on the ashes of the dead, since We do not wish to seek gains that can be obtained through deadly sins. Let buildings protect the ashes, and columns or marble adorn the sepulchers: Let not those who have left behind the cares of the living hold on to riches. It is right for gold to be taken from sepulchers where there is no master (*dominus*): Indeed, it is a kind of offense to leave behind hidden treasures for the dead, through which the life of the living can sustain itself. It is not greed to take away that for which there is no master to lament the loss of.[43]

[42] Éric Rebillard, *The Care of the Dead in Late Antiquity*, trans. Elizabeth Trapnell Rawlings and Jeanine Routier-Pucci (Ithaca, NY, 2009), chapter 4.

[43] Cass., *Var.* 4.34 (507/11): "Prudentiae mos est in humanos usus terris abdita talenta revocare commerciumque viventium non dicere mortuorum, quia et nobis infossa pereunt et illis in nullam partem profutura linquuntur. metallorum quippe ambitus solacia sunt hominum . . . Atque ideo moderata iussione decernimus, ut ad illum locum, in quo latere plurima suggeruntur, sub publica testificatione convenias: et si aurum, ut dicitur, vel argentum fuerit tua indagatione detectum, compendio publico fideliter vindicabis: ita tamen ut abstineatis manus a cineribus mortuorum, quia nolumus lucra quaeri, quae per funesta possunt scelera reperiri. aedificia tegant cineres, columnae vel marmora ornent sepulcra: talenta non teneant, qui vivendi commercia reliquerunt.

As Cassiodorus notes, this sanction applied only to graves that did not have a "master" (*dominus*): "*aurum enim sepulcris iuste detrahitur ubi dominus non habetur.*" This was not, therefore, an open call to rob burial sites indiscriminately on the grounds that the living benefited from the grave goods more than the dead did. If we are to take the term *dominus* to mean "patron" or "heir" of the deceased rather than the actual occupant of the grave, this proscription can be interpreted as an attempt by the crown to limit the appropriation of gold and other valuables to the graves of individuals who lacked guardians, whether kin or members of the local clergy, who might otherwise lay claim to any valuables.[44] This would be in keeping with Theoderic's instructions to the *comes* Annas calling for the investigation into allegations of grave robbing levied against the Arch-priest Laurentius.[45]

While the preservation of Italy's ancient urban landscape was a concern for Theoderic, so, too, was the protection of town-dwellers against the sorts of dangers associated with living in an urban setting. The two chief hazards of urban life were, as they had long been and were long to remain, fire and disease. Most houses, we may believe, would have been humble structures of wood, or wood and stone, and therefore at severe risk in the event of fire. Precisely because of the disastrous general effect which his action might therefore have, an arsonist was subject to the harshest penalties: a fiery death for slaves and tenants; fines, flogging, and banishment for freemen.[46]

Theoderic's contempt for the erstwhile arsonist is further illustrated in a letter of general admonition to the members of the Roman Senate, wherein he censures the inhabitants of the city for their involvement in the burning of a synagogue and likens the incident to an act of sedition:

> The propriety of manners which is characteristic of the City of Rome, not the customs of foreigners, must be upheld. Taking lightly the act of sedition, and to embrace the fiery destruction of your own city is not a quality of those who wish to be Roman. Therefore, the strictness of the laws must be observed

Aurum enim sepulcris iuste detrahitur, ubi dominus non habetur: immo culpae genus est inutiliter abditis relinquere mortuorum, unde se vita potest sustentare viventium. non est enim cupiditas eripere, quae nullus se dominus ingemiscat amisisse."

[44] *Contra* Nehlsen, who has instead interpreted this case as permitting private individuals the legal right to appropriate grave goods: "Der Grabfrevel in den germanischen Rechtsaufzeichnungen: Zugleich ein Beitrag zur Diskussion um Todesstrafe und Friedlosigkeit bei den Germanen," in H. Jankuhn, H. Nelsen and H. Roth (eds.), *Zum Grabfrevel in vorund frühgeschichtlicher Zeit: Untersuchungen zu Grabraub und "Haugbrot" in Mittel- und Nordeuropa.* Abhandlungen der Akademie der Wissenschaften in Göttingen, philologisch-historische Klasse, dritten Folge 113 (Göttingen, 1978), 107–68, esp. 112–14. See further Bonnie Effros, *Caring for Body and Soul: Burial and the Afterlife in the Merovingian World* (University Park, PA, 2002), 52.

[45] Cass., *Var.* 4.18. [46] *ET* 97.

when punishing the authors of the deed, lest the sight of their action inspires the crowd to imitate such a nefarious thing.[47]

Despite the reasons behind the burning of the synagogue (namely, the punishment inflicted upon Christian servants convicted of killing their Jewish masters), Theoderic chastens the Senators to restore order and bring the arsonists to justice. Absent here is the customary respect and flattery that typify all other letters written on behalf of the King to the senatorial elite. Obviously, the matter of arson was of such concern for Theoderic that it outweighed any political fallout that *might* have resulted from such an act of epistolary effrontery against Rome's Senators.

The other great danger for the town-dweller was disease, especially plague. During the Roman Empire, periodic outbreaks of smallpox and measles devastated cities and towns. The Antonine Plague (165–80), for instance, claimed nearly one-third of the population in some areas, and the historian Cassius Dio reports that during the height of the outbreak 2,000 people a day were dying in Rome alone. Between 251 and 266 the city was struck by a second, more virulent pestilence that at its peak claimed approximately 5,000 inhabitants every day.[48] Another epidemic – widely considered to be the first documented case of bubonic plague – struck Constantinople around 542. Procopius, who witnessed first-hand the devastating effects that the disease had on the city, provides this account:

> During these times, there was a pestilence, by which the whole human race came near to being annihilated. Now in the case of all other scourges sent from heaven some explanation of a cause might be given by daring men, such as the many theories propounded by those who are clever in these matters, for they love to conjure up causes which are absolutely incomprehensible to men . . . But for this calamity, it is quite impossible either to express in words or to conceive in thought any explanation, except indeed to refer it to God.[49]

47 Cass., *Var.* 4.43: "Urbis Romanae celebris opinio suo conservanda est nihilominus instituto, nec vitia peregrina capit, quae se semper de morum probitate iactavit. Levitates quippe seditionum et ambire propriae civitatis incendium non est velle Romanum. Ideoque in auctoribus facti legum est servanda districtio, ne detestabilis aspectus incendii ad imitationem nefandam vulgi pectora comprehendat." Similarly Anon. Val. 14.81, where Theoderic ordered the Roman population of Ravenna to pay for the rebuilding of the synagogue they burned down; those unable to pay were flogged publicly.

48 Cassius Dio, *Historia Romana*, ed. and trans. Earnest Cary, *Dio's Roman History*, 9 vols., Loeb Classical Library (Cambridge, MA, 1914–27), LXXII 14.3–4; Robert J. Littman and Maxwell L. Littman, "Galen and the Antonine Plague," *American Journal of Philology* 94 (1973), 254–5.

49 Proc., *BG*, II. xxii. 1–2 (trans. Dewing, 451–2): "Ὑπὸ δὲ τοὺς χρόνους τούτους λοιμὸς γεγονεν, ἐξ οὗ δὴ ἅπαντα ὀλίγου ἐδέησε τὰ ἀνθρώπεια ἐξίτηλα εἶναι. ἅπασι μὲν οὖν τοῖς ἐξ οὐρανοῦ ἐπισκήπτουσιν ἴσως ἂν καὶ λέγοιτό τις ὑπ' ἀνδρῶν τολμητῶν αἰτίου λόγος, οἷα πολλὰ φιλοῦσιν οἱ ταῦτα δεινοὶ αἰτίας τερατεύεσθαι οὐδαμῆ ἀνθρώπῳ καταληπτὰς οὖσας . . . τούτῳ μέντοι τῷ κακῷπρόφασίντινα ἢ λόγῳ εἰπεῖν ἢ διανοίᾳ λογίσασθαι μηχανή τις οὐδεμία ἐστί, πλήν γε δὴ ὅσαὲς τὸν θεὸν ἀναφέρεσθαι."

One modern estimate places the total death toll at 244,000 people out of a pre-plague population of 508,000.[50]

That Theoderic took seriously the threat posed by disease and plague is evidenced by his prerogative that physicians constituted a privileged class which, under the rules of *praescriptio fori*, received special jurisdiction in legal proceedings. As the *formula* for the Count of the Chief Physicians (*comes archiatorum*) stipulates, disputes involving physicians were to be settled by this officer:

> Therefore, hence forth adorn [yourself] with the rank of Count of the Chief Physicians, so that among doctors you alone shall be considered exceptional, and all who pain themselves with a desire of mutual contention shall submit to your judgment. Be the judge of this eminent profession, and end their quarrels, which result alone used to judge.[51]

The importance of physicians was such that the state could not allow them to put aside their duties to attend courts other than those of their presiding officer.

Whatever may be thought of the economic role of towns in Theoderic's Italy, there can be little doubt that the center of the economic picture was occupied by the villages and *villae* of the countryside. As to the quality of life in these places and the kinds of problems faced by the average landholder, the *ET* offers important clues. To be sure, the position of the landholder was a precarious one, made even more so by periodic droughts, famines, and wars, as well as a general lack of resources. An important consequence resulting from the shortage of available manpower was the development of a highly competitive labor market, wherein desperate landowners were forced to take on fugitives as free workers or tenants, no questions asked, in an attempt to preserve their accustomed standard of living. *ET* 142 speaks to the sorts of problems facing the landowner as a result of the manpower shortage, and the steps some of them took to compensate for it:

> An owner shall be permitted to transfer rustic slaves of each sex, even if they are *originarii*, which he possesses physically and lawfully, from his properties to locales which he owns, or to enjoin them to urban services, provided that they are returned to those regions where they first departed in accordance with the will of the owner, and rightfully be considered to be members of his

[50] Dionysios Ch. Stathakopolous, *Famine and Pestilence in the Late Roman and Early Byzantine Empire: A Systematic Survey of Subsistence Crises and Epidemics* (London, 2004).

[51] Cass., *Var.* 6.19: "Quapropter a praesenti tempore comitivae archiatrorum honore decorare, ut inter salutis magistros solus habearis eximius et omnes iudicio tuo cedant, qui se ambitu mutuae contentionis excruciant. esto arbiter artis egregiae eorumque discinge conflictus, quos iudicare solus solebat effectus."

> household staff in the city; and no judicial challenge on any grounds (for example under the opposition of origin) may arise concerning the actions and orderly arrangements of this measure. Moreover, it shall be permitted for owners of the aforementioned circumstance, under the attestation of their will, to transfer [slaves] from any portion of their land, or surrender, sell, or grant them to anyone they wish.[52]

Here, the owner was permitted to transfer his slaves to areas where they were most needed, whether to perform domestic duties in town or provide agricultural labor in the fields, as a means to maximize production; he could even lend them to other landholders at his discretion. In such instances, however, the slave remained the property of the original master; should he end up in the employ of another, he was to be returned to the original owner upon his request.

In the same way, *ET* 150 recognized the need for landholders to share resources between them, but severe fines punished anyone who did so without express permission. Those found guilty were to pay (presumably to the aggrieved owner) a *solidus* for every day he so employed another's slave or ox:

> Let no one demand work or service from another's farmhand without the consent of the owner, or to make use of his slave or ox unless that farmhand, or his chief tenant, or owner willingly offers this. Anyone who contradicts this precept shall give [the owner] one gold *solidus* for every day he so imposed burdens on [his] farmhand or ox without permission.[53]

The provision clearly speaks to the possibly widespread problem of landholders using other people's slaves without paying for the services. In light of the fact that in the sixth century an average person could survive on some three to four *solidi* a year,[54] this was a particularly harsh penalty. There is no parallel for this in Roman sources, and it appears to be an innovation on the part of the compilers. Both it and *ET* 142 attest to the fact that Italy at this

[52] *ET* 142: "Liceat unicuique domino ex praediis, quae corporaliter et legitimo iure possidet, rustica utriusque sexus mancipia, etiamsi originaria sint, ad iuris sui loca transferre, vel urbanis ministeriis adplicare, ita ut et illis praediis adquirantur, ad quae voluntate domini migrata fuisse constiterit, et inter urbanos famulos merito censeantur: nec de eiusmodi factis atque ordinationibus, velut sub oppositione originis, quaestio ulla nascatur. Alienare etiam supradictae conditionis liceat dominis, absque terrae aliqua portione, sub scripturae adtestatione, vel cedere, vendere cui libuerit vel donare."

[53] *ET* 150: "Nulli liceat invito [domino] rustico alieno operas aut obsequium imperare, nec eius mancipio aut bove uti, nisi hoc forte idem rusticus aut conductor ipsius, vel dominus sua voluntate praestiterit. Qui contra fecerit det pro unius rustici, vel unius bovis diurna opera, quam praesumpsit, auri solidum unum."

[54] Arnold H. M. Jones, *The Later Roman Empire, 284–602: A Social, Economic and Administrative Survey*, 3 vols. (Oxford, 1964), 1, 447–8.

time was plagued by acute labor shortages and a general lack of resources through which produce-bearing land could be effectively maintained.

For some landholders, a potential source of economic gain was the institution of the colonate. In the early Empire, agricultural tenants were often hired by landholders on short-term leases and were free to travel about in search of work. With the introduction of Diocletian's tax reforms, however, this came to an end. Diocletian's legislation required peasants to be registered in their villages or estates, an innovation that led ultimately to the position of the tenant farmer becoming a hereditary occupation. Around the middle of the fourth century we begin to have imperial laws that explicitly bound tenants, *coloni*, to their *origo*, that is, their place of tax registration, in order for them to fulfill their fiscal obligations. Eventually, these tied *coloni*, or *adscriptii*, became subject to their owners/masters (*domini*), and even came to resemble slaves in terms of social status.[55]

As in the late Empire, the colonate of early sixth-century Italy was inextricably linked with the credit system of rural estates.[56] It was a solution for destitute farmers in need of credit; it would have embodied a permanent obligation that was even stronger than one established through a private law contract. For property owners, the colonate would have had the same advantage that debt-slavery had over a labor contract in which merely food and lodgings were supplied in return for services. A labor contract involved only the contracting parties, but in debt–slavery the debtor–slave could be transferred to another person at the discretion of the master. The colonate operated much in the same way. Registered farmers, that is *coloni*, were tied to the land and would be transferred with it if need be, thus

[55] Arnold H. M. Jones, *The Roman Economy: Studies in Ancient Economic and Administrative History*, ed. P. A. Brunt (Oxford, 1974), 293–307; Jones *LRE*, 2, 795–803; Francesco De Martino, "Il colonato fra economia e diritto," in *Storia di Roma, III: L'eta tardoantica. I crisi e transformazioni* (Turin, 1993), 789–822, esp. 791–803; Arnaldo Marcone, "Il lavoro nelle campagne," in *Storia di Roma*, III.1 (Turin, 1993), 823–43, esp. 825–8. On the colonate in the later Roman Empire: M. Mirković, *The Later Roman Colonate and Freedom* (Philadelphia, PA, 1997); Walter Scheidel, "Slaves of the Soil," *JRA* 13 (2000), 727–32; Walter Goffart, *Caput and Colonate. Towards a History of Late Roman Taxation* (Toronto, 1974); Adrian J. B. Sirks, "The Colonate in Justinian's Reign," *JRS* 98 (2008), 120–43; Kyle Harper, *Slavery in the Late Roman World AD 275–425* (Cambridge, 2011), 153–54. For a general history, see Wickham, *Framing the Early Middle Ages*, 520–7.

[56] A reference to this credit system is found in a western law of 371 (*CJ* 11.48.8). The law deals with registered farmers (individuals *cum emolumentis tributariis*, that is, for whom taxes were owed) who had fled. It ends with this provision: "si qui vero inter agricolas, ut solet, ex quibuscumque commerciis huiusmodi hominibus inveniuntur esse debitores, coram partibus constitutis iudex ab obnoxiis quod debetur exposcat." According to this, if a fugitive was a debtor "as is usually the case, as a result of any sort of dealings of this sort," the judge must insist that the fugitive repay the debt before he was returned to his original place of residence. For this and the discussion that follows, see Boudevijn Sirks, "The farmers, the landlord, and the law in the fifth century," in Ralph W. Mathisen (ed.), *Law, Society and Authority in Late Antiquity* (Oxford, 2001), 256–71.

allowing an owner to sell any property with the available manpower to work it.

This would be consistent with the idea of the colonate as a means of securing debts with the rendering of services. It would also explain *ET* 121:

> If a creditor lends money to another's procurator, chief tenant, *colonus* or slave without the consent or knowledge of the owner, no prejudice of any kind shall be placed against the owner or his assets; the demands of the creditor shall be exacted from the *peculium* of the slave or *colonus* after deduction of what is owed to the master.[57]

Analogous to *CTh* 2.31.1 and 2.32.1 of the Emperors Honorius and Theodosius II of 422, the provision stipulates that if someone gives a loan to a *colonus* without his master's knowing, the *colonus* was to repay out of his own *peculium*, adding the words, "after deduction of what is owed the master" (*considerata vel servata prius indemnitate domini*). Here, the emphasis is on the debts of the *colonus* to the landowner. Moreover, the reservation regarding the master's claims is not unconditional; it not only gives him a right of priority, but it also implies that the *colonus* owed him money. We may assume that the *peculium* served as security for the master. It created, so to speak, a floating charge to secure the repayment of the loan; in the event of non-fulfillment, the owner then became the priority creditor, provided, of course, he knew what the debts were. In this way, the colonate functioned as a form of continuing security for the payment and performance of all debts pertaining to the *coloni*.

The barbarian settlement

That the details of the picture of the Italian countryside changed dramatically from what they had been since the later Roman Empire is undeniable, as is the principal reason for this change – namely, the settlement of the Goths. The issue of barbarian settlement is a hotly contested one, made even more so by the contributions of Walter Goffart, who has argued that the barbarian forces that settled in the different regions of the West were not given shares in land through the implementation of the billeting system (i.e. the one-third or two-thirds of Roman estates that was the traditional

[57] *ET* 121: "Si procuratori vel conductori, sive colono vel servo alicuius, invito vel nesciente domino, mutuam pecuniam quis dederit, nec ipsi domino, nec rei eius aliquod praeiudicium comparetur: sed ex peculio servi vel coloni, considerata vel servata prius indemnitate domini, consulatur petitionibus creditoris."

picture of the *hospitalitas* settlements of the barbarians), but rather on a distribution of the main asset of the Roman state, namely, the proceeds of taxation and the property assessments on which the taxes were levied.[58] In other words, the barbarian armies remained salaried, though with tax shares associated with specific areas of land, of which each soldier was a *hospes*, a guest, and from where he collected the tax directly. Through such a process of accommodation, the capital costs of barbarian settlement were borne, not by private hosts, but by the Roman state. And this is why, Goffart explains, the settlement occasioned hardly a ripple of protest from the Roman provincials and why the few protests they aroused assumed the form they did.[59]

The problem with this theory is that no single text clearly supports it. To take as an example *Var.* 2.17 (*c.* 510), a letter on the granting of *sors* to the Gothic Priest Butila, which directly resulted in the lessening of the tax burden on the city of Trento:

> We do not wish Our generosity to be ruinous to anyone . . . wherefore, by the authority of the present edict, We declare that the *sors* which in Our generosity We have bestowed on the priest Butila, is not to be included in the tax assessment; you are to be relieved the same amount of *solidi* as are

[58] For traditional views, see, e.g., Hartmann, *Geschichte Italiens*, I, 93–4 (authoritative); Giulio Romano and A. Solmi, *La dominazione barbariche in Italia (395–888)* (Milan, 1940), 114, 123–5, 167–8; Heinrich Brunner, *Deutsche Rechtsgeschichte*, vol. I, 1906; vol. II completed by Claudius Frh. von Schwerin, 2nd edn. (Leipzig, 1906–28), I, 77; Ludwig Schmidt, *Die Ostgermanen, Geschichte der deutschen Stämme bis zum Ausgang der Völkerwanderung* (Munich, 1969), 316–17, 327–9, 362–3; Ensslin, *Theodorich*, 94–7, 205; Ernst Stein, *Histoire du Bas-Empire, II: De la disparition de L'Empire d'Occident à la mort Justinien (476–565)* (Paris, 1949), 2, 41–3, 119; Levy, *West Roman Vulgar Law*, 84–5.

[59] Walter Goffart, *Barbarians and Romans: Techniques of Accommodation,* AD *418–584* (Princeton, NJ, 1980), esp. chapter 3. Goffart's major adherent is Jean Durliat: see, e.g., Jean Durliat, "Le salaire de la paix sociale dans les royaumes barbares," in Herwig Wolfram and Andreas Schwarcz (eds.), *Anerkennung und Integration: zu den wirtschaftlichen Grundlagen der Völkerwanderungszeit 400–600* (Vienna, 1988), 17–70; Jean Durliat, "Cité, impôt et intégration des barbares," in Walter Pohl and H. Reimitz (eds.), *Strategies of Distinction: the Construction of Ethnic Communities, 300–800* (Leiden, 1988), 153–79; *contra* Chris Wickham, "The Fall of Rome Will Not Take Place," in Lester Little and Barbara Rosenwein (eds.), *Debating the Middle Ages: Issues and Readings* (Malden, MA, 1998), 45–57. In direct opposition to Goffart's work: Sam J. Barnish, "Taxation Land and Barbarian Settlement in the Western Empire," *PBSR* 54 (1986), 170–95; Evangelos Chrysos, "De Foederatis Iterum," in Walter Pohl (ed.), *Kingdoms of the Empire: The Integration of the Barbarians in Late Antiquity* (Leiden/New York, 1997), 185–206; John H. W. G. Liebeschuetz, "Cities, Taxes and the Accommodation of the Barbarians: The Theories of Durliat and Goffart," in Pohl (ed.), *Kingdoms of the Empire*, 135–51; Peter Heather, "*Gens* and *Regnum* among the Ostrogoths," in Hans-Werner Goetz, Jörg Jarnut, and Walter Pohl (eds.), *Regna and Gentes: the Relationship Between Late Antique and Early Medieval Peoples and Kingdoms in the Transformation of the Roman World* (Leiden/New York, 2003), 113; Wickham, *Land and Power*, 24 n. 21. For a useful review of the historiography: Matthew Innes, "Land, Freedom and the Making of the Medieval West," *Transactions of the RHS* 16 (2006), 39–74, esp. 43–4; Wickham, *Framing the Early Middle Ages*, 84–6.

> calculated in that gift through your contribution of the one-third allotments (*tertiae*).[60]

Goffart argues that this letter actually concerned the diversion of tax revenues from the local tax bureau to Butila, whose *sors* thus comprised the tax revenues from the stated estate. John Wolf Liebeschuetz, however, notes that it could equally mean that Butila's estate-portion was tax-exempt; taxation for Trento would still go down.[61] This seems the least contrived of the two theories, and there is no good reason to abandon the less complex reading that Theoderic was simply cancelling the liability on land granted out as a Gothic allotment.

Beyond the ambiguity of the evidence, the many references in the *Variae* to boundary disputes between Goths and Romans are difficult to explain unless there had been a physical division of land. The crucial witness to this land division is a letter written in Theoderic's name to the Senate in 509, nominating the young Roman nobleman Venantius for an honorary office. Significant here is a lengthy panegyric on Venantius' father Liberius, who had served as Theoderic's Praetorian Prefect *c.* 493–500. Aside from his loyalty, and his attentive service to the public purse, Liberius was praised particularly for ensuring the peaceful settlement of Goths in Italy:

> It pleases Us to mention how, in the assignment of *tertiae*, he [i.e. Liberius] joined both the estates and hearts of Goths and Romans. For, although men usually come into conflict over proximity, for them the sharing of estates seems to have been the cause of harmony. For it so happened that each nation, while living in common, came together in the same hope. Behold, a new and wholly praiseworthy achievement: the goodwill of the masters was joined by the division of soil; friendship of the two peoples was increased through losses, and a defender was purchased by a share of the land, so that the security of the property might remain intact.[62]

60 "Munificentiam nostram nulli volumus extare damnosam. . . et ideo praesenti auctoritate cognoscite, pro sorte quam Butilani presbytero nostra largitate contulimus, nullum debere persolvere fiscalis calculi functionem, sed in ea praestatione quanti se solidi comprehendunt, de tertiarum illationibus vobis noveritis esse relevandos."

61 Walter Goffart, *Barbarians and Romans: Techniques of Accommodation,* AD *418–584* (Princeton, NJ, 1980), 77–9; *contra* Liebeschuetz, "Cities, Taxes and the Accommodation of the Barbarians," 135–51, esp. 142–3.

62 Cass., *Var.* 2.16: "Iuvat nos referre quemadmodum in tertiarum deputatione Gothorum Romanorumque et possessiones iunxit et animos. nam cum se homines soleant de vicinitate collidere, istis praediorum communio causam videtur praestitisse concordiae: sic enim contigit, ut utraque natio, dum communiter vivit, ad unum velle convenerit. En factum novum et omnino laudabile: gratia dominorum de cespitis divisione coniuncta est; amicitiae populis per damna creverunt et parte agri defensor adquisitus est, ut substantiae securitas integra servaretur."

Panegyric is at best an imprecise source, and it may be that Cassiodorus here is simply attempting to flatter Liberius by exaggerating the difficulty of the task he had so skillfully accomplished. But the context seems clear: Liberius is being congratulated for effecting an orderly division of land, here presented as a useful and essential price to pay for the military protection afforded by the newly-settled Goths. For the native Italian landholders, the distribution of property was necessary for preserving their security.[63]

While Cassiodorus does show Gothic soldiers receiving donatives and payments funded out of tax, he also makes it clear that this form of reward complemented the grants of allotments (*sortes*) already made. In a letter of exhortation addressed in Athalaric's name to the Gothic settlers of Reate and Nursia, the King reminded them that "allotments of your own nourish you, and our gifts, God willing, will enrich you."[64] Clearly these donatives were not the basis for the original settlement. The Goths were nourished by their allotments, that is, land. It is hard to imagine ordinary Gothic soldiers thinking in terms other than land, and being satisfied with anything less, despite how sophisticated their leaders were in diplomacy and its rhetoric. But this does not mean that Roman landowners were left out in the cold. A single papyrus from Ravenna in 540 hints at agreements made between Roman landowners and provincial officials, through which the impact of land-division was mediated and negotiated. The document transfers ownership of a portion of an estate to the Church of Ravenna, guaranteeing that the property (now owned by the Church) was exempt from any public or private charge, and from transfer to barbarians as an "allotment."[65] The fact that this guarantee was given under a Roman regime after Justinian's reconquest suggests that immunity was granted on the basis of the estate's prior history, that is, it related to land that had already been subjected to the process of allocation and division, and thus should not be so subjected again.[66]

In the end, whether one opines to the traditional theories that suggest the Goths were effectively settled according to the rules of the Roman system of *hospitalitas*, or those proposed by Walter Goffart, who suggests rather that the Goths received a third of the sum collected in taxes, it is obvious that the settlement of the Goths had important implications for tax liabilities.[67] In a

[63] Innes, "Land, Freedom and the Making of the Medieval West," 55 n. 43.
[64] Cass., *Var.* 8.26: "cum vos et sortes alant propriae et munera nostra domino iuvante ditificent[.]"
[65] Tjäder, *Die nichtliterarischen Lateinischen Papyri Italiens aus der Zeit 445–700*, no. 31.
[66] Innes, "Land, Freedom and the Making of the Medieval West," 56.
[67] Goffart, *Barbarians and Romans*, 60–102; Barnish, "Taxation," 170–95; Fabien Thibault, "L'impôt direct dans les royaumes des Ostrogoths, des Wisigoths et des Burgundes," *RHDFE* 25 (1901), 699–728.

world where title to land was dependent on the ability to meet fiscal demands, this is hardly surprising.

What little information our sources offer concerning tax liability is profoundly obscure. But it is at least apparent that the basic taxes fell on lands, houses, and slaves, for it was the reception of precisely these objects of property which obliged the new owner, by implication of *ET* 144, to assume the liabilities of the alienator. At the same time, just as Roman soldiers enjoyed immunity from taxation, so, too, did Theoderic's Goths who, as it has already been pointed out, functioned as the military arm of the Roman state.[68] Because of this, those properties which some Goths received as allotments (*sortes*) were not to be taxed.[69] But Goths were free to use their personal resources to purchase additional property if they so desired. As Theoderic made clear in a letter addressed to the *saio* Gesila, concerning the Gothic settlers in Picenum and Tuscia, the King's periodic distribution of donatives in gold to his Goths enabled them to invest in additional real estate.[70] When they did, their ownership undoubtedly became the subject of public record. While the details for this are lacking, mention in *ET* 126 and *Var.* 1.18 of official warrants (*pittacia delegationis*) effecting and limiting transfer is suggestive of a regular and public process along similar lines as those described in a novel of Valentinian III of 445, where contracts involving the sale or transfer of moveable property were to be regulated by the issuance of written instruments called *pittacia*.[71]

Records of some kind were necessary for this to be achieved, and although no example of an official document type for Ostrogothic Italy has survived, it is not unreasonable to suggest that such documents were similar in form to the *polyptyca exactorum* mentioned in the *interpretatio* to *CTh* 11.26.2 or the catalogue document (*breve*) described by Gregory the Great.[72] In any event, Goths were obliged to assume the liabilities of the

[68] Roman soldiers: Yann Le Bohec, *The Imperial Roman Army* (London, 1994), 218. Goths: Goffart, *Barbarians and Romans*, 91–3.

[69] Goffart, *Barbarians and Romans*, 92. [70] Cass., *Var.* 4.14.

[71] *Nov. Val.* 15.1.3. In *CTh* 7.4 *pittacium* denotes the warrant or chit delivered by military *actuarii* to keepers of tax stores in return for ration supplies; that is to say, the *pittacium* documented the moment at which the tax *annona* turned into the ration *annona*. But it is not clear if *pittacium* retained this narrow definition in the sixth century. In *Var.* 12.20 it has the general sense of an acknowledgement of debt (*obligatio chirographi*) by the Bishop of Rome; the same in Gaetano Marini, *I Papiri Diplomatici* (Rome, 1805), 138 (503), where it appears to be a synonym for *cautio*; Ennodius (*Vita Ephiphanii*, ed. Hartel, 375) mentions *pictacia ad clusuras*, meaning "passports" or "exit permits."

[72] *Greg. ep.* 9.113 (March 599), a letter concerning the matter of intestate succession and addressed to Sergius, defender of the patrimonies of Calabria and Apulia (*Registrum epistolarum*, ed. Paul Ewald and Ludo Moritz Hartmann, *MGH Epistolae* 1–2, 2 vols. (Berlin, 1887–99); trans. John R. C. Martyn, *The Letters of Gregory the Great* (Toronto, 2004), 610). For a further reference to *breve* in Gregory's *Registrum*: *ep.* 14.14.

alienator when they purchased property. And if they failed to do so, others would be unjustly burdened with paying their tax – a situation that would not be tolerated. To Gesila, Cassiodorus has Theoderic proclaim:

> To burden others with debts that are not their own is the greatest kind of sin . . . it is fitting that each person look after his own debts, and he who is known to have acquired property shall pay the tax. Therefore, through your present authority We command that the Goths residing in Picenum and the two regions of Tuscia shall be compelled by your threats to pay their due obligations (*debitae functiones*).[73]

In two other letters, Cassiodorus underscores the point that Goths who own property in addition to their original allotments (*sortes*) were required to assume normal tax liability in the same way Romans were. The first, addressed in Theoderic's name to the sublime Saturninus and Verbusius, has the King instruct the addressees to compel those who are able but otherwise unwilling to contribute to the *fiscus Gothorum*: "Therefore, We command by your present authority, upon receiving the petition of the *curiales* from the city of Adriana, that whosoever shirks from paying the *fiscus Gothorum* you are to compel to pay that which is equitable; but lest a poor person be compelled to pay from his own holdings, it is prudent for him to retain a suitable amount for himself."[74]

In the second letter Cassiodorus has Theoderic instruct those Goths who had retired and settled on the Danube frontier, and who were now claiming tax exemption for property recently acquired through marriage with Roman women, that such exemptions were not permitted: "Old barbarians who have chosen to marry Roman women and obtained estates under any title whatsoever, shall be compelled to pay the fisc for the property held, in addition to any *superindicta* [extra levies] imposed."[75]

Just as Goths were not exempt from the operations of fiscal liability, so, too, were churches subject to taxation. In a letter in Theoderic's name to the Praetorian Prefect Faustus, Cassiodorus tells of an unnamed church that had for some time before been granted limited exemption from taxes due,

[73] Cass., *Var.* 4.14: "Magni peccati genus est alienis debitis alterum praegravare . . . sua quemque damna respiciant et is solvat tributum, qui possessionis noscitur habere compendium. Atque ideo praesenti tibi auctoritate delegamus, ut Gothi per Picenum sive Tuscias utrasque residentes te imminente cogantur exsolvere debitas functiones."

[74] Cass., *Var.* 1.19: "Et ideo praesenti vobis iussione praecipimus, ut Adrianae civitatis curialium insinuatione suscepta, quicumque Gothorum fiscum detrectat implere, eum ad aequitatem redhibitionis artetis, ne tenuis de proprio cogatur exsolvere, quod constat idoneos indebite detinere."

[75] Cass., *Var.* 5.14: "Antiqui barbari, qui Romanis mulieribus elegerunt nuptiali foedere sociari, quolibet titulo praedia quaesiverunt, fiscum possessi cespitis persolvere ac superindicticiis oneribus parere cogantur."

although its lands had continued to be subject to occasional extraordinary levies (*superindicta*).[76] The petition now presented to Theoderic by this church sought for remission of all taxation, including both *superindicta* and regular taxes imposed on lands that the church had acquired since its previous award: "Since the time of Cassiodorus the Patrician, the aforementioned church has been free from the burden of *superindicta*. But following this initial grant, property has been conveyed to Our church by others."[77] In response Theoderic liberated the church from *superindicta* with respect to the property that had formerly been exempted, but required that it was to pay regular and extraordinary taxes for all property that it had recently acquired:

> Let the church accept the onus of taxation that is common to all landholders, and it shall be subject to the same action that concerns all recently obtained rights of ownership. We cannot be pleased by the gains of the church, since it disadvantages the fisc. Let the proceeds of the [original] compensation be sufficient for the landholder: tributes belong to the purple, not the military cloak.[78]

In addition to the imposition of regular taxes, customs fees were no doubt still levied and *coemptiones* imposed. For instance, any possessor of grain could be required to sell at the purchase price all that he did not need for his family.[79] On other occasions, the government acquired marble, timber, slaves, military supplies, etc., against compensation.[80] The general gist of this policy of expropriation can fairly well be grasped from a letter in

76 Cass., *Var.* 1.26.2–3.

77 *Ibid.*: "quatinus superindicticiorum onera titulorum praefata ecclesia in ea summa non sentiat, qua usque a magnifici viri patricii Cassiodori . . . temporibus est soluta. Ea vero quae a tempore beneficii ad ecclesiam nostram ab aliquibus est translata professio."

78 *Ibid.*: "commune cum universis possessoribus onus solutionis agnoscat et illius subiaceat functioni, cuius nacta est iura dominii. Alioquin grata nobis augmenta eius esse non possunt, qui fisci damno proficiat. Sufficiat possessori compendium pensionis: tributa sunt purpurae, non lacernae."

79 E.g., Cass., *Var.* 9.5 (a letter of Athalaric to the Bishops and functionaries of an unidentified province, forcing this action in an attempt to lessen the effects of an ongoing famine); cf. 2.26 (an edict of Theoderic addressed to the Praetorian Prefect Faustus, regulating the sale of grain in southern Italy and requiring that maximum prices set on food were to be observed); 4.19 (relief of tax on imports of grain, wine and oil); 12.14 (*coemptiones*); 2.38 (a letter in Theoderic's name to the merchants of the city of Sipontum in Apulia calling for a two-year exemption on *coemptiones* in an effort to mitigate the losses associated with 'hostile incursions' – presumably a reference to the attack of a Byzantine fleet in 508). For secondary literature, see Dahn, *Könige*, III, 162–3, 279–80, also on maximum prices placed on food.

80 Cass., *Var.* 1.28 (marble); 4.8; 5.16–20 (timber); 5.16.4 (slaves); 12.5 (an edict of Cassiodorus, as Praetorian Prefect, recognizing that supplies seized by the army in the regions of Lucania and Bruttium would be valued in cash above the market rate and regarded as tax already paid).

Theoderic's name to the *saio* Avilf, instructing him to collect timber (for the navy) along the banks of the Po:

> You are to proceed at once to the designated places with the proper men, and whether the wood is found in crown land or private property, you are to procure it with utmost speed, since that which by God's help will service the common good We do not believe to be an impediment to anyone. But We want you to carry out these commands in such a way that upon diligent inquiry nothing seems to have been sought after to the detriment of a landholder; but only those things which are necessary for our purpose shall be taken. Nothing which is not said to be reckoned for public use is to be demanded from a lord. We order only forests to be felled; nothing from others' property is to be violently destroyed.[81]

In the same way, the government requisitioned labor and services. *Munera* appeared in most various forms.[82] Pits, for example, were to be dug for defense works,[83] camps to be fortified and houses built for the shelter of the neighboring population.[84] According to the *formula* for appointment, the Count of Ravenna had the authority to exact a certain amount of forced labor from the owners of merchant vessels.[85] Horses had to be provided for the *cursus publicus*; granaries, bridges, and aqueducts had to be constructed or repaired and kept in good shape; famine relief had to be provided for, and so on.[86]

Over the course of the sixth century, however, the central administration became increasingly incapable of effectively managing the system, which strained to meet the demands for more revenue from less territory and increasingly devastated populations as war, famine, and pestilence ravaged the Italian economy. The situation was exasperated by the tendency of

81 Cass., *Var.* 5.20: "Ad loca designata cum artificibus incunctanter accedas et, sive in domo regia seu in privata reperta fuerint, sine aliqua facies tarditate procurari, quia nulli grave credimus praebere, quod deo auxiliante pro communi utilitate praeparatur. Verum ita volumus te iniuncta peragere, ut nihil ad laedendum possessorem studiose videatur inquiri, sed tantum quae sunt necessaria utilitatis nostrae causa praesumantur. Non exquiratur aliquid a domino, quod postea publico non dicatur acceptum. Ligna silvestria iubemus caedi, non aliquid de alienis facultatibus violenter abscidi."

82 Dahn, *Könige* III, 147, 278–9; VI, 260.

83 Cass., *Var.* 12.17 (a letter in Cassiodorus' name to John, tax-collector at Ravenna, instructing him to have the residents dig a series of defensive ditches along the perimeter).

84 Cass., *Var.* 1.17 (addressed in Theoderic's name, Cassiodorus has the King instruct the Gothic and Roman inhabitants of Dertona (now Tortona) to fortify the existing castle with a series of battlements).

85 Cass., *Var.* 7.14.

86 Cass., *Var.* 4.47 (public horses); 3.29 (repair of granaries); 12.19 (a bridge of boats ordered to be constructed across the Tiber); 3.31, 5.38, 8.30 (aqueducts); 1.34, 2.26, 4.5, 7, 5.35 (famine relief); Anon. Val. 12.67 (*annonae*). On the subject of the *annonae* in general, see Jean Rougé, "Quelques aspects de la navigation en Méditerranée au Ve siècle et dans la première moitié du VIe siècle," *Cahiers d'histoire* 6 (196), 129–54, at 143.

government officials to extort unlawful services, as well as to levy taxes, for their own ends. The barbarian regime recognized and forbade the practice, but clearly was in no position to stop it. Cassiodorus, for example, tells of two tax collectors (*censitores*) in Sicily, Victor and Witigisdus, *viri spectabiles*, who refused a summons to the *comitatus* to face multiple charges of fraud, extortion, and oppression of the locals. The pair had been summoned by Theoderic to the *comitatus* to answer the charges, but had yet failed to appear. They were now being rebuked by Athalaric for their delay and instructed to remedy the situation on their own, with the warning that any further abuse would not go unnoticed.[87] In another instance of bureaucratic corruption, Gildilas, *comes* for Syracuse, used an alleged need for wall repairs to raise taxes and then did not rebuild the walls. He was chastened with a reminder that "the true praise of the Goths is respect of the civilized rule of law [*civilitas*]."[88] This was little more than a slap on the wrist, and underscores just how ineffective the Ostrogothic administration was at ensuring the integrity of its local officials. In the end, taxes, customs, levies, and *munera* gave way to direct payments to, and outright confiscations by, corrupt officers.

While the arrival of the Goths certainly had important implications for the existing Roman tax system, the greatest problem posed by this settlement was the unauthorized expropriation of properties and subsequent enslavement of the landholders at the hands of Gothic warlords and powerful Romans.[89] In conformity with the general prohibition against self-help, *ET* 10 adopts and amplifies the measures of *invasio* – the deliberate and unauthorized occupation of immoveables in the possession of another – prescribed in *CTh* 4.22.3 of the Emperors Valentinian II, Theodosius I, and Arcadius of 389:

ET 10	*CTh* 4.22.3
We decree that any property holder whatsoever is to be sued by use of a judicial summons, and the outcome of a proper trial is always to be awaited. And if anyone evicts any holder whatsoever from his property, let him also be deprived of the impartial right to sue for such presumption; let him of course	It has been discovered that many persons have forcibly seized property which belongs to Our privy purse and which had been acquired by due formality of confiscation. We order such property to be forcibly taken from such illegal holders and to be added to Our treasury. We punish those persons who assume, beyond

[87] Cass., *Var.* 9.12. [88] Cass., *Var.* 9.14.8: "Gothorum laus est civilitas custodita."
[89] Cass., *Var.* 5.29–30; Goffart, *Barbarians and Romans*, 97; Innes, "Land, Freedom and the Making of the Medieval West," 39–74.

restore the property which he seized and also pay twice the property's income for his insolence. And if he has taken possession of property to which he had no legal right at all, let him suffer this penalty: that he both return to its owner the property, along with its income, in the same condition as it was when it was seized; and let him be compelled to pay the value of the property he seized to the fisc.[90]

the measure which public decency permits, such contumacious haughtiness that when they were able to initiate a suit, they were unwilling to await a judgment, spurned the victory which the outcome of legal proceedings would have prescribed, and appropriated that which their audacity had given them.[91]

While both prohibited *invasio* and required the unlawfully seized property to be returned to the dispossessed, the *ET* went much further than the *CTh*. Where the offender was acting without any legal claim, he was to return the property and was fined the value of the property (to be paid to the fisc). If, on the other hand, he had a legal claim to the property and was acting in anticipation of a court order, he forfeited his claim and was required to pay the dispossessed twofold the value of the income. This is in accordance with *ET* 76:

> The suit regarding ownership being preserved, in accordance with the law of temporary possession, property occupied through force shall be returned within one year to that one who will hold the same property (which he lost through the presumption of another) neither violently, nor clandestinely, nor with permission [by the one who ejected him in the first place].[92]

[90] *ET* 10: "Qualemcumque cuiuslibet rei possessorem conveniri iudiciaria auctoritate decernimus et expectari semper iustae cognitionis eventus. Quod si quis qualemcumque possessorem possessione deiecerit, amissionem pro tanta praesumptione vel bonae litis incurrat; reformata scilicet possessione, quam occupaverit, fructus quoque duplos pro tanta temeritate persolvat. Quod si illam possessionem occupaverit, quae eidem minime debebatur, hanc poenam habeat, ut et rem cum fructibus in eo statu domino reddat invasam et aestimationem rei pervasae subire cogatur fisci viribus profuturam." Similarly *ET* 11.

[91] *CTh* 4.22.3: "Plerosque detectum est rem privatam nostram, quam publicatio celebrata quaesiverat, invasisse: quam nos a retentatoribus ereptam sociari iubemus aerario, punientes contumacius, quam decus publicum sinebat, erectos, ut, qui litem inferre potuissent, nollent exspectare iudicium ac spernerent victoriam, quam iustitiae praescripsisset eventus, et amplecterentur, quod dedisset audacia." For discussion of this and other laws that underscore the imperial government's difficulty in defining property rights in the later Roman Empire, see Dennis P. Kehoe, *Law and the Rural Economy in the Roman Empire* (Ann Arbor, MI, 2007), 156–60.

[92] *ET* 76: "Illis res occupata per violentiam intra annum momenti iure, salva proprietatis causa reddetur, qui eandem rem, quam alterius praesumptione perdidit, nec violenter, nec abscondite, nec precario possidet."

Property occupied by force could not be retained. It was to be returned to the dispossessed, if he met the conditions stipulated in the provision, namely that he had not reacquired it through violence or theft, or by permission from the one who dispossessed him in the first place. Otherwise, neither could have it. The implication is that it would go to the fisc, which was supposed to take estimation of its value in accordance with *ET* 10. It was no excuse, in other words, to plead mere anticipation of a court order.

Deviating in all these respects is *Var.* 3.20, a letter written in Theoderic's name to the *saio* Triwila and the *apparitor* Ferrocinctus:

> We have been swayed by the grievous disaster of Castorious, on whom the destructive malice of various men has to this point pressed. This has provided the opportunity for a salutary decree, so that the help of Our piety may be more useful than the evil cunning of the wicked. And therefore by the present decree We command that, if the magnificent Prefect Faustus has burdened the property of Castorius with titles of ownership, or has seized it by private usurpation, by your threats the occupier must quickly return that estate to him, together with another of equal value, so that with the remedy of Our piety We may take care of one so afflicted by such cruel losses.[93]

In keeping with the *interpretatio* to *CTh* 4.22.3, Theoderic's decision provided that the property, along with another of equal value, be returned to the dispossessed. Yet another variation is found in an edict of Athalaric, which fined a *pervasor* the value of the estate seized, and in case of default, banishment.[94] Despite such variances, as Cassiodorus makes clear and the *ET* confirms, there was no place for a provisional procedure with the issue of ownership set aside, unless royal pardon released the invader from the prescribed penalty. Such a reprieve was granted by Athalaric to the Goth Tanca, accused of seizing the estates of Constantius and Venerius and enslaving the pair in the process:

> If they [i.e. Constantius and Venerius] request it, the invaded property is initially to be restored to them by the right of interim possession, but in such a way that a party to the action shall not withdraw from the case. This violent presumption of the laws must cease, so that the case may be settled by the

[93] Cass., *Var.* 3.20.2: "Castorii igitur flebili calamitate permoti, quem exitialis hactenus diversorum pressit invidia, occasionem praebuit salutaribus constitutis, ut plus valeret nostrae pietatis auxilium quam iniqua calliditas improborum. Atque ideo praesenti vobis auctoritate decernimus, ut, si praefectus vir magnificus Faustus ea quae Castorius possidebat vel titulis ingravavit vel privata usurpatione detinuit, mox ei praedium cum alio eiusdem meriti vobis imminentibus a pervasore reddatur, ut crudelibus damnis afflicto pietatis nostrae remedio consulamus."

[94] Cass., *Var.* 9.18.1.

> decision of a judge, and the defendant [i.e. Tanca] either possess his proven slaves with the goods belonging to them, or leave them free men, unharmed in person and estate. For it is enough that We have relaxed the penalty for him who has presumed to cause such injury.[95]

Although we cannot be sure about the merits of the case reported, Boethius would seem to suggest that this was not an isolated incident: "How often have I protected, by jeopardizing my authority, such poor wretches as the unpunished greed of the barbarians harassed with interminable accusations."[96]

The related matter of tampering with the boundaries of estates also received the attention of the compilers. Property boundaries were marked by special landmarks (*arca*), which could include banks of earth (*arcaturae*), inscribed stones or trees, and in some circumstances where the geography permitted, rivers or streams and the like. These markers were of paramount importance in the resolution of disputes. In a letter written in the name of Theoderic to an unnamed illustrious *consularis*, Cassiodorus refers to their examination by a land surveyor (*agrimensor*) to settle a dispute between the neighboring *spectabiles* Leontius and Paschasius:

> As We have discovered from the all too bitter submission of the suppliants, a boundary dispute has arisen between the distinguished gentlemen Leontius and Paschasius, with the result that they presumed to vindicate the boundaries of their estates not by the laws, but by force. We are amazed by this, that something which must be defined by the witness either of boundary stones, mountain ridges, river banks, or of artificial marker ditches and other evident signs, has been contested with such animosity . . . Therefore, let your greatness likewise consult a highly-skilled land surveyor (*agrimensor*), whose name is derived from his art, so that by visible markers he will make known everything that has been separated by clear reasoning . . . Therefore, supported by Our authority, choose a man of such skill that, after his verdict, the parties may blush to continue with their brazen litigation. Thus, the rights of owners, for whom it is essential to cultivate their own land, may not be confused.[97]

95 Cass., *Var.* 8.28.3: "Momenti iure si competunt, primitus reddantur invasa, ita tamen, ut persona legitima disceptationibus non desistat. cesset violenta praesumptio, ut causa iudicis cognoscatur arbitrio et aut convictos servos cum rebus sibi competentibus possideat aut probatos liberos indemnes atque integros derelinquat. sufficit enim quod ei relaxamus poenam qui facere praesumpsit iniuriam."

96 Boethius, *Cons. Phil.* 1.4.35: "quotiens miseros quos infinitis calumniis impunita barbarorum semper avaritia vexabat, obiecta periculis auctoritate protexi."

97 Cass., *Var.* 3.52: "Sicut invidiosa nimis interpellantium suggestione comperimus, inter Leontium atque Paschasium spectabiles viros finalis orta contentio est, ita ut terminos casarum suarum non legibus, sed viribus crederent vindicandos. Unde miramur tanta animositate fuisse litigatum, quod aut terminis testibus aut iugis montium aut fluminum ripis aut arcaturis constructis aliisque signis

The rule was that all markers be left as they stand, and deliberate tampering with them was harshly treated. A guilty freeman was deprived of a third of his property to the benefit of the fisc; a slave or *colonus*, regardless of whether he acted on his own or at the behest of the master, was to be executed.[98] The loss or destruction of boundary markers to accident – during plowing for example – or some such natural occurrence was inevitable. In any such instance, new markers might be set up, but only in the presence of an authorized surveyor and the neighboring parties involved. To do otherwise, as *ET* 104 presupposes and the case of Leontius and Paschasius would seem to confirm, constituted an act of *invasio*.

The legal consequences of *invasio* were severe, and demonstrate the determined concern of the compilers both to protect property-holders against the open greed of others and to prevent the anarchy that would have threatened if private individuals had been permitted to take the law into their own hands. At the same time, however, they felt it prudent to observe the thirty year statute of limitations established by earlier Roman precedents, and repeatedly mentioned in special decrees of Theoderic between 507 and 526. For example, in a letter of general instruction to the Roman Domitianus and Gothic Wilia, Theoderic proclaimed:

> If, after the date [i.e. 489] when, by God's favor, We crossed the river Isonzo, and the realm of Italy first received Us, a barbarian occupier has seized the estate of a Roman, without there being a warrant [issued] from any assigning officer, let him restore it without delay to the former owner. But if he has evidently entered the property before that time, since the thirty year limitation is clearly an objection, We decree that the plaintiff's claim is void.[99]

Along similar lines is *Var.* 2.27, a letter in Theoderic's name, datable to the period 507–12, concerning a synagogue in Genoa. Here, the King granted the Jewish community permission to build a roof on the existing walls, but nothing else in the way of ornament or expansion; and only if no one had, at

evidentibus constat esse definitum ... Quapropter agrimensorem peritissimum, cui ab arte nomen est, vestra nihilominus adhibeat magnitudo, ut iam omnia, quae manifesta ratione distincta sunt, per evidentia debeat documenta monstrare ... Quapropter auctoritate nostra suffulti talem eligite, post quem partes erubescant impudenti fronte litigare, quatenus possessorum iura confusa esse non debeant, quibus est necessarium rebus propriis adhibere culturam." On this letter and surveying in Late Antiquity, see Oswald A. W. Dilke, *The Roman Land Surveyors: an Introduction to the 'Agrimensoles'*, (London, 1971), 44–6.

98 *ET* 104.

99 Cass., *Var.* 1.18.2: "Si Romani praedium, ex quo deo propitio Sonti fluenta transmisimus, ubi primum Italiae nos suscepit imperium, sine delegatoris cuiusquam pittacio praesumptor barbarus occupavit, eum priori domino summota dilatione restituat. Quod si ante designatum tempus rem videtur ingressus, quoniam praescriptio probatur obviare tricennii, petitionem iubemus quiescere pulsatoris."

any time in the last thirty years, legally challenged their right to possess the synagogue on that place and in its current form. Similarly, *ET* 12, which was based in part on a novel of Valentinian III of 452 (*Nov.* 35) that reiterated an earlier law of Theodosius on prescription of actions (*CTh* 4.14.1 (424)), prohibited attempts to contest title from being made if the current possessor could demonstrate long and uninterrupted enjoyment of the property for a period of thirty years or more.[100] The purpose of this thirty year prescription was to protect current landholders (presumably Goths) against actions of individuals (presumably Romans) attempting to reclaim property seized during the initial settlement of the Goths under Odovacer, to assert their continuing title to lands which now housed barbarian settlers, even to claim rights over waste or woodland brought under the plow by these barbarian newcomers.

Law of the land

The issue of ownership brings us to the larger matter of land and the conditions attending upon it. The *ET* makes a clear distinction between private and public land. Public land, that is, property of the fisc, presumably originally comprising the old imperial estates, and to be distinguished from those belonging personally to the King, receives special attention from the compilers. In accordance with Roman law, when land had for any cause become public or crown property, it was to be affixed with *tituli*, to denote the fact and to warn off all other claimants:

> Absolutely no one shall put titles [of ownership] onto another's property or his own; since it is clear that this privilege is granted to the fisc alone for properties which it holds by right or by fact.[101]

Powerful men who had dispossessed weaker claimants used to imitate this practice – a tradition that clearly carried on into the sixth century. Here, they are strictly prohibited from doing so. Analogous to this provision is a rescript of the Emperors Arcadius and Honorius of 400 (*CTh* 2.14.1), which imposes forfeiture of the legal *and* factual control over property upon anyone who, as a defendant in a lawsuit, alleges it to belong to a *potentior* (presumably in an effort to bolster his claim in court).

Similarly, it was an offense for a defendant who, while entitled to the property claimed by a plaintiff, passed himself off as someone else (especially

[100] Fifty years was the norm in Visigothic law: *CE* 277.1.

[101] *ET* 45: "Nullus alienae rei vel suae titulos prorsus adfigat: cum soli fisco hoc privilegium, his quae possidet iure vel corpore, videatur esse concessum."

a *potentior*) by placing titles of ownership in another's name on the land in question.[102] If convicted, an individual was punished with the immediate forfeiture of the contested property, and was forbidden from challenging the ruling on appeal. But the law's primary concern was the unlawful seizure of public land, for this was a major source of revenue for the crown, essential for defraying the various expenses related to the operation of the government, such as upkeep of the court and army, together with extraordinary expenditure in the form of the endowment of churches and rewarding of supporters with real estate. To that end, the illegal usurpation of crown land constituted a capital offense and offenders were punished capitally.[103]

There was a further distinction made between private and public land through the law's treatment of *superficies*.[104] Conditions of life in early sixth-century Italy were such that the government was forced to concede generous building privileges in an effort to stimulate private initiative. Following closely the tradition begun by the Emperor Julian in 362 (*CTh* 15.1.9), Theoderic held out ownership to anyone initiating a building program on public grounds. The substance of this policy can be observed in Cassiodorus's *formula de competitionibus*:

> Anyone who wants to acquire ownership of public property may do so in this way: if the squalid property is made beautiful and that which has long since been in a state of disrepair is adorned. Wherefore, We grant you that place you seek with full ownership rights, except the brass or lead or marble, if they should be discovered there. Carry on in such a way that that which has fallen into neglect through careless age may acquire beauty through your actions; insofar as you may be deserving to discover the praise of a good citizen if you adorn the face of your city, you will also secure for others or transmit to posterity that which has been accomplished through your efforts.[105]

The *formula* is careful to point out that the subject of this grant was not the erection of a new building but rather the improvement of an old one. That the fisc under these circumstances retained its title in the building is likely, but the builder certainly acquired some *de iure* measure of ownership, which might be either temporary or in perpetuity and hereditary. This fact presents itself plainly enough in Cassiodorus's heading *de competitionibus*,

[102] *ET* 46. [103] *ET* 47. [104] Levy, *West Roman Vulgar Law*, 49–55.

[105] Cass., *Var.* 7.44: "Qui loca desiderat publica possidere hoc enim ita fieri decet, si res squalida in meliorem loci faciem transferatur et revocetur ad ornatum quod pridem iacere videbatur incultum. atque ideo desideranti tibi illum locum proprietario iure concedimus, praeter aes aut plumbum vel marmora, si tamen ibi fuerint latere comperta. Age itaque ut per te decorem sumat quod neglectum incuriosa vetustate iacuerat, quatenus boni civis laudem invenire merearis, si faciem tuae civitatis ornaveris, securus etiam ad quoslibet vel ad posteros transmissurus quod proprio fuerit labore compositum."

which denotes the purpose of the *formula*, namely to preclude claims of competing private parties.

Building on private land, however, was an altogether separate issue. In classical law, a person building on the private land of another, while retaining his rights in the materials, did not acquire ownership in the building made of them. The building accrued to the owner of the soil and to him alone. In this respect, it did not matter whether or not the constructor built with the owner's consent, whether or not he believed himself to be the owner of the ground. However, a *bona fide* constructor might keep the building until his expenses were reimbursed. Elements of this classical arrangement can be found in *ET* 137. According to the provision, a person retained no legal claim of ownership to a building he unknowingly constructed on another's land. Presumably, ownership accrued to the landholder. He was, however, to be reimbursed for the expenses, although the procedural details for this are not made clear. In the event that the proprietor had allowed another to build on his land, the provision provides no remedy. It is entirely likely, however, that it took for granted the development in post-classical law that recognized the builder in these circumstances as the legal owner and not the landowner.[106]

Not all freemen held their lands in full ownership. We hear from Cassiodorus, for example, that Theoderic made use of grants *in stipendio*. One such arrangement involved a certain *vir honestus* Thomas, who had failed to make good on the rent he owed for properties leased out to him by Theoderic.[107] And elsewhere, Theoderic is adamant that rent for crown land be properly assessed and paid. To the illustrious Ampelius and Liveria, commissioned to put a stop to various abuses committed at the hands of the King's tax-collectors in the Ostrogothic territories of Spain, he instructs: "We command that the farmers of the Lord's domain, whether they be Roman or barbarian, must pay the rent imposed upon them. And lest their labor may seem ungrateful to anyone, We wish their rents to be established by your fairness in accordance with the quality of the land."[108] These were remunerative concessions of land, made also by patrons to their private soldiery and by the Church to its servants, whether clerical or lay;[109] and

[106] *Gai Institutionum Epitome* 2.1.4, in *FIRA*, vol. II, 229–57; Levy, *West Roman Vulgar Law*, 53–4.

[107] Cass., *Var.* 5.7.

[108] Cass., *Var.* 5.39: "Conductores domus regiae, quacumque gente sint editi, ad liquidum veritate discussa tantum decernimus solvere, quantum nostra praedia constiterit pensitare. Et ne cuiquam labor suus videatur ingratus, solaria eis pro qualitate locatae rei vestra volumus aequitate constitui."

[109] E.g., Proc., *BG* V. xii. 50–4 (concerning the nobleman Theudis who raised a private army on his own land); Tjäder, *P-Ital* no. 3: in this example from the region of Padua and dating to *c.* 550, tenants (*coloni*) of the church were obliged to undertake heavy labor services for the land they received.

held conditionally upon the obedience and service of the grantee.[110] In that these concessions were of indefinite duration and economically gratuitous, they corresponded in character to those concessions made *iure precario* in classical times, but they differed from these in that they might not be revoked at will but only when the stipendiary was in breach of his obligations, such as rent, services, or both.

It can be reasonably assumed that peasants paid rents in kind, just as they paid taxes in kind; most peasants did not have sufficiently easy access to long-distance markets that they could obtain the metal for money-rents on a regular basis. These rents might be assessed in monetary terms, and then converted to kind in a process defined by Gregory the Great as *comparatio*, performed at the moment of rent-paying on his Sicilian estates.[111] At any rate, it was produce that was mostly extracted from cultivators, which could then be sold, either by *conductores* or landowners, presumably to cities, including Rome itself, as a supplement to the *annona*. Modeled on the imperial practice of *coemptio*, whereby the state purchased goods at fixed prices, this system provided tax assessors yet another opportunity to defraud peasants by unfair pricing and false weights.[112] To help limit these sorts of abuses, a corrupt tax official convicted of having used improperly balanced weights was fined fourfold the original amount.[113] In comparison to late imperial legislation that punished corrupt tax collectors capitally, this was an exceptionally lenient punishment.[114] Like the case of the taxmen Victor and Witigisdus, accused and rebuked for various acts of fraud while conducting official business in Sicily, it demonstrates that while the government displayed an interest in such matters, it clearly lacked the capability or desire to deal harshly with its tax officials – no doubt because it relied so heavily on their services.

The law's concern for land and landholders underscores the predominantly rural character of the early medieval Italian economy. Of primary importance to this rural economy was livestock, as some of the laws regulating the privileges and duties of travelers will already have shown. But this is perhaps best illustrated by the comparatively large number of provisions in the *ET* that deal with assorted breaches of a man's rights and

[110] Wickham, *Framing the Early Middle Ages*, 268–9, 271, 277–8, 293–4.

[111] Greg., *ep.* 142. On the subject of rent paid in kind but assessed in money, see also Domenico Vera, "Forme e funzioni della rendita fondiaria nella tarda antichità," in A. Giardina (ed.), *Società romana e impero tardoantico* (Rome and Bari, 1986), 435–7; Domenico Vera, "Strutture agrarie e strutture patrimoniali nella tarda Antichità: l'aristocrazia romana fra agricoltura e commercio," *Opus* 2 (1983), 489–533, esp. 516–21; and, classically, Lellia Ruggini, *Economia e società*, 131 and *passim* for agricultural exchange.

[112] Wickham, *Framing the Early Middle Ages*, 271. [113] *ET* 149. [114] E.g., *Nov. Maj.* 7.1.15 (458).

obligations to his animals. The general rule was that the man who caused the loss – through killing, theft, or otherwise misuse – of another's animal(s) was to compensate the owner accordingly.[115] But individual provisions established a variety of distinct consequences for particular offenses. The convicted cattle rustler was to be punished capitally, and compensation to the victim in the form of fourfold restitution – in money or kind the provision does not specify – was to be exacted from his estate.[116] In the event that his slave committed the act, the owner had the choice of paying the fourfold restitution himself or delivering up the malefactor to be punished accordingly.[117] In the event that he opted for the second prescription, he was nevertheless obligated to return all which he demonstrably received through the commission of the theft.[118]

The fourfold restitution could vary considerably according to the type of animal absconded. *ET* 57 provides a rough breakdown:

> If a rustler is proven to have stolen anywhere from one steed, two mares, and the same number of cows, and as many as ten she-goats and five pigs, whether he led them away through deception or by force from a pasture or stable, he shall be punished most severely: he shall be punished for the crime of theft and pay back fourfold the number of animals or pigs mentioned above which he stole from another.[119]

Here, an adult steed was deemed equal in value to two mature mares or two cows, five pigs, or ten she-goats. According to this formula, then, the value of an adult mare was on par with that of a mature cow, and both animals approximated the value accorded to two adult pigs and one suckling, or five she-goats; and lastly, one mature pig equaled the price of two adult she-goats. Beyond attesting to the diversification practiced by stock-raisers in early sixth-century Italy, the provision makes it clear that the horse was the most highly prized of all animals. It is likely that their importance stemmed primarily from their military role, but they were certainly used for the post and for personal travel, for threshing and carrying, and in the case of mares, for the breeding of mules. Horseracing, too, continued to thrive, undoubtedly placing an even higher premium on horses.[120]

Just as the rights of an owner of livestock were protected by the law, so, too, were his responsibilities subject to legislation. Any damage caused by

[115] *ET* 56–8, 88, 117, 150–2. [116] *ET* 88. [117] *ET* 56. [118] *ET* 118.

[119] "Abactor si usque ad unum equum, duas equas, totidemque boves, et usque ad decem capras, et quinque porcos tulisse tam de stabulis, quam de pascuis fuerit adprobatus, sive per surreptionem, sive ea violenter abduxerit, severissime puniatur: quidquid vero intra suprascriptum numerum animalium vel porcorum a quocunque sublatum fuerit, tanquam furtum sub quadrupli poena solvatur."

[120] On the survival of the games: Cass., *Var.* 1.20, 27, 30; 3.51; 5.42; 6.4; Anon. Val. 12.60, 67.

his animals had to be made good or compensated for.[121] That some kind of penal sanction was involved in the event that the animals' owner was directly responsible, by willful action or gross negligence, for the ill-effects of their behavior is likely. In the Visigothic kingdom, for instance, an individual who deliberately sent his animals into a meadow of young grass had to repay the value of the crop which would otherwise have been produced, and pay an additional *tremis* or *solidus* (according to his status) for every two beasts. Different only in detail was the treatment of the person who sent his animals into a vineyard or onto arable land.[122]

Conclusions

It cannot be doubted that Theoderic was responsible for a measure of economic recovery in Italy. But his reign, and especially those of his successors, must be viewed in the context of a dying or defunct empire, and relative to the harsh economic conditions that characterized much of the Italian peninsula during the first half of the sixth century. Many towns had been in a period of decline long before the official capitulation of the imperial administration in 476, and others were, over the course of the fifth and sixth centuries, destroyed, abandoned, or replaced by military fortifications called *castella*.[123] Even the many buildings Theoderic is alleged to have built have either not been found by archaeologists, or else turn out to be nothing more than restored ancient buildings: the palaces built in Ravenna, Verona, and Pavia appear to be adaptations of existing Roman structures.[124] Thus, rather than an active and attentive promoter of urban renewal as contemporary accounts make him out to be, Theoderic was, as the archaeological evidence suggests, a much more modest figure in this regard.

[121] *ET* 117.

[122] *LV* 8.3.12; 8.3.10. Injury caused by an animal to the person of a man or to another animal was treated in much the same way. Either the offending beast was transferred or composition was paid: the choice was that of the owner (*LV* 8.4.12).

[123] E.g., Cass., *Var.* 2.35 (Como) and *Var.* 3.49 (Catana). See further Marazzi, "The Last Rome," 279–301. On the construction of military fortifications: Cass., *Var.* 1.17, 3.48. For archaeological evidence for the destruction of cities and emergence of *castella* between the fifth and sixth century, see Brogiolo, "Dwellings and Settlements in Gothic Italy," 114–17, 122.

[124] Anon. Val. 12.71. For the archaeological evidence, see Brogiolo, "Dwellings and Settlements," 113–33; Christina La Rocca, "Perceptions of an Early Medieval Urban Landscape," in Peter Linehan and Janet Nelson (eds.), *The Medieval World* (London, 2001), 416–31, esp. 417–25. On Theoderic's building program in general, see Johnson, "Toward a History of Theoderic's Building Program," 73–96.

In the end, the favorable impression created by Cassiodorus' selective missives must be weighed against the far more authoritative evidence of the *ET*, which underscores the depressed economic conditions that characterized much of Italy in the early sixth century, as the peninsula continued to be beleaguered by an acute shortage of men, resources, and problems associated with the inability of the central administration to protect individuals against the open greed of powerful nobles and corrupt local officials.

Epilogue

In early sixth-century Italy, when a Goth or Roman required clarification or remedy in such matters as the payment of loans, distributions of property, boundaries, the status of slaves, succession, sales, gifts, and so on, they could turn to the *ET*. Given its straightforward style and focus on everyday matters, it is not difficult to imagine that they did. As a guidebook intended to supplement existing, but increasingly outdated, Roman law from previous centuries, it did not have to be comprehensive, only relevant. Thus, the compilers approached the Roman sources with a selective eye for the most useful and applicable. In the process they ignored a good deal. Their selections represent changed cultural, political, and economic circumstances: a society in which a King attempted to maintain peace and order through a much attenuated officer corps; a land of warlords (disingenuously described as patrons) running amok with their private armies; a largely rural place where the vast majority of people scratched out a living through the direct exploitation of the land. All of this was to be held together by a set of rules that presupposed a population still concerned with formalities that had their origins in a distant and bygone culture, and still with access to institutional resources at the local level by which they could be governed.

Indeed, the *ET* preserves the essence of classical law to a remarkable degree. But this was not the law of the third or fourth century. It was the law as it was intended to function in the towns and countryside of Theoderic's Italy. As such, the *ET* is of intrinsic historical importance, for it reveals a world that can only be glimpsed behind the smokescreen of Roman *civilitas* offered up by Cassiodorus, whose picture of Ostrogothic Italy, and in particular the reign of Theoderic, has left us with an image of a peaceful and prosperous time – an Indian summer of Roman renewal that contrasted sharply with the winter of discontent ushered in by Justinian's wars of reconquest. To be sure, Theoderic restored a degree of stability and allowed normal life to resume its course following nearly a century of political unrest and economic decline. However, while civic life continued, as did the administrative bureaucracy that regulated it, it did so on a much smaller scale and in an entirely debased form. Cities and towns were abandoned or despoiled, and in their place military fortifications were established. Commerce and industry continued to decline as population levels dwindled further and further. At the same time, much of the Roman administrative machinery that Theoderic inherited was either not fully utilized or abandoned altogether; Cassiodorus' version of a highly-differentiated administration composed of civil and military officers with clearly defined and separate functions gave way to one where authority was exercised by a smaller number of military officers.

For Theoderic, governing over the famous lands of Italy whose cities, monuments, and amenities he was scarcely able to maintain, Roman law was a source of prestige and authority through which he sought to define and justify his rule. It was an ancient institution that symbolized a connection between his reign and those of other glorious Emperors of the past, thereby reinforcing an ideology that his rule truly witnessed a renewal of all the hallmarks that once defined classical culture, such as law, civility, art, and philosophy. Writing to his new Gallic subjects shortly after taking control of a large portion of southern Gaul in 510, Theoderic described his rule as Roman, contrasting it explicitly with the "barbarous" rule of the Visigoths:

> You, who have been restored to it after so long a time, should gladly obey Roman custom, for it is gratifying to return to that place from where your ancestors undoubtedly took their rise. And therefore, as by God's grace you have been recalled to ancient liberty, adorn yourselves in the morals of the toga, cast off barbarism, throw aside savagery of the mind, for it does not befit you to abide by foreign customs while living in the justice of Our time.[1]

But the *ET* serves as ample proof that while Roman law withstood the social, political, and economic upheaval that brought an end to the western Roman Empire, it was not the law of Constantine or even Theodosius. It was a much simplified law of a barbarian King, created by Roman jurists who were acutely aware of the fact that – despite ideological statements of Cassiodorus to the contrary – the Roman world characterized at the height of its power as a highly-civilized urban culture and governed through an effective administrative and legal apparatus, had long since passed by.

[1] Cass., *Var.* 3.17: "Libenter parendum est Romanae consuetudini, cui estis post longa tempora restituti, quia ibi regressus est gratus, ubi provectum vestros constat habuisse maiores. Atque ideo in antiquam libertatem deo praestante revocati vestimini moribus togatis, exuite barbariem, abicite mentium crudelitatem, quia sub aequitate nostri temporis non vos decet vivere moribus alienis." See also Cass., *Var.* 4.26, 4.33, and 9.19 for references to Gothic Kings as the successors of the Roman legal heritage.

Appendix: Edict of King Theoderic

INDEX OF TITLES

1. If a judge accepts money to render a false judgment
2. If a judge accepts money to render a decision to the detriment of a person's status or property
3. If a judge receives anything unjustifiably from provincials
4. If the staff of any judge whatsoever receives anything beyond its mandate
5. If a judgment is delivered against those not present
6. The manner in which judgments are executed shall be the business of the staff of the judge and the judge's own sense of responsibility
7. A judge shall render a true decision after the charges and proofs of each party have been examined
8. No freeborn man is to be held without the authorization of a judge
9. Concerning those who presume to do anything contrary to this
10. One must sue the holder of property of any type with the authorization of a judge, and await the outcome of the trial
11. If a landholder is defeated in a suit, and does not return the property that has been claimed
12. Concerning those who have possessed any property without interruption for thirty years
13. Concerning those who accuse another with any crime
14. Let no one make a criminal accusation on behalf of another
15. Concerning an assailant who advances against another
16. Concerning those who advance violently against another's property (an approaching aggressor)
17. Concerning the abductor (*raptor*) of a freeborn woman or virgin
18. Concerning the parent or guardian of an abducted girl
19. Concerning a slave who discovers that the complaint of abduction (*raptus*) has been concealed

20. Within what time the crime of abduction is to be prosecuted
21. If anyone abducts another's *ancilla* or *originaria* with a gang
22. Concerning a knowledgeable or complicit chief tenant
23. Concerning those who die intestate
24. When the fisc is obligated to act
25. Disputes involving a landholder and the fisc must be settled before a judge
26. Concerning intestate clerics or religious persons
27. If a curial dies intestate without a successor
28. Concerning the liberty of testamentary rights
29. If a testator is either illiterate or otherwise unable to provide a signature
30. Concerning forgers
31. Let no one contradict another who wants to make a will
32. Concerning barbarians who wish to make a lawful will
33. Concerning those who can inherit from another who has died intestate
34. Concerning theft, whether committed by a Roman or barbarian
35. Concerning informers
36. If anyone plans to contract an illegitimate marriage
37. If a woman marries within a year of her husband's death
38. Concerning an adulterer and an adulteress
39. Anyone who offers a house so that adultery might occur
40. Anyone who unknowingly makes a false allegation
41. Anyone who produces or uses a forgery
42. Anyone who delivers conflicting or false testimony
43. No one shall transfer their actions at law to a powerful Roman or barbarian
44. No Roman or barbarian is to stand as a defense lawyer or supporter in another's trial
45. No one shall put titles on another's property or his own
46. If anyone, upon being summoned before a judge, places titles [of ownership] on the property which he possesses as a means of defense against his [legal] opponent
47. If anyone seizes estates which are designated by titles as belonging to another
48. Freedmen, *originarii*, or slaves are not to be heard against their patrons or the children of such patrons
49. This must also be observed concerning domestic servants (*familiarii*)
50. Concerning hidden and secret accusations
51. Concerning the publication of the donations of properties
52. If anyone bequeaths a rural or urban estate
53. On transferring ownership (*traditio*)

54. Marriages are not to be dissolved indiscriminately; only when certain charges are proven may couples withdraw from the marriage
55. A judge is obligated to hear all appeals
56. Concerning the rustler of assorted animals
57. If a rustler is proven to have stolen anywhere from one steed, two mares and the same number of cows, ten she-goats, and five pigs
58. Anyone who finds a cow, horse, or other livestock wandering about
59. Anyone who forcibly defiles a freeborn virgin
60. If anyone should commit *stuprum* against an unwilling widow
61. If a widowed matron is defiled by another's depravity
62. If a widowed matron is willingly defiled by a slave
63. If another's slave or *originarius* forcibly defiles a freeborn virgin
64. If anyone defiles another's virgin slave woman or *originaria*
65. Whenever a freeborn man, *originarius*, or slave comingles with a slave woman
66. Whenever another's slave or a freeborn man comingles with an *originaria*
67. If another's *originarius* comingles with an *originaria*
68. If an *originaria* flees from a freeborn man
69. If anyone takes possession of a decurion, guild member, or servant of the state for a period of thirty years
70. If a slave should take refuge in a church
71. If anyone flees to a church on account of a public debt
72. On the registration of wills
73. Concerning the execution of judicial directives
74. Concerning a dishonest plaintiff
75. On fighting armed men if they come violently to a property
76. Concerning the restoration of the temporary possession of seized properties
77. If slaves are convicted of inflicting violence
78. On stealing a freeborn man
79. If anyone holds a freeborn man under terms
80. If anyone induces another's slave to flee
81. If anyone unknowingly purchases slaves from a slave trader (*plagiator*)
82. If a freeborn man is sold
83. Anyone who conceals, sells, or knowingly purchases a freeborn man
84. Anyone who knowingly receives another's fugitive slave or *colonus*
85. If anyone receives slaves that have been induced to flight or furtively taken by another
86. Anyone who detains another's slave at his residence against the wishes of the owner

87. [Concerning] a slave in flight
88. If a cattle rustler, seducer (of slaves), or thief dies before he can be prosecuted
89. If anyone assembles an armed force on his own behalf to incite terror
90. If anyone changes another's testament, codicil, records, accounts, transcripts of registered instruments, documents, bonds or letters for the purposes of fraud
91. Anyone who bribes witnesses to commit perjury
92. If a betrothed woman, upon being persuaded by the one with whom she is betrothed, should take up residence with him before she has formally been given away in marriage
93. A father cannot be compelled to give away his child unwillingly to another in marriage
94. Parents who are compelled by necessity to sell their children
95. And it shall not be permitted for parents to give away their children as a pledge
96. If those who live as free are claimed as slaves
97. Anyone who sets fire to a house, villa, or dwelling
98. [Concerning] a fire that a slave or *colonus* heedlessly sets in his [owner's] field
99. Anyone who kills a man or urges that he be killed without a hearing before a judge
100. Another's slave cannot be tortured [to testify] to the detriment of another
101. Anyone who purchases a slave in order to prevent him from giving evidence under torture against him
102. If a slave is freed so that he is not tortured
103. A crime must be prosecuted in the place where it is committed
104. Concerning boundaries that have been dug up or trees marking boundaries
105. Boundaries between two estates must be observed
106. Concerning a suit that is completed with oaths
107. Concerning the instigator of sedition
108. Concerning those who make a sacrifice according to the pagan rite
109. If a slave or *colonus* should seize anything violently without the knowledge of his owner
110. Whoever destroys a grave
111. If anyone buries corpses within the city of Rome
112. Concerning the property of those condemned for any crime
113. If a condemned curial should leave behind children

140. [A vendor] who undergoes a judicial challenge concerning the purchase of property
141. Anyone who sells a runaway slave to an unknowing party
142. An owner shall be permitted to transfer his slaves, even *originarii*, to other regions, or do whatever he wants [in regards to them]
143. Concerning the preservation of the privileges of Jews
144. On recording the sureties of tax receipts
145. If a barbarian should refuse to appear in court after being summoned for a third time
146. Concerning stolen produce
147. Concerning sales exercised in good faith
148. Concerning slaves or *coloni* returned from the enemy
149. Concerning public measures and weights
150. No one may exercise control over another's farmhand or ox
151. Concerning a damaged crop or felled tree
152. If a person's slave is killed by someone else
153. A wife must not be prosecuted in the place of her husband
154. Concerning the Lord's Day and the days of Easter

PROLOGUE[1]

Many complaints have come to Our attention that some people within the provinces are trampling upon the rules of law. Even though the authority of the laws can in no way be used to defend unjust actions, however, We, taking into consideration the [desired] peace of the state, and having before Our eyes the irregularities that can often occur, command that the present edicts be posted for ending matters of this sort, so that both barbarians and Romans, while maintaining the respect due to the public laws and dutifully preserving in their entirety the rights of everyone, may clearly know what they are obligated to follow concerning the items specified in the present edicts.

[1] The *Edict* of Athalaric (*Var.* 9.18) begins in much the same way, noting in typical legal rhetoric that the King's court has long been inundated with reports of the laws being flouted: "For a long while, now, complaints from all parts have sounded in Our ears with frequent whispering that certain people, having spurned *civilitas*, aim to live in bestial savagery." ("diu est, quod diversorum querellae nostris auribus crebris susurrationibus insonarunt quosdam civilitate despecta affectare vivere beluina saevitia...") In the next letter (*Var.* 9.19), Cassiodorus has Athalaric confirm that the existing law (*residuum ius*), perhaps a reference to the *ET* (described in similar fashion by the Anonymous Valesianus as "*ius*"), is to be confirmed rather than abrogated by his *Edict*: "Let this revered edict seem not to diminish from the existing law, but rather strengthen it." ("... quae custodita residuum ius non debilitare, sed potius corroborare videantur.")

1. IF A JUDGE ACCEPTS MONEY TO RENDER A FALSE JUDGMENT[2]

In the first place We have decreed that if a judge accepts money to pass judgment which imperils the life or civil status of an innocent person against the ordinances and provisions of the public law, let him be subjected to a capital penalty.

2. IF A JUDGE ACCEPTS MONEY TO RENDER A DECISION TO THE DETRIMENT OF A PERSON'S STATUS OR PROPERTY[3]

If a judge accepts money in order to render a decision to the detriment of a person's status or property, and is convicted of this crime in a fair hearing, he shall pay fourfold the amount which he previously accepted in his eagerness for corrupt gain; and it will benefit the individual who received an unfair judgment as a result of the bribe.

3. IF A JUDGE RECEIVES ANYTHING UNJUSTIFIABLY FROM PROVINCIALS[4]

A judge that unjustifiably takes anything from provincials shall lose the office which he abused, and shall return at least fourfold the amount to those from whom clearly something was unjustifiably taken; and if the judge has died, let this penalty be sought from his heirs.

4. IF THE STAFF OF ANY JUDGE WHATSOEVER RECEIVES ANYTHING BEYOND ITS MANDATE[5]

Let the staff of any judge whatsoever that has exacted anything beyond what it has been mandated be compelled, under the penalty of being beaten, to

[2] Similarly *PS* 5.23.10; *Dig.* 48.8.1.1 *in fine* (Marcian. lib. 14 *Inst.*).

[3] Similarly *PS* 5.23.11 (10). Here, the guilty judge faced exile and confiscation of property (it is not stated whether this was to go to the victim or the fisc): "A judge who accepts a bribe to the detriment of the *caput* and property of an innocent man shall be deprived of his property and be deported to an island." ("Iudex, qui in caput fortunasque hominis pecuniam accepit, in insulam bonis ademptis deportetur.") This underwent substantial interpolation by the compilers of Justinian's *Digest* (*Dig.* 48.8.1.1): "A trial magistrate or judge who accepts a bribe in a capital case will be guilty in accordance with the public custom." ("quive magistratus iudexve quaestionis ob capitalem causam pecuniam acceperit ut publica lege reus fieret.") On the subject of judicial corruption in Late Antiquity, see Jill Harries, *Law and Empire in Late Antiquity*, (Cambridge, 1999), ch. 8; Michael H. Hoeflich, "Regulation of Judicial Misconduct from Late Antiquity to the Early Middle Ages," *Law and History Review* 2 (1984), 79–104.

[4] *CTh* 9.27.3.

[5] Similarly *CTh* 9.27.3.

pay fourfold to those from whom property was shown clearly to have been taken.

5. IF A JUDGMENT IS DELIVERED AGAINST THOSE NOT PRESENT[6]

A judgment delivered against parties not present shall be of no consequence, unless it is shown to have been rendered against an individual who, despite being summoned and formally called upon for the third time by judicial directives,[7] has refused to appear [in court].

6. THE MANNER IN WHICH JUDGMENTS ARE EXECUTED SHALL BE THE BUSINESS OF THE STAFF OF THE JUDGE AND THE JUDGE'S OWN SENSE OF RESPONSIBILITY[8]

It is the responsibility of the judge's staff and the judge's own sense of propriety to bring to a conclusion with a verdict issued in writing suits tried before them; and let them order the judgment to be executed.

7. A JUDGE SHALL RENDER A TRUE DECISION AFTER THE CHARGES AND PROOFS OF EACH PARTY HAVE BEEN EXAMINED

When the claims and proofs of each party have been examined, a judge must render a decision only on that which he perceives to be in accordance with justice and law.

8. NO FREEBORN MAN IS TO BE HELD WITHOUT THE AUTHORIZATION OF A JUDGE

Without the authorization[9] of a judge exercising the appropriate jurisdiction, no freeborn man shall endure the injustice of detention, or be delivered for judgment, or be held in confinement in a private place on account of the presumption of anyone at all.

[6] *PS* 5. *5a*.6; similarly *CJ* 7.43.9; *Dig.* 49.8.1, 3 (Macer. lib. 2 *de appelat.*). See also *Dig.* 48.19.5 pr. (Ulp. lib. 10 *de off. procons.*), the key Roman text on contumacy that is based on a rescript of Trajan. On the criminal and civil context of the Roman law of contumacy see Lucia Fanizza, *L'Assenza dell'Accusato nei Processi di Età Imperiale*, Studi Juridica 85 (Rome, 1992).

[7] These are *edicta peremptoria* issued by judges. [8] Similarly *CTh* 4.17.1; *CJ* 7.44.

[9] Since the fourth century the use of written documents was a widespread (and increasing) phenomenon. *Praeceptum* here could be referring to an oral command, or as is more likely a document. On this subject see Harries, *Law and Empire*, 108.

9. CONCERNING THOSE WHO PRESUME TO DO ANYTHING CONTRARY TO THIS

But if anyone has committed any of those offenses, let him have no doubt that he shall be arrested and charged with inflicting violence – a capital offense.

10. ONE MUST SUE THE LANDHOLDER OF ANY TYPE WITH THE AUTHORIZATION OF A JUDGE, AND AWAIT THE OUTCOME OF THE TRIAL[10]

We decree that any landholder[11] whatsoever is to be sued by use of a judicial summons, and the outcome of a proper trial is always to be awaited. And if anyone evicts any holder whatsoever from his property, let him also be deprived of the impartial right to sue for such presumption; let him of course restore the property which he seized and also pay twice the property's income[12] for his insolence. And if he has taken possession of property to which he had no legal right at all, let him suffer this penalty: that he both return to its owner the property, along with its income, in the same condition as it was when it was seized; and let him be compelled to pay the value of the property he seized to the fisc. We command all those judges, appointed in the provinces[13] or in the Venerable City, and their staffs, to be guardians of this just and lawful decree,[14] in such a manner that if there is any reason they should think themselves incapable of exacting the penalty referred to above, they shall send their report to Our bureaus[15] so that, if

[10] *CTh* 4.22.3; similarly *CJ* 8.4.7; *Nov. Val.* 8.1; similarly an edict of Athalaric (Cass., *Var.* 9.18.1), which cites *Nov. Val.* 8.1 (not, as Mommsen suggested, *CTh* 4.22.3 (389)). For examples of specific cases in the *Variae*: 3.20; 4.10; 8.18. The far more lenient punishment proscribed in *Var.* 3.20 is perhaps indicative of the status of the accused in the case, namely the Praetorian Prefect Faustus. Similarly, Cass., *Var.* 4.39 and 5.12, where the accused is none other than Theoderic's own nephew.

[11] Landholder (*possessor*): the owner or possessor of a landholding. During the Empire great landholders were capable of exercising a tremendous amount of authority in direct defiance of the central authority, either by defying the laws or evading them through connivance or collusion of the corrupt bureaucracy. On this subject see Chapter 3. Further references in the *ET* to *possessores*: *ET* 11, 25, 132, 136, 144.

[12] *Fructus*: in Roman law the term comprises primarily the natural produce of fields and gardens, animals, and any other proceeds obtained from the property.

[13] Province (*provincia*): an administrative and judicial district that was under the control of a Governor. At the basis of the administrative organization of the Empire lay the division into Prefectures, dioceses, provinces, and municipalities. At the end of the fourth century, there were thousands of municipalities scattered throughout 120 provinces. These were divided into fourteen dioceses that formed the four Prefectures of Gaul, Italy, Illyricum, and the Orient.

[14] Decree (*decretum*): a judicial decision rendered by any judge, including the Emperor.

[15] That is, the offices of the palace secretariat, the *magister officiorum*.

reason demands it, the penalty may be exacted (*vindicetur*)[16] more strictly by Us.

11. IF A LANDHOLDER IS DEFEATED IN A SUIT, AND DOES NOT RETURN THE PROPERTY THAT HAS BEEN CLAIMED[17]

But if a landholder is defeated in a suit and does not return the property that was claimed, and as an outcome of the trial a judgment has been delivered against him in accordance with the laws, he shall pay the costs of the litigation and living expenses incurred from the time he was summoned by judicial authority and gave his reply [to the claim]. Let this remedy prevent anyone from being tempted to go to court with a frivolous case.[18]

12. CONCERNING THOSE WHO HAVE POSSESSED ANY PROPERTY WITHOUT INTERRUPTION FOR THIRTY YEARS[19]

Anyone who is proven to be in possession of any property without interruption for thirty years shall be subject to no judicial challenge at all, whether on the part of a private party or the state. Moreover, We decree that the periods [of possession] of a previous holder, or the holder before that, must by law be [calculated] in favor of such a possessor. We add that if a suit has been brought within thirty years, and the end of the thirty years comes about before the suit is concluded, let that end the suit without any further ado; for We believe it is more than sufficient for anyone at all both to institute proceedings properly and bring them to completion within thirty years either through the judgment of a public court or the decision of private arbitration. There is this restriction: the exemptions granted by ancient and recent laws with regard to wards under puberty are to be preserved, and with regard to those persons who lawfully initiate their cases twenty-five and thirty years after a legal action could be taken. In this instance We approve the privilege of a five year extension as added in a recent law.[20]

[16] Interesting here is the occurrence of the term *vindicetur*. In classical law *vindicatio* denoted a lawsuit to recover something which one already owned but did not possess at that particular time. Generally speaking, in post-classical law the term was used much more freely in the sense to "acquire" or "assert ownership rights," irrespective of whether one had already owned the property and whether one now actually possessed it or not. In *ET* 70, *vindicare* is even qualified to mean to retain as owner. The model *CTh* 9.45.3 has *revocentur*.

[17] *CTh* 4.22.3. [18] See below *ET* 74.

[19] *CTh* 4.14.1; *Nov. Val.* 35.13. For a specific cases involving the thirty year rule: Cass., *Var.* 1.18; 3.45.

[20] The recent law referred to here is a *novel* of the Emperor Valentinian III of 452 (*Nov. Val.* 35).

13. CONCERNING THOSE WHO ACCUSE ANOTHER WITH ANY CRIME[21]

Anyone who considers accusing another with any crime, let him not be heard first, nor let anything concerning the case be judged, unless he undertakes the bond of a preliminary inscription, and guarantees the following before a judge exercising the appropriate jurisdiction: that if he does not prove what he claims, he will suffer a similar penalty which the accused, when convicted according to law, can receive. And let both the accused and accuser be held in similar custody until the outcome of the trial has been reached; unless either the charges are minor, in which cases a guarantor must be produced, or the accused is sufficiently noble[22] or of distinguished enough honor that he ought to be entrusted to his rank.

14. LET NO ONE MAKE A CRIMINAL ACCUSATION ON BEHALF OF ANOTHER[23]

Let no one make a criminal accusation on behalf of another, since We judge it improper that someone should prosecute in the interests or wishes of another under the pretext of a criminal accusation.[24]

[21] *CTh* 9.1.11; 9.1.19.

[22] *Nobilis*: it occurs in one other instance – *ET* 59 (on the forcible defilement of a freeborn virgin). It is impossible to define the nobles in precise terms. There are, of course, certain general features of the nobility, and certain defined groups who belonged to it, but no concise, formal statement of what identified the *nobilior* can be achieved. That some combination of social, political, and economic factors, which can be distinguished only in the broadest terms, served as the basis of decision is evident. To Cassiodorus, *nobilitas* was a very vague concept, based on wealth, power, and general eminence rather than ancestry. But more than anything else, membership of the aristocracy was defined by the holding of imperial offices and dignities, and aristocrats were in general synonymous with the governing elite, the *optimates*, rather than a cohesive nobility based on its high birth. Procopius' war narrative consistently uses three terms to designate an inner elite of the Gothic army that were responsible for making important policy decisions: *aristoi* ("the best"), *dokimoi* ("the notable"), and *logimoi* ("the worthy"). These three terms at least confirm the existence of a broader elite, what we may identify as nobility, among the Ostrogothic army. See further Peter Heather, "*Gens* and *Regnum* Among the Ostrogoths," in Hans-Werner Goetz, Jörg Jarnut, and Walter Pohl (eds.), *Regna and Gentes: The Relationship Between Late Antique and Early Medieval Peoples and Kingdoms in the Transformation of the Roman World* (Leiden/New York, 2003), 96–8; Peter Heather, "Merely an Ideology? – Gothic Identity in Ostrogothic Italy," in Sam J. Barnish and Federico Marazzi (eds.), *The Ostrogoths from the Migration Period to the Sixth Century: An Ethnographic Perspective* (Woodbridge, 2007), 42, 44, 45, 50.

[23] *CTh* 9.1.15.

[24] The compilers ignored as unnecessary the requirement in the original (*CTh* 9.1.15) that this did not apply to instances where an individual witnessed the unlawful flogging of an innocent man at the hands of a judge (and the subsequent covering up by his office staff). In all such instances, an action could be brought forward by a third party.

15. CONCERNING AN ASSAILANT WHO ADVANCES AGAINST ANOTHER[25]

Let the action of one who with a weapon repels an assailant advancing against him not be considered homicide, since someone defending himself is considered in no way to have committed an offense.

16. CONCERNING THOSE WHO ADVANCE VIOLENTLY AGAINST ANOTHER'S PROPERTY (AN APPROACHING AGGRESSOR)[26]

If anyone gathers a large band and attacks another's property, and he or someone from that band should happen to be killed as the attack is being repulsed, let the person who through necessity committed this act be considered free from the fear of punishment.

17. CONCERNING THE ABDUCTOR (*RAPTOR*) OF A FREEBORN WOMAN OR VIRGIN[27]

We decree, in accordance with established custom, that an abductor of a freeborn woman or virgin, together with his accomplices or assistants, shall be executed once his crimes have been proven; if the abducted consents to her abductor, she, too, shall be killed.

18. CONCERNING THE PARENT OR GUARDIAN OF AN ABDUCTED GIRL[28]

If perhaps the parents or guardian[29] of the abducted (*rapta*) girl neglect to prosecute and take legal measures against the guilty party of such a deed, by making an illicit pact concerning this crime, they shall suffer the penalty of exile.

[25] *CJ* 9.16.2; similarly 9.16.3(4).

[26] Similarly *CTh* 9.14.2. In the analogous text there are two specific references made to armed soldiers. That the compilers ignore this point could be taken as an indication of their reluctance to make such an explicit association, as soldiering at this time was an occupation exclusively reserved for the Goths.

[27] *CTh* 9.24.1. Cf. Cass., *Var.* 3.46, where Adeodatus, wrongly convicted for the abduction of the maiden Valeriana, suffered such extreme torture that death was surely inevitable had Theoderic not intervened.

[28] *CTh* 9.24.1.

[29] Curator (*curator*): in Roman law the legal guardian of a person between the ages of puberty and twenty-five years old, and of other persons who were deemed mentally or physically incompetent to manage their own affairs.

19. CONCERNING A SLAVE WHO DISCOVERS THAT THE COMPLAINT OF ABDUCTION (*RAPTUS*) HAS BEEN CONCEALED[30]

If a slave learns that a complaint of abduction (*raptus*)has been concealed by his owners and the crime passed over by connivance, and reports this to the courts, he shall be freed.

20. WITHIN WHAT PERIOD OF TIME THE CRIME OF ABDUCTION IS TO BE PROSECUTED[31]

Let it be permitted for all to make an accusation of abduction (*raptus*) within a period of five years, but after this period let no one initiate an investigation of this crime, even if it is shown that a legal action could have been brought forward within the period of time prescribed above: particularly since all the children from this marriage [which has been contracted by the crime of abduction] are protected both by the authority and privilege of legitimacy after a period of five years has passed.

21. IF ANYONE ABDUCTS ANOTHER'S *ANCILLA* OR *ORIGINARIA* WITH A GANG[32]

If anyone violently abducts another's *ancilla* or *originaria*[33] with a gang, should he be of freeborn status let him be punished with that penalty reserved for an abductor,[34] since he has committed the crime of violence; should he be a slave or *colonus*, and has committed such an act willingly, let him be punished in the same manner.[35]

22. CONCERNING A KNOWLEDGEABLE OR COMPLICIT CHIEF TENANT[36]

If anyone commits this deed [abduction] with the knowledge, instruction, complicity, or permission of a chief tenant,[37] the chief tenant himself shall

[30] *CTh* 9.24.1. [31] *CTh* 9.24.3. [32] Similarly *CJ* 9.13.1.

[33] *Originaria/originarius*: designates the status of ignoble birth and can be used interchangeably with *colonus* to denote a person of low (free) status. For further references in the *ET*: 48, 56, 63, 64, 65, 66, 67, 68 80, 97, 142.

[34] *ET* 17 (a capital offense).

[35] For a discussion of this law and its history, see Adolf Berger, *Encyclopedic Dictionary of Roman Law*, vol. 43, part 2 (Philadelphia, PA, 1953), 376.

[36] Similarly *CJ* 9.13.1.

[37] Chief tenant (*conductor*): was a leaseholder or a lessee of a large landholding, who divided it into smaller landholdings which he sublet to small farmers, chiefly *coloni*.

be punished just as if he was guilty of the crime. And if someone perpetrates this crime with the knowledge or bidding of an owner, the owner shall forfeit forthwith, to the benefit of the fisc, that property from where the abductor has fled.

23. CONCERNING THOSE WHO DIE INTESTATE

If someone dies intestate, let the closest in degree and title amongst the agnates[38] and cognates[39] of the deceased succeed, excepting that the rights of children and grandchildren must be preserved.

24. WHEN THE FISC IS OBLIGATED TO ACT[40]

In accordance with the precepts of the ancient laws, the fisc shall act at that time when neither a parent, child, grandchild, relative, kin, wife, or husband can be found to succeed: provided that whenever the fisc discovers an instance that it has a right to succession, or seeks something which it has a legal right of ownership to, it shall put forth an action [to claim it] without the formality of titles or benefice; for the fisc can deservedly, and without causing injury through the oppression of another, demand for itself any property whatsoever, provided that during a proper hearing a judgment was rendered in its favor. And We desire, just as the Emperors willed also, that this [property] law be universal.

38 Everyone who was subject to the authority of *paterfamilias* was related to him and to one another through a relationship known as *agnatio*. Even after the death of the *paterfamilias*, agnates remained in this relationship. The agnatic system had ancient origins, and remained the basis of family legal relationships for most of Rome's history. Being an agnate had important implications in the law, especially in regards to rights and obligations concerning inheritance and guardianship. Hence, it was of vital importance to know how the agnatic relationship broke down. In the later Empire greater emphasis was accorded to cognatic relationships (i.e., those based on blood) in part no doubt because of the artificiality of the agnatic relationship. On the agnatic system in Roman law see Andrew Borkowski and Paul Du Plessis, *Textbook on Roman Law*, 3rd edn. (Oxford, 2005), 112.

39 Cognate (*cognatus*): a relative related by blood kinship, either through males or females; sometimes related through females only, as contrasted with agnates who were related exclusively through males.

40 Similarly *CTh* 5.1.9. By Caracalla's time (198–217), *caduca* were going into the imperial fisc rather than the *aerarium*, and Caracalla also apparently abolished the right of all but the closest relatives (within three degrees of kinship) to claim *caduca*. With the transfer of *caduca* from the *aerarium* to the *fiscus*, an *advocatus fisci* was created who could look out for losses to the imperial treasury. For the history see Riccardo Astolfi, *La Lex Iulia et Papia*, 2nd edn. (Padua, 1986), 250–4; Buckland, *A Textbook of Roman Law*, 319–20; Judith Evans Grubbs, *Law and Family in Late Antiquity* (Oxford, 1995), 109–10. For a specific reference in our sources involving caducous property: Cass., *Var.* 5.24.

25. DISPUTES INVOLVING A LANDHOLDER AND THE FISC MUST BE SETTLED BEFORE A JUDGE[41]

We decree that when the possession of a landholder is subject to petition by the fisc, the case must be settled before a judge exercising appropriate jurisdiction.

26. CONCERNING INTESTATE CLERICS OR RELIGIOUS PERSONS[42]

We prescribe that clerics or religious persons who become intestate whenever a lawful successor has died are to bequeath their belongings to their church in accordance with the laws.

27. IF A CURIAL DIES INTESTATE WITHOUT A SUCCESSOR[43]

If a curial dies intestate without a legally recognized successor, let his municipal council (*curia*) succeed; the fisc is excluded from making a claim.

28. CONCERNING THE LIBERTY OF TESTAMENTARY RIGHTS[44]

We grant the universal right to make a will to all whom the laws permit to do so: provided that seven or five witnesses who are freeborn and of adult age shall at his request and at the same time subscribe the document in the presence of the testator.

29. IF A TESTATOR IS EITHER ILLITERATE OR OTHERWISE UNABLE TO PROVIDE A SIGNATURE[45]

If a testator is unable to provide his signature because he is either illiterate or gravely ill, then there shall be summoned on his behalf an eighth witness whose credibility cannot be challenged in any way. But let witnesses, and particularly the testator himself, know that if, under examination [of the document], anything should be proven false, they shall not be able to avoid

[41] *ET* 25 upholds the right of private individuals in regards to claims of the fisc over caducous land, to receive a hearing before a judge exercising appropriate authority. However, it presupposes the entire issue of caducous land, which is the basis of the analogous texts – two rescripts of the Emperor Constantius (*CTh* 10.10.27, 30–1(421, 422)) that outline in detail how the matter is to be carried out.

[42] *CTh* 5.3.1. [43] *CTh* 5.2.1.

[44] *CTh* 4.4.1, 3; *CJ* 6.23.9; *Nov. Th.* 16.2; similarly *Nov. Val.* 21.1.3–4. [45] *Nov. Th.* 16.3.

the punishment which is stipulated by the authority of the laws concerning forgers.

30. CONCERNING FORGERS[46]

Moreover, let an appointed heir, legatee, or freedman[47] know that if anything of this sort is attempted through their complicity or knowledge, not only shall they be deprived of the very profit and income of that testamentary provision, but they shall not be able to avoid the penalty of forgery.[48] Anyone who makes an effort or applies himself to drafting such testaments will be guilty of this offense, since We wish the desire of the dead to remain unimpeded, and nothing should be appropriated for another's benefit because of a difference of opinion [concerning the validity of the document].

31. LET NO ONE CONTRADICT ANOTHER WHO WANTS TO MAKE A WILL

Let no one deter or contradict another who wants to make a will, or witnesses [to such a document], under any pretense: this We uphold by denying [the ability to initiate] a legal action to a contradictor even if he is the heir.

32. CONCERNING BARBARIANS WHO WISH TO MAKE A LAWFUL WILL[49]

We grant the freedom of making wills to barbarians who are known to have performed military service for the state, in any way they wish and are able, whether they are at home or at a military camp.[50]

46 Similarly *Dig.* 48.10.6 pr. (African. lib. 3 *quaest.*).

47 Freedman (*libertus*): a person who has been legally manumitted from slavery. Their manumitters became their patrons, to whom the freedmen and freedwomen owed many obligations, such as services and reverential obedience. The relationship between patron (or patroness) and freedman was one of the most interesting and arcane areas of Roman civil law. For a discussion see John A. Crook, *Law and Life of Rome* (London, 1967), who describes (p. 50) freedmen as "the nearest thing Rome ever had to a middle class." Freedom could be granted in a will, either as a direct legacy to the slave, or by way of a trust imposed on the heir or a legatee to manumit him. The most common form of manumission was by will (hence the specific reference to freedmen in the provision here). See Borkowski and Du Plessis, *Textbook on Roman Law*, 96–100.

48 *ET* 41.

49 Similarly *Dig.* 29.1.1 pr. (Ulp. lib. 45 *ad Edict.*).

50 The reference to barbarians at home or stationed in military camps is a differentiation between retired and active soldiers. See further William W. Buckland, *A Manual of Roman Private Law*, (Cambridge, 1925), 224; Thomas S. Burns, *A History of the Ostrogoths*, (Bloomington, IN, 1984), 127. On wills and will-making in Roman law in general, see Nonn, "Merowingische Testamente," 14–15.

33. CONCERNING THOSE WHO CAN INHERIT FROM ANOTHER WHO HAS DIED INTESTATE[51]

Anyone who expects an inheritance from another who has died intestate, should he have prevented the testator from making a will as he wished, let his inheritance be confiscated just as if he was unworthy (*indignus*).

34. CONCERNING THEFT, WHETHER COMMITTED BY A ROMAN OR BARBARIAN

Let no one, whether Roman or barbarian, obtain another's property which (if he acquires it through theft) he will be unable to return, and does not think he will return together with its income. Our previous edicts above ratify this with an end to preserving the law.

35. CONCERNING INFORMERS[52]

Anyone who comes forth as an informer[53] to do [what he thinks] necessary as though under the pretext of the public interest, whom nevertheless We affirm We utterly curse, shall be prohibited in accordance with the laws from being heard during a suit, although he may even be reporting factual events; nevertheless, if upon being interrogated during the proceedings he is unable to prove those things which he conveyed to public ears, let him be consumed by flames.

36. IF ANYONE PLANS TO CONTRACT AN ILLEGITIMATE MARRIAGE[54]

If anyone plans to contract an illegitimate marriage, let him not escape the thorough censure of the laws; he shall know that he has neither a just marriage nor legitimate children.

[51] *PS* 5.12.2; similarly *Dig.* 29.6.1 pr. (Ulp. lib. 48 *ad Edict.*). [52] *CTh* 10.10.2.

[53] Informer (*delator*): an individual who provided information to the imperial fisc concerning property or money that the state had a claim to (e.g., caducous property, attempted tax evasion); or a person who informed the authorities of the commission of a crime or of a plot to commit some crime, particularly the crime of high treason (*maiestas*). Such informers were held in great disrepute throughout the Empire, and subject to severe penalties if their testimony failed to convict the accused person, or if they abandoned an action before the case was ended. For legislation outlawing informers: *CTh* 10.10.12.2 (380); 28 (418 west).

[54] Similarly *CJ* 5.5.6: the analogue refers to incestuous and prohibited unions. On legitimizing illegitimate children, see Cass. *Var.* 7.40 (*formula de matrimonio confirmando et liberis legitimis faciendis*).

37. IF A WOMAN MARRIES WITHIN A YEAR OF HER HUSBAND'S DEATH[55]

No woman shall marry for a second time within a year of her husband's death; and she shall not associate herself secretly with the man to whom she shall be married after a year's time; for, in so doing she seems to have been willing to circumvent the laws. For this reason, We stipulate that each one of them is guilty of *stuprum*. We grant this complaint to children and near relatives alone so that they may carry out what is lawfully admissible in such matters.

38. CONCERNING AN ADULTERER AND AN ADULTERESS[56]

Adulterers and adulteresses, upon being convicted during a trial, shall not escape a violent death; collaborators or those knowledgeable of that crime must be punished in the same way.

39. ANYONE WHO OFFERS A HOUSE SO THAT ADULTERY MIGHT OCCUR[57]

Anyone who offers a house or dwelling so that adultery may be committed, or anyone who persuades a wife to consent to adultery, shall be punished capitally.

40. ANYONE WHO UNKNOWINGLY MAKES A FALSE ALLEGATION[58]

Anyone who unknowingly makes a false allegation shall not be held for the punishment of *falsum*.[59]

[55] *CTh* 3.8.1. On the subject of the mourning period, see Michel Humbert, *Le Remariage à Rome: Étude d'histoire juridique et sociale* (Milan, 1970), 113–31, 378–87; Susan Treggiari, *Roman Marriage: Iusti Coniuges from the Time of Cicero to the Time of Ulpian* (Oxford, 1991), 493–5; Evans Grubbs, *Law and Family*, 94.

[56] Similarly *CTh* 9.40.1. In a case of adultery concerning the wife of a soldier, Cassiodorus has Theoderic instruct the *dux* Wilitanch (whose position granted him authority over cases involving Goths), to deal with the adulterers, if proven guilty, as the laws prescribe ("sicut iura nostra praecipiunt"). Presumably, the reference here is to *ET* 38, just as the *Edict* of Athalaric (9.18.5) requires that all the statutes of the late King (Theoderic) concerning the crime of adultery be observed: "ceterum in adulteris totum districtissime volumus custodiri, quicquid divali potuit commotione decerni." For the details of the case, see Cass., *Var.* 5.33.

[57] *Dig.* 48.5.9 pr. (Papinian). [58] *PS* 1.12.2 (3).

[59] *Falsum* was a criminal act that covered any kind of forgery, falsification or counterfeiting. The fundamental statute on *falsum* was the *Lex Cornelia de falsis* by Sulla (81 BC). The statute was gradually extended to include crimes that were not originally mentioned in it. The statute was still in force by the time Justinian's *Digest* was compiled. See further Berger, *Encyclopedic Dictionary of Roman Law*, 467.

41. ANYONE WHO PRODUCES OR USES A FORGERY[60]

Anyone who produces or knowingly uses a forgery, or persuades or compels another to make one, shall suffer a capital penalty [i.e. exile].

42. ANYONE WHO DELIVERS CONFLICTING OR FALSE TESTIMONY[61]

Those who deliver conflicting or false testimony, or provide such testimony to either party [in a suit], shall be sent into exile.

43. NO ONE SHALL TRANSFER THEIR ACTIONS AT LAW TO A POWERFUL ROMAN OR BARBARIAN[62]

No one shall transfer their legal suit under any title to a powerful Roman or barbarian.[63] But if he should do this, let the litigant lose the suit, and he who receives the suit shall be compelled to bear half the value of the matter under dispute as evaluated by the fisc. We stipulate that even those who try to transfer the property in dispute to a person of this sort are to be held by this penalty, since We desire that the litigants contend with the same opportunity when the more powerful person has been removed. But after the conclusion of the case, We grant to the litigants the power of giving what they won to any person they wish.

44. NO ROMAN OR BARBARIAN IS TO STAND AS A DEFENSE LAWYER OR SUPPORTER IN ANOTHER'S TRIAL[64]

No powerful Roman or barbarian shall involve himself as a representative (*defensor*) or supporter (*suffragator*) in [another's] trial.

[60] *PS* 4.7.2: the penalty here was deportation (presupposed by *PS* 4.7.1).

[61] *PS* 5.5.5; similarly *Dig.* 22.5.16 (Paul lib. 5 *sententiarum*).

[62] *CTh* 2.13.1. Here, the compilers make the point explicit that this was prohibited whether the *potens* was Roman or barbarian: the original makes no such differentiation. For a specific case: Cass., *Var.* 4.20 (*pignoratio*).

[63] Powerful person (*potens*): a person of the higher classes, either because of his wealth or official position or both. In the later Empire such persons were renowned for plundering and oppressing the lower classes at will, and were usually able to evade punishment.

[64] *CTh* 2.13.1; similarly 2.12.6. The original applied to members of the imperial civil service, whereas here, the compilers extended the prohibition to include Roman and barbarian *potentes*.

45. NO ONE SHALL PUT TITLES ON ANOTHER'S PROPERTY OR HIS OWN[65]

Absolutely no one shall put titles [of ownership] onto another's property or his own; since it is clear that this privilege is granted to the fisc alone for properties which it holds by right or by fact.

46. IF ANYONE, UPON BEING SUMMONED BEFORE A JUDGE, PLACES TITLES [OF OWNERSHIP] ON THE PROPERTY WHICH HE POSSESSES AS A MEANS OF DEFENSE AGAINST HIS [LEGAL] OPPONENT[66]

Anyone who, upon being summoned before a judge, presumes that a title in the name of a powerful person affixed to the property which he owns will serve as a deterrent to his opponent, let him be punished with the loss of his holding or house which he has attempted to retain as owner under this fraud; and he shall not have the ability to initiate a civil action even if he is otherwise eligible to do so.

47. IF ANYONE SEIZES ESTATES WHICH ARE DESIGNATED BY TITLES AS BELONGING TO ANOTHER

But let anyone who seizes estates which are designated by titles as belonging to another be punished capitally.[67]

48. FREEDMEN, *ORIGINARII*, OR SLAVES ARE NOT TO BE HEARD AGAINST THEIR PATRONS OR CHILDREN OF SUCH PATRONS[68]

We prohibit freedmen, *originarii*, or slaves who inform against their patrons or the children of these patrons from being heard in any matter; for, persons of this sort are incapable of having a legitimate voice in civil or criminal cases

[65] Similarly *CTh* 2.14.1. In a letter written in Theoderic's name to the *saio* Triwila and the *apparitor* Ferrocinctus, Cassiodorus relates a case concerning allegations that the Praetorian Prefect Faustus had burdened the property of his neighbor, Castorius, with titles and henceforth seized it. The decision of the King was for the estate, along with another of equal value, to be returned. For details: Cass., *Var.* 3.20.

[66] *CTh* 2.14.1; *Var.* 9.18.2 (*Edict* of Athalaric). The punishment enumerated in *CTh* 2.14.1 was *infamia* for the complicit *potens*, and flogging and perpetual punishment of labor in the mines for the litigant who attempted this fraud.

[67] Since the use of titles to indicate ownership was limited to the fisc alone (*ET* 45), this provision applied exclusively to the unauthorized seizure of crown land.

[68] *CTh* 9.6.3. Here, the compilers made the point that the punishment for contravening the ban on hidden or secret accusations was capital, whereas the original did not.

involving their patrons, masters, or their children, even if they speak in their defense; those caught in the act must be cut down with swords at the commencement of the suit.

49. THIS MUST ALSO BE OBSERVED CONCERNING DOMESTIC SERVANTS (*FAMILIARII*)[69]

Moreover, We propose that this prohibition is to be observed with regard to domestic servants who, being intimately connected to another's household or home, come forth as informers or accusers; however, We except the crime of treason.

50. CONCERNING HIDDEN AND SECRET ACCUSATIONS[70]

No credence shall be given to hidden and secret accusations; but it is proper for the person who makes any [criminal] accusation to go before a judge so that if he is unable to prove that which he charges, he may be subjected to capital retribution.

51. CONCERNING THE PUBLICATION OF THE DONATIONS OF PROPERTIES[71]

We command that donations are to be made public under this formality: if moveable property of any value, or a slave, happens to be donated, the transaction shall be completed only upon delivery by the grantor; moreover, a record of the donation, which includes the signatures of witnesses, must be made public.

52. IF ANYONE BEQUEATHS A RURAL OR URBAN ESTATE[72]

But if anyone wishes to willingly make a gift of rural or urban estates, a record of the generosity, confirmed by the signatures of witnesses, shall be registered in the municipal records;[73] provided that three curials or municipal magistrates,[74] and a *defensor civitatis* on behalf of the municipal

[69] *CTh* 9.6.3. [70] *CTh* 10.10.4. [71] *CTh* 8.12.1. [72] *CTh* 8.12.8.

[73] The original specifies the office of the tax assessor. Both *ET* 126 and 144 mention this officer in particular.

[74] Municipal magistrate (*magistratus*): the head of municipalities, usually two in number, called *duumviri*.

magistrate together with three decurions or *duumviri*[75] or *quinquennales*[76] are present as witnesses for the drawing up of the records [of the gift]; but if these are not available, the registering of the transaction shall be fulfilled in another municipality which has these officials; or let a report of what was given be forwarded to the Governor of that province.

53. ON TRANSFERRING OWNERSHIP (*TRADITIO*)[77]

Concerning *traditio*, it is necessary for it to be conducted according to the laws in the district: if a municipal magistrate, *defensor*, *duumviri*, and *quinquennales* are not available, three decurions shall be sufficient for executing the records of transfers, provided that the performance of the material conveyance is carried out before knowledgeable men in the neighborhood.

54. MARRIAGES ARE NOT TO BE DISSOLVED INDISCRIMINATELY; ONLY WHEN CERTAIN CHARGES ARE PROVEN MAY COUPLES WITHDRAW FROM THE MARRIAGE[78]

We do not permit marriages to be dissolved indiscriminately. Wherefore, upon the issuance of a divorce notice, neither a wife nor husband shall withdraw from the marriage bond except on proven grounds which the laws recognize. Divorce is permitted only on the following grounds: if a wife proves in trial that her husband is a murderer, sorcerer,[79] or a violator of tombs. A husband, too, rightfully may divorce his wife who is convicted of these crimes, that is, if he is able to prove in a trial that she is an adulteress

[75] *Duumvir*: one of the two highest of the municipal magistrates. Their office was similar to the Roman Consulship, and was held for one year. In earlier times it was much sought after as an honor but in the later Empire it became burdensome and expensive and was evaded whenever possible; see below, *ET* 53.

[76] On these officers, see Halsey L. Royden, "The Tenure of Office of the Quinquennales in the Roman Professional Collegia," *American Journal of Philology* 110 (1989), 303–15.

[77] *CTh* 8.12.8. [78] *CTh* 3.16.1, 2; *Nov. Th.* 14.1. 2.

[79] Sorcerer (*maleficus*): a person who practiced the arts of the supernatural by invoking evil spells. In the *CTh*, the various terms indicating sorcerers/magicians are used almost synonymously, with little distinction except of degree and intention. The practice of magic was especially opposed by the Emperors who feared its effect would detract from their own authority. On the prohibition of magic in the *Theodosian Code*, the relevant provisions are found in 9.16 under the title *De maleficis et mathematicis et ceteris similibus* ("concerning magicians, astrologers, and all such like"). See further James B. Rives, "Magic in Roman Law: The Reconstruction of a Crime," *Classical Antiquity* 22.2 (2003), 313–39; Clyde Pharr, "The Interdiction of Magic in Roman Law," *Transactions and Proceedings of the American Philological Association* 63 (1932), 269–96, esp. 277–96. *ET* 108 prohibits the use of magic and the practice of soothsaying, and threatens anyone found guilty with the punishment of death.

(*adultera*), or sorceress (*malefica*), or what is commonly referred to as a procuress (*aggagula*). When these facts have been disclosed clearly, a husband shall both gain back the dower and receive or retain the dowry;[80] and in accordance with the laws, We order him to preserve intact property of both himself and his former wife for the children of that marriage. And in like manner, if a wife proves that her husband has been involved in the aforementioned crimes, she shall receive both the dowry and dower as profit. Moreover, she shall take back that which her husband bestowed upon her as a betrothal bounty for the benefit of the children; and in accordance with ancient customs, she shall obtain the freedom to marry again or not.

55. A JUDGE IS OBLIGATED TO HEAR ALL APPEALS[81]

Those provincial judges before whom pleas can be petitioned shall hear all appeals; since it befits their unsurpassed knowledge to hear even a superfluous appeal without hesitation,[82] provided that an ordained *cognitor*,[83] upon consideration of the laws, can render a judgment about the merit of an appeal. If a judge should secure his absence so as not to hear appellate petitions, We decree that he who intended to make an appeal must present his petition concerning the absence of the judge, and about his own appeal in well-known places. But let a judge who either refuses to hear an appeal, or at least takes the appellant into custody, or has him flogged or injured by some other grievance, be punished with the loss of ten pounds of gold; this sum We ordain to be amassed by the care of an ordained *cognitor* for the coffers of the fisc. Moreover, the office for which this is a concern will be subject to a lawful penalty.

80 *Dos*: in imperial Roman law this term always denoted the assets that the bride brought with her into the marriage. In the fourth century, it received a counterpart, *donatio nuptialis* (bride-gift), which was the groom's contribution. Eventually, through a development that is unclear, the bride-gift replaced the dowry in the western parts of the Empire. By the sixth century, the term was most commonly used to designate the bride-gift. In this provision, the term is used twice, and each time with different meanings: the first refers to the bride-gift, and the second to the traditional dowry. On the subject of the *dos* in general, see Antti Arjava, *Women and Law in Late Antiquity*, (Oxford, 1996), 52–62; Judith Evans Grubbs, "Marrying and Its Documentation in Later Roman Law," in P. L. Reynolds and J. Witte Jr. (eds.), *To Have and To Hold: Marrying and Its Documentation in Western Christendom, 400–1600* (Cambridge, 2007), 64–70.

81 *CTh* 11.30.42; 11.30.22.

82 *CTh* 11.30.42 made the same requirement that a judge was to hear even superfluous appeals – a flat contradiction of earlier prohibitions against such appeals.

83 Cognitor (*cognitor*): in this instance, a judge who held an investigating trial or cognizance. The term could also be used to refer to the Governor of a province who functioned as the judge of first instance.

56. CONCERNING THE RUSTLER OF ASSORTED ANIMALS[84]

The rustler of another's animals, flocks, and herds, whether he drives them off from stables or pastures, shall be punished by the sword; and the remuneration for the victim's loss, which is to be garnered from the property of the rustler, shall be fourfold. But if the rustler is a slave or *originarius*, his owner, upon being summoned before a judge for these crimes,[85] shall, if he prefer, either compensate [the victim] in accordance with what We have decreed above, or not delay to surrender those accused to a public judge to be punished by death.

57. IF A RUSTLER IS PROVEN TO HAVE STOLEN ANYWHERE FROM ONE STEED, TWO MARES AND THE SAME NUMBER OF COWS, TEN SHE-GOATS, AND FIVE PIGS[86]

If a rustler is proven to have stolen anywhere from one steed, two mares and the same number of cows, and as many as ten she-goats and five pigs, whether he led them away through deception or by force from a pasture or stable, he shall be punished most severely: he shall be punished for the crime of theft and pay back fourfold the number of animals or pigs mentioned above which he stole from another.

58. ANYONE WHO FINDS A COW, HORSE, OR OTHER LIVESTOCK WANDERING ABOUT[87]

Anyone who leads away a cow, horse, or other livestock wandering about must also be held guilty of the crime of theft, and he shall restore fourfold

[84] *PS* 5.18.2; similarly *Dig.* 47.14.1 pr. (Ulp. lib. 8 *de off. procons.*).

[85] Presumably, the participation of the master involved his testifying to the fact that he had no involvement in, or prior knowledge of the crime of his slave or *colonus*.

[86] *PS* 5.18.1; *Dig.* 47.14.1 pr. (Ulp. lib. 8 *de off. procons.*).

[87] *PS* 5.18.4; *Dig.* 47.14.1 pr. (Ulp. lib. 8 *de off. procons.*). While provisions like *ET* 56, 57, and 58 underscore the importance of livestock to the Ostrogothic economy, remarkably, there is no specific mention in the *ET* to the killing of animals. The silence of the compilers might be seen as perplexing, especially considering the depth of detail which the more or less contemporary Visigothic laws devoted to the matter. In the Visigothic kingdom, the killing of animals involved ninefold restitution (*LV* 7.2.23), while that of strays whose owner was unknown, a necessary repayment *in duplo* (*LV* 8.5.7). The law went so far as to provide remedy for the killing of unborn animals: when a mare was caused to miscarry, the offender had to deliver a yearling foal, but when some other animal was involved the rule was different. A cow, e.g., passed to the offender, who was required to hand over in its place a sound beast together with its calf (*LV* 8.4.5, 6). A possible explanation for the *ET*'s silence in this matter is the position of the law towards the crime of cattle rustling. As a general rule, the loss

the number of animals or livestock stolen; unless he acknowledges this fact in public or in well-known places, or before the official residence of a judge for seven continuous days since that day he found them; upon completion of this, let him not endure the detriment of any penalty.

59. ANYONE WHO FORCIBLY DEFILES A FREEBORN VIRGIN

Anyone who forcibly defiles a freeborn virgin, should he be supported by a suitable patrimony[88] and is of noble rank, shall be compelled to accept her as his wife; provided that he is of the understanding that a fifth of his patrimony is to be conferred to her under the title of a dower. But if he commits such acts while already having a wife, he shall be compelled under worthy and solemn (written) guarantee to give a third of his patrimony to that one whom he forcibly corrupted; so that she, who lost her modesty on account of him, may find a respectable husband. But the oppressor and violator of freeborn modesty shall be afflicted with the most extreme punishment if he is not supported either by a suitable patrimony or nobility.[89]

60. IF ANYONE SHOULD COMMIT *STUPRUM* AGAINST AN UNWILLING WIDOW

If anyone should commit *stuprum* against an unwilling widow, the corrupter, be him of whatever rank, shall perish under the penalty of adultery.

61. IF A WIDOWED MATRON IS DEFILED BY ANOTHER'S DEPRAVITY[90]

But if any slave commits this crime [*stuprum*], even if he does so with a willing and complicit widow, he shall be burned up by avenging flames; she,

of an animal to the actions of a rustler was considered permanent. Thus, it made no difference to an owner whether or not his animals were killed or absconded. That the compilers recognized this and accordingly treated the killing of animals in the same way as their theft seems entirely likely. The fact that the penalties reserved for cattle rustlers are on par with those faced by an individual convicted of killing another's *servus* or *rusticus* speaks to such a connection.

[88] Patrimony (*patrimonium*): a paternal inheritance.

[89] According to this, an offender could pay for his crime provided he was of sufficient means both in terms of material wealth and status to do so. Otherwise he was to be punished most severely (presumably this meant death). While this last provision finds many parallels in the Roman sources, the idea that a corrupter of freeborn chastity could escape capital punishment through the payment of a fine was in profound opposition to earlier Roman law on the subject, which generally applied the maximum penalty in all instances, regardless of the rank or wealth of the accused.

[90] *CTh* 9.24.2; 9.25.2. *CTh* 9.24.2 concerned acts of *raptus* involving a complicit virgin girl.

too, who was not ashamed to find pleasure with a slave, shall pay the penalty of adultery.

62. IF A WIDOWED MATRON IS WILLINGLY DEFILED BY A SLAVE[91]

If a widowed matron is willingly defiled by another's libidinous [slave], she has committed *stuprum*, unless she is common and low-class.[92] If anyone has intercourse with those consenting widows who are known to practice the work of a trade or service in public, neither he nor they shall be held accountable for this offense.

63. IF ANOTHER'S SLAVE OR *ORIGINARIUS* FORCIBLY DEFILES A FREEBORN VIRGIN

If another's slave or *originarius* should forcibly defile a freeborn virgin, or commit *stuprum* against a widow by force, upon the summoning of his master and when the facts of the case have been investigated and disclosed, let him be executed.

64. IF ANYONE DEFILES ANOTHER'S VIRGIN SLAVE WOMAN OR *ORIGINARIA*[93]

Any freeborn man (who is obligated to no municipality in any manner[94]), who defiles another's virgin slave woman or *originaria* of any age, and wishes to be united with her (provided the owner is also willing), he shall acknowledge this in the municipal records and remain under the authority of the woman's owner; [having done this] he shall not abandon the union with the woman he despoiled, nor be able to leave upon her death. If the owner of the slave woman does not consent, or the corruptor is unwilling to acknowledge this [in the municipal records], then he shall either give the owner two slaves of equal value should he suffer any financial loss as result of this; or, if he is unable to fulfill this, upon being flogged most severely with military rods,[95] he shall be judged by a board of magistrates of the nearest city; the

[91] *PS* 2.26.11; similarly *CJ* 9.9.22.

[92] The original, *PS* 2.26.11, qualifies this further to mean women who are known to work in taverns or inns.

[93] *Nov. Val.* 31.1.5. [94] That is, either as a decurion or guildsman.

[95] By the early Empire, the military staff, *fustis*, replaced the rods, *virgae* (traditionally carried by lictors), as the instrument of civilian beating. Beating was regarded as a rather severe sanction, principally because all forms of corporal punishment were held to be degrading. Yet, the man of small means might well find beating preferable.

judge of that place, mindful of his written statement,[96] will be obligated to ensure that this is carried out.

65. WHENEVER A FREEBORN MAN, *ORIGINARIUS*, OR SLAVE COMINGLES WITH A SLAVE WOMAN[97]

Whenever a freeborn man, *originarius*, or slave should comingle with a slave woman, it is mandatory that complete agnation follows the mother; that is, all children shall belong to the owner of the slave woman.

66. WHENEVER ANOTHER'S SLAVE OR A FREEBORN MAN COMINGLES WITH AN *ORIGINARIA*[98]

Moreover, whenever another's slave or a freeborn man comingles with an *originaria*, the children shall in the same way establish their descent from the mother.

67. IF ANOTHER'S *ORIGINARIUS* COMINGLES WITH AN *ORIGINARIA*[99]

If another's *originarius* should comingle with an *originaria*, the owner of the *originarius* shall acquire ownership over two thirds of the children, and the owner of the *originaria* a third.

68. IF AN *ORIGINARIA* FLEES FROM A FREEBORN MAN[100]

An *originaria* can be reclaimed by her former owner (ingenuous) only within a period of twenty years from the day she departed. But if after a period of twenty years has elapsed, and the *originaria* should be lost to her former owner as a result of this prescription, in keeping with the tenor of the new law any offspring which she gave birth to within this twenty year period must not be lost to her [former] owner.

[96] Written statement (*periculum*): a term denoting the written memorandum of a judicial statement. This was to be prepared and read by a judge as the valid pronouncement of his sentence. As was the case in Roman law (*CTh* 4.17), an oral pronouncement not read from a written document was deemed invalid. Praetorian Prefects were exempt from this requirement: Cass., *Var.* 6.3.3 (*formula* for the position).

[97] *CTh* 5.10.1. [98] *CTh* 6.10.1; similarly *CJ* 11.48 (47). 16; *Dig.* 1.5.19 (Cels. lib. 29 *digest.*).

[99] *CTh* 5.10.1. [100] *CTh* 5.10.1; *Nov. Val.* 31.2 (452) (referred to here as the *novella lex*).

69. IF ANYONE TAKES POSSESSION OF A DECURION, GUILD MEMBER, OR SERVANT OF THE STATE FOR A PERIOD OF THIRTY YEARS[101]

We order that decurions, guild members, or slaves that clearly have not contributed to their municipality [i.e. through the performance of compulsory public services] are to be retained by property owners who have been in possession of them for a period of thirty years; since We allow the beneficial decree of this thirty-year statute to be disturbed with respect to no one under any pretext, it is fitting that this law [of thirty years] maintain its legal force, in whatever way the laws prescribe, whether in matters involving a private citizen or the fisc. And since We know that such false accusations are frequently stirred up to the ruin of masters when rustics or decurions connive together to say that they have offered a contribution [to their municipality], We grant the following: if it is proven that a contribution was made with the knowledge of the property owner or his procurator[102] or chief tenant if the owner was overseas, this law will remain in full force.

70. IF A SLAVE SHOULD TAKE REFUGE IN A CHURCH[103]

If a slave of any nation should take refuge in a church, let him be returned immediately upon his owner promising pardon, for We forbid him from staying in that place for more than a single day. If he is unwilling to depart, the archdeacon of that church, or a priest and clerics shall compel him to return to his owner, and deliver him up without delay on the owner pardoning him. But if it happens that the abovementioned religious persons are unwilling to do this, they shall be compelled to give to the owner another slave of equal value; even the slave that remains within the retreats of the church may be claimed by his owner forthwith if he can be captured beyond church limits.

71. IF ANYONE FLEES TO A CHURCH ON ACCOUNT OF A PUBLIC DEBT[104]

If anyone flees to a church on account of a public debt, the archdeacon shall compel him to leave in order to render account according to the law; but if the debtor is unwilling to do this, let him deliver forthwith his property

[101] *Nov. Maj.* 7.1; similarly *Nov. Val.* 27.1.

[102] Procurator (*procurator*): a manager or overseer in charge of the property of another. He was usually a slave or freedman and often managed the property in the absence of his master.

[103] *CTh* 9.45.3.

[104] *CTh* 9.45.3, 5. Throughout the Empire most of the public debtors were delinquent taxpayers.

which he transferred to the church. Unless he does this, let the archdeacon be compelled to pay the debt: this is of great interest to the public good.

72. ON THE REGISTRATION OF WILLS

Testaments shall be registered as the laws[105] prescribe; in this way, the fulfillment of another's will shall not be able to falter.

73. CONCERNING THE EXECUTION OF JUDICIAL DIRECTIVES

Let office staffs carry out the directives of any judges, as well as the commands of any office or jurisdiction, provided local custom [jurisdiction] of the *civitas* is observed;[106] it is enough that the person sued promises to go before the court, and let the *apparitor* dare nothing beyond [extracting this promise].[107] And let the *apparitor* of that jurisdiction from which the precepts are issued handle the judgments. But if a *miles*[108] of another jurisdiction should attempt to implement the directive of another, let him be flogged and incur the loss of his position. And the plaintiff shall forthwith lose his case.

74. CONCERNING A DISHONEST PLAINTIFF[109]

If a plaintiff launches a wrongful lawsuit over some matter, and is refuted after a just examination, from the day the suit was formally set out the falsely accused shall receive from the plaintiff the costs and expenses of the litigation which he demonstrates he sustained when he was undeservedly sued; this shall be determined by the assessment of a judge or of knowledgeable good men appointed for that purpose. It is right that their sense of justice and deliberations determine what costs and expenses of the suit he who heedlessly led another into a public trial should pay.

105 E.g., *CTh* 4.4.1–3.

106 The phrase here, *sola publica servata civitate*, is difficult to interpret with any certainty. The fact that the *MGH* edition suggests *civilitate* as an alternative to *civitate* is indicative of the problem. *CTh* 11.7.6 (and there are other instances) uses the phrase *consuetudine servata regionum*, which seems to fit best here. An alternative reading of this phrase is: "provided the local customs of the *civitas* are observed."

107 That is, the judge cannot compel attendance.

108 *Miles*: a member of an imperial service whether it be civil or military in nature. See e.g. *CTh* 2.12.6, where the term *militans* is used to designate a member of the imperial service, either a civilian *apparitor* or a soldier. However, the Anonymous Valesianus (2.60) uses the term *militia* to describe the civil service of the Romans. As Moorhead notes (*Theoderic in Italy*, (Oxford, 1992), 71 n. 23), the term cannot possibly mean "military service."

109 *Dig.* 5.1.79 pr. (Ulp. lib. 5 *de off. procons.*). The context here suggests a civil action. For in criminal trials, under the rule of *inscriptio* (*CTh* 9.10.3) the accuser had to bind himself by a written undertaking (*inscriptionis vinculum*) to undergo the same penalty as that which faced the defendant, if proved innocent: *ET* 13.

75. ON FIGHTING ARMED MEN IF THEY COME VIOLENTLY TO A PROPERTY[110]

Moreover, anyone who with men, armed with swords, clubs, or stones, expels someone from his property, home, or villa[111] or attacks, blockades, and besieges him, and if on account of this matter he happens to furnish men of his own, or hires or assembles them and causes turmoil and insurrections and sets fire; or if through his property supplies, stations, and leads his men, and incites turmoil and insurrections and sets fire, he shall be held for the penalty of violence (which has been prescribed above).[112] If anyone prohibits a corpse from being buried, intending to claim the deceased as his debtor,[113] those who are *honestiores*[114] shall lose a third of their goods and be sent into exile for a period of five years; those who are *humiliores* shall be flogged and endure the penalty of perpetual exile.

76. CONCERNING THE RESTORATION OF THE TEMPORARY POSSESSION OF SEIZED PROPERTIES[115]

The suit regarding ownership being preserved, in accordance with the law of temporary possession,[116] property occupied through force shall be returned within one year to that one who will hold the same property (which he lost through the presumption of another) neither violently, nor clandestinely, nor with permission [by the one who ejected him in the first place].

[110] *PS* 5.26.3; similarly *Dig.* 48, 6, 3 pr. (Marcian. lib. 14 *Inst.*). 4 (Ulp. lib. 59 *ad Edict.*). The context of this seems to be illegal distraint of property because of debt. It follows *PS* quite closely, and seems to merge elements of *publica iudicia* of *vis publica* and *vis privata* (see *Dig.* 48.6, 7). The confiscation of one-third seems to belong to the latter. The Visigothic *Breviary of Alaric* combines the two under the same title but distinguishes them in chapters.

[111] Villa (*villa*): 1. a farmhouse; 2. a landed estate, often containing one or more villages, under the control of a great landholder.

[112] *ET* 9 (a capital offense).

[113] In his commentary on the *Book of Tobit* (*De Tobia*, ed. and trans. Lois M. Zucker, *De Tobia: A Commentary with an Introduction and Translation* (Washington, DC, 1933), c. 10), Ambrose of Milan mentions that the dead were sometimes denied burial until interest on any outstanding debt was paid.

[114] *Honestiores*: a term referring to members from the higher ranks of society, to be contrasted with their socially inferior counterparts, the *humiliores*. While this distinction was at first a social one, it came to take into account an increasing number of legal consequences, whereby *honestiores* could lawfully expect and demand preferential treatment in comparison with *humiliores*. These divisions appear in *ET* 83, 89, 91, 108, 145.

[115] Similarly *PS* 5.6.7; Cass., *Var.* 9.18.1 (*Edict* of Athalaric).

[116] Temporary or interim possession (*momentum*): this referred to the possession of property in dispute that is granted to one of the litigants until the case can be adjudicated; another interpretation is that this refers to property which is to be possessed immediately.

77. IF SLAVES ARE CONVICTED OF INFLICTING VIOLENCE[117]

If slaves are convicted of inflicting violence, or at the very least they confess to this, and it is proven under a just and diligent inquiry that this was committed through the instruction of the owner, when the owner has been held for the penalty of violence, any stolen incomes shall be returned; slaves, nevertheless, shall be punished by the extreme penalty if it is evident that they committed this violence through their own audacity.

78. ON STEALING A FREEBORN MAN[118]

Anyone who sells, gives away, or presumes to retain for his own service a freeborn man whom he has taken to another place by means of *plagium*, that is through solicitation, shall be put to death.

79. IF ANYONE HOLDS A FREEBORN MAN UNDER TERMS[119]

Anyone who holds a freeborn man in servitude and is unable to prove that he is [legally] bound to such a condition shall be held liable for trickery (*calumnia*) and the injuries incurred [by the victim].

80. IF ANYONE INDUCES ANOTHER'S SLAVE TO FLEE

Anyone who induces another's slave to flee shall render to the owner three others of equal value, and the original slave together with his *peculium*.[120] But if anyone is received by another under good faith whereby he claims that he is freeborn, it is necessary for the receiver to take these precautions: namely, to direct the claimant to the records offices where he can declare his freeborn status; upon completion of this, if the claimant is demanded by the owner and proven to be his slave or *originarius*, he shall be returned without any inconvenience to the one who received him [in the first place].

117 *CTh* 9.10.4; similarly *ET* 118.

118 The basis for the legal remedy stipulated here and in the following nine provisions is the *Lex Fabia*, a statute of unknown date (presumably the second or first century BC). Interestingly, in defining the term, the compilers added a few words of clarification for *plagium* ("*id est sollicitandum*") – an indication perhaps that they felt the meaning of the term was becoming, or had become, unclear at the time of their writing.

119 Similarly *CJ* 6.16.31. For a specific case: Cass., *Var.* 5.29.

120 *Peculium*: technically, the property acquired by any legally dependent person, such as a slave during his servitude or a son under the control of his father. Cassiodorus uses the term twice to refer to the property (cattle) of free persons: Cass., *Var.* 8.28, 33.

81. IF ANYONE UNKNOWINGLY PURCHASES SLAVES FROM A SLAVE TRADER (*PLAGIATOR*)[121]

If anyone unknowingly purchases slaves from a *plagiator*, he cannot be held liable for the offense of *plagium*.

82. IF A FREEBORN MAN IS SOLD[122]

If a freeborn man is sold he is not to incur the prejudice of his new status, unless perchance, being of the age of majority,[123] he kept the buyer in the dark by remaining silent about his freeborn status. For he could have brought an action against the seller in defense of himself, or injustices concerning the crime of *plagium*, except that he wanted the money that was given for him to be split between himself and the seller. In that case, he shall incur the prejudice of the condition which he created for himself through deceit and connivance.

83. ANYONE WHO CONCEALS, SELLS, OR KNOWINGLY PURCHASES A FREEBORN MAN[124]

Of those who conceal, sell, or knowingly purchase a freeborn man, *humiliores* shall be flogged and sentenced to perpetual exile; *honestiores* shall be deprived a third of their goods and shall also endure a penalty of exile for a period of five years.

84. ANYONE WHO KNOWINGLY RECEIVES ANOTHER'S FUGITIVE SLAVE OR *COLONUS*[125]

Anyone who knowingly receives or conceals another's fugitive slave or *colonus*[126] shall render to the owner that fugitive together with his (i.e. the slave's) income and *peculium*, as well as another slave of equal value. But if the one who first received the fugitive allowed him to be received

[121] *CJ* 9.20.10. [122] *Dig.* 40.13.

[123] Legal age for males in Roman law was twenty-five, although children could be released from *potestas*, through a procedure called *emancipatio*, which severed most legal ties with paternal relatives. For males, this could be granted at the age of twenty-one; for females at nineteen. See *CTh* 2.17.1, 2 (321; 324); *CTh* 2.16.2 (319). Cf. Cass., *Var.* 4.35, where minors are prohibited from entering into legal contracts of any sort – the implication being that once of age, a person was in a *de iure* position to decide any matter as they saw fit and as the law permitted.

[124] *PS* 5.30*b*.1; similarly *PS* 5.6.14. [125] *CTh* 5.9.4; similarly *CJ* 6.1.4.

[126] *Colonus*: a tenant farmer, a sharecropper, of ignoble status. Originally he was of freeborn condition, but over the course of the Empire his position gradually deteriorated until it was little better than that of a slave (*servus*). In the *ET* the two are often equated. Further references: *ET* 97, 98, 99, 109, 121, 128, 146.

for a second or third time, then that one shall render to the slave's owner three additional slaves, in addition to the fugitive along with his income. However, a slave must be tortured in examination lest perchance he has been sent by his owner to the home of the person who received him in order to cleverly and deceitfully profit; so that if through the interrogation of the one testifying it is established that he was fraudulently sent by his owner to another's home, the fisc may at once be compensated.

85. IF ANYONE RECEIVES SLAVES THAT HAVE BEEN INDUCED TO FLIGHT OR FURTIVELY TAKEN BY ANOTHER[127]

If someone knowingly receives slaves that have been induced to flight or furtively taken by another, not only must they be prosecuted concerning those received and return them, but they must also be detained to answer for the offense of theft (*actio furti*).[128]

86. ANYONE WHO DETAINS ANOTHER'S SLAVE AT HIS RESIDENCE AGAINST THE WISHES OF THE OWNER[129]

Anyone who holds another's slave at his residence against the wishes of the owner must be persecuted through an action of theft.

87. [CONCERNING] A SLAVE IN FLIGHT[130]

A slave in flight can neither be sold nor given away.

88. IF A CATTLE RUSTLER, SEDUCER (OF SLAVES), OR THIEF DIES BEFORE HE CAN BE PROSECUTED

If a cattle rustler, seducer (of slaves), or thief should die before he is convicted by the authority of a judge, his heirs shall in no way be held accountable for his offense, unless it is evident that by claiming these [stolen] things they came into possession of them.

[127] Similarly *CJ* 6.2.6; *Dig.* 11.3.11.2 (Ulp. lib. 23 *ad Edict.*).

[128] In classical law, it was a penal action in that the plaintiff could recover double or fourfold damages from the defendant, depending on the type of theft that had been committed, i.e., whether it was manifest or not. The specification is not made here.

[129] *CJ* 6.2.6. [130] *CJ* 9.20.6.

89. IF ANYONE ASSEMBLES AN ARMED FORCE ON HIS OWN BEHALF TO INCITE TERROR[131]

If anyone assembles an armed force on his behalf to terrify someone else, or assumes authority which he does not have, let those who are from the lower classes (*viliores*)[132] be flogged and endure the punishment of perpetual banishment; those who are *honestiores* shall suffer the inconveniences of exile.

90. IF ANYONE CHANGES ANOTHER'S TESTAMENT, CODICIL, RECORDS, ACCOUNTS, TRANSCRIPTS OF REGISTERED INSTRUMENTS, DOCUMENTS, BONDS, OR LETTERS FOR THE PURPOSES OF FRAUD[133]

Those who erase, change, add to or take away, burn or expunge another's testament, codicil, records, accounts, transcripts of registered instruments, documents, bonds, or letters in any place for the purposes of fraud, or give, sell, or substitute gilded bronze, silver, or iron for gold, and those who substitute tin for silver, or cut around the outer circle of a *solidus*, or those who prescribe or take pains that this may be done, shall endure the stipulated penalty for the crime of forgery.[134]

91. ANYONE WHO BRIBES WITNESSES TO COMMIT PERJURY[135]

Anyone who bribes witnesses so that they commit perjury, or at least remain silent about what they know, or suppress the truth, or those who bribe a judge so that he renders a judgment contrary to justice or not make a judgment at all, those who are *humiliores* shall be punished capitally; those who are *honestiores* shall suffer the deprivation of their possessions.[136]

[131] *PS* 5.25.12. The provision targeted individuals who assembled armed men or illegally assumed authority with the purpose of inciting terror: *humiliores* were to be flogged and exiled, and *honestiores* exiled. Whereas the compilers note the specific penalties for those *viliores* found guilty, the original simply states that they were to be punished capitally (presumably this meant exile).

[132] Synonymous with *humiliores*.

[133] *PS* 5.25.1, 5; similarly *CTh* 9.22.1. The provision classifies as *dolus* (fraud) the action of tampering with or destroying a genuine document, but treats the offense as *falsum* (forgery). An analogue to this is Constantine's law on forgery (*CTh* 9.22.1), which addresses the subject of decurions who tamper with a testament, codicil, or any will of a dying person; but applies the death penalty only in the most serious of offenses.

[134] *ET* 41 (a capital offense).

[135] *PS* 5.25.2.

[136] According to *ET* 1 and 2, the punishment for the corrupt judge in this instance could vary, depending on whether the case was capital or not. *PS* 5.25.2 stipulates that he was to be deported along with the offending *honestior*.

92. IF A BETROTHED WOMAN, UPON BEING PERSUADED BY THE ONE WITH WHOM SHE IS BETROTHED, SHOULD TAKE UP RESIDENCE WITH HIM BEFORE SHE HAS BEEN FORMALLY GIVEN AWAY IN MARRIAGE[137]

In the event that a betrothed woman, upon being persuaded by the man with whom she is betrothed, should take up residence with him before she has been formally given away in marriage, the bridegroom shall not be held criminally liable as an abductor.

93. A FATHER CANNOT BE COMPELLED TO GIVE AWAY HIS CHILD UNWILLINGLY TO ANOTHER IN MARRIAGE

A father shall not be compelled to give away his child unwillingly to another in marriage.

94. PARENTS WHO ARE COMPELLED BY NECESSITY TO SELL THEIR CHILDREN[138]

Parents who are compelled by necessity to sell their children for the sake of vital necessities shall not prejudice their *ingenuus* status; for the value of a free person is considered inestimable.

95. AND IT SHALL NOT BE PERMITTED FOR PARENTS TO GIVE AWAY THEIR CHILDREN AS A PLEDGE[139]

Moreover, parents cannot give away their children as a pledge to another; and if a creditor knowingly receives freeborn children from their parents as a pledge, he shall be sent into exile. Parents can only transfer the services of those children that are under their legal authority [*in potestate*].

[137] Similarly *CTh* 9.24.1. The context envisaged here is a *de iure* betrothal which has become a *de facto* marriage through the over-zealousness of the bridegroom, not to be confused with marriage by abduction (*raptus*) – a point which the compilers make clear.

[138] *PS* 5.1.1; similarly *CTh* 5.8.1. According to Roman law, parents might sell their children for a limited period (perhaps twenty-five years) without ultimate prejudice to their freedom: *CTh* 3.3 (391); *Nov. Val.* 33 (451). Cassiodorus notes a specific incident of parents selling their children (*Var.* 8.33). *CTh* 5.8.1, a rescript of the Emperors Valentinian II, Theodosius I, and Arcadius of 386, stipulates that a freeborn child so sold could reclaim his freedom at no cost (that is, he does not have to repay the purchase price).

[139] *PS* 5.1.1.

96. IF THOSE WHO LIVE AS FREE ARE CLAIMED AS SLAVES[140]

Anyone who while living as free is claimed as a slave shall take the part of the defendant: the burden of proof rests with the plaintiff or the one who says he is the owner, to demonstrate that this individual is his slave. But if [an enslaved] individual should claim that he is free, it is necessary for his *defensor* to prove his free status.

97. ANYONE WHO SETS FIRE TO A HOUSE, VILLA, OR DWELLING[141]

Anyone who sets fire to another's house, villa, or dwelling out of enmity, if they are a slave, *colonus*, slave woman, or *originarius*, they shall be consumed by fire. If a freeborn should do this, he shall repay any of the costs associated with the fire that he set, and he shall restore the building, and in addition, as a penalty for committing such an act, he shall be compelled to pay the value of the possessions destroyed; but if he is unable to raise this amount on account of his penury, let him be flogged and punished with the banishment of perpetual exile.

98. [CONCERNING] A FIRE THAT A SLAVE OR *COLONUS* HEEDLESSLY SETS IN HIS [OWNER'S] FIELD[142]

If, as a result of the fire heedlessly set by a slave or *colonus* in his owner's field, there is damage done to a neighbor's fruit-bearing trees, or woods, vineyards, or grainfield, or there results any loss, upon an assessment of the damage done the owner (of the one through whom a loss to the neighbor occurred) shall either repair the damages and pay compensation; or, if he chooses this alternative instead, shall deliver up to a judge the one who set the fire so that he may be punished for the faults of his deed.

[140] Similarly *Dig.* 40.12.7, 5 (Ulp. lib. 54 *ad Edict.*). *Dig.* 40.12 required that anyone who could show that a person was being held in slavery unjustly could bring a "suit for freedom" (*causa liberalis*). Enslaved persons could not bring the suit themselves; they needed to have an advocate who would bring the case for them. In Rome, the praetor heard claims for freedom; in the provinces, only the Governor could judge them.

[141] *PS* 5.20.2. The harshness of the penalty here, in comparison to that of the following provision, reflects the context for which the provision was drafted – namely an attack as opposed to an accident.

[142] *PS* 5.20.3–4.

99. ANYONE WHO KILLS A MAN OR URGES THAT HE BE KILLED WITHOUT A HEARING BEFORE A JUDGE[143]

Anyone who unjustly orders a man to be killed or urges that he be killed without a hearing before a judge, and lacking the permission or legal authority of a judge exercising the appropriate jurisdiction, shall himself be killed as one guilty of homicide.

100. ANOTHER'S SLAVE CANNOT BE TORTURED [TO TESTIFY] TO THE DETRIMENT OF ANOTHER[144]

Another's slave cannot be tortured [to testify] to the detriment of another, unless the informer or accuser, whose concern it is to prove what he claims, is prepared to stake the amount of the slave's value as determined by his owner.

101. ANYONE WHO PURCHASES A SLAVE IN ORDER TO PREVENT HIM FROM GIVING EVIDENCE UNDER TORTURE AGAINST HIM[145]

If anyone purchases a slave in order to prevent him from giving evidence under torture against him, when the payment has been returned and the sale cancelled, let the slave be forced to testify under torture against the one who fraudulently purchased him.

102. IF A SLAVE IS FREED SO THAT HE IS NOT TORTURED[146]

If a slave is freed so that he is not tortured, an interrogation under torture can in any event be held in respect to him.

103. A CRIME MUST BE PROSECUTED IN THE PLACE WHERE IT IS COMMITTED[147]

The formal accusation and prosecution of a crime is to happen in the place where the crime is alleged to have been committed. For those who are accused should not be transferred from one province to another, lest during the course of travel they are rescued or escape; and it is not a matter of

[143] *PS* 5.23.10 (11); *PS* 5.26.1. [144] *PS* 5.16.3 (*De servorum quaestionibus*). [145] *PS* 5.16.7.
[146] *PS* 5.16.9; similarly *Dig.* 48.18.1.13. [147] *Dig.* 48.2.7.4; *CTh* 9.1.10 (368).

concern if those who are reported to have committed something criminal are freeborn, freedmen, or slaves.[148]

104. CONCERNING BOUNDARIES THAT HAVE BEEN DUG UP OR TREES MARKING BOUNDARIES[149]

Those who dig up boundaries or plow up property lines,[150] specifically those which designate a perimeter, or destroy trees marking boundaries, if they are slaves or *coloni* and have acted without the consent or authority of their master, they shall be executed. If it is proven that this act was done at the owner's behest, that same owner is to be deprived of a third of his possessions to the benefit of the fisc as a requirement of the law; nevertheless, the slave or *colonus* must be punished capitally.

105. BOUNDARIES BETWEEN TWO ESTATES MUST BE OBSERVED[151]

The boundaries which the owner of different farms used to separate one property from another when he sold one of them must be observed; those which had at one time been used to separate the different farms are not to be observed.

106. CONCERNING A SUIT THAT IS COMPLETED WITH OATHS[152]

Whenever an oath is used to determine the outcome of some legal matter, whether in accordance with the consent of the litigants or the determination of the judge, the matter cannot be reconsidered; nor is it permitted for anyone to bring an action or start an inquiry concerning the possibility of perjury.[153]

148 The explanation offered here as to why a trial must take place where the alleged crime took place appears nowhere in either of the original sources. It appears to have been an addition of the compilers, as was the stipulation that it made no difference as to the status of the accused.

149 *PS* 5.22.2. In a letter written in the name of Theoderic to an unidentified illustrious *consularis*, Cassiodorus refers to such property markers and the examination thereof by a land surveyor (*agrimensor*) to settle a dispute between the neighboring *spectabiles* Leontius and Paschasius (Cass., *Var.* 3.52). See further Oswald A. W. Dilke, *The Roman Land Surveyors: An Introduction to the Agrimensores* (London, 1971), 44–6.

150 Under Roman law, a *fines* was not a simple line but a strip of land, five feet in width, that separated two properties.

151 *Dig.* 10.1.12 (Paul lib. 3 *respons.*).

152 Similarly *Dig.* 12.2.7 *in fine* (Ulpian lib. 22 *ad Edict.*); *Dig.* 42.1.56 (Ulpian lib. 27 *ad Edict.*).

153 On the subject of oath-taking in late Roman law, see Ian Wood, "Disputes in Late Fifth- and Early Sixth-century Gaul," in Wendy Davies and Paul Fouracre (eds.), *The Settlement of Disputes in Early Medieval Europe* (Cambridge, 1986), 7–22, esp. 15–18. For a further reference to oath-taking, see *ET* 119.

107. CONCERNING THE INSTIGATOR OF SEDITION[154]

Anyone who instigates sedition either among the people or in the army is to be burned alive.

108. CONCERNING THOSE WHO MAKE A SACRIFICE ACCORDING TO THE PAGAN RITE[155]

If anyone is apprehended while sacrificing according to the pagan rite, as well as diviners ([*h*]*arioli*) and necromancers (*umbrarii*) should they be discovered, upon conviction in a lawful trial they shall be punished capitally; of those individuals who are knowledgeable of the wicked arts, that is sorcerers (*malefici*), *honestiores*, upon being stripped of all their possessions that they might possess, shall be condemned to perpetual exile; and *humiliores* shall be punished capitally.

109. IF A SLAVE OR *COLONUS* SHOULD SEIZE ANYTHING VIOLENTLY WITHOUT THE KNOWLEDGE OF HIS OWNER[156]

If a slave or *colonus* should seize anything violently without the knowledge of his owner, the owner shall be sued fourfold the original amount within a year of the offense, and for the simple sum after a year; or in place of this, should the owner choose the following alternative, let him know that the offending slave or *colonus* is to be delivered up to a judge to be punished: provided that the owner return that which he came into possession of as a result of the violence of the slave. But if the one sued claims that his slave has fled, let it suffice for the claimant to seek legal satisfaction [in accordance with this provision].

110. WHOEVER DESTROYS A GRAVE[157]

Anyone who destroys a grave shall be killed.

154 *PS* 5.22.1.

155 *CTh* 16.10.6; 16.10.23. For a general history see Jocelyn N. Hillgarth (ed.), *Christianity and Paganism. The Conversion of Western Europe, 350–750* (Philadelphia, PA, 1986), 105–10; Peter Brown, *The Rise of Western Christendom. Triumph and Diversity, AD 200–1000*, 2nd edn. (Maldon, MA, 2003), 149.

156 *CJ* 3.41.4.

157 Similarly *PS* 5.19a (*Dig.* 47.12.11); *CTh* 9.17; *Nov. Val.* 23.3–4 (447). *PS* 1.21.5 defines the crime of tomb violation as damage to the tomb and punishes perpetrators with exile to an island or deportation to the mines, according to their status. Specific types of damage included (*PS* 1.21.8): the opening of a tomb, with or without breaking in, in order to introduce the body of a stranger; vandalizing inscriptions, damaging statues, stealing columns and other materials. *PS* 1.21.4 addresses

111. IF ANYONE BURIES CORPSES WITHIN THE CITY OF ROME[158]

Anyone who buries corpses within the city of Rome shall be compelled to allocate a fourth of his patrimony to the fisc; if he is destitute he shall be publicly flogged.

112. CONCERNING THE PROPERTY OF THOSE CONDEMNED FOR ANY CRIME[159]

The property of those who have been condemned for any crime[160] shall first be conferred on their children and parents, or relatives up to the third degree; but if the condemned should have no such relation as these, the fisc shall lay claim to their property.

the specific issue of profanation of the cadaver: "Anyone who strips a body that is permanently buried, or which has been deposited temporarily in some place, and exposes it to the rays of the sun, has committed a sin: and therefore, if he is an *honestior* he is usually exiled to an island; if he is a *humilior*, he is condemned to the mines." ("Qui corpus perpetuae sepulturae traditum vel ad tempus alicui loco commendatum nudaverit et solis radiis ostenderit, piaculum committit: atque ideo, si honestior sit, in insulam, si humilior in metallum dari solet.") For specific cases: Cass., *Var.* 4.34, a letter in Theoderic's name validating state-sponsored grave robbery as a means of increasing revenue. See also the case of the grave-robbing priest (Cass., *Var.* 4.18). Grave robbing and the destruction of tombs in general seem to have been a pernicious problem throughout Late Antiquity. In a letter to his nephew Secundus (III.xii.1–2), Sidonius Apollinaris recounts the violation of the tomb of his grandfather in 469. When he arrived at Clermont by the road from Lyons, he saw undertakers working at the site of his grandfather's grave, unaware what was there: "The field of burial itself had for a long time been so filled up with ashes from the pyres and with bodies that there was no more room for digging; but the earth which it is customary to pile upon the buried had spread out until the surface resumed its original flatness, the various heaps having gradually sunk down owing to the weight of snow and a long exposure to downpours of rain." At that moment, Sidonius came upon them and, in his own words, on the very spot of his grandfather's final resting place, "gave them such a beating that it would be able to provide for the care of the survivors and the security of the dead." ("... supra senis nostri ipsum opertorium torsi latrones, quantum sufficere posset superstitum curae, mortuorum securitati.") The action of the grave-diggers was, in Sidonius' opinion, a crime against the laws of the state (*publicum scelus*). Later, however, he explains that he should not have taken this initiative, but instead have handed the guilty over to the Bishop. In many of the other barbarian successor kingdoms, the exhumation and theft of grave objects constituted heinous crimes. Section 14 of the sixth-century recension of the *Pactus legis Salicae*, e.g., levied an indemnity of two hundred *solidi* against those convicted of exhuming and robbing a corpse. In addition to the heavy fine, those who did not admit their guilt faced the status of *wargus*, a term used during this period to designate an exile of the community. See, in general Éric Rebillard, *The Care of the Dead in Late Antiquity*, trans. Elizabeth Trapnell Rawlings and Jeanine Routier-Pucci (Ithaca, NY, 2009), ch. 4.

[158] *CTh* 9.17.6. [159] *CTh* 7.42.2.

[160] The implication here is a capital offense. The original source excludes the crimes of treason and magic.

113. IF A CONDEMNED CURIAL SHOULD LEAVE BEHIND CHILDREN[161]

If a condemned curial should leave behind children, they shall take possession of everything which he forfeits; if he has no children, his assets shall be conferred on the municipal council; an exception to this is the case of high treason when the precepts of the laws require that the property of all those condemned [for this crime] is to be conferred on the fisc alone and not their children (should they have any).

114. IF CLERICS OR ANY OTHERS SHOULD RELEASE A CONDEMNED PERSON[162]

If clerics or any others should forcibly release those who have been adjudged [guilty] and condemned in a criminal proceeding, they themselves shall be penalized or held liable for the fines which the judgment rendered against those convicted had stipulated; and if it is proven that this was perpetrated through the complicity or collusion of the judge, that same judge shall be compelled to pay five pounds of gold.

115. ANYONE WHO STEALS PUBLIC OR FISCAL MONEY[163]

Anyone who in their pursuit of plunder steals money belonging to the fisc or public accounts shall repay fourfold the original amount.[164]

116. IF ANYONE SHOULD RECEIVE AND KEEP PLUNDER FROM A THIEF[165]

Should anyone knowingly receive plunder from a robber (*raptor*) (that is a thief (*fur*)) for safekeeping, he shall be held to the same penalty accorded the robber.

161 *CTh* 7.42.24. 162 Similarly *CTh* 9.3.5. 163 *PS* 5.27.1.

164 Presumably the offender was subject to capital retribution in addition to the stipulated fine.

165 Similarly *CJ* 6.2.14. In classical tradition (e.g., *Dig.* 47.8.2.23 (Ulpian)), *rapina* had been nothing but *furtum* aggravated by the use or threat of violence, but the tendency in post-classical times had in fact been toward a blurring of the line which marked it off from simple theft, such as in *ET* 116. Elsewhere, however, the *ET* makes a distinction between acts of *rapina* and *furtum*, treating the thief, whose actions are defined by stealth, with far greater severity than the robber, whose actions are usually accompanied by force or menace. Generally speaking, thieves like tomb-raiders and cattle rustlers who would, we may assume, ply their trade at night or otherwise covertly were punished far more severely than the brazen robber who committed his acts openly. Compare, e.g., the capital punishment enumerated in *ET* 110 for destroying a tomb (presumably done with an end to stealing any contents), and the simple restitution stipulated in *ET* 124 for creditors who violently seize

117. IF A SLAVE SHOULD STEAL FROM [ANOTHER] OR OTHERWISE CAUSE ANOTHER TO SUFFER A LOSS[166]

If a slave should steal from [another] or otherwise cause another to suffer a loss, his owner, if he is not prepared to return or restore the equivalent of that person's property, must surrender his slave to be punished; he shall also observe this rule concerning his animals should they cause another to suffer losses.

118. IF AN OWNER IS SUED FOR THE THEFT COMMITTED BY HIS SLAVE[167]

If an owner, upon being sued for the theft committed by his slave, should elect to surrender his slave rather than defend him in a trial, he is equally enjoined to repay those things which he is proven to have acquired as a result of the theft.

119. IF ANYTHING IS LOST FROM A STABLE, SHIP, OR INN[168]

If anything is lost from an inn, [ship][169], or stable, it must be reclaimed from those who operate such places or do business in them. There is this

property of a defaulting debtor. Other barbarian peoples similarly treated robbery less severely than theft (see Heinrich Brunner, *Deutsche Rechtsgeschichete*, vol. II, completed by Claudius Frh. von Schwerin, 2nd edn. (Leipzig, 1906–28), 838–9). But it should be borne in mind that particular cases of theft or robbery were treated on their merits and punished in distinct fashion. The man who formed and led a band of robbers, for example, was punished capitally (*ET* 75). On the evolution of the concept of theft in Roman law, see Alan Watson, "The Definition of *Furtum* and the Trichotomy," *Tijdschrift voor Rechtsgeschiedenis = Revue d'histoire du droit* 28 (1960), 197–210; David Ibbetson, "The Danger of Definition: Contrectatio and Appropriation," in A. D. E. Lewis and D. Ibbetson (eds.), *The Roman Law Tradition* (Cambridge, 1994), 54–72.

166 *PS* 2.31.7. In a letter written in the name of Theoderic to the Senators of Rome recently caught up in the violence associated with rival circus factions (in connection with the Laurentian Schism), Cassiodorus has the King command that any slave accused of the murder of a free-born citizen is to be delivered up to the court by his master, under penalty of ten pounds of gold (Cass., *Var.* 1.30).

167 Similarly *Dig.* 9.4.33 (Pomp. *lib. ad Sabin.*).

168 *PS* 2.31.16. Ulpian discusses this subject at length (lib. 14 *ad edict.* (*Dig.* 4.9.1 pr.-1)): "The praetor says: 'I will give an action against seamen, innkeepers and stablekeepers in respect of what they have received and undertaken to keep safe, unless they restore it'. (1) This edict is of the greatest benefit, because it is necessary generally to trust these persons and deliver property into their custody." ("Ait praetor: 'nautae caupones stabularii quod cuiusque salvum fore receperint nisi restituent, in eos iudicium dabo'. (1) Maxima utilitas est huius edicti, quia necesse est plerumque eorum fidem sequi et res custodiae eorum committere.") As Ulpian notes, liability under this provision lay in respect of theft or damage committed by the employees of shippers, innkeepers, and stable keepers. In addition, innkeepers were liable for the acts of permanent residents but not casual guests or travelers. The distinction was justified, according to Ulpian, since the innkeeper chose his permanent residents but not passing travelers (*Dig.* 47.5.1.6).

169 Despite including this category in the title, the compilers omitted it in the provision.

provision: that if they take an oath concerning their good faith and that of their associates [regarding the matter], they shall not be compelled to pay anything; or at least, restore however much the claimant swears he lost in that place.

120. IF A SLAVE COMMITS THEFT AND IS MANUMITTED[170]

If a slave commits theft and is manumitted by his owner, or sold, or given to another, the one manumitted, or the one who purchases him, or the one to whom he was given shall then plead a case of theft; for the punishment that follows is always capital. Moreover, not only will the one who commits the theft be held liable for the act, but that one, too, through whose efforts and counsel the theft is committed, will also be held liable.

121. IF A CREDITOR LENDS MONEY TO ANOTHER'S PROCURATOR, OVERSEER, *COLONUS*, CHIEF TENANT, OR SLAVE WITHOUT THE CONSENT OR KNOWLEDGE OF THE OWNER[171]

If a creditor lends money to another's procurator, chief tenant, *colonus* or slave without the consent or knowledge of the owner, no prejudice of any kind shall be placed against the owner or his assets; the demands of the creditor shall be exacted from the *peculium* of the slave or *colonus* after deduction of what is owed to the master.

122. IF ANYONE TRANSFERS *CAUTIONES* OF THEIR DEBTORS TO A POWERFUL PERSON FOR THE PURPOSES OF COLLECTION[172]

Creditors who transfer *cautiones*[173] of their debtors to powerful persons and are more willing to secure the loan through them shall lose their claim of the debt.

123. CONCERNING THE ACQUISITION OF PLEDGES[174]

We deny an individual the permission to seize a pledge on his own unless in a credible case the presiding judge gives him the authority.

170 *PS* 2.31.8–10. 171 *CTh* 2.30.2; similarly 2.32.1.

172 *CTh* 2.13.1. The compilers ignored the moralizing reasoning for the basis of the law found in *CTh* 2.13.1 – namely the greed of the creditor.

173 *Cautio*: a written acknowledgement of debt guaranteeing that the debt will be paid back.

174 *PS* 5.26.4.

124. IF A CREDITOR SHOULD FORCIBLY SEIZE PROPERTY FROM HIS DEBTOR THAT IS NOT PLEDGED TO HIM[175]

If a creditor forcibly seizes from his debtor property that is not pledged to him, let him restore as penalty fourfold the amount previously taken if he is sued within a year of the offense being committed; but after a year, he will be obligated to pay back the simple sum. Even with respect to produce that has been forcibly removed the rule of law must also be observed.

125. IF ANYONE SHOULD REMOVE OTHER INDIVIDUALS FROM CHURCHES, THAT IS RELIGIOUS PLACES[176]

If anyone should remove other individuals from churches, that is religious places, or presumes to remove anything therein by force, let him be punished capitally.

126. NO CURIAL, TAX COLLECTOR, OR REGISTRAR SHALL ISSUE ASSIGNMENT WARRANTS (*PITTACIA* [*DELEGATIONIS*]) WITHIN A CHURCH

Hereafter no curial, registrar[177] or tax collector shall issue assignment warrants within a church; but if he recognizes someone as being a debtor to the fisc, from outside the church let him expose him [as a public debtor], or at least "delegate" [the fiscal debtor] so as to make the matter public in regards to the one who denies he is a debtor. But if anyone presumes to violently expel someone [from the church] against his will since he is a debtor and makes claims to the contrary, let him restore fourfold the amount that he has demanded.

127. NO ONE MAY BE UNWILLINGLY ASSIGNED TO A THIRD PARTY [WITH RESPECT TO A DEBT][178]

No one may be assigned unwillingly to another [with respect to a debt]; but if the person who is transferred by his creditor consents to the transfer, professes that he is in debt, and promises to repay, let him be compelled to pay what he promised.

[175] *PS* 5.26.4; similarly *Dig.* 4.2.14, 17 (Ulpian *lib. ad Edict.*). [176] Similarly *CJ* 1.12.2.

[177] Public registrar (*tabularius*): an official in charge of public records and archives, especially the records of tax accounts.

[178] Similarly *CJ* 8.41 (42).1.

128. IF A SON *IN POTESTATE*, OR A SLAVE, OR COLONUS ARE NOT DEFENDED BY THE FATHER OR OWNER AGAINST AN ACCUSATION[179]

If a son *in potestate*, or a slave, or *colonus* are not defended by the father or owner against an accusation of an offense or crime, they must be given over to a judge exercising the appropriate authority; but a son may choose to defend himself in court against an offense for which he has been sued.

129. ANYONE WHO OBTAINS SOMETHING THROUGH DECEIT OR THEFT[180]

Anyone who obtains something through deceit or theft, let him neither profit nor cause harm to another as a result.

130. IF SOMETHING IS PROMISED IN ORDER TO CATCH A THIEF[181]

That which has clearly been promised in order to catch a thief must deservedly and fittingly be paid.

131. CONCERNING THOSE WHO HAVE BEEN CONVICTED OR CONDEMNED IN COURT ON A CHARGE OF DEBT[182]

Those who have been convicted or condemned in court on a charge of debt must procure the payment within two months of the day when the judgment was rendered. If they do not do this, by the authority of a judge the property which they have pledged must be seized and sold off in accordance with the legal claim of the victor: so that what has been lawfully decided may be carried out.

132. [CONCERNING] A LANDHOLDER WHO IS SUMMONED TO APPEAR IN COURT[183]

A landholder who is summoned to appear in court shall not be compelled to set forth the legal basis for his title of ownership, nor is the burden of proof to be imposed upon him: for, it is the duty of the claimant rather, to prove how the property which he lays claim to in fact belongs to him.

179 Similarly *Dig.* 9.4.33 (Pomp. lib. 14 *ad Sab.*). 180 Similarly *CJ* 1.22.2. 181 *PS* 2.31.24, 25.
182 *PS* 5.5*a*.4; similarly *Dig.* 42.1.31 (Callistr. lib. 2 *cognit.*). 183 *CTh* 11.39.12.

133. IN THE EVENT THAT A WOMAN PROMISES BY WAY OF A GUARANTEE THAT SHE WILL REPAY ANOTHER'S DEBT

A woman is not to be held liable even if she promises by way of a guarantee that she will repay another's debt.[184]

134. ANYONE WHO EXTORTS FROM HIS DEBTOR ANYTHING MORE THAN THE 1 PERCENT ALLOWED BY LAW[185]

A creditor who presumes to demand from his debtor anything more than the 1 percent [per month] allowed by law shall forfeit his share of the debt.[186]

135. IF A GUARANTOR SHOULD ACQUIRE POSSESSION OF THE PLEDGED PROPERTY OF A DEBTOR ON WHOSE BEHALF HE HAS ASSUMED THE DEBT[187]

A guarantor who repays the creditor and acquires from him the pledged properties of the debtor on whose behalf he has made a pledge must return the pledged property to the debtor once the debt has been paid back.

136. IF ANYONE SHOULD ACQUIRE A PORTION OF HIS PROPERTY WITHOUT KNOWING THAT IT ALREADY BELONGS TO ANOTHER LANDHOLDER[188]

If anyone should acquire his property without knowing that it already belongs to another landholder, he is to suffer no prejudice; but he shall be able to bring forward an action concerning the matter of ownership.

137. IF ANYONE SHOULD ERECT AN EDIFICE ON ANOTHER'S LAND[189]

If anyone should unknowingly erect an edifice on another's land, he shall receive compensation for the costs which he incurred; but he shall forfeit ownership of that dwelling.

184 Cf. *ET* 153. 185 *CTh* 2.33.2.
186 The analogue imposed an additional fourfold fine on the rapacious creditor.
187 Similarly *CJ* 8.13 (14).21. 188 *CJ* 4.65.20. 189 Similarly *Dig.* 41.1.7.12 (Gaius lib. 2 *rer. Cott.*).

138. IF THE SAME PROPERTY IS PURCHASED BY DIFFERENT PEOPLE[190]

If the same property is purchased by different people at different times, the one who received it shall have a stronger case and shall more readily acquire ownership.

139. THE VENDOR SHALL OBSERVE THE JURISDICTION [OF THE BUYER][191]

The vendor, even if he has the privilege to claim the jurisdiction of his own court, shall nevertheless observe the jurisdiction of the buyer when he is to defend his sale.[192]

140. [A VENDOR] WHO UNDERGOES A JUDICIAL CHALLENGE CONCERNING THE PURCHASE OF PROPERTY[193]

[A vendor] who undergoes a judicial challenge concerning the purchase of property must respond to the claimant, [the purpose of which is] not to reject [the validity of the sale] on the basis of what was offered to the vendor: let him [i.e. the vendor] be mindful that he is obligated to do only this – namely, to defend his action in the sale.

141. ANYONE WHO SELLS A RUNAWAY SLAVE TO AN UNKNOWING PARTY[194]

Anyone who sells a slave with a history of escaping to another unaware of this, should the slave then flee the buyer, the vendor shall both return the payment and compensate [the buyer] for any losses he may have suffered as a result of that [fugitive] slave.

[190] *Epitome Codex Gregorianus Wisigotica* 3.6(2).4, ed. J. Baviera, *FIRA* II (Florence, 1940), 655–65.

[191] *Dig.* 5.1.49 (Paul lib. 3 *respons.*).

[192] The general principle of venue in Roman law was *actor sequatur forum rei*, that is, that the prosecutor or plaintiff, in criminal and in civil actions, had to proceed in the court which had jurisdiction over the accused or defendant (*CJ* 3.13.2 (293); *CTh* 2.1.4 (364)). In ordinary cases this meant the court within whose area the defendant was domiciled, that is, that of the Governor of the province in which the defendant lived. There were some exceptions to this rule, the most important of which was that in a criminal case, prosecution had to take place in the court within whose jurisdiction the alleged crime was committed (*ET* 103). In derogation of these general principles were rules of *praescriptio fori*, whereby soldiers, Senators, and others had privileges over where, and before whom, their cases should be conducted. Here, the vendor is explicitly prohibited from invoking any such privilege.

[193] Similarly *Dig.* 21.2.74.2. [194] *PS* 2.17.11.

142. AN OWNER SHALL BE PERMITTED TO TRANSFER HIS SLAVES, EVEN *ORIGINARII*, TO OTHER REGIONS, OR DO WHATEVER HE WANTS [IN REGARDS TO THEM][195]

An owner shall be permitted to transfer rustic slaves of each sex, even if they are *originarii*, which he possesses physically and lawfully,[196] from his properties to locales which he owns, or to enjoin them to urban services, provided that they are returned to those regions where they first departed in accordance with the will of the owner, and rightfully be considered to be members of his household staff in the city; and no judicial challenge on any grounds (for example under the opposition of origin) may arise concerning the actions and orderly arrangements of this measure. Moreover, it shall be permitted for owners of the aforementioned circumstance, under the attestation of their will, to transfer [slaves] from any portion of their land, or surrender, sell, or grant them to anyone they wish.

143. CONCERNING THE PRESERVATION OF THE PRIVILEGES OF JEWS[197]

The privileges conferred by the laws upon Jews shall be preserved: when disputes arise between those Jews who live in accordance with their own laws, they must have as judges those whom they consider to be teachers of their observance.

144. ON RECORDING THE SURETIES OF TAX RECEIPTS[198]

Those who are receivers of tax receipts, when recording the sureties of landholders, shall specifically record the names of each of the holders and their tax declaration (*professio*);[199] they shall also record the amount of money they receive. But if anyone should be unwilling to record the tax assessment of the property, the names of the owners, and sum of the money

[195] Similarly *Nov. Val.* 35.18. The provision addresses a scenario in which great landowners, facing acute labor shortages, pooled workers from several areas and transferred others from domestic duties in town to agricultural labor.

[196] The same distinction drawn between lawful and physical ownership is found in *ET* 45.

[197] Similarly *CTh* 16.8.13. We are told by Cassiodorus that on at least one other occasion Theoderic reaffirmed this privilege to the Jews of Milan (Cass., *Var.* 4.33).

[198] *CTh* 12.6.18; similarly *Nov. Val.* 1.3. On the subject of tax liability: Cass., *Var.* 1.14; 2.17; 4.14; 5.26–7; 6.24; 7.45; 8.26; Walter Goffart, *Barbarians and Romans: Techniques of Accommodation, AD 418–584* (Princeton, NJ, 1980), 60–102; Sam J. Barnish, "Taxation, Land and Barbarian Settlement in the Western Empire," *PBSR* 54 (1986), 170–95 Fabien Thibault, "L'impôt direct dans les royaumes des Ostrogoths, des Wisigoths et des Burgundes," *RHDFE* 25 (1901), 699–728.

[199] *Professio*: see Walter Goffart, "From Roman Taxation to Mediaeval Seigneurie: Three Notes," *Speculum* 47 (1972), 165–87, 170.

received in making these sureties, and is proven guilty of this offense in court, he shall be compelled to pay fourfold the amount of the money which the landholder proves he paid.[200] It is equally appropriate that this precept be observed concerning *discussores*[201] if, when publishing sureties concerning any titles, they are unwilling to record how much money they received from would-be possessors or those in arrears.

145. IF A BARBARIAN SHOULD REFUSE TO APPEAR IN COURT AFTER BEING SUMMONED FOR A THIRD TIME

If any barbarian, upon being summoned for a third time by the authority of a judge exercising the appropriate jurisdiction, and duly called upon by judicial directives refuses to come to the judge by whose command he has been summoned, he shall deservedly receive a sentence of contempt after examination of the case; and moreover he shall be judged to have lost the case concerning which he was summoned. There must be these conditions: that either the reliability of the guarantee issued by the defendant shows, or the testimony of freeborn and honorable men confirms, that he who was summoned for the third time was one of the *capillati*; and that it is clearly obvious to those giving testimony that he who lost by judicial decree disdained to give a response and had no wish to come before the court.

200 The compilers made the point explicit that the taxpayer was to prove the amount which he claims he brought to the office of tax collector or receiver. This requirement does not appear in the original source (*CTh* 12.6.18).

201 In the later Empire, it was the task of the officers of the Privy Purse to employ more stringent means of coercing recalcitrant taxpayers and enforcing the collection of arrears. *Exactores*, *compulsores*, and *discussores* were sent out from the palace as representatives of the Count of the Privy Purse (*CTh* 8.8.7), armed with extraordinary powers that allowed them abundant opportunities for fraud and oppression. Of all these, those most open to corruption were the *discussores*, officers who were responsible for discovering and collecting arrears of taxation. By demanding old tax receipts which had been lost (*CTh* 11.26.2; Amm. Marc., 26.6.17), by over-exaction (*CTh* 11.8), by tampering with the census lists (*Nov. Just.* 30.3), the *discussor* was in a position to oppress the provincials for great personal profit. In the ordinary scheme of things these officers were appointed on a regular basis (*Nov. Val.* 1.3), and normally people would not be very willing to undertake so onerous a task, but in the later Empire, as the administration became increasingly incapable of effectively managing its affairs, the position became highly sought after by individuals looking to profit at the expense of taxpayers (*Nov. Val.* 3.1; and *CTh* 8.8.9). In legislation of the Emperor Valentinian of 369, *discussores* were compelled to refund whatever the amount they had illegally exacted on fictitious claims (*CTh* 11.26.1); this restitution was quadrupled by a law of Honorius (*CTh* 13.11.11), who also prohibited *discussores* from demanding old tax receipts that had been registered in the public records (*polyptycha*) but were subsequently lost by the taxpayer (*CTh* 11.26.2). For discussion on the corruption of late imperial governments, see George R. Monks, "The Administration of the Privy Purse," *Speculum* 32 (1957), 748–79, esp. 763–5; Peter Heather, *The Fall of the Roman Empire: A New History of Rome and the Barbarians* (Oxford, 2006), 100–110.

146. CONCERNING STOLEN PRODUCE[202]

Both a *colonus* and owner can bring forward an action concerning produce stolen from the property, since this matter is a concern for each.

147. CONCERNING SALES EXERCISED IN GOOD FAITH[203]

A sale agreed upon in good faith and concluded cannot be challenged by the vendor; but he may demand from the buyer any outstanding payment.

148. CONCERNING SLAVES OR *COLONI* RETURNED FROM THE ENEMY[204]

Slaves or *coloni* that have been captured by enemies and returned shall be restored to their owner: provided that another did not already purchase them when they were sold by enemies in a valid transaction (*commercium*).[205]

149. CONCERNING PUBLIC MEASURES AND WEIGHTS[206]

If, while matters of the fisc are being carried out, a [tax] collector or receiver should use a greater measure or heavier weight than what the long-standing regulation of public ordination has established, he shall at once be led to court[207] along with his measures and weights; so that, if he is convicted in regards to their imbalance, he may thereupon pay fourfold the value of the goods he fraudulently received in favor of the one he superexacted. Moreover, We decree that this must also be observed in regards to private businessmen should it be proven that they used improper weights or measures in the course of their transactions.[208]

150. NO ONE MAY EXERCISE CONTROL OVER ANOTHER'S FARMHAND OR OX

Let no one demand work or service from another's farmhand (*rusticus*) without the consent of the owner, or to make use of his slave or ox unless

[202] *PS* 2.31.30. [203] Similarly *CJ* 4.44.3; *CTh* 3.1.7. [204] Similarly *CJ* 8.50 (51).10.

[205] The reference to sale here would seem to reflect the caveat in the second half of *CJ* 8.50 (51).10 in the clause "si . . . ancilla nec commercio redempta est."

[206] *CTh* 11.8.1. 3; similarly *Nov. Maj.* 7.1.15 (458). In a letter (*Var.* 5.39) written in the name of Theoderic concerning various misdeeds of revenue officers in Spain, Cassiodorus states that the land-tax collectors are accused of using false weights in collecting the quotas of produce from provincials. Cf. Cass., *Var.* 9.12.

[207] Presumably by the *defensor civitatis*, as stipulated in the corresponding imperial decree (*CTh* 11.8.3).

[208] The application of this provision to private businessmen was an addition made by the compilers.

that farmhand, or his chief tenant or owner willingly offers this. Anyone who contradicts this precept shall give [the owner] one gold *solidus*[209] for every day he so imposed burdens on [his] farmhand or ox without permission.

151. CONCERNING A DAMAGED CROP OR FELLED TREE[210]

If another's crop or tree is destroyed, or any loss results from someone's cunning, fourfold the amount of damages shall be awarded [the victim] in the name of the person who did this.

152. IF A PERSON'S SLAVE IS KILLED BY SOMEONE ELSE

If a person's slave or farmhand is killed by someone else, his owner shall have the power either to act according to criminal procedure concerning the death of his slave and accuse[211] the murderer of a criminal offense; or, in accordance with civil procedure, propose an action concerning the loss of his dead slave, in such a way that he shall receive two slaves of the same value as that of the murdered slave.

153. A WIFE CANNOT BE SUED IN THE PLACE OF HER HUSBAND[212]

A wife must not be sued in place of her husband; in accordance with the prudence and moderation of the laws, only his property or espousal largesse shall be demanded for his financial liability.

154. CONCERNING THE LORD'S DAY AND THE DAYS OF EASTER[213]

We order that no one is to be sued on the day of the sun, which is called the Lord's Day,[214] as well as the days of Easter; anyone who contradicts this precept shall be considered guilty of sacrilege.

[209] *Solidus*: the standard gold coin, 1/72 of a Roman pound. [210] *PS* 2.31.24.

[211] The term *accusare* is used here in connection with laying a criminal charge. Elsewhere, the compilers are not so technical.

[212] Similarly *CJ* 4.12.2. [213] *CTh* 2.8.18; 8.8.4.

[214] This is a specific reference to Constantine's purposeful identification in *CTh* 2.8.18 between the pagan day for the worship of the sun and the Lord's Day of the Christians.

Epilogue

We have brought together these [edicts], advantageous to all barbarians as well as Romans, as much as Our labors could permit or We could address at this time; all loyal barbarians and Romans must abide by them. Those matters which either the brief scope of the *Edict,* or [Our] attention to [other] public business have prevented Us from including are to be settled as they arise by the usual path of the laws. Let no one with any rank, wealth, power, office, or honor presume in any way to oppose these beneficial precepts. We have gathered these laws to some extent from recent law (*lex*) and the sanctity of ancient Roman custom (*ius*). And all judges and those who pronounce the law shall know that if they allow these edicts to be violated in any way, they shall be deservedly struck by the punishment of proscription and exile. But if it happens that a person of considerable influence or his procurator, deputy, or even chief tenant, whether barbarian or Roman, does not allow the present edicts (which have been decreed for the good of all) to be heeded in a case of some kind, and the judge involved is unable to withstand or prevent this, let that judge, if he has his own interests at heart, draw up an account of everything, lay aside any appearance of fear, and without delay send a report to Us. Only in this way can he be absolved of blame. For it is the duty of the whole to uphold that which has been provided for the security of all provincials.

Bibliography

PRIMARY SOURCES

Ambrose, *DeTobia*, ed. and trans. Lois M. Zucker, *De Tobia: A Commentary with an Introduction and Translation* (Washington, DC: The Catholic University of America Press, 1933).

Ambrosiaster, *Quaestiones Veteris et Novi Testamenti cxxvii*, ed. A. Souter, *CSEL* 50 (Vienna: Verlag der Österreichischen Akademie der Wissenschaften, 1908).

Ammianus Marcellinus, *Res Gestae*, ed. and trans. John C. Rolfe. *Ammianus Marcellinus: Res Gestae* 3 vols. Loeb Classical Library (Cambridge, MA: Harvard University Press, 1935–40).

Anonymi Valesiani pars posterior, ed. Theodor Mommsen, *MGH AA* 9 (Berlin, 1892; repr. Munich, 1981); trans. John C. Rolfe, *Ammianus Marcellinus: Res Gestae*, vol. 3., Loeb Classical Library (Cambridge, MA: Harvard University Press, 1940).

Appendices Legis romanae visigothorum, ed. Johannes Baviera, *FIRA*, vol. II, Auctores, 2nd edn., (Florence: S.A.G. Barbèra, 1940).

Augustine of Hippo, *Confessions*, ed. James J. O'Donnell, 3 vols. (Oxford University Press, 1992).

Aurelius Victor, *Liber de Caesaribus = Sexti Aurelii Victoris Liber de Caesaribus*, ed. Franciscus Pichlmayr (Leipzig: Teubner, 1911); trans. H.W. Bird, *Sextus Aurelius Victor: Liber de Caesaribus*, Translated Texts for Historians 17 (Liverpool University Press, 1994).

Boethius, *Consolatio Philosophiae*, ed. L. Bieler, *CCSL* 94, 2nd edn. (Turnhout: Brepols, 1984).

Cassiodorus, *Historia ecclesiastica tripatita*, ed. W. Jacob and R. Hanslik, *CSEL* 71 (Vienna: Verlag des Österreichischen Akademie des Wissenschaften, 1952).

Variae, ed. Theodor Mommsen, *MGH AA* 12 (Berlin: Weidmann, 1894); trans. (partial) Thomas Hodgkin, *The Letters of Cassiodorus Being a Condensed Translation of the Variae Epistolae of Magnus Aurelius Cassiodorus Senator* (London: Henry Frowde, 1886); trans. (select) Sam. J. Barnish, *The Variae of Cassiodorus Senator*, Translated Texts for Historians (Liverpool University Press, 1992).

Cassius Dio, *Historia Romana*, ed. and trans. Earnest Cary, *Dio's Roman History*, 9 vols. Loeb Classical Library (Cambridge, MA: Harvard University Press, 1914–27).

Cicero, *Pro Caecina*, ed. and trans. H. Grose Hodge, Loeb Classical Library (Cambridge, MA: Harvard University Press, 1927).

Codices Latini Antiquiores. A Palaeographical Guide to Latin Manuscripts Prior to the Ninth Century I–XI plus supplement, ed. E. A. Lowe (Oxford University Press, 1934–71).

Concilia Galliae a. 511-a. 695, ed. C. De Clercq, *CCSL* (Turnhout: Brepols, 1963).

Concilium Epaonense, ed. C. De Clercq, *CCSL* 148A (Turnhout: Brepols, 1963).

Corpus Inscriptionum Latinarum. ed. Theodor Mommsen *et al.* 16 vols. and supplements (Berlin: G. Reimerum, 1862–).

Corpus Iuris Civilis, ed. Paul Krueger and R. Schoell, 3 vols. (Berlin: Weidmann, 1912–22).

Cyprian, Firminus, Viventius, Messianus, and Stephen, *Vita Caesarii Arelatensis* (*BHL*, 1508–9), ed. Germain Morin, *S. Caesarii episcapi Arelatensis opera omnia*, 2 vols. (Maredsous, Belgium, 1957–42, repr. in *CCSL* 1–3 and 104 (Turnhout: Brepols, 1953)).

Edictum Theoderici regis, ed. Friedrich Bluhme, *MGH Leges nationum Germanicarum* 5 (Hannover: Hahn, 1889), 149–70; repr. by J. Baviera, *FIRA*, vol. II (Florence: S. A. G. Barbèra, 1940), 683–710; repr. Pier Luigi Falaschi, *Edictum Theoderici regis Italiae* (Milan: Giuffrè, 1966).

Ennodius, *Epistulae*, ed. and trans. Stéphane Gioanni, *Ennode de Pavie: Lettres*. vol. 1: Livres I et II (Paris: Les Belles Lettres, 2006).

Magni Felicis Ennodii Opera, ed. Friedrich Vogel, *MGH AA* 7 (Berlin: Weidmann, 1885).

Panegyricus dictus clementissimo regi Theoderico, ed. and trans. Christian Rohr, *Der Theoderich–Panegyricus des Ennodius. MGH* Studien und Texte 12 (Hannover: Hahnische Buchhandlung, 1995).

Epistolae Theodericianae Variae, ed. Theodor Mommsen, *MGH AA* 12 (Berlin: Weidmann, 1894), 387–92.

Vita Epiphanii, ed. W. Hartel, *CSEL* 6 (Ennodius, *Opera*) (Vienna: Verlag der Österreichischen Akademie der Wissenschatter, 1882).

Epitome Codex Gregorianus Wisigotica, ed. J. Baviera, *FIRA* vol. II (Florence: S. A. G. Barbèra, 1940).

Ferrandus Diaconus, *Vita s. Fulgentii*, ed. and trans. G.–G. Lapeyre (Paris: Belles Lettres, 1929).

Fragmenta Vaticana, ed. J. Baviera, *FIRA* vol. II (Florence: S. A. G. Barbèra, 1940), 463–540.

Gaetano Marini, *I Papiri Diplomatici* (Rome: Stampira della sac. Congr. de Prop. Fide, 1805).

Gai Institutionum Epitome, ed. J. Baviera, *FIRA* vol. II (Florence: S.A.G. Barbèra, 1940), 229–57.

Gelasius I, *Epistulae*, ed. Andreas Thiel, *Epistulae Romanorum Pontificum genuinae et quae ad eos scriptae sunt a S. Hilaro usque ad Pelagium*, vol. I (Brausnberg: Peter, 1868; repr. New York, 1974).

Gregory of Tours, *Decem Libri Historiarum*, ed. Bruno Krusch and Wilhelm Levison, *MGH SRM* 1.1, 2nd edn. (Hanover: Hahn, 1951); trans.

Lewis Thorpe, *Gregory of Tours: The History of the Franks* (London: Penguin Books, 1974).

Gregory the Great, *Dialogi*, ed. U. Moricca, *Gregorii Magni dialogi libri IV*. Fonti per la storia d'Italia 57 (Rome, 1924; repr. Turin, 1960).

Registrum epistolarum, ed. Paul Ewald, and Ludo Moritz Hartmann, *MGH Epistolae* 1–2, 2 vols. (Berlin: Weidmann, 1887–99); trans. John R. C. Martyn, *The Letters of Gregory the Great*, 3 vols. (Toronto: Pontifical Institute of Mediaeval Studies, 2004).

Inscriptiones Latinae Selectae, ed. Hermann Dessau, 3 vols. (Berlin: Weidmann, 1974).

Isidore of Seville, *Historia Gothorum Wandalorum Sueborum*, ed. Theodor Mommsen, *MGH AA* 11 (Berlin: Weidmann, 1894).

John Malalas, *Chronographia*, ed. Ludwig Dindorf (Bonn, Habelt: 1831); trans. (with new material and improved apparatus) Elizabeth Jeffreys, Michael Jeffreys, and Roger Scott (eds.), *The Chronicle of John Malalas* (Melbourne: Australian Association for Byzantine Studies, 1986).

John of Antioch, ed. and trans. Sergei Mariev, *Ioannis Antiocheni Fragmenta Quae Supersunt Ommia* (Berlin: Walter de Gruyter & Co., 2008).

Jordanes, *Romana et Getica*, ed. Theodor Mommsen, *MGH AA* 5.1 (Berlin: Weidmann, 1882).

Leges Visigothorum, ed. K. Zewmer, *MGH Leges* vol. 1. (Hannover: Hahn, 1902).

Lex Baiuvariorum, ed. E. Van Schwind, *MGH Leges* vol. 2 (Hannover: Hahn, 1926).

Lex Romana Burgundiorum, ed. F. Bluhme in *MGH Leges* vol. 3 (Hannover: Hahn, 1863), 675–9.

*Lex Romana Visigothorum (*or *Breviarium Alarici)*, ed. G. Haenel (Leipzig: Teubner, 1849; repr. Aalen: Scientia, 1962), 33–456.

Lex Salica, ed. K. A. Eckhardt, *MGH Leges nationum Germanicarum* 4–2 (Hannover: Hahn, 1969).

Libanius, *Orations*, ed. R. Foerster, *Libanii opera*, 4 vols. (Leipzeg: Teubner, 1903–8); ed. and trans. A. F. Norman, *Selected works* II (Cambridge, MA: Harvard University Press, 1977).

Liber Constitutionum, ed. L. R. von Salis, *MGH Leges nationum Germanicarum* I (Hannover: Hahn, 1902), 1–122.

Liber historiae Francorum, ed. B. Krusch, *MGH SRM* vol. 2 (Hannover: Hahn, 1888), 215–328.

Maximus of Turin, *Sermones*, ed. and trans. Boniface Ramsey, *Ancient Christian Writers* 50 (Mahwah, NJ: Newman Press, 1989).

Mosaicarum et Ramanorum Legum Collatio, ed. J. Baviera, *FIRA* vol. II (Florence: S. A. G. Barbèra, 1940), 544–89.

Notitia Dignitatum omnium tam civilium quam militarium, ed. Otto Seeck (Berlin: Weidmann, 1876; repr. Frankfurt, 1962).

Novellae, ed. Rudolf Schoell and Wilhelm Kroll, *Corpus Iuris Civilis*, 3 (Berlin: Weidmann, 1895; repr. 1967).

Novellae ad Theodosianum pertinentes, ed. Paul M. Meyer and Theodor Mommsen (Berlin: Weidmann, 1905).

Pactus Legis Salicae, ed. K. A. Eckhardt, *MGH Leges nationum Germanicarum* 4.1 (Hannover: Hahn, 1962).

Patrologiae Cursus Completus, Series Latina, ed. Jacques-Paul Migne (Paris: Garnieri Fratres, 1844–91).

Pauli Sententiae, ed. J. Baviera, *FIRA*, vol. II (Florence: S.A.G. Barbèra, 1940; repr. 1964), 319–417.

Pliny, *Natural History*, ed. J. Newsome (Oxford: Clarendon Press, 1964).

Procopius, *History of the Wars*, ed. J. Haury, and trans. H. B. Dewing, 5 vols., Loeb Classical Library (Cambridge, MA: Harvard University Press, 1914–28).

The Anecdota or Secret History, ed. J. Haury, and trans. H. B. Dewing, Loeb Classical Library (Cambridge, MA: Harvard University Press, 1935).

Ravennas Anonymus, *Cosmographia*, ed. Joseph Schnetz, *Itineraria Romana*, vol. 2: *Ravennatis Anonymi Cosmographia* (Leipzig, 1929–40; repr. Berlin: De Gruyter, 1990).

Regesta Pontificum Romanorum, 2 vols., ed. Phillippe Jaffé (repr. Graz: Akademische Druck –u. Verlag, 1956).

Regulae Ulpiani, ed. Paul Krüger, Theoder Mommsen, and Wilhelm Studemund, *Collectio Librarum Iuris Anteiustiniani* vol. 2 (Berlin: Weidemann, 1878).

Salvian, *De Gubernatione Dei Libri VIII*, ed. F. Pauly, *CSEL* 8 (Vienna: Verlag der Österreichischen Akademie der Wissenschaften, 1883).

Sidonius Apollinaris, *Epistulae et Carmina*, ed. Christian Lütphanne, *MGH Auctor*, vol. VIII (Berlin: Weidemann, 1887).

Theodoret of Cyrrhus, *Historia Ecclesiastica*, ed. L. Parmentier, *GCS* 44, 2nd edn. (Berlin: Akedemie-Verlag, 1954).

Theodosiani libri XVI cum constitutionibus Sirmondianis et Leges Novellae ad Theodosianum Pertinentes, ed. Theodor Mommsen, Paul Meyer, and Paul Krueger, 2 vols. (Berlin, Weidmann: 1905; repr. 1971).

Tituli ex corpore Ulpiani, ed. and trans. J. T. Abdy and Bryan Walker, *The Commentaries of Gaius and Rules of Ulpian* (Cambridge University Press, 1885).

Zeno of Verona, *Tractatus*, ed. B. Löftstedt, *CCSL* 22 (Turnhout: Brepols, 1971).

SECONDARY SOURCES

Alchermes, Joseph, "Spolia in Roman Cities of the Late Empire: Legislative Rationales and Architectural Reuse," *Dumbarton Oaks Papers* 48 (1994), 167–78.

Alföldi, Maria R., "Il medaglione d'oro di Teodorico," *Rivista italiana di Numismatica e scienze affini* 80 (1978), 133–41.

Alfödy, Geza, *The Social History of Rome*, trans. David Braund and Frank Pollock (Baltimore, MD: Johns Hopkins University Press, 1988).

Amory, Patrick, *People and Identity in Ostrogothic Italy, 489–554*, Cambridge Studies in Medieval Life and Thought: Fourth Series (Cambridge University Press, 1997).

"The Meaning and Purpose of Ethnic Terminology in the Burgundian Laws," *Early Medieval Europe* 2 (1993), 1–28.

Andaloro, Maria, "Tendenze figurative a Ravenna nell'età di Teodorico," in *Teoderico il Grande e i Goti d'Italia: atti del XIII Congresso internazionale di studi sull'Alto Medioevo, Milano 2–6 novembre 1992* (Spoleto: Centro italiano di studi sull'alto Medioevo, 1993), 555–83.

Ando, Clifford, "Decline, Fall, and Transformation," *Journal of Late Antiquity* 1.1 (2008), 31–60.

Andreolli, Bruno, "La corvée precarolinga," in *Le prestazioni d'opera nelle campagne italiane del Medioevo* (Bologna: Loescher, 1987), 15–33.

Arjava, Antti, "Divorce in Later Roman Law," *Arctos* 22 (1988), 5–21.

"Paternal Power in Late Antiquity," *JRS* 88 (1998), 147–65.

"The Survival of Roman Family Law After the Barbarian Settlements," in Ralph W. Mathisen (ed.), *Law, Society and Authority in Late Antiquity* (Oxford University Press, 2001), 33–51.

Women and Law in Late Antiquity (Oxford University Press, 1996).

Arthur, Paul and H. Patterson, "Local Pottery in Southern Puglia in the Sixth and Seventh Centuries," in L. Saguì (ed.), *Ceramica in Italia:* VI-VII *secolo. Atti del convegno in onore di J.W. Hayes*, May 11–13, 1995. Arch. Medievale 14 (Florence: All'insegna del giglio, 1998), 511–30.

Ashburner, Walter, "Farmer's Law. I," *JHS* 30 (1910), 68–108.

"Farmer's Law. II," *JHS* 32 (1912), 68–95.

Astolfi, Riccardo, *La Lex Iulia et Papia*, 2nd edn. (Padua: Antonio Milani, 1986).

Atzeri, Lorena, *Gesta senatus Romani de Theodosiano publicando. Il Codice Teodosiano e la sua diffusione ufficiale in Occidente* (Berlin: Duncker & Humblot, 2008).

Auerbach, Erich, *Literary Language & Its Public in Late Antiquity and in the Middle Ages* (Princeton University Press, 1993).

Bagnall, Roger S., *Egypt in Late Antiquity* (Princeton University Press, 1993).

Baldwin, Barry, "Illiterate Emperors," *Historia* 38 (1989), 124–6.

Barnes, Timothy, *Constantine and Eusebius* (Cambridge, MA: Harvard University Press, 1981).

Barnish, Sam J., "Pigs, Plebeians and *Potentes*: Rome's Economic Hinterland, c. 350–600 AD," *PBSR* 55 (1987), 157–85.

"Sacred Texts of the Secular: Writing, Hearing, and Reading Cassiodorus' *Variae*," *Studia Patristica* 38 (2001), 362–70.

"Taxation, Land and Barbarian Settlement in the Western Empire," *PBSR* 54 (1986), 170–95.

"The *Anonymous Valesianus* II as a source for the last years of Theoderic," *Latomus* 42 (1983), 572–96.

The Variae of Cassiodorus Senator, Translated Texts for Historians (Liverpool University Press, 1992).

"Transformation and Survival in the Western Senatorial Aristocracy, *c.* AD 400–700," *PBSR* 56 (1988), 120–55.

Barnwell, Paul S., "Emperors, Jurists and Kings: Law and Custom in the Late Roman and Early Medieval West," *Past and Present* 168 (2000), 6–29.

Emperors, Prefects and Kings: The Roman West, 395–565 (London: Duckworth, 1992).

Bartlett, Richard, "The Dating of Ennodius' Writings," in Edoardo D'Angelo (ed.), *Atti della Seconda Giornata Ennodiana* (Naples: Pubblicazioni del Dipartimento di Filologia Classica dell'Università degli Studi di Napoli Federico II, 2003), 53–74.

Bauman, Richard A., *Crime and Punishment in Ancient Rome* (London: Routledge, 1996).

"*Leges Iudiciorum Publicorum*," in H. Temporini (ed.), *Aufstieg und Niedergang der römischen Welt* ii., 13 (Berlin: Walter de Gruyter & Co., 1980; repr. 1994), 103–233.

Beaucamp, Joëlle, *Le statut de la femme à Byzance (4e-7e siècles) vol. 1, Le droit impérial* (Paris: De Boccard, 1990).

Becker, Hans-Jürgen, "Edictum Theoderici," in *Handwörterbuch zur deutschen Rechtsgeschichte* 1 (Berlin: E. Schmidt, 1971), 801–3.

Berger, Adolf, *Encyclopedic Dictionary of Roman Law*, vol. 43, part 2 (Philadelphia, PA: The American Philosophical Society, 1953).

Bianchi Fossati Vanzetti, Maria (ed.), *Pauli Sententiae. Testo e interpretatio* (Padua: Cedam, 1995).

Bierbrauer, Volker, *Die Ostgotischen Grab- und Schatzfunde in Italien* (Spoleto: Centro italiano di Studi sull'Alto Medioevo, 1975).

Bjornlie, Shane, "What Have Elephants to Do with Sixth-Century Politics? A Reappraisal of the 'Official' Governmental Dossier of Cassiodorus," *Journal of Late Antiquity* 2.1 (2009), 143–71.

Bonnassie, Pierre, *From Slavery to Feudalism in South-Western Europe*, trans. Jean Birrell (Cambridge University Press, 2009).

Borkowski, Andrew and Paul Du Plessis, *Textbook on Roman Law*, 3rd edn. (Oxford University Press, 2005).

Boswell, John, *The Kindness of Strangers: The Abandonment of Children in Western Europe from Late Antiquity to the Renaissance* (New York: Pantheon Books, 1988).

Bovini, Giuseppe, "Note sul presunto ritratto musivo di Giustiniano in S. Apollinare Nuovo di Ravenna," *Annales Universitatis Saraviensis. Philosophie, Lettres* 5 (1956), 50–3.

Bradley, Keith R., *Slaves and Masters in the Roman Empire: A Study in Social Control* (Oxford University Press, 1987).

Brogiolo, Gian Pietro, "Dwellings and Settlements in Gothic Italy," in Sam J. Barnish and Federico Marazzi (eds.), *The Ostrogoths from the Migration Period to the Sixth Century: An Ethnographic Perspective* (Woodbridge: Boydell Press, 2007), 113–33.

Brown, Peter, *Power and Persuasion in Late Antiquity: Towards a Christian Empire* (Madison: University of Wisconsin Press, 1992).

Society and the Holy in Late Antiquity (Berkeley, CA: University of California Press, 1982).

The Body and Society: Men, Women and Sexual Renunciation in Early Christianity (New York: Columbia University Press, 1988).

The Making of Late Antiquity (Cambridge University Press, 1978).

"The Rise and Function of the Holy Man in Late Antiquity," *JRS* 61 (1971), 80–101.

The Rise of Western Christendom. Triumph and Diversity, AD *200–1000*, 2nd edn. (Maldon, MA: Blackwell, 2003).

The World of Late Antiquity: AD *150–750*, rev. edn. (London: Thames and Hudson, 1989).

The World of Late Antiquity: From Marcus Aurelius to Muhammad (London: Thames and Hudson, 1971).

Brown, Thomas S., "Everyday Life in Ravenna under Theoderic: an Example of his 'Tolerance' and 'Prosperity'?," in *Teoderico il Grande e i Goti d'Italia: atti del XIII Congresso internazionale di studi sull'Alto Medioevo, Milano 2–6 novembre 1992* (Spoleto: Centro italiano di studi sull'alto Medioevo, 1993).

Gentlemen and Officers: Imperial Administration and Aristocratic Power in Byzantine Italy, AD *554–800*, (Rome: British School at Rome, 1984).

Brunner, Heinrich, *Deutsche Rechtsgeschichte*, vol. I, 1906; vol. II completed by Claudius Frh. von Schwerin, 2nd edn., (Leipzig: Systematisches Handbuch der deutschen Rechtswissenschaft, 1906–28).

Forschungen zur Geschichte des deutschen und französischen Rechtes (Stuttgart: Scientia-Verl., 1894).

Zur Rechtsgeschichte der römischen und germanischen Urkunde, I, Das Privaturkunde Italiens; das angelsächischen Landbuch; die fränkische Privaturkunde (Berlin: Weidmann, 1880).

Brunt, Peter A., *Italian Manpower 225* BC–AD *14* (Oxford: Clarendon Press, 1971).

Buckland, William W., *A Manual of Roman Private Law* (Cambridge University Press, 1925).

The Roman Law of Slavery (Cambridge University Press, 1908).

Burdese, Alberto, *Manuale di diritto pubblico romano* (Turin: UTET, 1987; repr. 1994).

Burdon, Joan, "Slavery as a Punishment in Roman Criminal Law," in Léonie Archer (ed.), *Slavery and Other Forms of Unfree Labor* (London: Routledge, 1988), 68–85.

Burns, Thomas S., *A History of the Ostrogoths* (Bloomington, IN: Indiana University Press, 1984).

"Calculating Ostrogothic Population," *Acta Antiqua Academiae Scientiarum Hungaricae* 26 (1978), 457–64.

Bury, James B., *History of the Later Roman Empire*, 2 vols. (New York: Dover Publications, Inc., 1958).

Cameron, Averil, *Procopius and the Sixth Century* (London: Duckworth, 1985).

The Later Roman Empire, AD *284–430* (Cambridge, MA: Harvard University Press, 1993; repr. 2001).

The Mediterranean World in Late Antiquity, AD *395–600* (London: Routledge, 1993).

Caner, Daniel, *Wandering, Begging Monks: Spiritual Authority and the Promotion of Monasticism in Late Antiquity* (Berkeley, CA: University of California Press, 2002).

Cesa, Maria, "Odoacre nelle fonti letterarie dei secoli V e VI," in Paolo Delogu (ed.), *Le invasioni barbariche nel meridione dell'impero: Visigoti, Vandali, Ostrogoti: atti del convegno svoltosi alla Casa delle culture di Consenza dal 24 al 26 luglio 1998* (Soveria Mannelli: Rubbettino, 2001), 41–59.

Chadwick, Henry, *Boethius: The Consolations of Music, Logic, Theory, Philosophy* (Oxford: Clarendon Press, 1981).

Cherry, David, "Intestacy and the Roman Poor," *Traditio* 64 (1996), 155–72.

Christensen, Arne Søby, *Cassiodorus, Jordanes and the History of the Goths: Studies in a Migration Myth* (Copenhagen: Museum Tusculanum Press, University of Copenhagen, 2002).

Christie, Neil, *From Constantine to Charlemagne. An Archaeology of Italy* AD *300–800* (Aldershot: Ashgate, 2006).

Chrysos, Evangelos, "De Foederatis Iterum," in Walter Pohl (ed.), *Kingdoms of the Empire: The Integration of the Barbarians in Late Antiquity* (Leiden/New York: Brill 1997), 185–206.

"Justinian and the Senate of Rome under Ostrogothic Rule," *Byzantina Symmeikta* 15 (2008), 33–8.

Cimma, Maria R., *L'episcopalis audientia nelle constituzioni imperiali da Costantino à Giustiniano* (Turin: Giappichelli, 1989).

Clark, Gillian, *Women in Late Antiquity. Pagan and Christian Lifestyles* (Oxford University Press, 1993).

Classen, Peter, "Fortleben und Wandel spätrömischen Urkundenwesens im frühen Mittelalter," in Peter Classen, *Recht und Schrift im Mittelalter*, Vorträge und Forschungen 23 (Sigmaringen: Thorbecke, 1977), 13–54.

"Kaiserrescript und Königsurkunde: Diplomatische Studien zum römisch-germanischen Kontinuitätsproblem," *Archiv für Diplomatik* 1 (1955), 1–87; 2 (1956), 1–115.

"Spätrömischen Grundlagen mittelalterlichen Kanzlein," (1974), repr. J. Fleckenstein (ed.), *Ausgewählte Aufsätze von Peter Classen*, Vortäge und Forschungen 28 (Sigmaringen: Thorbecke, 1983), 67–84.

Claude, Dietrich, "Comes," *Reallexikon der germanischen Altertumskunde* 5 (New York/Berlin: Walter de Gruyter & Co., 1982), 65–7.

Der Handel im westlichen Mittelmeer während des Frühmittelalters. Abhandlungen der Akademie der Wissenschaften in Göttingen, Phil.-hist. Kl. III 144 (Göttingen: Abhandlungen der Academie der Wissenschaften, 1985).

"Freedmen in the Visigothic Kingdom," in E. James (ed.), *Visigothic Spain: New Approaches* (Oxford University Press, 1980), 159–88.

Clavadetscher, Otto P., "Churrätien im Übergang von der Spätantike zum Mittelalter nach den Schriftquellen," *Vortäge und Forschungen* 25 (Sigmaringen: Thorbecke, 1979), 159–78.

Clemente, Guido, *La Notitia Dignitatum*, Saggi di storia e letterature 4 (Cagliari: Editrice Sarda Fossataro, 1968).

Coates-Stephens, Robert, "The Walls and Aqueducts of Rome in the Early Middle Ages, AD 500–1000," *JRS* 88 (1998), 167–78.

Cohen, David, "The Augustan Law on Adultery: The Social and Cultural Context," in David Kertzer and R. P. Saller (eds.), *The Family in Italy from Antiquity to the Present* (New Haven, CT: Yale University Press, 1991), 109–26.

Collins, Roger, "Law and Ethnic Identity in the Western Kingdoms in the Fifth and Sixth Centuries," in Alfred P. Smyth (ed.), *Medieval Europeans: Studies in Ethnic Identity and National Perspectives in Medieval Europe* (New York: Palgrave MacMillan, 1998), 1–28.

Visigothic Spain (London: Routledge, 2004).

Contreni, John, *Carolingian Learning, Masters and Manuscripts* (Aldershot: Ashgate, 1992).

Coon, Lynda, *Sacred Fictions: Holy Women and Hagiography in Late Antiquity* (Philadelphia, PA: University of Pennsylvania Press, 1997).

Cooper, Kate, *The Fall of the Roman Household* (Cambridge University Press, 2007).

Corbett, Percy E., *The Roman Law of Marriage* (Oxford: Clarendon Press, 1930).

Corcoran, Simon J., *The Empire of the Tetrarchs: Imperial Pronouncements and Government* AD *284–324* (Oxford: Clarendon Press, 1996).

Costambeys, Marios, "Burial Topography and the Power of the Church in Fifth- and Sixth-Century Rome," *PBSR* 69 (2001), 169–89.

Croke, Brian, "AD 476: The Manufacture of a Turning Point," *Chiron* 13 (1983), 81–119.

Count Marcellinus and his Chronicle (Oxford University Press, 2001).

Crook, John A., *Law and Life of Rome* (London: Thames and Hudson, 1967).

"Women in Roman Succession," in B. Rawson (ed.), *The Family in Ancient Rome: New Perspectives* (Ithaca, NY: Cornell University Press, 1986), 58–82.

Csillag, Pal, *The Augustan Laws of Family Relations* (Budapest: Akademiai Kiado, 1976).

Dahn, Felix, *Die Könige der Germanen: Das Wesen des ältesten Königsthums der germanischen Stämme und seine Geschichte bis auf die Feudalzeit*, 4 vols. (Leipzig: Teubner, 1879).

Daube, David, "The Preponderance of Intestacy in Rome," *Tulane Law Review* 35 (1964–5), 253–62.

Deichmann, Friedrich Wilhelm, *Ravenna: Hauptstadt des spätantiken Abendlandes*, vol. 1 (Wiesbaden: F. Steiner, 1969).

Delbrueck, Richard, *Die Consulardiptychen und verwandte Denkmäler*, 2 vols. (Berlin: Walter de Gruyter & Co., 1929).

Deliyannis, Deborah M., "The Mausoleum of Theoderic and the Seven Wonders of the World," *Journal of Late Antiquity* 3.2 (2010), 365–85.

Delmaire, Roland, *Les Institutions du Bas-Empire romain, de Constantin à Justinien*, 1, *Les Institutions palatines* (Paris: Cerf, 1995).

Demandt, Alexander, *Die Spätantike: Römischen Geschichte von Diocletian bis Justinian 284–565 n. Chr.*, Müller's Handbuch, vol. 3, part 6 (Munich: C. H. Beck, 1989; repr. 2007).

De Martino, Francesco, "Il colonato fra economia e diritto," in *Storia di Roma, III: L'età tardoantica. I. Crisi e transformazioni* (Turin: Einaudi, 1993), 789–822.

De Sainte Croix, Geoffrey E. M., *The Class Struggle in the Ancient Greek World: From the Archaic Age to the Arab Conquests* (London: Duckworth, 1981; repr. New York, 1989).

Desanti, Lucetta, "Costantino, il ratto e il matrimonio riparatore," *SDHI* 52 (1986), 195–217.

Dietl, Albert, *Defensor civitatis: der Stadtpatron in romanischen Reliefzyklen Oberitaliens* (Munich: Fink, 1998).

Di Giuseppe, Helga, "La Fornace di Calle di Tricarico," in L. Saguì (ed.), *Ceramica in Italia: VI-VII secolo. Atti del convegno in onore di J. W. Hayes* (Rome, May 11–13, 1995) Arch. Medievale 14 (Florence: All'insegna del giglio, 1998), 735–52.

Dilke, Oswald A. W., *The Roman Land Surveyors: An Introduction to the Agrimensores* (London: David & Charles plc, 1971).

Dopsch, Alfons, *The Economic and Social Foundations of European Civilization*, trans. M. G. Beard and N. Marshall (London: K. Paul, Trench, Trubner, & Co., 1937; repr. Berlin, 1969).

D'Ors, Alvaro, *El Código de Eurico* (Madrid: Rivadengra, 1960).

Duby, Georges and Michelle Perrot, *A History of Women in the West, vol. II: Silences of the Middle Ages* (Cambridge, MA: Harvard University Press, 1992).

Dupont, Clémence, "Les Donations dans les constitutions de Constantin," *RIDA* 9 (1962), 291–324.

Le Droit criminel dans les constitutions de Constantin, i. Les Infractions (Lille: Imprimerie Morel et Corduant, 1953).

Le Droit criminel dans les constitutions de Constantin, ii. Les Peines (Lille: Imprimerie Morel et Corduant, 1955).

Durliat, Jean, "Cité, impôt et intégration des barbares," in Walter Pohl and H. Reimitz (eds.), *Strategies of Distinction: the Construction of Ethnic Communities, 300–800* (Leiden: Brill, 1998), 153–79.

"Le salaire de la paix sociale dans les royaumes barbares," in Herwig Wolfram and Andreas Schwarcz (eds.), *Anerkennung und Integration: zu den wirtschaftlichen Grundlagen der Völkerwanderungszeit 400–600* (Vienna: Verlag der Österreichischen Akademie der Wissenschaften, 1988), 17–70.

Effros, Bonnie, *Caring for Body and Soul: Burial and the Afterlife in the Merovingian World* (University Park, PA: Penn State University Press, 2002).

Ensslin, Wilhelm, "Beweise der Romverbundenheit in Theoderichs des Grossen Aussen – und Innenpolitik," in *Settimane di studio del Centro italiano di studi sull'alto medioevo*, 3 (Spoleto: Presso la sede del Centro, 1956), 509–11.

"Rex Theodericus inlitteratus?" *Historisches Jahrbuch* 60 (1940), 391–6.

Theoderich der Grosse, 2nd edn. (Munich: F. Bruckmann, 1959).

Evans Grubbs, Judith, "Abduction Marriage in Antiquity: A Law of Constantine (*CTh* IX. 24. 1) and its Social Context," *JRS* 79 (1989), 59–83.

"Hidden in Plain Sight: *Expositi* in the Community," delivered at the vth Roman Family Conference: Secrets de familles, familles secretes: mémoire et identité familiales (Université de Fribourg, June 15, 2007), SSRN, 1–17.

Law and Family in Late Antiquity (Oxford: Clarendon Press, 1995).

"'Marriage More Shameful than Adultery': Slave-Mistress Relationships, 'Mixed Marriages', and Late Roman Law," *Phoenix* 47 (1993), 125–54.

"Marrying and Its Documentation in Later Roman Law," in P. L. Reynolds and J. Witte Jr. (eds.), *To Have and To Hold: Marrying and Its Documentation in Western Christendom, 400–1600* (Cambridge University Press, 2007), 64–70.

Women and the Law in the Roman Empire: A Sourcebook on Marriage, Divorce, and Widowhood (London: Routledge, 2002).

Everett, Nicholas *Literacy in Lombard Italy c 568–774* (Cambridge University Press, 2003).

Fanizza, Lucia, *L'Assenza dell'Accusato nei Processi di Età Imperiale*, Studi Juridice 85 (Rome, Università di Bari/Bretschneides, 1992).

Fantham, Elaine, "*Stuprum*: Public Attitudes and Penalties for Sexual Offenses in Republican Rome," *EMC/CV NS* 10 (1991), 267–91.

Finley, Moses I., *Ancient Slavery and Modern Ideology* (Harmondsworth: Penguin, 1980).

Fischer-Drew, Katherine, *Law and Society in Early Medieval Europe. Studies in Legal History* (London: Variorum, 1988).

"Law, German: Early Germanic Codes," in J. R. Strayer (ed.), *Dictionary of the Middle Ages*, vol. 7 (New York: Charles Scribner's Sons, 1986), 468–75.

"The Barbarian Kings as Lawgivers and Judges," in R. S. Hoyt (ed.), *Life and Thought in Early Middle Ages* (Minneapolis, MN: University of Minnesota Press, 1967), 7–29.

"The Germanic Family of the *Leges Burgundionum*," *Mediaevalia et Humanistica* 15 (1963), 5–14.

Fouracre, Paul, "'Placita' and Disputes in Later Merovingian Francia," in Wendy Davies and Paul Fouracre (eds.), *The Settlement of Disputes in Early Medieval Europe* (Cambridge University Press, 1986).

"Space, Culture and Kingdoms in Early Medieval Europe," in Peter Linehan and Janet Nelson (eds.), *The Medieval World* (New York: Routledge, 2003), 366–80.

Frakes, Robert M. *Contra Potentium Iniurias: The Defensor Civitatis and Late Roman Justice* (Munich: Beck, 2001).

"Late Roman Social Justice and the Origins of the *Defensor Civitatis*," *The Classical Journal* 89 (1994), 337–48.

"Some Hidden *Defensores Civitatum* in the *Res Gestae* of Ammianus Marcellinus," *ZSS (RA)* 109 (1992), 526–32.

Frank, Richard I., "Augustus' Legislation on Marriage and Children," *California Studies in Classical Antiquity* 8 (1975), 41–52.

Fridh, Åke, *Terminologie et formules dans les Variae de Cassiodore: étude sur le développement du style administratif aux derniers siècles de l'antiquité* (Stockholm: Almqvist & Wiksell, 1956).

Frye, David, "Gundobad, the *Leges Burgundionum* and the Struggle for Sovereignty in Burgundy," *Classica et Mediaevalia* 41 (1990), 199–212.

Fuchs, Siegfried, *Kunst der Ostgotenzeit* (Berlin: Walter de Gruyter & Co., 1944).

Fuenteseca, Pablo, "Maternum patrimonium (Revisión de CTh. 8,18,1 y 8,18,2)," *Atti dell'Accademia Romanistica Costantiniana:* IX *Convegno internazionale* (Naples: Edizioni scientifiche italiane, 1993), 331–47.

Ganshof, François L. (ed.), *The Carolingians and the Frankish Monarchy*, trans. Janet Sondheimer (Ithaca, NY: Cornell University Press, 1971).

Ganz, David, "Bureaucratic Shorthand and Merovingian Learning," in Patrick Wormald with Donald Bullough and Roger Collins (eds.), *Ideal and Reality in Frankish and Anglo-Saxon Society* (Oxford University Press, 1983), 58–75.

Gardner, Jane, *Women in Roman Law, and Society* (Bloomington, IN: Indiana University Press, 1986).

Gardner, Jane and Thomas Wiedemann, *The Roman Household. A Sourcebook* (London: Routledge, 1991).

Garnsey, Peter, *Social Status and Legal Privilege in the Early Empire* (Oxford: Clarendon Press, 1970).

Garnsey, Peter and Richard P. Saller, *The Roman Empire: Economy, Society and Culture* (Berkeley, CA: University of California Press, 1987).

Gaudemet, Jean, *La formation du droit séculier et du droit de l'Église aux* IV*e et* V*e siècles*, 2nd edn. (Paris: Sirey, 1979).

"Le mariage en droit romain: *iustum matrimonium*," in Jean Gaudemet (ed.), *Sociétés et mariage* (Strasbourg: Cerdic, 1980), 46–103.

Gaudenzi, Augusto, *Gli editti di Teodorico e di Atalarico nel Diritto Romano nel Regno degli Ostrogoti* (Bologna: Loescher, 1884).

Gaupp, Ernst Theodor, *Die germanischen Ansiedlungen und Landtheilungen in den Provinzen des römischen Westreiches* (Breslau: Josef Max, & Co., 1844).

Geary, Patrick, "Peasant Religion in Medieval Europe," *Cahiers d'Extrême Asie* 12 (2001), 185–209.

Giardina, Andrea, *Aspetti della burocrazia nel Basso Impero* (Rome: dell'Ateneo & Bizzari, 1977).

L'Italia romana: Storie di un'identità incompiuta (Rome and Bari: Laterza, 1997).

(ed.), *Società romana e impero tardoantico* (Rome and Bari: Laterza, 1986).

"The Family in the Late Roman World," in Averil Cameron, Bryan Ward-Perkins and Michael Whitby (eds.), *The Cambridge Ancient History,* vol. 14: *Late Antiquity: Empire and Successors,* AD *425–600* (Cambridge University Press, 2000), 392–415.

Gibbon, Edward, *The History of the Decline and Fall of the Roman Empire*, 6 vols., ed. and abbr. Hans-Friedrich Mueller, Modern Library (Toronto and New York: Random House, 2003).

Gillett, Andrew, *Envoys and Political Communication in the Late Antique West, 411–533* (Cambridge University Press, 2003).

"The Purposes of Cassiodorus' *Variae*," in A. C. Murray (ed.), *After Rome's Fall: Narrators and Sources of Early Medieval History. Essays Presented to Walter Goffart* (University of Toronto Press, 1998), 37–50.

Goetz, Hans-Werner, Jörg Jarnut, and Walter Pohl (eds.), *Regna and Gentes: The Relationship between Late Antique and Early Medieval Peoples and Kingdoms in the Transformation of the Roman World* (Leiden/New York: Brill, 2003).

Goffart, Walter, *Barbarians and Romans: Techniques of Accommodation,* AD *418–584* (Princeton University Press, 1980).

Barbarian Tides: The Migration Age and the Later Roman Empire (Philadelphia, PA: University of Pennsylvania Press, 2006).

Caput and Colonate. Towards a History of Late Roman Taxation (University of Toronto Press, 1974).

"From Roman Taxation to Mediaeval Seigneurie: Three Notes," *Speculum* 47 (1972), 165–87.

Greatrex, Geoffrey, "Lawyers and Historians in Late Antiquity," in Ralph W. Mathisen (ed.), *Law, Society and Authority in Late Antiquity* (Oxford University Press, 2001), 148–61.

Grieser, Heike, *Sklaverei im spätantiken und frühmittelalterlichen Gallien (5.-7. Jh.): das Zeungis der christlichen Quellen* (Stuttgart: F. Steiner, 1997).

Grey, Campbell Ainsworth, "Contextualizing *Colonatus*: The *Origo* of the Late Roman Empire," *JRS* 97 (2007), 155–75.

"Revisiting the 'Problem' of *agri deserti* in the Late Roman Empire," *JRA* 20 (2007), 362–76.

Grodzynski, Denise, "Ravies et coupables: Un essai d'interprétation de la loi 9,24,1 du Code Théodosien," *MEFRA* 96 (1984), 697–726.

Grundmann, Herbert, "Litteratus-illiteratus," *Archiv für Kulturgeschichte* 40 (1958), 1–65.

Guarino, Antonio, *Storia del diritto romano* (Naples: E. Jovene, 1996).

Hahn, Wolfgang, *Moneta Imperii Byzantini*, 3 vols. (Vienna: Verlag der Österreichischen Akademie der Wissenschaften, 1973).

Haldon, John F., *Byzantium in the Seventh Century: The Transformation of a Culture* (Cambridge University Press, 1990).

Halsall, Guy, *Barbarian Migrations and the Roman West, 376–568*, Cambridge Medieval Textbooks (Cambridge University Press, 2007).

Hannestad, Knud, *L'évolution des ressources agricoles de l'Italie du quatrième au sixième siècle de notre ère*. Historisk-filosofiske Meddelelser af det Koneglige Danske Videnskabernes Selskab 40/41 (Copenhagen: The Royal Danish Society of Sciences and Letters, 1962).

Harper, Kyle, "Slave Prices in Late Antiquity (And in the Very Long Term)," *Historia* 59 (2010), 206–38.

Slavery in the Late Roman World, AD *275–425* (Cambridge University Press, 2011).

Harries, Jill, *Law and Crime in the Roman World* (Cambridge University Press, 2007).

Law and Empire in Late Antiquity (Cambridge University Press, 1999).

"Resolving Disputes: The Frontiers of Law in Late Antiquity," in Ralph W. Mathisen (ed.), *Law, Society and Authority in Late Antiquity* (Oxford University Press, 2001), 68–82.

Sidonius Apollinaris and the Fall of Rome AD *407–485* (Oxford: Clarendon Press, 1994).

"The Roman Imperial Quaestor from Constantine to Theodosius II," *JRS* 78 (1988), 148–72.

"'Not the Theodosian Code': Euric's Law and Late Fifth-Century Gaul," in Jill Harries and Ian Wood (eds.), *The Theodosian Code. Studies in the Imperial Law of Late Antiquity* (London: Duckworth, 1993), 39–51.

"Violence, Victims, and the Legal Tradition in Late Antiquity," in H. A. Drake (ed.), *Violence in Late Antiquity: Perceptions and Practices* (Burlington, VT: Ashgate, 2006), 85–102.

Harries, Jill and lan Wood (eds.), *The Theodosian Code. Studies in the Imperial Law of Late Antiquity* (London: Duckworth, 1993).

Harris, William V., "The Roman Father's Power of Life and Death," in Roger. S. Bagnall and William V. Harris (eds.), *Studies in Roman Law in Memory of A. A. Schiller* (Leiden: Brill, 1986), 81–95.

Hartmann, Ludo Moritz, *Geschichte Italiens im Mittelalter*, 2 vols. (Leipzig: G.H. Wigand, 1897; repr. 1923).

Heather, Peter, "*Gens* and *Regnum* among the Ostrogoths," in Hans-Werner Goetz, Jörg Jarnut, and Walter Pohl (eds.), *Regna and Gentes: the Relationship Between Late Antique and Early Medieval Peoples and Kingdoms in the Transformation of the Roman World* (Leiden/New York: Brill, 2003), 88–133.

Goths and Romans, 332–489 (Oxford: Clarendon Press, 1991).

"Literacy and Power in the Migration Period," in A. K. Bowman and Greg Woolf (eds.), *Literacy and Power in the Ancient Roman World* (Cambridge University Press, 1994), 177–97.

"Merely an Ideology? – Gothic Identity in Ostrogothic Italy," in Sam. J. Barnish and Federico Marazzi (eds.), *The Ostrogoths from the Migration Period to the Sixth Century: An Ethnographic Perspective* (Woodbridge: Boydell Press 2007), 31–60.

"State, Lordship and Community in the West (c. AD 400–600)," in Averil Cameron, Bryan Ward-Perkins, and Michael Whitby (eds.), *Cambridge Ancient History*, vol. 14, 2nd edn. (Cambridge University Press, 2000), 437–68.

The Fall of the Roman Empire: A New History of Rome and the Barbarians (Oxford University Press, 2006).

The Goths (Oxford: Blackwell, 1996).

"Theoderic, King of the Goths," *Early Medieval Europe* 4.2 (1995), 145–73.
Heather, Peter and John Matthews, *The Goths in the Fourth Century* (Liverpool University Press, 1991).
Hen, Yitzhak, *Culture and Religion in Merovingian Gaul,* AD *481–751* (Leiden/New York: Brill, 1995).
Hillgarth, Jocelyn N. (ed.), *Christianity and Paganism. The Conversion of Western Europe, 350–750* (Philadelphia, PA: University of Pennsylvania Press, 1986).
Hoeflich, Michael H., "Regulation of Judicial Misconduct from Late Antiquity to the Early Middle Ages," *Law and History Review* 2 (1984), 79–104.
Honoré, Tony, "Ausonius and Vulgar Law," *Iura* 35 (1984), 79–82.
"Conveyances of Land and Professional Standards in the Later Empire," in Peter Birks (ed.), *New Perspectives in the Roman Law of Property. Essays for Barry Nicholas* (Oxford University Press, 1989), 137–52.
Emperors and Lawyers (London: Duckworth 1981).
"Roman Law AD 200–400: From Cosmopolis to Rechtstaat?" in Simon Swain and Mark Edwards (eds.), *Approaching Late Antiquity. The Transformation from Early to Late Empire* (Oxford University Press, 2004), 109–32.
"Some Quaestors of the Reign of Theodosius II," in Jill Harries and Ian Wood (eds.), *The Theodosian Code. Studies in the Imperial Law of Late Antiquity* (London: Duckworth, 1993), 68–94.
Tribonian (London: Duckworth, 1978).
Ulpian: Pioneer of Human Rights (Oxford University Press, 1982; repr. 2002).
Howard-Johnson, James and Paul Antony Hayward (eds.), *The Cult of Saints in Late Antiquity and the Middle Ages: Essays on the Contribution of Peter Brown* (Oxford University Press, 1999).
Humbert, Michel, *Le Remariage à Rome: Étude d'histoire juridique et sociale* (Milan: Giuffrè, 1970).
Humfress, Caroline, "Judging by the Book: Christian Codices and Late Antique Legal Culture," in William E. Klingshirn and Linda Safran (eds.), *The Early Christian Book* (Washington, DC: The Catholic University of America Press, 2007), 141–58.
Orthodoxy and the Courts in Late Antiquity (Oxford University Press, 2007).
"Poverty and Roman Law," in Margaret Atkins and Robin Osborne (eds.), *Poverty in the Roman World* (Cambridge University Press, 2006), 183–203.
Humphries, Mark, "From Emperor to Pope? Ceremonial, Space, and Authority in Rome from Constantine to Gregory the Great," in Kate Cooper and J. Hillner (eds.), *Religion, Dynasty, and Patronage in Early Christian Rome, 300–900* (Cambridge University Press, 2007), 21–58.
Ibbetson, David, "The Danger of Definition: Contrectatio and Appropriation," in A. D. E. Lewis and D. Ibbetson (eds.), *The Roman Law Tradition* (Cambridge University Press, 1994), 54–72.
Innes, Matthew, "Land, Freedom and the Making of the Medieval West," *Transactions of the RHS* 16 (2008), 39–74.

James, Edward, *The Origins of France: From Clovis to the Capetians, 500–1000* (London: MacMillan, 1989).

Jenal, Georg, *Italia ascetica atque monastica. Das Asketen- und Mönchtum in Italien von den Anfängen bis zur Zeit der Langobarden (c.a. 150/250–604)*, 2 vols. (Stuttgart: Hiersemann, 1995).

Johnson, Mark J., "Toward a History of Theoderic's Building Program," *Dumbarton Oaks Papers* 42 (1988), 73–96.

Johnston, David, *Roman Law in Context* (Cambridge University Press, 1999).

Jolowicz, Herbert F., and Barry Nicholas, *A Historical Introduction to the Study of Roman Law*, 3rd edn. (Cambridge University Press, 1972; repr. 2008).

Jones, Allen E., *Social Mobility in Late Antique Gaul: Strategies and Opportunities for the Non-Elite* (Cambridge University Press, 2009).

Jones, Arnold H. M., "Slavery in the Ancient World," in Moses I. Finley (ed.), *Slavery in Classical Antiquity* (Cambridge University Press, 1960), 1–15.

"The Caste System in the Later Roman Empire," in Peter Brunt (ed.), *The Roman Economy* (Oxford University Press, 1974), 396–418.

"The Constitutional Position of Odoacer and Theoderic," *JRS* 52 (1962), 126–30.

The Later Roman Empire, 284–602: A Social, Economic and Administrative Survey, 3 vols. (Oxford: Blackwell, 1964).

"The Roman Civil Service (Clerical and Sub-Clerical Grades)," *JRS* 39 (1949), 38–55.

Jones, Michael E., *The End of Roman Britain* (Ithaca, NY: Cornell University Press, 1996).

"The Legacy of Roman Law in Post-Roman Britain," in Ralph W. Mathisen (ed.), *Law, Society and Authority* (Oxford, 2001), 45–57.

Jones, Philip J., "L'Italia agraria nell' alto medioevo: problemi di cronologia e di continuità," in *Settimane di studio del Centro italiano di studi sull'alto medioevo*, 13 (Spoleto: Presso la sede del Centro 1969), 57–92.

The Italian City-State: From Commune to Signoria (Oxford University Press, 1997).

Kaplan, Michel, *Les propriétés de la couronne et de l'église dans l'empire byzantin (ve-vie siècles)* (Paris: Sorbonne, 1976).

Kampen, Natalie, *Image and Status: Roman Working Women in Ostia* (Berlin: Mann, 1981).

Kaser, Michael, *Das römische Privatrecht, 1: Das altrömische, das vorklassiche und klassiche Recht*, trans. Rolf Dannenbring, *Roman Private Law*, 6th edn. (London: Butterworths, 1968).

Das römische Zivilprozessrecht, 2nd edn. (Munich: Beck, 1996).

Römische Rechtsgeschichte (Göttingen: Vandenhoeck & Ruprecht, 1976; repr. 1993).

Kehoe, Dennis P., *Law and the Rural Economy in the Roman Empire* (Ann Arbor, MI: University of Michigan Press, 2007).

Kelly, Christopher, *Ruling the Later Roman Empire* (Cambridge, MA: Harvard University Press, 2004).

Kelly, John M., *Roman Litigation* (Oxford University Press, 1966).

Kennell, Stefanie A. H., *Magnus Felix Ennodius: A Gentleman of the Church* (Ann Arbor, MI: University of Michigan Press, 2000).
King, Paul D., *Law and Society in the Visigothic Kingdom* (Cambridge University Press, 1972).
Kirschenbaum, Aaron, *Sons, Slaves and Freedmen in Roman Commerce* (Washington, DC: Catholic University of America Press, 1987).
Kramer, Bärbel, "Liste der Syndikoi, Ekdikoi und Defensores in den Papyri Ägyptens," *Miscellanea Papyrologica* 19 (Florence, 1990), 305–29.
Krause, Jens-Uwe, *Spatäntike Patronatsformen im Westen der römischen Reiches* (Munich: Beck, 1987).
Krautschick, Stefan, *Cassiodor und die Politik seiner Zeit*. Habelts Dissertationsdrucke, Reihe Alte Geschichte 17 (Bonn: Habelt, 1983).
Kreuter, Nicole, *Römisches Privatrecht im 5. Jh. N. Chr.: Die Interpretatio zum westgotischen Gregorianus und Hermogenianus* (Berlin: Duncker & Humblot, 1993).
Kübler, Berhard, *Geschichte des römischen Rechts* (Leipzig: Scientia, 1925).
Kulikowski, Michael, "The 'Notitia Dignitatum' as a Historical Source," *Historia* 49.3 (2000), 358–77.
Kunkel, Wolfgang, *An Introduction to Roman Legal and Constitutional History*, trans. J. M. Kelly, 2nd edn., based on the sixth German edition of *Römische Rechtsgeschichte* (Oxford University Press, 1973).
Kunkel, Wolfgang and Martin Josef Schermaier, *Römische Rechtsgeschichte* (Cologne: Böhlau, 2001).
Laistner, Max L. W., *Thought and Letters in Western Europe,* AD *500 to 900* (Ithaca, NY: Cornell University Press, 1966).
Lambertini, Renzo, *Introduzione allo studio esegetico del diritto romano* (Bologna: Loescher, 1993).
Lamoreaux, John C., "Episcopal Courts in Late Antiquity," *JECS* 3 (1995), 143–67.
Lançon, Bertrand, *Rome in Late Antiquity,* AD *313–604* (Edinburgh University Press, 2000).
La Rocca, Christina, "Perceptions of an Early Medieval Urban Landscape," in Peter Linehan and Janet Nelson (eds.), *The Medieval World* (London: Routledge, 2001), 416–31.
Le Bohec, Yann, *The Imperial Roman Army* (London: B.T. Batsford, 1994).
Lenel, Otto, *Palingenesia iuris civilis* I-II (Leipzig: Tauchnitz, 1889; repr. Rome, 2000 with additions by L. E. Sierl).
Das Edictum perpetuum. Ein Versuch seiner Wiederherstellung, 3rd edn. (Leipzig: Tauchnitz, 1927; repr. Aalen, 1956, 1974).
Lenski, Noel, "Evidence for the *Audientia episcopalis* in the New Letters of Augustine," in Ralph W. Mathisen (ed.), *Law, Society and Authority in Late Antiquity* (Oxford University Press, 2001), 83–97.
Failure of Empire: Valens and the Roman State in the Fourth Century AD (Berkeley, CA: University of California Press, 2002).

Levy, Ernst, *Gesammelte Schriften: Zu seinem achtzigsten Geburstag mit Unterstützung der Akademien der Wissenschaften zu Göttingen, Heidelberg und München sowie von Basler Freunden ihm dargebracht* (Cologne: Böhlau, 1963).

Pauli sententiae: A Palingenesia of the Opening Titles as a Specimen of Research in West Roman Vulgar Law (Ithaca, NY: Rothman Reprints, 1945; repr. 1969).

"Vulgarization of Roman Law in the Early Middle Ages," *Mediaevalia et Humanistica* 1 (1963), 14–40.

West Roman Vulgar Law: The Law of Property (Philadelphia, PA: American Philosophical Society, 1952).

Weströmisches Vulgarrecht. Das Obligationenrecht, Forschungen zum römischen Recht (Weimar: H. Böhlaus Nachfolger, 1956).

Liebeschuetz, John H. W. G., "Cities, Taxes and the Accommodation of the Barbarians," in Walter Pohl (ed.), *Kingdoms of the Empire: The Integration of the Barbarians in Late Antiquity* (Leiden/New York: Brill, 1997), 135–51.

The Decline and Fall of the Roman City (Oxford University Press, 2003).

Liebs, Detlef, *Die Jurisprudenz im spätantiken Italien (260–640 n. Chr.)*, Freiburger Rechtsgeschichtliche Abhandlungen, n.f. 8 (Berlin: Duncker & Humblot, 1987).

"Die pseudopaulinischen Sentenzen," *ZSS (RA)* 112 (1995), 151–71.

(ed.), *Das Gesetz in Spätantike und frühem Mittelalter* (Göttingen: Abhandlungen der Akademie der Wissenschaften, 1992).

"Roman Vulgar Law in Late Antiquity" in A. J. B. Sirks (ed.), *Aspects of Law in Late Antiquity* (Oxford: All Souls College, 2008), 35–53.

Römische Jurisprudenz in Africa mit Studien zu den pseudopaulinischen Sentenzen (Berlin: Duncker & Humblot, 2005).

"Römische Jurisprudenz in Afrika im 4. Jh. n. chr," *ZSS (RA)* 106 (1989), 201–17.

Römische Jurisprudenz in Gallien (2 bis 8 Jahrhundert) (Berlin: Duncker & Humblot, 2002).

Vor den Richtern Roms. Berühmte Prozesse der Antike (Berlin: Beck, 2007).

Linder, Amnon, *The Jews in the Legal Sources of the Early Middle Ages* (Detroit: Wayne State University Press, 1997).

Lindsay, Hugh, *Adoption in the Roman World* (Cambridge University Press, 2009).

Littman, Robert J., and Maxwell L. Littman, "Galen and the Antonine Plague," *American Journal of Philology* 94 (1973), 254–5.

Lizzi, Rita, *Vescovi e strutture ecclesiastiche nella città tardoantica: L'Italia Annonaria nel* IV-V *secolo d.C.* (Como: Edizioni New Press, 1989).

Loyen, André, *Sidoine Apollinaire*, 2 vols. (Paris: Les Belles Lettres, 1970).

Lutz, Cora, "Musonius Rufus: 'The Roman Socrates'," *Yale Classical Studies* 10 (1947), 3–147.

Lynch, Joseph H., *Godparents and Kingship in Early Medieval Europe* (Princeton University Press, 1986).

MacGeorge, Penny, *Late Roman Warlords* (Oxford University Press, 2002).

MacMullen, Ramsay, *Corruption and the Decline of Rome* (New Haven, CT: Yale University Press, 1988).

"Late Roman Slavery," *Historia* 36 (1987), 359–82.

"Roman Bureaucratese," *Traditio* 18 (1962), 364–78.

Roman Government's Response to Crisis AD *235–337* (New Haven, CT: Yale University Press, 1976).

Maigne d'Arnis, W. H. and Jacques-Paul Migne, *Lexicon manuale ad scriptores mediae et infimae latinitas* (Paris: J.P. Migne, 1858, repr. 1977).

Mannino, Vincenzo, *Ricerche sul "Defensor Civitatis"* (Milan: Giuffrè, 1984).

Marazzi, Federico, "The Destinies of the Late Antique Italies," in Richard Hodges and William Bowden (eds.), *The Sixth Century. Production, Distribution and Demand* (Leiden/New York: Brill, 1998), 119–59.

"The Last Rome: From the End of the Fifth to the End of the Sixth Century," in Sam J. Barnish and Federico Marazzi (eds.), *The Ostrogoths from the Migration Period to the Sixth Century* (Woodbridge: Boydell 2007), 279–301.

Marcone, Arnaldo, "Il lavoro nelle campagne," in *Storia di Roma,* III*: L'età tardoantica.* I*. Crisi e transformazioni* (Turin: Einaudi, 1993), 823–43.

Martindale, Janet R., "The French Aristocracy in the Early Middle Ages: A Reappraisal," *Past and Present* 75 (1977), 5–45.

Martindale, John, *The Prosopography of the Later Roman Empire, vol. 2:* AD *395–527* (Cambridge University Press, 1980).

Matthews, John F., "Interpreting the *Interpretationes* of the *Breviarium,*" in Ralph W. Mathisen (ed.), *Law, Society and Authority in Late Antiquity* (Oxford University Press, 2001), 11–32.

Laying Down the Law: A Study of the Theodosian Code (New Haven, CT: Yale University Press, 2000).

"Roman Law and Barbarian Identity in the Late Roman West," in S. Mitchell and G. Greatrex (eds.), *Ethnicity and Culture in Late Antiquity* (London: Duckworth, 2000), 31–45.

"The Making of the Text," in Jill Harries and Ian Wood (eds.), *The Theodosian Code. Studies in the Imperial Law of Late Antiquity* (London: Duckworth, 1993), 19–44.

Western Aristocracies and Imperial Court, AD *364–425* (Oxford: Clarendon Press, 1992).

Mathisen, Ralph W., (ed.), *Law, Society and Authority in Late Antiquity* (Oxford University Press, 2001).

Roman Aristocrats in Barbarian Gaul: Strategies for Survival in the Age of Transition (Austin, TX: University of Texas Press, 1993).

Mazzarino, Santo, "Si può parlare di rivoluzione sociale alla fine del mondo antico," in *Il passagio dall'antichità al medioevo in Occidente,* Settimane di Studi del Centro Italiano di Studi sull'Alto Medioevo 9 (Spoleto: Presso la sede del Centro, 1961), 410–25.

McCormick, Michael, *Eternal Victory: Triumphal Rulership in Late Antiquity, Byzantium, and the Early Medieval West* (Cambridge University Press, 1986).

McGinn, Thomas A. J., "Concubinage and the *Lex Julia* on Adultery," *TAPA* 121 (1991), 335–75.

Prostitution, Sexuality and the Law in Ancient Rome (Oxford University Press, 1998).

McKitterick, Rosamond, *The Carolingians and the Written Word* (Cambridge University Press, 1989).

(ed.), *The Uses of Literacy in Early Medieval Europe* (Cambridge University Press, 1990).

Melicher, Teophil, *Der Kampf zwischen Gesetzes- und Gewohnheitsrecht im Westgotenreich* (Weimer: Hermann Bohlaus, 1930).

Melillo, Generoso, Antonio Palma, and Carmela Pennacchio (eds.), *Lessico dell' «Edictum Theoderici Regis»* (Rome and Naples: Edizioni scientifiche italiane, 1990).

Merêa, Paulo, "Le mariage '*sine consensu parentum*' dans le droit romain vulgaire occidental," *RIDA* 5 (1950), 203–17.

Metzger, Ernest, *Litigation in Roman Law* (Oxford University Press, 2005).

Meyer, Elizabeth A., *Legitimacy and Law in the Roman World. Tabulae in Roman Belief and Practice* (Cambridge University Press, 2004).

Meyer-Marthaler, Elisabeth, *Römisches Recht in Rätien im frühen und hohen Mittelalter* (Zurich: Leemann, 1968).

Millar, Fergus, "Condemnation to Hard Labor in the Roman Empire, from the Julio-Claudians to Constantine," *PBSR* 52 (1984), 124–47.

Mirković, Miroslava, *The Later Roman Colonate and Freedom* (Philadelphia, PA: American Philosophical Association, 1997).

Mitteis, Ludwig, *Reichsrecht und Volksrecht in den östlichen Provinzen des römischen Kaiserreichs: Mit Beiträge zur Kenntniss des griechischen Rechts und der spätrömischen Rechtsentwicklung* (Leipzig: Teubner, 1891; repr. Hildesheim, 1963).

Momigliano, Arnaldo, "La caduta senza rumore di un impero nel 476 d.C," *Annali della Scuola Normale Superiore di Pisa*, ser. III, vol. III.2 (1973), 397–418.

Sesto contributo alla storia degli studi classici e del mondo antico, I (Rome: Edizioni di Storia e Letteratura, 1980).

Mommsen, Theodor, *Gesammelte Schriften*, 8 vols. (Berlin: Weidmann, 1904).

Römisches Strafrecht, trans. J. Duquesne, *Le Droit pénal romain*, 3 vols. (Paris, 1907).

Monks, George R., "The Administration of the Privy Purse," *Speculum* 32 (1957), 748–79.

Moorhead, John, "The Last Years of Theoderic," *Historia* 32 (1983), 106–20.

Theoderic in Italy (Oxford University Press, 1992).

"Theoderic, Zeno and Odovacer," *Byzantinische Zeitschrift* 77 (1984), 261–6.

Morton, Catherine, "Marius of Avenches, the *Excerpta Valesiana* and the Death of Boethius," *Traditio* 38 (1982), 107–36.

Mousourakis, George, *The Historical and Institutional Context of Roman Law* (Aldershot: Ashgate, 2003).

Myres, John N. L., "Pelagius and the End of Roman Rule in Britain," *JRS* 50 (1960), 21–36.

Nehlsen, Hermann, "Aktualität und Effektivität der ältesten germanischen Rechtsaufzeichnungen," in P. Classen (ed.), *Recht und Schrift im Mittelalter*, Vorträge und Forschungen, xxiii (Sigmaringen: Thorbecke, 1977), 449–502.

"Der Grabfrevel in den germanischen Rechtsaufzeichnungen: Zugleich ein Beitrag zur Diskussion um Todesstrafe und Friedlosigskeit bei den Germanen," in H. Jankuhn, H. Nelsen, and H. Roth (eds.), *Zum Grabfrevel in vorund frühgeschichtlicher Zeit: Untersuchungen zu Grabraub und "Haugbrot" in Mittel- und Nordeuropa*. Abhandlungen der Akademie der Wissenschaften in Göttingen, philologisch-historische Klasse, dritten Folge 113 (Göttingen: Vandenhoeck & Ruprecht, 1978), 107–68.

"*Edictum Theoderici*," *Zeitschrift der Savigny-Stiftung für Rechtsgeschichte, Germanistische Abteilung* 86 (1969), 246–60.

Sklavenrecht zwischen Antike und Mittelalter: germanisches und römisches Recht in den germanischen Rechtsaufzeichnungen 1, *Ostgoten, Westgoten, Franken, Langobarden, Göttinger Studien zur Rechtsgeschichte* 7 (Göttingen: Musterscmidt, 1972).

Überlieferung, Aufbau und Stil von Gai Institutiones (Leiden: Brill, 1981).

Nicholas, Barry, *An Introduction to Roman Law* (Oxford: Clarendon Press, 1991).

Nixon, Charles E. V., "Relations between Visigoths and Romans in Fifth-Century Gaul," in J. Drinkwater and H. Elton (eds.), *Fifth-Century Gaul: A Crisis of Identity?* (Cambridge University Press, 1992), 64–74.

Noble, Thomas F. X. (ed.), *From Roman Provinces to Medieval Kingdoms* (London/ New York: Routledge, 2006).

Nonn, Ulrich, "Merowingische Testamente: Studien zum Fortleben einer römischen Urkundenform in Frankreich," *Archiv für Diplomatik* 18 (1972), 14–15.

Nörr, Dieter, "Planung in der Antike: Über die Ehegesetze des Augustus," in Horst Baier (ed.), *Freiheit und Sachzwang: Beiträge zu Ehren Helmut Schelskys* (Braunschweig and Opladen: Westdeutscher Verlag, 1977), 309–43.

O'Donnell, James, *Cassiodorus* (Berkeley, CA: University of California Press, 1979).

"Liberius the Patrician," *Traditio* 37 (1981), 31–72.

Osborne, John, "Death and Burial in Sixth-Century Rome," *EMC/CV* 3.2 (1984), 291–9.

Ostrogorsky, George, *History of the Byzantine State*, 2nd edn. (Oxford: Blackwell, 1968).

"La commune rurale byzantine: Loi agraire – Traité fiscal – Cadastre de Thèbes," *Byzantion* 32 (1962), 140–7.

Paradisi, Bruno, "Critica e mito dell'editto teodericano," *Bollettino dell'Istituto di diritto romano* 68 (1965), 1–47.

Patlagean, Evelyne, *Pauvreté économique et pauvreté sociale à Byzance, 4e-7e siècles* (Paris: Mouton, 1977).

Patterson, Orlando, *Slavery and Social Death: A Comparative Study* (Cambridge, MA: Harvard University Press, 1985).

Percival, John, "P.Ital. 3 and Roman Estate Management," *Latomus* 102 (1969), 607–15.

"Seigneurial aspects of late Roman estate management," *EHR* 84 (1969), 449–73.

Pergami, Federico, *L'appello nella legislazione del tardo impero, AARC, Materiali per una palingenesi delle costituzioni tardo-imperiali*, serie terza 2 (Milan: Guiffré, 2000).

Peters, Edward, *Torture* (Oxford: Blackwell, 1985).

Pharr, Clyde, "The Interdiction of Magic in Roman Law," *Transactions and Proceedings of the American Philological Association* 63 (1932), 269–96.

Phillipson, Donald, "Development of the Roman Law of Debt Security," *Stanford Law Review* 6 (1968), 1230–48.

Piganiol, André, *L'empire chrétien (325–395), Histoire Romaine 4* (Paris: Presses universitaires de France, 1947).

Pohl, Walter (ed.), *Kingdoms of the Empire: The Integration of the Barbarians in Late Antiquity* (Leiden/New York: Brill, 1997).

"Perceptions of Barbarian Violence," in H. A. Drake (ed.), *Violence in Late Antiquity. Perceptions and Practices* (Burlington, VT: Ashgate, 2006), 15–26.

Posner, Ernst, *Archives in the Ancient World* (Cambridge University Press, 1972).

Potter, Timothy W., and Anthony C. King, *Excavations at the Mola di Monte Gelato* (London: British School at Rome, 1997).

Ramin, Jaques and Paul Veyne, "Droit romain et société: Les hommes libres qui passent pour esclaves et l'esclavage volontaire," *Historia* 30 (1981), 472–97.

Rapp, Claudia, *Holy Bishops in Late Antiquity: The Nature of Christian Leadership in an Age of Transition* (Berkeley, CA: University of California Press, 2005).

Rasi, Piero, "Sulla paternità del c.d. Edictum Theodorici Regis," *Archivio giuridico* 145 (1953), 105–62.

Rawson, Beryl, "Roman Concubinage and Other de facto Marriages," *TAPA* 104 (1974), 279–305.

"*Spurii* and the Roman View of Illegitimacy," *Antichthon* 23 (1989), 10–41.

Rea, Rossella (ed.), *Rota Colisei: La valle del Colosseo attraverso i secoli* (Milan: Electa, 2002).

Rebillard, Éric *The Care of the Dead in Late Antiquity*, trans. Elizabeth Trapnell Rawlings and Jeanine Routier-Pucci (Ithaca, NY: Cornell University Press, 2009).

Reinhold, Meyer, "Usurpation of Status and Status Symbols in the Roman Empire," *Historia* 20 (1971), 275–302.

Reiss, Edmund, "The Fall of Boethius and the Fiction of the *Consolatio Philosophiae*," *The Classical Journal* 77 (1981), 37–47.

Riché, Pierre, *Education and Culture in the Barbarian West: From the Sixth through the Eighth Century*, translated from the 3rd French edn. by John Contreni (Columbia, SC: University of South Carolina Press, 1962).

Richlin, Amy, "Approaches to the Sources on Adultery at Rome," in H. Foley (ed.), *Reflections of Women in Antiquity* (New York: Gordon and Breach Science Publishers, 1981), 379–404.

Riggsby, Andrew M., *Roman Law and the Legal World of the Romans* (Cambridge University Press, 2010).

Rives, James B., "Magic in Roman Law: The Reconstruction of a Crime," *Classical Antiquity* 22.2 (2003), 313–39.

The Sources of Roman Law: Problems and Methods for Ancient Historians (London: Routledge, 1997).

Robinson, Olivia F., *Penal Practice and Penal Policy in Ancient Rome* (London: Routledge, 2006).

Romano, Giulio and A. Solmi, *La dominazione barbariche in Italia (395–888)* (Milan: F. Villardi, 1940).

Rougé, Jean, "Quelques aspects de la navigation en Méditerranée au Ve siècle et dans la première moitié du VIe siècle," *Cahiers d'histoire* 6 (1961), 129–54.

Royden, Halsey L., "The Tenure of Office of the Quinquennales in the Roman Professional Collegia," *American Journal of Philology* 110 (1989), 303–15.

Ruggini, Lellia, *Economia e società nell' "Italia annonaria"* (Milan: Giuffrè, 1961).

"Ebrei e Orientali nell'Italia settentrionale fra il IV e il VI secolo d. Cr.," *Studia et documenta historiae et iuris* 25 (1959), 186–308.

Saller, Richard, *Patriarchy, Property and Death in the Roman Family* (Cambridge University Press, 1994).

Personal Patronage Under the Early Empire (Cambridge University Press, 1982).

Schäfer, Christoph, *Der weströmische Senat als Träger antiker Kontinuät unter den Ostgotenkönigen (490–540 n.Chr.)* (St. Katharinen, Hamburg: Scripta Mercaturae Verlag, 1991).

Scheidel, Walter, "Slaves of the Soil," *JRA* 13 (2000), 727–32.

Schiller, Arthur A., *Roman Law: Mechanisms of Development* (New York: Mouton, 1978).

Schlosser, Hans, *Grundzüge der neueren Privatrechtsgeschichte*, 4th edn. (Heidelberg: Uni-Taschenbücher, 1982).

Schmidt, Ludwig, "Die comites Gothorum: ein Kapitel zur ostgotischen Verfassungsgeschichte," *Mitteilungen des Instituts für Österreichische Geschichtsforschung* 40 (1925), 127–33.

Die Ostgermanen, Geschichte der deutschen Stämme bis zum Ausgang der Völkerwanderung (Munich: Beck, 1969).

Schott, Clausidieter, "Der Stand der Leges-Forschung," *Frühmittelalterliche Studien* 13 (1979), 29–55.

Schröder, Richard, *Lehrbuch der deutschen Rechtsgeschichte* (Leipzig: Veit, 1907).

Schulz, Fritz, *Classical Roman Law* (Oxford: Clarendon Press, 1954).

History of Roman Legal Science (Oxford: Clarendon Press, 1967).

Seeck, Otto, "Comites," *RE* 17 (1900), 622–4.

Regesten der Kaiser und Päpste für di Jähre 311 bis 476 n. Chr.: Vorarbeit zu einer Prosopographie der christlichen Kaiserzeit (Frankfurt: Minerva, 1964 repr.).

Serfass, Adam, "Slavery and Pope Gregory the Great," *Journal of Early Christian Studies* 14 (2006), 77–103.

Sinnigen, William, "Administrative Shifts of Competence under Theoderic," *Traditio* 21 (1965), 456–67.

Sirks, Adrian J. B., "Shifting Frontiers in the Law: Romans, Provincials and Barbarians," in Ralph W. Mathisen and H. Sivan (eds.), *Shifting Frontiers in Late Antiquity* (Aldershot: Variorum, 1996), 146–57.

"The Colonate in Justinian's Reign," *JRS* 98 (2008), 120–43.

"The Farmers, the Landlord, and the Law in the Fifth Century," in Ralph W. Mathisen (ed.), *Law, Society and Authority in Late Antiquity* (Oxford University Press, 2001), 256–71.

Sivan, Hagith S., "Why Not Marry a Jew? Jewish–Christian Marital Frontiers in Late Antiquity," in Ralph W. Mathisen (ed.), *Law, Society and Authority in Late Antiquity* (Oxford University Press, 2001), 208–19.

Small, Alastair M., and R. J. Buck, *The Excavations of S. Giovanni di Ruotix*, I (University of Toronto Press, 1994).

Smith, Christopher J., *The Roman Clan: the Gens from Ancient Ideology to Modern Anthropology* (Cambridge University Press, 2006).

Soraci, Rosario, *Ricerche sui conubia tra Romani e Germani nei secoli IV-VI* (Catania: N. Giannota, 1968; repr. 1974).

Staab, Franz, "Ostrogothic Geographers at the Court of Theoderic the Great: A Study of Some Sources of the Anonymous Cosmographer of Ravenna," *Viator* 7 (1976), 27–64.

Stathakopolous, Dionysios Ch., *Famine and Pestilence in the Late Roman and Early Byzantine Empire: A Systematic Survey of Subsistence Crises and Epidemics* (London: Ashgate, 2004).

Stein, Ernst, *Histoire du Bas-Empire, II: De la disparition de l'Empire d'Occident à la mort Justinien (476–565)* (Paris: Desclée, 1949).

Untersuchungen über das Officium der Prätorianerpräfektur seit Diokletian (Amsterdam: A. M. Hakkert, 1962).

Stein, Peter, *Roman Law in European History* (Cambridge University Press, 1999).

Sullivan, Richard E. (ed.), *"The Gentle Voices of Teachers": Aspects of Learning in the Carolingian Age* (Columbus, OH: University of Ohio Press, 1995).

Tabata, Kayoko, "I comites Gothorum e l'amministrazione municipale in epoca Ostrogota," in J.-M. Carrié and R. Lizzi Testa (eds.), *'Humana Sapit'. Études d'Antiquité Tardive Offertes à Lellia Cracco Ruggini* (Bibliothèque de l'Antiquité Tardive, 3) (Turnhout: Brepols 2002), 67–78.

Talamanca, Mario (ed.), *Lineamenti di storia del diritto romano* (Milan: Giuffrè, 1989).

Tate, Joshua C., "Inheritance Rights of Nonmarital Children in Late Roman Law," *Roman Legal Tradition* 4 (2008), 1–36.

Thibault, Fabien, "L'impôt direct dans les royaumes des Ostrogoths, des Wisigoths et des Burgundes," *RHDFE* 25 (1901), 699–728.

Thomas, Yan, "Droit domestique et droit politique à Rome: Remarques sur le pécule et les honores des fils de famille," *MEFRA* 94 (1982), 527–80.

"Vitae necisque potestas. Le père, la cité, la mort," in *Du châtiment dans la cité: Supplices corporels et peine de mort dans le monde antique*, organisée par l'Ècole française de Rome avec le concours du Centre national de la recherche scientifique (Rome, November 9–11) (Rome: École française de Rome, 1984), 499–548.

Thompson, Edward A., *Romans and Barbarians: The Decline of the Western Roman Empire* (Madison, WI, University of Wisconsin Press, 1982).

Timpe, Dieter, "Comes," *Reallexikon der germanischen Altertumskunde*, vol. 5, 2nd edn. (Berlin/New York: Walter de Gruyter & Co., 1982), 63–5.

Tjäder, Jan-Olof, *Die nichtliterarischen Lateinischen Papyri Italiens aus der Zeit 445–700,* Acta Instituti Romani Regni Sueciae, series in 4° 19, 2 vols. (Uppsala: C. W. K. Gleerup, 1955; repr. Stockholm, 1982).

Toubert, Pierre, *Les structures du Latium médiéval* (Rome: École française de Rome, 1973).

Treggiari, Susan, "*Contubernales* in *CIL* 6," *Phoenix* 35 (1981), 42–69.

Roman Marriage: Iusti Coniuges from the Time of Cicero to the Time of Ulpian (Oxford: Clarendon Press, 1991).

Ullman, Walter, *The Carolingian Renaissance and the Idea of Kingship* (London: Methuen, 1969).

Van Dam, Raymond, *Leadership and Community in Late Antique Gaul* (Berkeley, CA: University of California Press, 1985).

Saints and their Miracles in Late Antique Gaul (Princeton University Press, 1993).

Vandendriessche, Sarah, *Possessio und Dominium im postklassischen römischen Recht. Eine Überprüfung von Levy's Vulgarrechtstheorie anhand der Quellen des Codex Theodosianus und der Posttheodosianischen Novelle* (Hamburg: Kovač, 2006).

Venturini, Carlo, "'*Accusatio Adulterii*' e politica constantiniana (Per un riesame di CTH 9,7,2)," *SDHI* 54 (1988), 66–109.

Vera, Domenico, "Dalla 'villa perfecta' alla villa di Palladio," *Athenaeum* 83 (1995), part 1: 189–211; part 2: 331–56.

"Essere 'schiavi della terra' nell'Italia tardoantica: la razionalitá di una dipendenza," *Studia historica* 25 (2007), 489–505.

"Forme e funzioni della rendita fondiaria nella tarda antichità," in A. Giardina (ed.), *Società romana e impero tardoantico* (Rome and Bari: Laterza, 1986), 367–447.

"Schiavitù rurale, colonate e transformazioni agrarie nell'Italia imperial," *Scienze dell'antichità, VI-VII* (Rome: Università degli studi di Roma, 1992–3), 291–339.

"Strutture agrarie e strutture patrimoniali nella tarda Antichità: l'aristocrazia romana fra agricoltura e commercio," *Opus* 2 (1983), 489–533.

Verhulst, Adriaan, "Quelques remarques à propos des corvées de colons à l'époque du Bas-Empire et du Haut Moyen Age," in *Revue de l'Université de Bruxelles* (Brussels: Bruylant-Christophe, 1977), 1, 89–95.

Rural and Urban Aspects of Early and Medieval Northwest Europe (Aldershot: Variorum, 1992).

Vidén, Gunhild, *The Roman Chancery Tradition: Studies in the Language of Codex Theodosianus and Cassiodorus' 'Variae'* (Göteborg: Acta Universitatis Gothoburgensis, 1984).

Vismara, Giulio, "Edictum Theoderici," *Ius Romanum Medii Aevi*, part I, 2 b aa α (Milan: Giuffrè, 1967).

"Romani e Goti di fronte al diritto nel regno ostrogoto," *Settimanae di studio del Centro Italiano di studi sull'alto medioevo 3 [= I Goti in occidente: problemi]* (Spoleto: Presso la sede del Centro, 1956), 407–63.

Voci, Pasquale, "Il diritto ereditario Romano nell'età di tardo impero: il IV secolo (prima parte)," *Iura* 29 (1978), 17–113.

Volterra, Edoardo, "Intorno ad alcune costituzioni di Costantino," *Rendiconti dell'Accademia Nazionale dei Lincei. Classe di Scienze morali, storiche e filologiche*, series 8, vol. 13 (1958), 61–89.

"Quelques remarques sur le style des constitutions de Constantin," *Mélanges Levy-Bruhl* (Paris: Sirey, 1959), 325–34.

Von Lorentz, Friedrich, "Theoderich -nicht Iustinian," *Mitteilungen des Deutschen Archäologischen Instituts, Römische Abteilung* 50 (1935), 339–47.

Wallace-Hadrill, Andrew, "Family and Inheritance in the Augustan Marriage Laws," *Proceedings of the Cambridge Philological Society* 207 (1981), 58–80.

(ed.), *Patronage in Ancient Society* (London: Routledge, 1989).

Wallace-Hadrill, John Michael, *Early Germanic Kingship in England and on the Continent* (Oxford University Press, 1971).

The Barbarian West, 400–1000, 3rd edn. (London: Hutchison, 1967).

The Long-Haired Kings, and Other Studies in Frankish History (London, Methuen, 1962).

Ward-Perkins, Bryan, *From Classical Antiquity to the Middle Ages: Urban Public Building in North and Central Italy, AD 300–850* (Oxford University Press, 1985).

"Land, Labor and Settlement," in Averil Cameron, Bryan Ward-Perkins and Michael Whitby (eds.), *The Cambridge Ancient History,* vol. 14: *Late Antiquity: Empire and Successors, AD 425–600* (Cambridge University Press, 2000), 315–46.

"Specialized Production and Exchange," in Averil Cameron, Bryan Ward-Perkins, and Michael Whitby (eds.) *The Cambridge Ancient History* (Cambridge University Press, 2008).

The Fall of Rome and the End of Civilization (Oxford University Press, 2005).

Watson, Alan, *Roman Slave Law* (Baltimore, MD: Johns Hopkins Press, 1987).

Society and Legal Change (Edinburgh: Scottish Academic Press, 1977).

"The Definition of *Furtum* and the Trichotomy," *Tijdschrift voor Rechtsgeschiedenis = Revue d'histoire du droit* 28 (1960), 197–210.

The Evolution of Western Private Law (Baltimore, MD: Johns Hopkins Press, 1985).

Weaver, Paul R. C., "The Status of Children in Mixed Marriages," in B. Rawson (ed.), *The Family in Ancient Rome: New Perspectives* (Ithaca, NY: Cornell University Press, 1986), 145–69.

Welles, C. Bradford, *The Excavations at Dura-Europos, Final Report V. Part I: The Parchments and Papyri* (New Haven, CT: Yale University Press, 1959).

Whittaker, C. Richard, "Landlords and Warlords in the Later Roman Empire," in J. Rich and G. Shipley (eds.), *Warfare and Society in the Roman World* (London: Routledge, 1993), 277–302.

Whittow, Mark, *The Making of Orthodox Byzantium, 600–1025* (Basingstoke: Macmillan, 1996).

Wickham, Chris, *Early Medieval Italy: Central Power and Local Society 400–1000* (London: Macmillan, 1981).

Framing the Early Middle Ages: Europe and the Mediterranean, 400–800 (Oxford University Press, 2005).

Land and Power: Studies in Italian and European Social History, 400–1200 (London: British School at Rome, 1994).

"Specialized Production and Exchange," in Averil Cameron, Bryan Ward-Perkins, and Michael Whitby (eds.), *The Cambridge Ancient History*, vol. 14 (Cambridge, 2000), 346–91.

"The Fall of Rome Will Not Take Place," in Lester Little and Barbara Rosenwein (eds.), *Debating the Middle Ages: Issues and Readings* (Malden, MA: Blackwell, 1998), 45–57.

Wieacker, Franz, "Le droit romain de la mort d'Alexandre Sévère á l'avènement de Dioclétien," *RHDFE* 49 (1971), 201–23.

Römische Rechtsgeschichte (Munich: Beck, 1988 and 2006).

"'Vulgarrecht' und 'Vulgarismus'. Alte und Neue Probleme und Diskussionen, lecture in Siena 4th December 1979," in *Studi in onore di Arnaldo Biscardi I* (Milan: La Goliardica, 1982), 33–51.

Wolfram, Herwig, "Gotisches Studien I/II," *Mitteilungen des Instituts für Österreichische Geschichtsforschung* 83 (1975), 1–32, 289–324.

History of the Goths, trans. Thomas J. Dunlap, 2nd edn. (Berkeley, CA: University of California Press, 1988).

The Roman Empire and Its Germanic Peoples, trans. Thomas Dunlap (Berkeley, CA: University of California Press, 1997).

Wood, Ian, "Administration, Law and Culture in Merovingian Gaul," in Rosamond McKitterick (ed.), *The Uses of Literacy in Early Medieval Europe* (Cambridge University Press, 1990), 63–81.

"Disputes in Late Fifth- and Early Sixth-Century Gaul: Some Problems," in Wendy Davies and Paul Fouracre (eds.), *The Settlement of Disputes in Early Medieval Europe* (Cambridge University Press, 1986), 7–22.

"*Gentes*, Kings and Kingdoms – The Emergence of States: The Kingdom of the Gibichungs," in Hans-Werner Goetz, Jörg Jarnut, and Walter Pohl (eds.), *Regna and Gentes: The Relationship Between Late Antique and Early Medieval Peoples and Kingdoms in the Transformation of the Roman World* (Leiden/New York: Brill, 2003), 243–69.

"The Fall of the Western Empire and the End of Roman Britain," *Britannia* 18 (1987), 251–62.

The Merovingian Kingdoms, 450–751 (London/New York: Longman, 1994).

Wormald, Patrick, "*Lex Scripta* and *verbum Regis*: Legislation and Germanic Kingship, from Euric to Cnut," in P. H. Sawyer and I. N. Wood (eds.), *Early Medieval Kingship* (Leeds: The Editors, 1977), 105–38.

"The *Leges Barbarorum*: Law and Ethnicity in the Post-Roman West," in Hans-Werner Goetz, Jörg Jarnut, and Walter Pohl (eds.), *Regna and Gentes: The Relationship Between Late Antique and Early Medieval Peoples and Kingdoms in the Transformation of the Roman World* (Leiden/New York, 2003), 21–53.

Zimmermann, Odo J., *The Late Latin Vocabulary of the 'Variae' of Cassiodorus* (Washington, DC: The Catholic University of America Press, 1944).

Zimmerman, Reinhard, *The Law of Obligations: Roman Foundations of the Civilian Tradition* (Capetown: Juta, 1992; repr. Oxford University Press, 1996).

Index

For EU product safety concerns, contact us at Calle de José Abascal, 56–1°, 28003 Madrid, Spain or eugpsr@cambridge.org.

www.ingramcontent.com/pod-product-compliance
Lightning Source LLC
LaVergne TN
LVHW011528200926
848484LV00001B/183

* 9 7 8 1 1 0 7 0 2 8 3 4 0 *